Mastering Blockchain
Second Edition

Distributed ledger technology, decentralization, and smart contracts explained

Imran Bashir

BIRMINGHAM - MUMBAI

Mastering Blockchain
Second Edition

Acquisition Editors: Ben Renow-Clarke, Suresh M Jain
Project Editor: Suzanne Coutinho
Content Development Editor: Alex Sorrentino
Technical Editor: Bhagyashree Rai
Indexer: Tejal Daruwale Soni
Graphics: Tom Scaria
Production Coordinator: Aparna Bhagat

First published: March 2017
Second edition: March 2018

Production reference: 1290318

Published by Packt Publishing Ltd.
Livery Place
35 Livery Street
Birmingham
B3 2PB, UK.

ISBN 978-1-78883-904-4

www.packtpub.com

`mapt.io`

Mapt is an online digital library that gives you full access to over 5,000 books and videos, as well as industry leading tools to help you plan your personal development and advance your career. For more information, please visit our website.

Why subscribe?

- Spend less time learning and more time coding with practical eBooks and Videos from over 4,000 industry professionals

- Improve your learning with Skill Plans built especially for you

- Get a free eBook or video every month

- Mapt is fully searchable

- Copy and paste, print, and bookmark content

PacktPub.com

Did you know that Packt offers eBook versions of every book published, with PDF and ePub files available? You can upgrade to the eBook version at `www.PacktPub.com` and as a print book customer, you are entitled to a discount on the eBook copy. Get in touch with us at `service@packtpub.com` for more details.

At `www.PacktPub.com`, you can also read a collection of free technical articles, sign up for a range of free newsletters, and receive exclusive discounts and offers on Packt books and eBooks.

Contributors

About the author

Imran Bashir has an M.Sc. in Information Security from Royal Holloway, University of London, and has a background in software development, solution architecture, infrastructure management, and IT service management. He is also a member of the Institute of Electrical and Electronics Engineers (IEEE) and the British Computer Society (BCS).

Imran has sixteen years' of experience in the public and financial sectors. He worked on large scale IT projects in the public sector before moving to the financial services industry. Since then, he has worked in various technical roles for different financial companies in Europe's financial capital, London. He is currently working for an investment bank in London as Vice President in the Technology department.

I would like to thank the talented team at Packt, including Ben Renow-Clarke, Suzanne Coutinho, Alex Sorrentino, Gary Schwartz, and Bhagyashree Rai, who provided prompt guidance and valuable feedback throughout this project. I am also extremely thankful to the reviewer, Pranav Burnwal, who provided constructive and very useful feedback that helped me tremendously to improve the material in this book.

I thank my wife and children for putting up with my all-night and weekend-long writing sessions.

Above all, I would like to thank my parents, whose blessings have made everything possible for me.

About the reviewer

Pranav Burnwal has a background in Research and Development, and he has been working with cutting-edge technologies for the past few years. The technologies he works on range from blockchain, big data, analytics (log and data), cloud, to message queues, NoSQL, web servers, and so on. He has worked across various domains ranging from BFSI, HLS, FMCG, and automobiles to name a few.

Pranav is an active community member in multiple communities. He is the Regional Head for Blockchain Education Network (BEN), a registered NGO and a worldwide network of people of blockchain. He has also organized multiple meetups and a start-up weekend in India.

Pranav has also been an active trainer in the blockchain space for an exciting period of three years now, for an audience ranging from junior developers to senior VPs. This has also given him insights into how people understand a new and complex technology, which helped him frame this book in the best interest of the readers.

Packt is searching for authors like you

If you're interested in becoming an author for Packt, please visit `authors.packtpub.com` and apply today. We have worked with thousands of developers and tech professionals, just like you, to help them share their insight with the global tech community. You can make a general application, apply for a specific hot topic that we are recruiting an author for, or submit your own idea.

Table of Contents

Preface

This book has one goal, to introduce theoretical and practical aspects of the blockchain technology. This book contains all material that is necessary to become a blockchain technical expert. Since the publication of the first edition of this book, a lot has changed and progressed further with regards to blockchain; therefore, a need to update the book has arisen.

The multitude of benefits envisaged by the implementation of blockchain technology has sparked profound interest among researchers from academia and industry who are tirelessly researching this technology. As a result, many consortia, working groups, projects, and professional bodies have emerged, which are involved in the development and further advancement of this technology. The second edition of this book will provide in-depth insights into decentralization, smart contracts, and various blockchain platforms such as Ethereum, Bitcoin, and Hyperledger Fabric. After reading this book, readers will be able to develop a deep understanding of inner workings of the blockchain technology and will be able to develop blockchain applications.

This book covers all topics relevant to the blockchain technology, including cryptography, cryptocurrencies, Bitcoin, Ethereum, and various other platforms and tools used for blockchain development. It is recommended that readers have a basic understanding of computer science and basic programming experience to benefit fully from this book. However, if that is not the case then still this book can be read easily, as relevant background material is provided where necessary.

Who this book is for

This book is for anyone who wants to understand blockchain in depth. It can also be used as a reference by developers who are developing applications for blockchain. Also, this book can be used as a textbook for courses related to blockchain technology and cryptocurrencies. It can also be used as a learning resource for various examinations and certifications related to cryptocurrency and blockchain technology.

What this book covers

Chapter 1, *Blockchain 101*, introduces the basic concepts of distributed computing on which blockchain technology is based. It also covers history, definitions, features, types, and benefits of blockchains along with various consensus mechanisms that are at the core of the blockchain technology.

Chapter 2, *Decentralization*, covers the concept of decentralization and its relationship with blockchain technology. Various methods and platforms that can be used to decentralize a process or a system have also been introduced.

Chapter 3, *Symmetric Cryptography*, introduces the theoretical foundations of symmetric cryptography, which is necessary to understand that how various security services such as confidentiality and integrity are provided.

Chapter 4, *Public Key Cryptography*, introduces concepts such as public and private keys, digital signatures and hash functions with practical examples. Finally, an introduction to financial markets is also included as there are many interesting use cases for blockchain technology in the financial sector.

Chapter 5, *Introducing Bitcoin*, covers Bitcoin, the first and largest blockchain. It introduces technical concepts related to bitcoin cryptocurrency in detail.

Chapter 6, *Bitcoin Network and Payments*, covers Bitcoin network, relevant protocols and various Bitcoin wallets. Moreover, advanced protocols, Bitcoin trading and payments is also introduced.

Chapter 7, *Bitcoin Clients and APIs*, introduces various Bitcoin clients and programming APIs that can be used to build Bitcoin applications.

Chapter 8, *Alternative Coins*, introduces alternative cryptocurrencies that were introduced after the invention of Bitcoin. It also presents examples of different altcoins, their properties, and how they have been developed and implemented.

Chapter 9, *Smart Contracts*, provides an in-depth discussion on smart contracts. Topics such as history, the definition of smart contracts, Ricardian contracts, Oracles, and the theoretical aspects of smart contracts are presented in this chapter.

Chapter 10, *Ethereum 101*, introduces the design and architecture of the Ethereum blockchain in detail. It covers various technical concepts related to the Ethereum blockchain that explains the underlying principles, features, and components of this platform in depth.

Chapter 11, *Further Ethereum*, continues the introduction of Ethereum from pervious chapter and covers topics related to Ethereum Virtual Machine, mining and supporting protocols for Ethereum.

Chapter 12, *Ethereum Development Environment*, covers the topics related to setting up private networks for Ethereum smart contract development and programming.

Chapter 13, *Development Tools and Frameworks*, provides a detailed practical introduction to the Solidity programming language and different relevant tools and frameworks that are used for Ethereum development.

Chapter 14, *Introducing Web3*, covers development of decentralized applications and smart contracts using the Ethereum blockchain. A detailed introduction to Web3 API is provided along with multiple practical examples and a final project.

Chapter 15, *Hyperledger*, presents a discussion about the Hyperledger project from the Linux Foundation, which includes different blockchain projects introduced by its members.

Chapter 16, *Alternative Blockchains*, introduces alternative blockchain solutions and platforms. It provides technical details and features of alternative blockchains and relevant platforms.

Chapter 17, *Blockchain – Outside of Currencies*, provides a practical and detailed introduction to applications of blockchain technology in fields others than cryptocurrencies, including Internet of Things, government, media, and finance.

Chapter 18, *Scalability and Other Challenges*, is dedicated to a discussion of the challenges faced by blockchain technology and how to address them.

Chapter 19, *Current Landscape and What's Next*, is aimed at providing information about the current landscape, projects, and research efforts related to blockchain technology. Also, some predictions based on the current state of blockchain technology have also been made.

To get the most out of this book

- All examples in this book have been developed on Ubuntu 16.04.1 LTS (Xenial) and macOS version 10.13.2. As such, it is recommended to use Ubuntu or any other Unix like system. However, any appropriate operating system, either Windows or Linux, can be used, but examples, especially those related to installation, may need to be changed accordingly.

- Examples related to cryptography have been developed using the OpenSSL 1.0.2g 1 Mar 2016 command-line tool.

- Ethereum Solidity examples have been developed using Remix IDE, available online at `https://remix.ethereum.org`

- Ethereum Byzantine release is used to develop Ethereum-related examples. At the time of writing, this is the latest version available and can be downloaded from `https://www.ethereum.org/`.

- Examples related to IoT have been developed using a Raspberry Pi kit by Vilros, but any aapropriate latest model or kit can be used. Specifically, Raspberry Pi 3 Model B V 1.2 has been used to build the hardware example of IoT. Node.js V8.9.3 and npm V5.5.1 have been used to download related packages and run Node js server for IoT examples.

- The Truffle framework has been used in some examples of smart contract deployment, and is available at `http://truffleframework.com/`. Any latest version available via npm should be appropriate.

Download the example code files

You can download the example code files for this book from your account at `www.packtpub.com`. If you purchased this book elsewhere, you can visit `www.packtpub.com/support` and register to have the files emailed directly to you.

You can download the code files by following these steps:

1. Log in or register at `www.packtpub.com`.
2. Select the **SUPPORT** tab.
3. Click on **Code Downloads & Errata**.
4. Enter the name of the book in the **Search** box and follow the onscreen instructions.

Once the file is downloaded, please make sure that you unzip or extract the folder using the latest version of:

- WinRAR/7-Zip for Windows
- Zipeg/iZip/UnRarX for Mac
- 7-Zip/PeaZip for Linux

The code bundle for the book is also hosted on GitHub at `https://github.com/PacktPublishing/Mastering-Blockchain-Second-Edition`. In case there's an update to the code, it will be updated on the existing GitHub repository.

We also have other code bundles from our rich catalog of books and videos available at `https://github.com/PacktPublishing/`. Check them out!

Download the color images

We also provide a PDF file that has color images of the screenshots/diagrams used in this book. You can download it here: `http://www.packtpub.com/sites/default/files/downloads/MasteringBlockchainSecondEdition_ColorImages.pdf`.

Conventions used

There are a number of text conventions used throughout this book.

`CodeInText`: Indicates code words in text, database table names, folder names, filenames, file extensions, pathnames, dummy URLs, user input, and Twitter handles. Here is an example: "After executing the command, a file named `privatekey.pem` is produced, which contains the generated private key as follows."

A block of code is set as follows:

```
pragma solidity ^0.4.0;
contract TestStruct {
  struct Trade
  {
    uint tradeid;
    uint quantity;
    uint price;
    string trader;
  }

  //This struct can be initialized and used as below
```

```
    Trade tStruct = Trade({tradeid:123, quantity:1, price:1,
trader:"equinox"});

}
```

When we wish to draw your attention to a particular part of a code block, the relevant lines or items are set in bold:

```
pragma solidity ^0.4.0;
contract TestStruct {
  struct Trade
  {
    uint tradeid;
    uint quantity;
    uint price;
    string trader;
  }

  //This struct can be initialized and used as below

  Trade tStruct = Trade({tradeid:123, quantity:1, price:1,
trader:"equinox"});

}
```

Any command-line input or output is written as follows:

```
$ sudo apt-get install solc
```

Bold: Indicates a new term, an important word, or words that you see onscreen. For example, words in menus or dialog boxes appear in the text like this. Here is an example: "Enter the password and click on **SEND TRANSACTION** to deploy the contract."

Warnings or important notes appear like this.

Tips and tricks appear like this.

Get in touch

Feedback from our readers is always welcome.

General feedback: Email `feedback@packtpub.com` and mention the book title in the subject of your message. If you have questions about any aspect of this book, please email us at `questions@packtpub.com`.

Errata: Although we have taken every care to ensure the accuracy of our content, mistakes do happen. If you have found a mistake in this book, we would be grateful if you would report this to us. Please visit `www.packtpub.com/submit-errata`, selecting your book, clicking on the Errata Submission Form link, and entering the details.

Piracy: If you come across any illegal copies of our works in any form on the Internet, we would be grateful if you would provide us with the location address or website name. Please contact us at `copyright@packtpub.com` with a link to the material.

If you are interested in becoming an author: If there is a topic that you have expertise in and you are interested in either writing or contributing to a book, please visit `authors.packtpub.com`.

Reviews

Please leave a review. Once you have read and used this book, why not leave a review on the site that you purchased it from? Potential readers can then see and use your unbiased opinion to make purchase decisions, we at Packt can understand what you think about our products, and our authors can see your feedback on their book. Thank you!

For more information about Packt, please visit `packtpub.com`.

Blockchain 101 1

If you are reading this book, it is very likely that you already have heard about blockchain and have some fundamental appreciation of its enormous potential. If not, then let me tell you that this is a technology that has promised to positively alter the existing paradigms of nearly all industries including, but not limited to IT, finance, government, media, medical, and law.

This chapter serves an introduction to blockchain technology, its technical foundations, the theory behind it, and various techniques that have been combined together to build what is known today as blockchain.

In this chapter, we first describe the theoretical foundations of distributed systems. Next, we address the precursors of Bitcoin by which blockchain technology was introduced to the world. Finally, we introduce you to blockchain technology. This approach is a logical way to understanding blockchain technology, as the roots of blockchain are in distributed systems. We will cover a lot of ground quickly here, but don't worry—we will go over a great deal of this material in much greater detail as you move through the book.

The growth of blockchain technology

With the invention of Bitcoin in 2008, the world was introduced to a new concept, which is now likely to revolutionize the whole of society. It is something that promises to have an impact on every industry, including but not limited to the financial sector, government, media, law, and arts. Some describe blockchain as a revolution, whereas another school of thought believes that it is going to be more evolutionary, and it will take many years before any practical benefits of blockchain reach fruition. This thinking is correct to some extent, but in my opinion, the revolution has already begun.

Many prominent organizations all around the world are already writing proofs of concept using blockchain technology, as its disruptive potential has now been fully recognized. However, some organizations are still in the preliminary exploration stage, though they are expected to progress more quickly as the technology matures. It is a technology that has an impact on current technologies too and possesses the ability to change them at a fundamental level.

If we look at the last few years, we notice that in 2013 some ideas started to emerge that suggested usage of blockchain in other areas than cryptocurrencies. Around that time the primary usage of blockchain was cryptocurrencies, and many new coins emerged during that time. The following graph shows a broad-spectrum outline of year wise progression and adaption trend of blockchain technology. Years shown on the x axis indicate the range of time in which a specific phase of blockchain technology falls. Each phase has a name which represents the action and is shown on the x axis starting from the period of **IDEAS & THOUGHTS** to eventually **MATURITY & FURTHER STANDARDIZATION**. The y axis shows level of activity, involvement and adoption of blockchain technology. The graph shows that eventually, roughly around **2025** blockchain technology is expected to become mature with a high number of users.

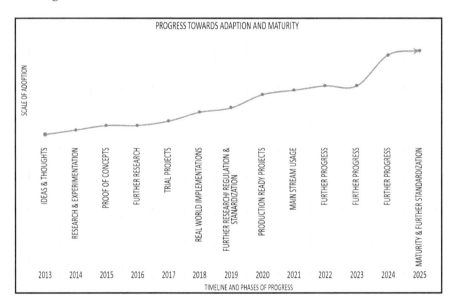

Blockchain technology adoption and maturity

The preceding graph shows that in 2013 **IDEAS & THOUGHTS** emerged related to other usages of blockchain technology apart from cryptocurrencies. Then in 2014 some **RESEARCH & EXPERIMENTATION** started which led to **PROOF OF CONCEPTS**, **FURTHER RESEARCH**, and full-scale **TRIAL PROJECTS** between 2015 and 2017. In 2018 we will see **REAL WORLD IMPLEMENTATIONS**. Already many projects are underway and set to replace existing systems, for example, **Australian Securities Exchange** (**ASX**) is soon to become the first organization to replace its legacy clearing and settlement system with blockchain technology.

 More information on this topic can be found at
`https://www.asx.com.au/services/chess-replacement.htm`.

It is expected that during 2019 more research will be carried out along with some interest towards regulation and standardization of blockchain technology. After this, production ready projects and off the shelf products utilizing blockchain technology will be available from 2020 and by 2021 mainstream usage of blockchain technology is expected to start. Progress in blockchain technology almost feels like the internet *dot-com boom* of the late 1990s. More research is expected to continue along with adaption and further maturity of blockchain technology, and finally, in 2025 it is expected that the technology will be mature enough to be used on day to day basis. Please note that the timelines provided in the chart are not strict and can vary as it is quite difficult to predict that when exactly blockchain technology will become mature. This graph is based on the progress made in the recent years and the current climate of research, interest and enthusiasm regarding this technology which suggests that by 2025 blockchain technology is expected to become mature.

Interest in blockchain technology has risen quite significantly over the last few years. Once dismissed as simply geek money from a cryptocurrency point of view, or as something that was just not considered worth pursuing, blockchain is now being researched by the largest companies and organizations around the world. Millions of dollars are being spent to adapt and experiment with this technology. This is evident from recent actions taken by European Union where they have announced plans to increase funding for blockchain research to almost 340 million euros by 2020.

 Interested readers can read more about this at
`https://www.irishtimes.com/business/technology/boost-for-blockch`
`ain-research-as-eu-increases-funding-four-fold-1.3383340`.

Another report suggests that global spending on blockchain technology research could reach 9.2 billion dollars by 2021.

More information regarding this can be found at
`https://bitcoinmagazine.com/articles/report-suggests-global-spen`
`ding-blockchain-tech-could-reach-92-billion-2021/`.

There are various consortiums such as **Enterprise Ethereum Alliance (EEA)**, **Hyperledger**, and **R3**, which have been established for research and development of blockchain technology. Moreover, a large number of start-ups are providing blockchain-based solutions already. A simple trend search on Google reveals the immense scale of interest in blockchain technology over the last few years. Especially, since early 2017 the increase in the search term *blockchain* is quite significant, as shown in the following graph:

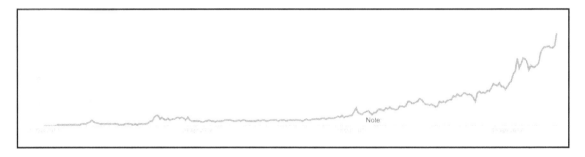

Google trend graph for blockchain

Various benefits of this technology are envisioned, such as decentralized trust, cost savings, transparency, and efficiency. However, there are multiple challenges too that are an area of active research on blockchain, such as scalability and privacy.

In this book, we are going to see how blockchain technology can help bring about the benefits mentioned earlier. You are going to learn about what exactly is blockchain technology, and how it can reshape businesses, multiple industries, and indeed everyday life by bringing about a plenitude of benefits such as efficiency, cost saving, transparency, and security. We will also explore what is distributed ledger technology, decentralization, and smart contracts and how technology solutions can be developed and implemented using mainstream blockchain platforms such as Ethereum, and Hyperledger. We will also investigate that what challenges need to be addressed before blockchain can become a mainstream technology.

Chapter 18, *Scalability and Other Challenges*, is dedicated to a discussion of the limitations and challenges of blockchain technology.

Distributed systems

Understanding distributed systems is essential to the understanding of blockchain technology, as blockchain is a distributed system at its core. It is a distributed ledger which can be centralized or decentralized. A blockchain is originally intended to be and is usually used as a decentralized platform. It can be thought of as a system that has properties of both decentralized and distributed paradigms. It is a decentralized-distributed system.

Distributed systems are a computing paradigm whereby two or more nodes work with each other in a coordinated fashion to achieve a common outcome. It is modeled in such a way that end users see it as a single logical platform. For example, Google's search engine is based on a large distributed system, but to a user, it looks like a single, coherent platform.

A **node** can be defined as an individual player in a distributed system. All nodes are capable of sending and receiving messages to and from each other. Nodes can be honest, faulty, or malicious, and they have memory and a processor. A node that exhibits irrational behavior is also known as a **Byzantine node** after the Byzantine Generals Problem.

The Byzantine Generals problem

In 1982, a thought experiment was proposed by Lamport and others in their research paper, *The Byzantine Generals Problem* which is available at: `https://www.microsoft.com/en-us/research/publication/byzantine-generals-problem/` whereby a group of army generals who lead different parts of the Byzantine army are planning to attack or retreat from a city. The only way of communicating among them is via a messenger. They need to agree to strike at the same time in order to win. The issue is that one or more generals might be traitors who could send a misleading message. Therefore, there is a need for a viable mechanism that allows for agreement among the generals, even in the presence of the treacherous ones, so that the attack can still take place at the same time. As an analogy to distributed systems, the generals can be considered nodes, the traitors as Byzantine (malicious) nodes, and the messenger can be thought of as a channel of communication among the generals.

This problem was solved in 1999 by Castro and Liskov who presented the **Practical Byzantine Fault Tolerance** (**PBFT**) algorithm, where consensus is reached after a certain number of messages are received containing the same signed content.

This type of inconsistent behavior of Byzantine nodes can be intentionally malicious, which is detrimental to the operation of the network. Any unexpected behavior by a node on the network, whether malicious or not, can be categorized as Byzantine.

A small-scale example of a distributed system is shown in the following diagram. This distributed system has six nodes out of which one (**N4**) is a Byzantine node leading to possible data inconsistency. **L2** is a link that is broken or slow, and this can lead to partition in the network.

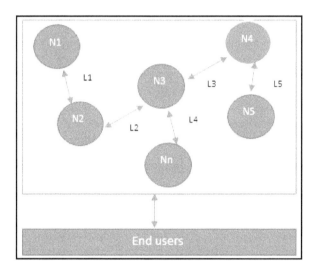

Design of a distributed system: N4 is a Byzantine node, L2 is broken or a slow network link

The primary challenge in distributed system design is coordination between nodes and fault tolerance. Even if some of the nodes become faulty or network links break, the distributed system should be able to tolerate this and continue to work to achieve the desired result. This problem has been an active area of distributed system design research for many years, and several algorithms and mechanisms have been proposed to overcome these issues.

Distributed systems are so challenging to design that a hypothesis known as the **CAP theorem** has been proven, which states that a distributed system cannot have all three of the much-desired properties simultaneously; that is, consistency, availability, and partition tolerance. We will dive into the CAP theorem in more detail later in this chapter.

The history of blockchain and Bitcoin

Blockchain was introduced with the invention of Bitcoin in 2008. Its practical implementation then occurred in 2009. For the purposes of this chapter, it is sufficient to review Bitcoin very briefly, as it will be explored in great depth in `Chapter 5`, *Introducing Bitcoin*. However, it is essential to refer to Bitcoin because, without it, the history of blockchain is not complete.

Electronic cash

The concept of electronic cash or digital currency is not new. Since the 1980s, e-cash protocols have existed that are based on a model proposed by David Chaum.

Just as understanding the concept of distributed systems is necessary to comprehend blockchain technology, the idea of electronic cash is also essential in order to appreciate the first and astonishingly successful application of blockchain, Bitcoin, or more broadly cryptocurrencies in general.

Two fundamental e-cash system issues need to be addressed: accountability and anonymity.

Accountability is required to ensure that cash is spendable only once (double-spend problem) and that it can only be spent by its rightful owner. Double spend problem arises when same money can be spent twice. As it is quite easy to make copies of digital data, this becomes a big issue in digital currencies as you can make many copies of same digital cash. **Anonymity** is required to protect users' privacy. As with physical cash, it is almost impossible to trace back spending to the individual who actually paid the money.

David Chaum solved both of these problems during his work in 1980s by using two cryptographic operations, namely **blind signatures** and **secret sharing**. These terminologies and related concepts will be discussed in detail in `Chapter 3`, *Symmetric Cryptography* and `Chapter 4`, *Public Key Cryptography*. For the moment, it is sufficient to say that *blind signatures* allow for signing a document without actually seeing it, and *secret sharing* is a concept that enables the detection of double spending, that is using the same e-cash token twice (double spending).

In 2009, the first practical implementation of an electronic cash (e-cash) system named Bitcoin appeared. The term cryptocurrency emerged later. For the very first time, it solved the problem of distributed consensus in a trustless network. It used **public key cryptography** with a **Proof of Work** (**PoW**) mechanism to provide a secure, controlled, and decentralized method of minting digital currency. The key innovation was the idea of an ordered list of blocks composed of transactions and cryptographically secured by the PoW mechanism. This concept will be explained in greater detail in Chapter 5, *Introducing Bitcoin*.

Other technologies used in Bitcoin, but which existed before its invention, include Merkle trees, hash functions, and hash chains. All these concepts are explained in appropriate depth in Chapter 4, *Public Key Cryptography*.

Looking at all the technologies mentioned earlier and their relevant history, it is easy to see how concepts from electronic cash schemes and distributed systems were combined to create Bitcoin and what now is known as blockchain. This concept can also be visualized with the help of the following diagram:

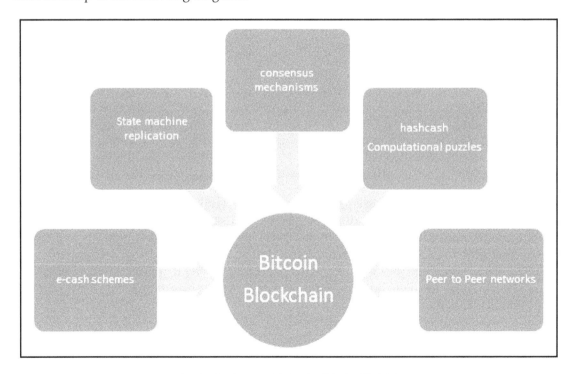

The various ideas that supported the invention of Bitcoin and blockchain

Blockchain

In 2008, a groundbreaking paper entitled *Bitcoin: A Peer-to-Peer Electronic Cash System* was written on the topic of peer-to-peer electronic cash under the pseudonym *Satoshi Nakamoto*. It introduced the term **chain of blocks**. No one knows the actual identity of Satoshi Nakamoto. After introducing Bitcoin in 2009, he remained active in the Bitcoin developer community until 2011. He then handed over Bitcoin development to its core developers and simply disappeared. Since then, there has been no communication from him whatsoever, and his existence and identity are shrouded in mystery. The term *chain of blocks* evolved over the years into the word *blockchain*.

As stated earlier, blockchain technology incorporates a multitude of applications that can be implemented in various economic sectors. Particularly in the finance sector, significant improvement in the performance of financial transactions and settlements is seen as resulting in desirable time and cost reductions. Additional light will be shed on these aspects of blockchain in Chapter 17, *Blockchain – Outside of Currencies* where practical use cases will be discussed in detail for various industries. For now, it is sufficient to say that parts of nearly all economic sectors have already realized the potential and promise of blockchain and have embarked, or will do so soon, on the journey to capitalize on the benefits of blockchain technology.

Blockchain defined

Layman's definition: Blockchain is an ever-growing, secure, shared record keeping system in which each user of the data holds a copy of the records, which can only be updated if all parties involved in a transaction agree to update.
Technical definition: Blockchain is a peer-to-peer, distributed ledger that is cryptographically-secure, append-only, immutable (extremely hard to change), and updateable only via consensus or agreement among peers.

Now let's examine the preceding definitions in more detail. We will look at all keywords in the definitions one by one.

Peer-to-peer

The first keyword in the technical definition is *peer-to-peer*. This means that there is no central controller in the network, and all participants talk to each other directly. This property allows for cash transactions to be exchanged directly among the peers without a third-party involvement, such as by a bank.

Distributed ledger

Dissecting the technical definition further reveals that blockchain is a *distributed ledger*, which simply means that a ledger is spread across the network among all peers in the network, and each peer holds a copy of the complete ledger.

Cryptographically-secure

Next, we see that this ledger is *cryptographically-secure*, which means that cryptography has been used to provide security services which make this ledger secure against tampering and misuse. These services include non-repudiation, data integrity, and data origin authentication. You will see how this is achieved later in Chapter 3, *Symmetric Cryptography* which introduces the fascinating world of cryptography.

Append-only

Another property that we encounter is that blockchain is *append-only*, which means that data can only be added to the blockchain in *time-ordered sequential order*. This property implies that once data is added to the blockchain, it is almost impossible to change that data and can be considered practically immutable. Nonetheless, it can be changed in rare scenarios wherein collusion against the blockchain network succeeds in gaining more than 51 percent of the power. There may be some legitimate reasons to change data in the blockchain once it has been added, such as the *right to be forgotten* or *right to erasure* (also defined in **General Data Protection** (**GDPR**) ruling, https://gdpr-info.eu/art-17-gdpr/).

However, those are individual cases that need to be handled separately and that require an elegant technical solution. For all practical purposes, blockchain is indeed immutable and cannot be changed.

Updateable via consensus

Finally, the most critical attribute of a blockchain is that it is *updateable* only via consensus. This is what gives it the power of decentralization. In this scenario, no central authority is in control of updating the ledger. Instead, any update made to the blockchain is validated against strict criteria defined by the blockchain protocol and added to the blockchain only after a consensus has been reached among all participating peers/nodes on the network. To achieve consensus, there are various consensus facilitation algorithms which ensure that all parties are in agreement about the final state of the data on the blockchain network and resolutely agree upon it to be true. Consensus algorithms are discussed later in this chapter and throughout the book as appropriate.

Blockchain can be thought of as a layer of a distributed peer-to-peer network running on top of the internet, as can be seen in the following diagram. It is analogous to SMTP, HTTP, or FTP running on top of TCP/IP.

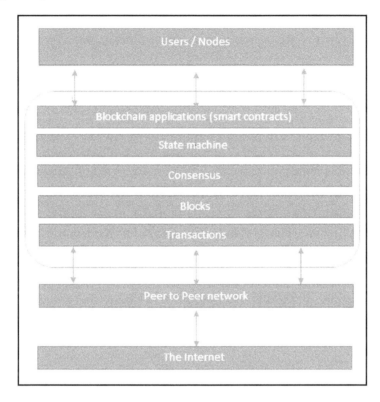

The network view of a blockchain

At the bottom layer in the preceding diagram, there is the internet, which provides a basic communication layer for any network. In this case, a peer-to-peer network runs on top of the internet, which hosts another layer of blockchain. That layer contains transactions, blocks, consensus mechanisms, state machines, and blockchain smart contracts. All of these components are shown as a single logical entity in a box, representing blockchain above the peer-to-peer network. Finally, at the top, there are users or nodes that connect to the blockchain and perform various operations such as consensus, transaction verification, and processing. These concepts will be discussed in detail later in this book.

From a business standpoint, a blockchain can be defined as a platform where peers can exchange value / electronic cash using transactions without the need for a centrally-trusted arbitrator. For example, for cash transfers, banks act as a trusted third party. In financial trading, a central clearing house acts as an arbitrator between two trading parties. This concept is compelling, and once you absorb it, you will realize the enormous potential of blockchain technology. This disintermediation allows blockchain to be a decentralized consensus mechanism where no single authority is in charge of the database. Immediately, you'll see a significant benefit of decentralization here, because if no banks or central clearing houses are required, then it immediately leads to cost savings, faster transaction speeds, and trust.

A **block** is merely a selection of transactions bundled together and organized logically. A **transaction** is a record of an event, for example, the event of transferring cash from a sender's account to a beneficiary's account. A block is made up of transactions, and its size varies depending on the type and design of the blockchain in use.

A reference to a previous block is also included in the block unless it is a genesis block. A **genesis block** is the first block in the blockchain that is hardcoded at the time the blockchain was first started. The structure of a block is also dependent on the type and design of a blockchain. Generally, however, there are just a few attributes that are essential to the functionality of a block: the block header, which is composed of pointer to previous block, the timestamp, nonce, Merkle root, and the block body that contains transactions. There are also other attributes in a block, but generally, the aforementioned components are always available in a block.

A **nonce** is a number that is generated and used only once. A nonce is used extensively in many cryptographic operations to provide replay protection, authentication, and encryption. In blockchain, it's used in PoW consensus algorithms and for transaction replay protection.

Merkle root is a hash of all of the nodes of a Merkle tree. Merkle trees are widely used to validate the large data structures securely and efficiently. In the blockchain world, Merkle trees are commonly used to allow efficient verification of transactions. Merkle root in a blockchain is present in the block header section of a block, which is the hash of all transactions in a block. This means that verifying only the Merkle root is required to verify all transactions present in the Merkle tree instead of verifying all transactions one by one. We will elaborate further on these concepts in `Chapter 4`, *Public Key Cryptography*.

The generic structure of a block.

This preceding structure is a simple block diagram that depicts a block. Specific block structures relative to their blockchain technologies will be discussed later in the book with greater in-depth technical detail.

Generic elements of a blockchain

Now, let's walk through the generic elements of a blockchain. You can use this as a handy reference section if you ever need a reminder about the different parts of a blockchain. More precise elements will be discussed in the context of their respective blockchains in later chapters, for example, the Ethereum blockchain. The structure of a generic blockchain can be visualized with the help of the following diagram:

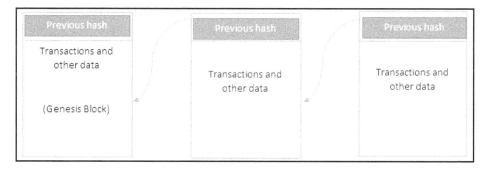

Generic structure of a blockchain

Elements of a generic blockchain are described here one by one. These are the elements that you will come across in relation to blockchain:

- **Address**: Addresses are unique identifiers used in a blockchain transaction to denote senders and recipients. An address is usually a public key or derived from a public key. While addresses can be reused by the same user, addresses themselves are unique. In practice, however, a single user may not use the same address again and generate a new one for each transaction. This newly-created address will be unique. Bitcoin is, in fact, a pseudonymous system. End users are usually not directly identifiable, but some research in removing the anonymity of Bitcoin users has shown that they can be identified successfully. A good practice is for users to generate a new address for each transaction in order to avoid linking transactions to the common owner, thus preventing identification.

- **Transaction**: A transaction is the fundamental unit of a blockchain. A transaction represents a transfer of value from one address to another.

- **Block**: A block is composed of multiple transactions and other elements, such as the previous block hash (hash pointer), timestamp, and nonce.

- **Peer-to-peer network**: As the name implies, a peer-to-peer network is a network topology wherein all peers can communicate with each other and send and receive messages.

- **Scripting or programming language**: Scripts or programs perform various operations on a transaction in order to facilitate various functions. For example, in Bitcoin, transaction scripts are predefined in a language called **Script**, which consist of sets of commands that allow nodes to transfer tokens from one address to another. Script is a limited language, however, in the sense that it only allows essential operations that are necessary for executing transactions, but it does not allow for arbitrary program development. Think of it as a calculator that only supports standard preprogrammed arithmetic operations. As such, Bitcoin script language cannot be called *Turing complete*. In simple words, Turing complete language means that it can perform any computation. It is named after Alan Turing who developed the idea of Turing machine that can run any algorithm however complex. Turing complete languages need loops and branching capability to perform complex computations. Therefore, Bitcoin's scripting language is not Turing complete, whereas Ethereum's Solidity language is.

To facilitate arbitrary program development on a blockchain, Turing complete programming language is needed, and it is now a very desirable feature of blockchains. Think of this as a computer that allows development of any program using programming languages. Nevertheless, the security of such languages is a crucial question and an essential and ongoing research area. We will discuss this in greater detail in `Chapter 5`, *Introducing Bitcoin*, `Chapter 9`, *Smart Contracts*, and `Chapter 13`, *Development Tools and Frameworks*, later in this book.

- **Virtual machine**: This is an extension of the transaction script introduced earlier. A *virtual machine* allows Turing complete code to be run on a blockchain (as smart contracts); whereas a transaction script is limited in its operation. However, virtual machines are not available on all blockchains. Various blockchains use virtual machines to run programs such as **Ethereum Virtual Machine** (**EVM**) and **Chain Virtual Machine** (**CVM**). EVM is used in Ethereum blockchain, while CVM is a virtual machine developed for and used in an enterprise-grade blockchain called **Chain Core**.

- **State machine**: A blockchain can be viewed as a state transition mechanism whereby a state is modified from its initial form to the next one and eventually to a final form by nodes on the blockchain network as a result of a transaction execution, validation, and finalization process.

- **Node**: A node in a blockchain network performs various functions depending on the role that it takes on. A node can propose and validate transactions and perform mining to facilitate consensus and secure the blockchain. This goal is achieved by following a **consensus protocol** (most commonly PoW). Nodes can also perform other functions such as simple payment verification (lightweight nodes), validation, and many other functions depending on the type of the blockchain used and the role assigned to the node. Nodes also perform a transaction signing function. Transactions are first created by nodes and then also digitally signed by nodes using private keys as proof that they are the legitimate owner of the asset that they wish to transfer to someone else on the blockchain network. This asset is usually a token or virtual currency, such as Bitcoin, but it can also be any real-world asset represented on the blockchain by using tokens.

- **Smart contract**: These programs run on top of the blockchain and encapsulate the business logic to be executed when certain conditions are met. These programs are enforceable and automatically executable. The smart contract feature is not available on all blockchain platforms, but it is now becoming a very desirable feature due to the flexibility and power that it provides to the blockchain applications. Smart contracts have many use cases, including but not limited to identity management, capital markets, trade finance, record management, insurance, and e-governance. Smart contracts will be discussed in more detail in `Chapter 9`, *Smart Contracts*.

How blockchain works

We have now defined and described blockchain. Now let's see how a blockchain actually works. Nodes are either *miners* who create new blocks and mint cryptocurrency (coins) or *block signers* who validates and digitally sign the transactions. A critical decision that every blockchain network has to make is to figure out that which node will append the next block to the blockchain. This decision is made using a *consensus mechanism*. The consensus mechanism will be described later in this chapter.

Now we will look at the how a blockchain validates transactions and creates and adds blocks to grow the blockchain.

How blockchain accumulates blocks

Now we will look at a general scheme for creating blocks. This scheme is presented here to give you a general idea of how blocks are generated and what the relationship is between transactions and blocks:

1. A node starts a transaction by first creating and then digitally signing it with its private key. A transaction can represent various actions in a blockchain. Most commonly this is a data structure that represents transfer of value between users on the blockchain network. Transaction data structure usually consists of some logic of transfer of value, relevant rules, source and destination addresses, and other validation information. This will be covered in more detail in specific chapters on Bitcoin and Ethereum later in the book.
2. A transaction is propagated (flooded) by using a flooding protocol, called Gossip protocol, to peers that validate the transaction based on preset criteria. Usually, more than one node are required to verify the transaction.

3. Once the transaction is validated, it is included in a block, wh propagated onto the network. At this point, the transaction is confirmed.

4. The newly-created block now becomes part of the ledger, and itself cryptographically back to this block. This link is a hash p stage, the transaction gets its second confirmation and the blo confirmation.

5. Transactions are then reconfirmed every time a new block is created. Usually, six confirmations in the Bitcoin network are required to consider the transaction final.

It is worth noting that steps 4 and 5 are considered non-compulsory, as the transaction itself is finalized in step 3; however, block confirmation and further transaction reconfirmations, if required, are then carried out in step 4 and step 5.

This completes the basic introduction to blockchain. In the next section, you will learn about the benefits and limitations of this technology.

Benefits and limitations of blockchain

Numerous advantages of blockchain technology have been discussed in many industries and proposed by thought leaders around the world who are participating in the blockchain space. The notable benefits of blockchain technology are as follows:

- **Decentralization**: This is a core concept and benefit of the blockchain. There is no need for a trusted third party or intermediary to validate transactions; instead, a consensus mechanism is used to agree on the validity of transactions.

- **Transparency and trust**: Because blockchains are shared and everyone can see what is on the blockchain, this allows the system to be transparent. As a result, trust is established. This is more relevant in scenarios such as the disbursement of funds or benefits where personal discretion in relation to selecting beneficiaries needs to be restricted.

- **Immutability**: Once the data has been written to the blockchain, it is extremely difficult to change it back. It is not genuinely immutable, but because changing data is so challenging and nearly impossible, this is seen as a benefit to maintaining an immutable ledger of transactions.

- **High availability**: As the system is based on thousands of nodes in a peer-to-peer network, and the data is replicated and updated on every node, the system becomes highly available. Even if some nodes leave the network or become inaccessible, the network as a whole continues to work, thus making it highly available. This redundancy results in high availability.
- **Highly secure**: All transactions on a blockchain are cryptographically secured and thus provide network integrity.
- **Simplification of current paradigms**: The current blockchain model in many industries, such as finance or health, is somewhat disorganized. In this model, multiple entities maintain their own databases and data sharing can become very difficult due to the disparate nature of the systems. However, as a blockchain can serve as a single shared ledger among many interested parties, this can result in simplifying the model by reducing the complexity of managing the separate systems maintained by each entity.
- **Faster dealings**: In the financial industry, especially in post-trade settlement functions, blockchain can play a vital role by enabling the quick settlement of trades. Blockchain does not require a lengthy process of verification, reconciliation, and clearance because a single version of agreed-upon data is already available on a shared ledger between financial organizations.
- **Cost saving**: As no trusted third party or clearing house is required in the blockchain model, this can massively eliminate overhead costs in the form of the fees which are paid to such parties.

As with any technology, some challenges need to be addressed in order to make a system more robust, useful, and accessible. Blockchain technology is no exception. In fact, much effort is being made in both academia and industry to overcome the challenges posed by blockchain technology. The most sensitive blockchain problems are as follows:

- Scalability
- Adaptability
- Regulation
- Relatively immature technology
- Privacy

All of these issues and possible solutions will be discussed in detail in Chapter 18, *Scalability and Other Challenges*.

Tiers of blockchain technology

In this section, various layers of blockchain technology are presented. It is thought that due to the rapid development and progress being made in blockchain technology, many applications will evolve. Some of these advancements have already been realized, while others are anticipated in the near future based on the current rate of advancement in blockchain technology.

The three levels discussed here were initially described in the book *Blockchain: Blueprint for a New Economy* by *Melanie Swan, O'Reilly Media, 2015* as blockchain tiers categorized by applications in each category. This is how blockchain is evolving, and this versioning shows different tiers of evolution and usage of blockchain technology. In fact, all blockchain platforms, with limited exceptions, support these functionalities and applications. This versioning is just a logical segregation of various blockchain categories based on the way that they are currently being used, are evolving, or predicted to evolve.

Also note that this versioning is being presented here for completeness and for historic reasons, as these definitions are somewhat blurred now, and with the exception of Bitcoin (Blockchain 1.0), all newer blockchain platforms that support smart contract development can be programmed to provide the functionalities and applications mentioned in all blockchain tiers: 1.0, 2.0, 3.0, and beyond.

In addition to Tier 1, Tier 2 and Tier 3, or Tier X in the future, the following represents my own vision of what blockchain technology eventually could become as this technology advances:

- **Blockchain 1.0**: This tier was introduced with the invention of Bitcoin, and it is primarily used for cryptocurrencies. Also, as Bitcoin was the first implementation of cryptocurrencies, it makes sense to categorize this first generation of blockchain technology to include only cryptographic currencies. All alternative cryptocurrencies as well as Bitcoin fall into this category. It includes core applications such as payments and applications. This generation started in 2009 when Bitcoin was released and ended in early 2010.
- **Blockchain 2.0**: This second blockchain generation is used by financial services and smart contracts. This tier includes various financial assets, such as derivatives, options, swaps, and bonds. Applications that go beyond currency, finance, and markets are incorporated at this tier. Ethereum, Hyperledger, and other newer blockchain platforms are considered part of Blockchain 2.0. This generation started when ideas related to using blockchain for other purposes started to emerge in 2010.

- **Blockchain 3.0**: This third blockchain generation is used to implement applications beyond the financial services industry and is used in government, health, media, the arts, and justice. Again, as in Blockchain 2.0, Ethereum, Hyperledger, and newer blockchains with the ability to code smart contracts are considered part of this blockchain technology tier. This generation of blockchain emerged around 2012 when multiple applications of blockchain technology in different industries were researched.

- **Blockchain X.0**: This generation represents a vision of blockchain singularity where one day there will be a public blockchain service available that anyone can use just like the Google search engine. It will provide services for all realms of society. It will be a public and open distributed ledger with general-purpose rational agents (*Machina economicus*) running on a blockchain, making decisions, and interacting with other intelligent autonomous agents on behalf of people, and regulated by code instead of law or paper contracts. This does not mean that law and contracts will disappear, instead law and contracts will be implementable in code.

Machina Economicus is a concept which comes from the field of **Artificial Intelligence** (**AI**) and computational economics. It can be defined as a machine that makes logical and perfect decisions. There are various technical challenges that need to be addressed before this dream can be realized.

 Discussion of Machina Economicus is beyond the scope of this book, interested readers can refer to `https://www.infosys.com/insights/purposeful-ai/Documents/machina-economicus.pdf`, for more information.

This concept in the context of blockchain and its convergence with AI will be elaborated on in `Chapter 19`, *Current Landscape and What's Next*.

Features of a blockchain

A blockchain performs various functions which are supported by various features. These functions include but are not limited to transfer of value, managing assets and agreements. All of the blockchain tiers described in the previous section perform these functions with the help of features offered by blockchain, but with some exceptions. For example, smart contracts are not supported by all blockchain platforms, such as Bitcoin. Another example is that not all blockchain platforms produce cryptocurrency or tokens, such as Hyperledger Fabric, and MultiChain.

The features of a blockchain are described here:

- **Distributed consensus**: Distributed consensus is the primary underpinning of a blockchain. This mechanism allows a blockchain to present a single version of the truth, which is agreed upon by all parties without the requirement of a central authority.
- **Transaction verification**: Any transactions posted from the nodes on the blockchain are verified based on a predetermined set of rules. Only valid transactions are selected for inclusion in a block.
- **Platform for smart contracts**: A blockchain is a platform on which programs can run to execute business logic on behalf of the users. Not all blockchains have a mechanism to execute *smart contracts*; however, this is a very desirable feature, and it is available on newer blockchain platforms such as Ethereum and MultiChain.

Smart Contracts

Blockchain technology provides a platform for running smart contracts. These are automated, autonomous programs that reside on the blockchain network and encapsulate the business logic and code needed to execute a required function when certain conditions are met. For example, think about an insurance contract where a claim is paid to the traveler if the flight is canceled. In the real world, this process normally takes a significant amount of time to make the claim, verify it, and pay the insurance amount to the claimant (traveler). What if this whole process were automated with cryptographically-enforced trust, transparency, and execution so that as soon as the smart contract received a feed that the flight in question has been canceled, it automatically triggers the insurance payment to the claimant? If the flight is on time, the smart contract pays itself.

This is indeed a revolutionary feature of blockchain, as it provides flexibility, speed, security, and automation for real-world scenarios that can lead to a completely trustworthy system with significant cost reductions. Smart contracts can be programmed to perform any actions that blockchain users need and according to their specific business requirements.

- **Transferring value between peers**: Blockchain enables the transfer of value between its users via tokens. Tokens can be thought of as a carrier of value.

- **Generation of cryptocurrency**: This feature is optional depending on the type of blockchain in use. A blockchain can create cryptocurrency as an incentive to its miners who validate the transactions and spend resources to secure the blockchain. We will discuss cryptocurrencies in great detail in Chapter 5, *Introducing Bitcoin*.

- **Smart property**: It is now possible to link a digital or physical asset to the blockchain in such a secure and precise manner that it cannot be claimed by anyone else. You are in full control of your asset, and it cannot be double-spent or double-owned. Compare this with a digital music file, for example, which can be copied many times without any controls. While it is true that many **Digital Rights Management** (**DRM**) schemes are being used currently along with copyright laws, but none of them is enforceable in such a way as blockchain based DRM can be. Blockchain can provide DRM functionality in such a way that it can be enforced fully. There are famously broken DRM schemes which looked great in theory but were hacked due to one limitation or another. One example is Oculus hack (http://www.wired.co.uk/article/oculus-rift-drm-hacked).

Another example is PS3 hack, also copyrighted digital music, films and e-books are routinely shared on the internet without any limitations. We have copyright protection in place for many years, but digital piracy refutes all attempts to fully enforce the law on a blockchain, however, if you own an asset, no one else can claim it unless you decide to transfer it. This feature has far-reaching implications, especially in DRM and electronic cash systems where double-spend detection is a crucial requirement. The double-spend problem was first solved without the requirement of a trusted third party in Bitcoin.

- **Provider of security**: The blockchain is based on proven cryptographic technology that ensures the integrity and availability of data. Generally, confidentiality is not provided due to the requirements of transparency. This limitation is the leading barrier to its adoption by financial institutions and other industries that require privacy and confidentiality of transactions. As such, the privacy and confidentiality of transactions on the blockchain is being researched very actively, and advancements are already being made. It could be argued that, in many situations, confidentiality is not needed and transparency is preferred. For example, with Bitcoin, confidentiality is not an absolute requirement; however, it is desirable in some scenarios. A more recent example is Zcash, which provides a platform for conducting anonymous transactions. This scheme will be discussed in detail in Chapter 8, *Alternative Coins*. Other security services, such as non-repudiation and authentication, are also provided by blockchain, as all actions are secured using private keys and digital signatures.

- **Immutability**: This is another critical feature of blockchain: once records are added to the blockchain, they are immutable. There is the remote possibility of rolling back changes, but this is to be avoided at all costs as doing so would consume an exorbitant amount of computing resources. For example, with Bitcoin if a malicious user wants to alter previous blocks, then it would require computing the PoW once again for all those blocks that have already been added to the blockchain. This difficulty makes the records on a blockchain essentially immutable.

- **Uniqueness**: This blockchain feature ensures that every transaction is unique and has not already been spent (double-spend problem). This feature is especially relevant with cryptocurrencies, where detection and avoidance of double spending are a vital requirement.

Types of blockchain

Based on the way that blockchain has evolved over the last few years, it can be divided into multiple categories with distinct though sometimes partially-overlapping attributes. You *should* note that the tiers described earlier in the chapter are a different concept whereby the logical categorization of blockchain based on its evolution and usage is presented.

In this section, we will examine the different types of blockchains from a technical and business usage perspective. These blockchain types can occur on any blockchain tier, as there is no direct relationship between those tiers and the various types of blockchain.

In this section we'll examine:

- Distributed ledgers
- Distributed Ledger Technology (DLT)
- Blockchains
- Ledgers

Distributed ledgers

First, I need to clarify an ambiguity. It should be noted that a *distributed ledger* is a broad term describing shared databases; hence, all blockchains technically fall under the umbrella of shared databases or distributed ledgers. Although all blockchains are fundamentally distributed ledgers, all distributed ledgers are not necessarily a blockchain.

A critical difference between a distributed ledger and blockchain is that a distributed ledger does not necessarily consist of blocks of transactions to keep the ledger growing. Rather, a blockchain is a special type of shared database that is comprised of blocks of transactions. An example of a distributed ledger that does not use blocks of transactions is R3's Corda. Corda is a distributed ledger which is developed to record and manage agreements and is especially focused on financial services industry. On the other hand, more widely-known blockchains like Bitcoin and Ethereum make use of blocks to update the shared database.

As the name suggests, a distributed ledger is distributed among its participants and spread across multiple sites or organizations. This type of ledger can be either private or public. The fundamental idea here is that, unlike many other blockchains, the records are stored contiguously instead of being sorted into blocks. This concept is used in Ripple which is a blockchain and cryptocurrency based global payment network.

Distributed Ledger Technology

It should be noted that over the last few years, the terms distributed ledger or **Distributed Ledger Technology** (**DLT**) have grown to be commonly used to describe blockchain in finance industry. Sometimes, blockchain and DLT are used interchangeably. Though this is not entirely accurate, it is how the term has evolved recently, especially in the finance sector. In fact, DLT is now a very active and thriving area of research in the financial sector. From a financial sector point of view, DLTs are permissioned blockchains that are shared and used between known participants. DLTs usually serve as a shared database, with all participants known and verified. They do not have a cryptocurrency or do not require mining to secure the ledger.

Public blockchains

As the name suggests, public blockchains are not owned by anyone. They are open to the public, and anyone can participate as a node in the decision-making process. Users may or may not be rewarded for their participation. All users of these *permissionless* or *unpermissioned* ledgers maintain a copy of the ledger on their local nodes and use a distributed consensus mechanism to decide the eventual state of the ledger. Bitcoin and Ethereum are both considered public blockchains.

Private blockchains

As the name implies, private blockchains are just that—private. That is, they are open only to a consortium or group of individuals or organizations who have decided to share the ledger among themselves. There are various blockchains now available in this category, such as HydraChain and Quorum. Optionally, both of these blockchains can also run in public mode if required, but their primary purpose is to provide a private blockchain.

Semiprivate blockchains

With *semiprivate blockchains*, part of the blockchain is private and part of it is public. Note that this is still just a concept today, and no real world POCs have yet been developed. With a semi-private blockchain, the private part is controlled by a group of individuals, while the public part is open for participation by anyone.

This hybrid model can be used in scenarios where the private part of the blockchain remains internal and shared among known participants, while the public part of the blockchain can still be used by anyone, optionally allowing mining to secure the blockchain. This way, the blockchain as a whole can be secured using PoW, thus providing consistency and validity for both the private and public parts. This type of blockchain can also be called a *semi-decentralized* model, where it is controlled by a single entity but still allows for multiple users to join the network by following appropriate procedures.

Sidechains

More precisely known as *pegged sidechains,* this is a concept whereby coins can be moved from one blockchain to another and moved back again. Typical uses include the creation of new *altcoins* (alternative cryptocurrencies) whereby coins are burnt as a proof of an adequate stake. *Burnt* or *burning the coins* in this context means that the coins are sent to an address which is unspendable and this process makes the *burnt* coins irrecoverable. This mechanism is used to bootstrap a new currency or introduce scarcity which results in increased value of the coin.

This mechanism is also called **Proof of Burn** (**PoB**) and is used as an alternative method for distributed consensus to PoW and **Proof of Stake** (**PoS**). The aforementioned example for burning coins applies to a **one-way pegged sidechain**. The second type is called a **two-way pegged sidechain**, which allows the movement of coins from the main chain to the sidechain and back to the main chain when required.

This process enables the building of smart contracts for the Bitcoin network. Rootstock is one of the leading examples of a sidechain, which enables smart contract development for Bitcoin using this paradigm. It works by allowing a two-way peg for the Bitcoin blockchain, and this results in much faster throughput.

Permissioned ledger

A *permissioned ledger* is a blockchain where participants of the network are already known and trusted. Permissioned ledgers do not need to use a distributed consensus mechanism; instead, an agreement protocol is used to maintain a shared version of the truth about the state of the records on the blockchain. In this case, for verification of transactions on the chain, all verifiers are already preselected by a central authority and typically there is no need for a mining mechanism.

By definition, there is also no requirement for a permissioned blockchain to be private, as it can be a public blockchain but with regulated access control. For example, Bitcoin can become a permissioned ledger if an access control layer is introduced on top of it that verifies the identity of a user and then allows access to the blockchain.

Shared ledger

This is a generic term that is used to describe any application or database that is shared by the public or a consortium. Generally, all blockchains, fall into the category of a shared ledger.

Fully private and proprietary blockchains

There is no mainstream application of these types of blockchains, as they deviate from the core concept of decentralization in blockchain technology. Nonetheless, in specific private settings within an organization, there could be a need to share data and provide some level of guarantee of the authenticity of the data.

An example of this type of blockchain might be to allow for collaboration and the sharing data between various government departments. In that case, no complex consensus mechanism is required, apart from simple state machine replication and an agreement protocol with known central validators. Even in private blockchains, tokens are not really required, but they can be used as means of transferring value or representing some real-world asset.

Tokenized blockchains

These blockchains are standard blockchains that generate cryptocurrency as a result of a consensus process via mining or initial distribution. Bitcoin and Ethereum are prime examples of this type of blockchain.

Tokenless blockchains

These blockchains are designed in such a way that they do not have the basic unit for the transfer of value. However, they are still valuable in situations where there is no need to transfer value between nodes and only the sharing of data among various trusted parties is required. This is similar to full private blockchains, the only difference being that use of tokens is not required. This can also be thought of as a shared distributed ledger used for storing data. It does have its benefits when it comes to immutability, security, and consensus driven updates but are not used for common blockchain application of value transfer or cryptocurrency.

This ends our examination of the various type of blockchain, we'll now move in the next section to discuss the concept of census.

Consensus

Consensus is the backbone of a blockchain and, as a result, it provides decentralization of control through an optional process known as **mining**. The choice of the **consensus algorithm** is also governed by the type of blockchain in use; that is, not all consensus mechanisms are suitable for all types of blockchains. For example, in public permissionless blockchains, it would make sense to use PoW instead of a simple agreement mechanism that is perhaps based on proof of authority. Therefore, it is essential to choose an appropriate consensus algorithm for a particular blockchain project.

Consensus is a process of agreement between distrusting nodes on the final state of data. To achieve consensus, different algorithms are used. It is easy to reach an agreement between two nodes (in client-server systems, for example), but when multiple nodes are participating in a distributed system and they need to agree on a single value, it becomes quite a challenge to achieve consensus. This process of attaining agreement common state or value among multiple nodes despite the failure of some nodes is known as **distributed consensus**.

Consensus mechanism

A **consensus mechanism** is a set of steps that are taken by most or all nodes in a blockchain to agree on a proposed state or value. For more than three decades, this concept has been researched by computer scientists in industry and academia. Consensus mechanisms have most recently come into the limelight and gained considerable popularity with the advent of blockchain and Bitcoin.

There are various requirements that must be met to provide the desired results in a consensus mechanism. The following describes these requirements:

- **Agreement**: All honest nodes decide on the same value
- **Termination**: All honest nodes terminate execution of the consensus process and eventually reach a decision
- **Validity**: The value agreed upon by all honest nodes must be the same as the initial value proposed by at least one honest node
- **Fault tolerant**: The consensus algorithm should be able to run in the presence of faulty or malicious nodes (Byzantine nodes)
- **Integrity**: This is a requirement that no node can make the decision more than once in a single consensus cycle

Types of consensus mechanisms

All consensus mechanisms are developed to deal with faults in a distributed system and to allow distributed systems to reach a final state of agreement. There are two general categories of consensus mechanisms. These categories deal with all types of faults (fail stop type or arbitrary). These common types of consensus mechanisms are as follows:

- **Traditional Byzantine Fault Tolerance (BFT)-based**: With no compute-intensive operations, such as partial hash inversion (as in Bitcoin PoW), this method relies on a simple scheme of nodes that are publisher-signed messages. Eventually, when a certain number of messages are received, then an agreement is reached.
- **Leader election-based consensus mechanisms**: This arrangement requires nodes to compete in a leader-election lottery, and the node that wins proposes a final value. For example, the PoW used in Bitcoin falls into this category.

Many practical implementations of consensus protocols have been proposed. **Paxos** is the most famous of these protocols. It was introduced by Leslie Lamport in 1989. With Paxos, nodes are assigned various roles such as Proposer, Acceptor, and Learner. Nodes or processes are named replicas, and consensus is achieved in the presence of faulty nodes by agreement among a majority of nodes.

An alternative to Paxos is RAFT, which works by assigning any of three states; that is, follower, candidate, or leader to the nodes. A leader is elected after a candidate node receives enough votes, and all changes then have to go through the leader. The leader commits the proposed changes once replication on the majority of the follower nodes is completed. More detail on the theory of consensus mechanisms from a distributed system point of view are beyond the scope of this chapter. Later in this chapter, however, a full section is dedicated to the introduction of consensus protocols. Specific algorithms will be discussed in chapters dedicated to Bitcoin and other blockchains later in this book.

Consensus in blockchain

Consensus is a distributed computing concept that has been used in blockchain in order to provide a means of agreeing to a single version of the truth by all peers on the blockchain network. This concept was previously discussed in the distributed systems section of this chapter. In this section, we will address consensus in the context of blockchain technology. Some concepts presented here are still relevant to distributed systems theory, but they are explained from a blockchain perspective.

Roughly, the following describes the two main categories of consensus mechanisms:

- Proof-based, leader-election lottery based, or the Nakamoto consensus whereby a leader is elected at random (using an algorithm) and proposes a final value. This category is also referred to as the *fully decentralized* or *permissionless* type of consensus mechanism. This type is well used in the Bitcoin and Ethereum blockchain in the form of a PoW mechanism.
- BFT-based is a more traditional approach based on rounds of votes. This class of consensus is also known as the *consortium* or *permissioned* type of consensus mechanism.

BFT-based consensus mechanisms perform well when there are a limited number of nodes, but they do not scale well. On the other hand, leader-election lottery based (PoW) type consensus mechanisms scale very well but perform very slowly. As there is significant research being conducted in this area, new types of consensus mechanism are also emerging, such as the semi-decentralized type, which is used in the Ripple network. Ripple network will be discussed in detail in Chapter 16, *Alternative Blockchains*. There are also various other proposals out there, which are trying to find the right balance between scalability and performance. Some notable projects include PBFT, Hybrid BFT, BlockDAG, Tezos, Stellar, and GHOST.

The consensus algorithms available today, or that are being researched in the context of blockchain, are presented here. The following is not an exhaustive list, but it includes all notable algorithms.

- **Proof of Work (PoW)**: This type of consensus mechanism relies on proof that adequate computational resources have been spent before proposing a value for acceptance by the network. This scheme is used in Bitcoin, Litecoin, and other cryptocurrency blockchains. Currently, it is the only algorithm that has proven to be astonishingly successful against any collusion attacks on a blockchain network, such as the Sybil attack. The Sybil attack will be discussed in Chapter 5, *Introducing Bitcoin*.
- **Proof of Stake (PoS)**: This algorithm works on the idea that a node or user has an adequate stake in the system; that is, the user has invested enough in the system so that any malicious attempt by that user would outweigh the benefits of performing such an attack on the network. This idea was first introduced by Peercoin, and it is going to be used in the Ethereum blockchain version called *Serenity*. Another important concept in PoS is **coin age**, which is a criterion derived from the amount of time and number of coins that have not been spent. In this model, the chances of proposing and signing the next block increase with the coin age.

- **Delegated Proof of Stake (DPoS)**: This is an innovation over standard PoS, whereby each node that has a stake in the system can delegate the validation of a transaction to other nodes by voting. It is used in the BitShares blockchain.

- **Proof of Elapsed Time (PoET)**: Introduced by Intel in 2016, PoET uses a **Trusted Execution Environment** (**TEE**) to provide randomness and safety in the leader election process via a guaranteed wait time. It requires the Intel **Software Guard Extensions** (**SGX**) processor to provide the security guarantee for it to be secure. This concept is discussed in more detail in `Chapter 15`, *Hyperledger*, in the context of the Intel's *Sawtooth Lake* blockchain project.

- **Proof of Deposit (PoD)**: In this case, nodes that wish to participate in the network have to make a security deposit before they can mine and propose blocks. This mechanism is used in the Tendermint blockchain.

- **Proof of Importance (PoI)**: This idea is significant and different from PoS. PoI not only relies on how large a stake a user has in the system, but it also monitors the usage and movement of tokens by the user in order to establish a level of trust and importance. It is used in the NEM coin blockchain. More information about this coin is available at NEM's website `https://nem.io`.

- **Federated consensus or federated Byzantine consensus**: This mechanism is used in the stellar consensus protocol. Nodes in this protocol retain a group of publicly-trusted peers and propagate only those transactions that have been validated by the majority of trusted nodes.

- **Reputation-based mechanisms**: As the name suggests, a leader is elected by the reputation it has built over time on the network. It is based on the votes of other members.

- **PBFT**: This mechanism achieves state machine replication, which provides tolerance against Byzantine nodes. Various other protocols including PBFT, PAXOS, RAFT, and **Federated Byzantine Agreement** (**FBA**) are also being used or have been proposed for use in many different implementations of distributed systems and blockchains.

- **Proof of Activity** (**PoA**): This scheme is a combination of PoS and PoW, which ensures that a stakeholder is selected in a pseudorandom but uniform fashion. This is a comparatively more energy-efficient mechanism as compared to PoW. It utilizes a new concept called *Follow the Satoshi*. In this scheme, PoW and PoS are combined together to achieve consensus and good level of security. This scheme is more energy efficient as PoW is used only in the first stage of the mechanism, after the first stage it switches to PoS which consumes negligible energy. We will discuss these ideas further in `Chapter 6`, *Bitcoin Network and Payments* where protocols are reviewed in the context of advanced Bitcoin protocols.

- **Proof of Capacity (PoC)**: This scheme uses hard disk space as a resource to mine the blocks. This is different from PoW, where CPU resources are used. In in PoC, hard disk space is utilized for mining and as such is also known as *hard drive mining*. This concept was first introduced in the Burstcoin cryptocurrency.
- **Proof of Storage (PoS)**: This scheme allows for the outsourcing of storage capacity. This scheme is based on the concept that a particular piece of data is probably stored by a node *which* serves as a means to participate in the consensus mechanism. Several variations of this scheme have been proposed, such as Proof of Replication, Proof of Data Possession, Proof of Space, and Proof of Space-Time.

CAP theorem and blockchain

CAP theorem, also known as Brewer's theorem, was introduced by Eric Brewer in 1998 as conjecture. In 2002, it was proven as a theorem by Seth Gilbert and Nancy Lynch. The theory states that any distributed system cannot have consistency, availability, and partition tolerance simultaneously:

- **Consistency** is a property which ensures that all nodes in a distributed system have a single, current, and identical copy of the data.
- **Availability** means that the nodes in the system are up, accessible for use, and are accepting incoming requests and responding with data without any failures as and when required. In other words, data is available at each node and the nodes are responding to requests.
- **Partition tolerance** ensures that if a group of nodes is unable to communicate with other nodes due to network failures, the distributed system continues to operate correctly. This can occur due to network and node failures.

It has been proven that a distributed system cannot have consistency, availability, and partition tolerance simultaneously. This is explained with the following example. Let's imagine that there is a distributed system with two nodes. Now let us apply the three theorem properties on this smallest of possible distributed systems only with two nodes.

- **Consistency** is achieved if both nodes have the same shared state; that is, they have the same up-to-date copy of the data.
- **Availability** is achieved if both nodes are up and running and responding with the latest copy of data.
- **Partition tolerance** is achieved if communication does not break down between two nodes (either due to network issues, Byzantine faults, and so forth), and they are able to communicate with each other.

Now think of scenario where a partition occurs and nodes can no longer communicate with each other. If no new updated data comes in, it can only be updated on one node only. In that case, if the node accepts the update, then only that one node in the network is updated and therefore consistency is lost. Now, if the update is rejected by the node, that would result in loss of availability. In that case due to partition tolerance, both availability and consistency are unachievable.

This is strange because somehow blockchain manages to achieve all of these properties—or does it? This will be explained shortly. To achieve fault tolerance, replication is used. This is a standard and widely-used method to achieve fault tolerance. Consistency is achieved using consensus algorithms in order to ensure that all nodes have the same copy of the data. This is also called **state machine replication**. The blockchain is a means for achieving state machine replication. In general, there are two types of faults that a node can experience. Both of these types fall under the broader category of faults that can occur in a distributed system:

- **Fail-stop fault**: This type of fault occurs when a node merely has crashed. Fail-stop faults are the easier ones to deal with of the two fault types. Paxos protocol, introduced earlier in this chapter, is normally used to deal with this type of fault. These faults are simple to deal with

- **Byzantine faults**: The second type of fault is one where the faulty node exhibits malicious or inconsistent behavior arbitrarily. This type is difficult to handle since it can create confusion due to misleading information. This can be a result of an attack by adversaries, a software bug, or data corruption. State machine replication protocols such as PBFT was developed to address this second type of faults.

Strangely, it seems that the CAP theorem is violated in the blockchain, especially in its most successful implementation, Bitcoin. However, this is not the case. In blockchains, consistency is sacrificed in favor of availability and partition tolerance. In this scenario, **Consistency (C)** on the blockchain is not achieved simultaneously with **Partition tolerance (P)** and **Availability (A)**, but it is achieved over time. This is called eventual consistency, where consistency is achieved as a result of validation from multiple nodes over time. The concept of mining was introduced in Bitcoin for this purpose. **Mining** is a process that facilitates the achievement of consensus by using the PoW consensus algorithm. At a higher level, mining can be defined as a process that is used to add more blocks to the blockchain. More on this later in `Chapter 5`, *Introducing Bitcoin*.

Summary

In this chapter, we introduced you to the blockchain technology at an advanced level. First, we discussed some basic concepts of distributed systems, and then we reviewed the history of blockchain. We also discussed concepts such as electronic cash.

Furthermore, we presented various definitions of blockchain from different point of views. We also introduced you to few applications of blockchain technology. Next, we explored different types of blockchain. Finally, we examined the benefits and limitations of this new technology. Few topics such as blockchain scalability and adaptability issues were intentionally introduced only briefly, as these will be discussed in depth, in later chapters.

In the next chapter, we will introduce you to the concept of decentralization, which is central to the idea behind blockchains and their vast number of applications.

Decentralization 2

Decentralization is not a new concept. It has been used in strategy, management, and the government, for a long time. The basic idea of decentralization is to distribute control and authority to the peripheries of an organization instead of one central body being in full control of the organization. This configuration produces several benefits for organizations, such as increased efficiency, expedited decision making, better motivation, and a reduced burden on top management.

In this chapter, we will discuss the concept of decentralization in the context of blockchain. The fundamental basis of blockchain is that no single central authority is in control, and, in this chapter, we will present examples of various methods of decentralization and routes to achieve this. Furthermore, we will discuss the decentralization of the blockchain ecosystem, decentralized applications, and platforms for achieving decentralization, in detail. Also, we will introduce you to numerous exciting applications and ideas that emerge out of the decentralized blockchain technology.

Decentralization using blockchain

Decentralization is a core benefit and service provided by blockchain technology. By design, blockchain is a perfect vehicle for providing a platform that does not need any intermediaries and that can function with many different leaders chosen via consensus mechanisms. This model allows anyone to compete to become the decision-making authority. This competition is governed by a consensus mechanism, and the most commonly used method is known as **Proof of Work** (**PoW**).

Decentralization is applied in varying degrees from a semi-decentralized model to a fully decentralized one depending on the requirements and circumstances. Decentralization can be viewed from a blockchain perspective as a mechanism that provides a way to remodel existing applications and paradigms, or to build new applications, in order to give full control to users.

Information and Communication Technology (**ICT**) has conventionally been based on a centralized paradigm whereby database or application servers are under the control of a central authority, such as a system administrator. With Bitcoin and the advent of blockchain technology, this model has changed and now the technology exists, which allows anyone to start a decentralized system and operate it with no single point of failure or single trusted authority. It can either be run autonomously or by requiring some human intervention, depending on the type and model of governance used in the decentralized application running on blockchain.

The following diagram shows the different types of systems that currently exist: central, decentralized, and distributed. This concept was first published by Paul Baran in *On Distributed Communications: I. Introduction to Distributed Communications Networks* (Rand Corporation, 1964):

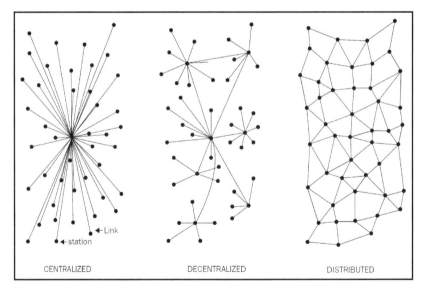

Different types of networks/systems

Centralized systems are conventional (client-server) IT systems in which there is a single authority that controls the system, and who is solely in charge of all operations on the system. All users of a centralized system are dependent on a single source of service. The majority of online service providers including Google, Amazon, eBay, Apple's App Store, and others use this conventional model for delivering services.

A **distributed system**, data and computation are spread across multiple nodes in the network. Sometimes, this term is confused with *parallel computing*. While there is some overlap in the definition, the main difference between these systems is that in a parallel computing system, computation is performed by all nodes simultaneously in order to achieve the result; for example, parallel computing platforms are used in weather research and forecasting, simulation and financial modeling. On the other hand, in a distributed system, computation may not happen in parallel and data is replicated across multiple nodes that users view as a single, coherent system. Variations of both of these models are used with to achieve fault tolerance and speed. In the parallel system model, there is still a central authority that has control over all nodes, which governs processing. This means that the system is still centralized in nature.

The critical difference between a decentralized system and distributed system is that in a distributed system, there still exists a central authority that governs the entire system; whereas, in a decentralized system, no such authority exists.

A **decentralized system** is a type of network where nodes are not dependent on a single master node; instead, control is distributed among many nodes. This is analogous to a model where each department in an organization is in charge of its own database server, thus taking away the power from the central server and distributing it to the subdepartments who manage their own databases.

A significant innovation in the decentralized paradigm that has given rise to this new era of decentralization of applications is **decentralized consensus**. This mechanism came into play with Bitcoin, and it enables a user to agree on something via a consensus algorithm without the need for a central, trusted third party, intermediary, or service provider.

Methods of decentralization

Two methods can be used to achieve decentralization: disintermediation and competition (Contest-driven decentralization). These methods will be discussed in detail in the sections that follow.

Disintermediation

The concept of **disintermediation** can be explained with the aid of an example. Imagine that you want to send money to a friend in another country. You go to a bank who, for a fee, will transfer your money to the bank in that country. In this case, the bank maintains a central database that is updated, confirming that you have sent the money. With blockchain technology, it is possible to send this money directly to your friend without the need for a bank. All you need is the address of your friend on the blockchain. This way, the intermediary; that is, the bank, is no longer required, and decentralization is achieved by *disintermediation*. It is debatable, however, how practical decentralization through disintermediation is in the financial sector due to massive regulatory and compliance requirements. Nevertheless, this model can be used not only in finance but in many different industries as well.

Contest-driven decentralization

In the method involving **competition**, different service providers compete with each other in order to be selected for the provision of services by the system. This paradigm does not achieve complete decentralization. However, to a certain degree, it ensures that an intermediary or service provider is not monopolizing the service. In the context of blockchain technology, a system can be envisioned in which smart contracts can choose an external data provider from a large number of providers based on their reputation, previous score, reviews, and quality of service.

This method will not result in full decentralization, but it allows smart contracts to make a free choice based on the criteria just mentioned. This way, an environment of competition is cultivated among service providers where they compete with each other to become the data provider of choice.

In the following diagram, varying levels of decentralization are shown. On the left-hand side, the conventional approach is shown where a central system is in control; on the right-hand side, complete disintermediation is achieved as intermediaries are entirely removed. Competing intermediaries or service providers are shown in the center. At that level, intermediaries or service providers are selected based on reputation or voting, thus achieving partial decentralization.

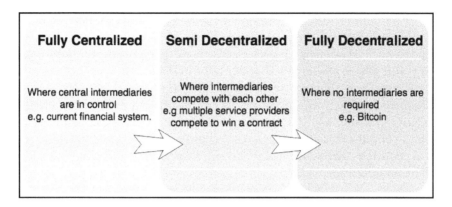

Scale of decentralization

While there are many benefits of decentralization, including transparency, efficiency, cost saving, development of trusted ecosystems, and in some cases privacy and anonymity, some challenges, such as security requirements, software bugs, and human errors need to be examined thoroughly.

For example, in a decentralized system such as Bitcoin or Ethereum where security is normally provided by private keys, how can one ensure that a smart property associated with these private keys cannot be rendered useless if the private keys are lost or, due to a bug in the smart contract code or the decentralized application becomes vulnerable to attack? Before embarking on a journey to decentralize everything using blockchain and decentralized applications, it is essential that you understand that not everything can or needs to be decentralized.

This view raises few fundamental questions. Is a blockchain really needed? When is a blockchain required? In what circumstances is blockchain preferred over traditional databases? To answer these questions, go through the simple set of questions presented here:

1. Is high data throughput required? If the answer to this question is yes, then use a traditional database.
2. Are updates centrally controlled? If yes, then use a conventional database.
3. Do users trust each other? If yes, then use a traditional database.
4. Are users anonymous? If yes, then use a public blockchain; if not, then use a private blockchain.
5. If consensus is required to be maintained within a consortium then use a private blockchain, otherwise use a public blockchain.

Answering all of these questions can provide an understanding of whether or not a blockchain is required. Beyond the questions posed in this model there are many other issues to consider, such as latency, choice of consensus mechanisms, whether consensus is required or not, and where consensus is going to be achieved. If consensus is maintained internally by a consortium, then a private blockchain should be used; otherwise, if consensus is required publicly among multiple entities, then a public blockchain solution should be considered. Other aspects like immutably should also be considered while making a decision about whether to use a blockchain or a traditional database. If strict data immutability is required, then a public blockchain should be used; otherwise, a central database may be an option.

As blockchain technology matures, there will be more questions raised regarding this model. For now, however, this set of questions is sufficient to decide whether a blockchain-based solution is required or not.

Routes to decentralization

Even though there were systems that pre-existed blockchain and Bitcoin, including BitTorrent and the Gnutella file sharing system, which to a certain degree could be classified as decentralized. However, with the advent of blockchain technology, many initiatives are now being taken to leverage this new technology for achieving decentralization. The Bitcoin blockchain is typically the first choice for many, as it has proven to be the most resilient and secure blockchain and has a market cap of nearly $145 billion at the time of this writing. Alternatively, other blockchains, such as Ethereum, serve as the tool of choice for many developers for building decentralized applications. As compared to Bitcoin, Ethereum has become a more prominent choice because of the flexibility it allows for programming any business logic into the blockchain by using *smart contracts*.

How to decentralize

Arvind Narayanan and others have proposed a framework in their book, *Bitcoin and Cryptocurrency Technologies, Princeton University Press*, that can be used to evaluate the decentralization requirements of a variety of issues in the context of blockchain technology. The framework raises four questions whose answers provide a clear understanding as to how a system can be decentralized:

1. What is being decentralized?
2. What level of decentralization is required?
3. What blockchain is used?
4. What security mechanism is used?

The first question simply asks you to identify what system is being decentralized. This can be any system, such as an identity system or a trading system.

The second question asks you to specify the level of decentralization required by examining the scale of decentralization as discussed earlier. It can be full disintermediation or partial disintermediation.

The third question asks developers to determine which blockchain is suitable for a particular application. It can be Bitcoin blockchain, Ethereum blockchain, or any other blockchain that is deemed fit for the specific application.

Finally, a fundamental question that needs to be addressed is how the security of a decentralized system will be guaranteed. For example, the security mechanism can be atomicity-based, where either the transaction executes in full or does not execute at all. This deterministic approach ensures the integrity of the system. Other mechanisms may include one based on reputation, which allows for varying degrees of trust in a system.

The decentralization framework example

Let's evaluate a money transfer system as an example of an application selected to be decentralized. The four questions discussed previously are used to evaluate the decentralization requirements of this application. The answers to these questions are as follows:

1. Money transfer system
2. Disintermediation
3. Bitcoin
4. Atomicity

The responses indicate that the money transfer system can be decentralized by removing the intermediary, implemented on the Bitcoin blockchain, and that a security guarantee will be provided via atomicity. Atomicity will ensure that transactions execute successfully in full or not execute at all. We have chosen Bitcoin blockchain because it is the longest established blockchain which has stood the test of time.

Similarly, this framework can be used for any other system that needs to be evaluated in terms of decentralization. The answers to these four simple questions help clarify what approach to take to decentralize the system.

Blockchain and full ecosystem decentralization

To achieve complete decentralization, it is necessary that the environment around the blockchain also be decentralized. The blockchain is a distributed ledger that runs on top of conventional systems. These elements include storage, communication, and computation. There are other factors, such as identity and wealth, which are traditionally based on centralized paradigms, and there's a need to decentralize these aspects as well in order to achieve a sufficiently decentralized ecosystem.

Storage

Data can be stored directly in a blockchain, and with this fact it achieves decentralization. However, a significant disadvantage of this approach is that a blockchain is not suitable for storing large amounts of data by design. It can store simple transactions and some arbitrary data, but it is certainly not suitable for storing images or large blobs of data, as is the case with traditional database systems.

A better alternative for storing data is to use **Distributed Hash Tables** (**DHTs**). DHTs were used initially in peer-to-peer file sharing software, such as BitTorrent, Napster, Kazaa, and Gnutella. DHT research was made popular by the CAN, Chord, Pastry, and Tapestry projects. BitTorrent is the most scalable and fastest network, but the issue with BitTorrent and the others is that there is no incentive for users to keep the files indefinitely. Users generally don't keep files permanently, and if nodes that have data still required by someone leave the network, there is no way to retrieve it except by having the required nodes rejoin the network so that the files once again become available.

Two primary requirements here are high availability and link stability, which means that data should be available when required and network links also should always be accessible. **InterPlanetary File System** (**IPFS**) by Juan Benet possesses both of these properties, and its vision is to provide a decentralized World Wide Web by replacing the HTTP protocol. IPFS uses Kademlia DHT and Merkle **Directed Acyclic Graph** (**DAG**) to provide storage and searching functionality, respectively. The concept of DHTs and DAGs will be introduced in detail in `Chapter 4`, *Public Key Cryptography*.

The incentive mechanism for storing data is based on a protocol known as Filecoin, which pays incentives to nodes that store data using the Bitswap mechanism. The Bitswap mechanism lets nodes keep a simple ledger of bytes sent or bytes received in a one-to-one relationship. Also, a Git-based version control mechanism is used in IPFS to provide structure and control over the versioning of data.

There are other alternatives for data storage, such as Ethereum Swarm, Storj, and MaidSafe. Ethereum has its own decentralized and distributed ecosystem that uses Swarm for storage and the Whisper protocol for communication. MaidSafe aims to provide a decentralized World Wide Web. All of these projects are discussed later in this book in greater detail.

BigchainDB is another storage layer decentralization project aimed at providing a scalable, fast, and linearly-scalable decentralized database as opposed to a traditional filesystem. BigchainDB complements decentralized processing platforms and file systems such as Ethereum and IPFS.

Communication

The internet (the communication layer in blockchain) is considered to be decentralized. This belief is correct to some extent, as the original vision of the internet was to develop a decentralized communications system. Services such as email and online storage are now all based on a paradigm where the service provider is in control, and users trust such providers to grant them access to the service as requested. This model is based on unconditional trust of a central authority (the service provider) where users are not in control of their data. Even user passwords are stored on trusted third-party systems.

Thus, there is a need to provide control to individual users in such a way that access to their data is guaranteed and is not dependent on a single third party. Access to the internet (the communication layer) is based on **Internet Service Providers** (**ISPs**) who act as a central hub for internet users. If the ISP is shut down for any reason, then no communication is possible with this model.

An alternative is to use **mesh networks**. Even though they are limited in functionality when compared to the internet, they still provide a decentralized alternative where nodes can talk directly to each other without a central hub such as an ISP.

 An example of a Meshnet is FireChat (`http://www.opengarden.com/firechat.html`), which allows iPhone users to communicate with each other directly in a peer-to-peer fashion without an internet connection.

Now imagine a network that allows users to be in control of their communication; no one can shut it down for any reason. This could be the next step toward decentralizing communication networks in the blockchain ecosystem. It must be noted that this model may only be vital in a jurisdiction where the internet is censored and controlled by the government.

As mentioned earlier, the original vision of the internet was to build a decentralized network; however, over the years, with the advent of large-scale service providers such as Google, Amazon, and eBay, control is shifting towards these big players. For example, email is a decentralized system at its core; that is, anyone can run an email server with minimal effort and can start sending and receiving emails. There are better alternatives available, for example, Gmail and Outlook.com, which already provide managed services for end users, so there is a natural inclination toward selecting from these large centralized services as they are more convenient and free. This is one example that shows how the internet has moved toward centralization.

Free services, however, are offered at the cost of exposing valuable personal data, and many users are unaware of this fact. Blockchain has once again given this vision of decentralization to the world, and now concerted efforts are being made to harness this technology and take advantage of the benefits that it can provide.

Computing power and decentralization

Decentralization of computing or processing power is achieved by a blockchain technology such as Ethereum, where smart contracts with embedded business logic can run on the blockchain network. Other blockchain technologies also provide similar processing-layer platforms, where business logic can run over the network in a decentralized manner.

The following diagram shows a decentralized ecosystem overview. At the bottom layer, the internet or Meshnets provide a decentralized communication layer. On the next layer up, a storage layer uses technologies such as IPFS and BigchainDB to enable decentralization. Finally, at the next level up, you can see that blockchain serves as a decentralized processing (computation) layer. Blockchain can, in a limited way, provide a storage layer too, but that severely hampers the speed and capacity of the system. Therefore, other solutions such as IPFS and BigchainDB are more suitable to store large amounts of data in a decentralized way. The Identity, Wealth layers are shown at the top level. Identity on the internet is a vast topic, and systems such as BitAuth and OpenID provide authentication and identification services with varying degrees of decentralization and security assumptions:

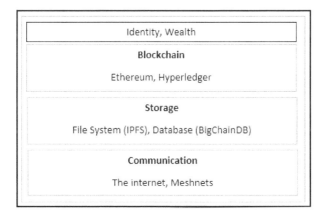

Decentralized ecosystem

The blockchain is capable of providing solutions to various issues relating to decentralization. A concept relevant to identity known as **Zooko's Triangle** requires that the naming system in a network protocol be secure, decentralized, and is able to provide human-meaningful and memorable names to the users. Conjecture has it that a system can have only two of these properties simultaneously. Nevertheless, with the advent of blockchain in the form of Namecoin, this problem was resolved. It is now possible to achieve security, decentralization, and human-meaningful names with the Namecoin blockchain. However, this is not a panacea, and it comes with many challenges, such as reliance on users to store and maintain private keys securely. This opens up other general questions about the suitability of decentralization to a particular problem.

Decentralization may not be appropriate for every scenario. Centralized systems with well-established reputations tend to work better in many cases. For example, email platforms from well reputed companies such as Google or Microsoft would provide a better service as compared to a scenario where individual email servers are hosted by users on the internet.

There are many projects underway that are developing solutions for a more comprehensive distributed blockchain system. For example, Swarm and Whisper are developed to provide decentralized storage and communication for Ethereum blockchain. We will discuss Swarm and Ethereum in more detail in Chapter 11, *Further Ethereum*.

With the emergence of the decentralization paradigm, different terminologies and buzzwords are now appearing in the media and academic literature. With the advent of blockchain technology, it is now possible to build software versions of traditional physical organizations in the form of **Decentralized Organizations** (**DOs**) and other similar constructs, which we will examine in detail shortly.

The following concepts are worth discussion in the context of decentralization.

Smart contracts

A **smart contract** is a decentralized program. Smart contracts do not necessarily need a blockchain to run; however, due to the security benefits that blockchain technology provides, blockchain has become a standard decentralized execution platform for smart contracts.

A smart contract usually contains some business logic and a limited amount of data. The business logic is executed if specific criteria are met. Actors or participants in the blockchain use these smart contracts, or they run autonomously on behalf of the network participants.

More information on smart contracts will be provided in `Chapter 9`, *Smart Contracts*.

Decentralized Organizations

DOs are software programs that run on a blockchain and are based on the idea of actual organizations with people and protocols. Once a DO is added to the blockchain in the form of a smart contract or a set of smart contracts, it becomes decentralized and parties interact with each other based on the code defined within the DO software.

Decentralized Autonomous Organizations

Just like DOs, a **Decentralized Autonomous Organization** (**DAO**) is also a computer program that runs atop a blockchain and embedded within it are governance and business logic rules. DAO and DO are fundamentally the same thing. The main difference, however, is that DAOs are autonomous, which means that they are fully automated and contain artificially-intelligent logic. DOs, on the other hand, lack this feature and rely on human input to execute business logic.

The Ethereum blockchain led the way with the initial introduction of DAOs. In a DAO, the code is considered the governing entity rather than people or paper contracts. However, a human curator maintains this code and acts as a proposal evaluator for the community. DAOs are capable of hiring external contractors if enough input is received from the token holders (participants).

The most famous DAO project is The DAO, which raised $168 million in its crowdfunding phase. The DAO project was designed to be a venture capital fund aimed at providing a decentralized business model with no single entity as owner. Unfortunately, this project was hacked due to a bug in the DAO code, and millions of dollars' worth in **Ether currency** (**ETH**) was siphoned out of the project and into a child DAO created by hackers. A hard fork was required on the Ethereum blockchain to reverse the impact of the hack and initiate the recovery of the funds. This incident opened up the debate on the security, quality, and need for thorough testing of the code in smart contracts in order to ensure their integrity and adequate control. There are other projects underway, especially in academia, which are seeking to formalize smart contract coding and testing.

Currently, DAOs do not have any legal status, even though they may contain some intelligent code that enforces certain protocols and conditions. However, these rules have no value in the real-world legal system at present. One day, perhaps an **Autonomous Agent (AA)**; that is, a piece of code that runs without human intervention, commissioned by a law enforcement agency or regulator will contain rules and regulations that could be embedded in a DAO for the purpose of ensuring its integrity from a legalistic and compliance perspective. The fact that DAOs are purely-decentralized entities enables them to run in any jurisdiction. Thus, they raise a large question as to how the current legal system could be applied to such a varied mix of jurisdictions and geographies.

Decentralized Autonomous Corporations

Decentralized Autonomous Corporations (**DACs**) are similar to DAOs in concept, though considered to be a smaller subset of them. The definitions of DACs and DAOs may sometimes overlap, but the general distinction is that DAOs are usually considered to be nonprofit; whereas DACs can earn a profit via shares offered to the participants and to whom they can pay dividends. DACs can run a business automatically without human intervention based on the logic programmed into them.

Decentralized Autonomous Societies

Decentralized Autonomous Societies (**DASs**) are a concept whereby an entire society can function on a blockchain with the help of multiple, complex smart contracts and a combination of DAOs and **Decentralized Applications** (**DApps**) running autonomously. This model does not necessarily translate to a free-for-all approach, nor is it based on an entirely libertarian ideology; instead, many services that a government commonly offers can be delivered via blockchains, such as government identity card systems, passports, and records of deeds, marriages, and births. Another theory is that, if a government is corrupt and central systems do not provide the satisfactory levels of trust that a society needs, then that society can start its own virtual one on a blockchain that is driven by decentralized consensus and transparency. This concept might look like a libertarian's or cypherpunk's dream, but it is entirely possible on a blockchain.

Decentralized Applications (DApps)

All ideas mentioned up to this point come under the broader umbrella of DApps. DAOs, DACs, and DOs are DApps that run on top of a blockchain in a peer-to-peer network. They represent the latest advancement in decentralization technology. DApps, on the other hand, are software programs that can run on their respective blockchains, use an existing established blockchain, or use only the protocols of an existing blockchain. These are called Type I, Type II, and Type III DApps.

Requirements of a Decentralized Application

For an application to be considered decentralized, it must meet the following criteria. This definition was provided in the whitepaper by Johnston and others, *The General Theory of Decentralized Applications, Dapps*:

- The DApp should be fully open source and autonomous, and no single entity should be in control of a majority of its tokens. All changes to the application must be consensus-driven based on the feedback given by the community.
- Data and records of operations of the application must be cryptographically secured and stored on a public, decentralized blockchain to avoid any central points of failure.
- A cryptographic token must be used by the application to provide access and rewards to those who contribute value to the applications, for example, miners in Bitcoin.
- The tokens must be generated by the DApp according to a standard cryptographic algorithm. This generation of tokens acts as a proof of the value to contributors (for example, miners).

Operations of a DApp

Establishment of consensus by a DApp can be achieved using consensus algorithms such as PoW and PoS. So far, only PoW has been found to be incredibly resistant to 51% attacks, as is evident from Bitcoin. Furthermore, a DApp can distribute tokens (coins) via mining, fundraising, and development.

DApp examples

Examples of some decentralized applications are provided here.

KYC-Chain

This application provides the facility to manage **Know Your Customer** (**KYC**) data securely and conveniently based on smart contracts.

OpenBazaar

This is a decentralized peer-to-peer network that enables commercial activities directly between sellers and buyers instead of relying on a central party, such as eBay and Amazon. It should be noted that this system is not built on top of a blockchain; instead, DHTs are used in a peer-to-peer network to enable direct communication and data sharing among peers. It makes use of Bitcoin and various other cryptocurrencies as a payment method.

Lazooz

This is the decentralized equivalent of Uber. It allows peer-to-peer ride sharing and users to be incentivized by proof of movement, and they can earn Zooz coins.

 Many other DApps have been built on the Ethereum blockchain and are showcased at `http://dapps.ethercasts.com/`.

Platforms for decentralization

Today, there are many platforms available for decentralization. In fact, the fundamental feature of blockchain networks is to provide decentralization. Therefore, any blockchain network such as Bitcoin, Ethereum, Hyperledger Fabric, or Quorum can be used to provide decentralization service. Many organizations around the world have introduced platforms that promise to make distributed application development easy, accessible, and secure. Some of these platforms are described next.

Ethereum

Ethereum tops the list as being the first blockchain to introduce a Turing-complete language and the concept of a virtual machine. This is in stark contrast to the limited scripting language in Bitcoin and many other cryptocurrencies. With the availability of its Turing-complete language called Solidity, endless possibilities have opened for the development of decentralized applications. This blockchain was first proposed in 2013 by Vitalik Buterin, and it provides a public blockchain to develop smart contracts and decentralized applications. Currency tokens on Ethereum are called **Ethers**.

MaidSafe

MaidSafe provides a **Secure Access For Everyone** (**SAFE**) network that is made up of unused computing resources, such as storage, processing power, and the data connections of its users. The files on the network are divided into small chunks of data, which are encrypted and distributed randomly throughout the network. This data can only be retrieved by its respective owner. One key innovation of MaidSafe is that duplicate files are automatically rejected on the network, which helps reduce the need for additional computing resources needed to manage the load. It uses Safecoin as a token to incentivize its contributors.

Lisk

Lisk is a blockchain application development and cryptocurrency platform. It allows developers to use JavaScript to build decentralized applications and host them in their respective sidechains. Lisk uses the **Delegated Proof of Stake** (**DPOS**) mechanism for consensus whereby 101 nodes can be elected to secure the network and propose blocks. It uses the Node.js and JavaScript backend, while the frontend allows the use of standard technologies, such as CSS3, HTML5, and JavaScript.

Lisk uses **LSK** coin as a currency on the blockchain. Another derivative of Lisk is Rise, which is a Lisk-based decentralized application and digital currency platform. It offers a greater focus on the security of the system.

A more practical introduction to these platforms and others will be supplied in later chapters.

Summary

In this chapter, we introduced the concept of decentralization, which is the core service offered by blockchain technology. Although the concept of decentralization is not new, it has gained renewed significance in the world of the blockchain. Consequently, various applications based on a decentralized architecture have recently been introduced.

We began the chapter with an introduction to the concept of decentralization. Next, we discussed decentralization from the blockchain perspective. Moreover, we introduced you to ideas relating to the different layers of decentralization in the blockchain ecosystem and to the several new concepts and terms that have emerged with the advent of blockchain technology and decentralization from the blockchain perspective, including DAOs, DACs, and DApps. Finally, we looked at few examples of decentralized applications.

In the next chapter, we will present the fundamental concepts necessary to understanding the blockchain ecosystem; principally, we will introduce you to cryptography, which provides a crucial foundation for blockchain technology.

Symmetric Cryptography

3

In this chapter, you will be introduced to the concepts, theory, and practical aspects of *symmetric cryptography*. We will focus more on the elements that are specifically relevant in the context of blockchain technology. We will provide you with concepts that are required to understand the material covered in later chapters.

You will also be introduced to applications of cryptographic algorithms so that you can gain hands-on experience in the practical implementation of cryptographic functions. For this, we'll use the OpenSSL command-line tool. Before starting with the theoretical foundations, we'll look at the installation of OpenSSL in the following section, so that you can do some practical work as you read through the conceptual material.

Working with the OpenSSL command line

On the Ubuntu Linux distribution, OpenSSL is usually already available. However, it can be installed using the following command:

```
$ sudo apt-get install openssl
```

Examples in this chapter have been developed using OpenSSL version 1.0.2g.

 It is available at https://packages.ubuntu.com/xenial/openssl.

You are encouraged to use this specific version, as all examples in the chapter have been developed and tested with it. The OpenSSL version can be checked using the following command:

```
$ openssl version
```

You will see the following output:

```
OpenSSL 1.0.2g  1 Mar 2016
```

Now, you are all set to run the examples provided in this chapter. If you are running a version other than 1.0.2g, the examples may still work but that is not guaranteed, as older versions lack the features used in the examples and newer versions may not be backward compatible with version 1.0.2g.

In the sections that follow, the theoretical foundations of cryptography are first discussed and then a series of relevant practical experiments will be presented.

Introduction

Cryptography is the science of making information secure in the presence of adversaries. It does so under the assumption that limitless resources are available to adversaries. **Ciphers** are algorithms used to encrypt or decrypt data, so that if intercepted by an adversary, the data is meaningless to them without **decryption**, which requires a secret key.

Cryptography is primarily used to provide a confidentiality service. On its own, it cannot be considered a complete solution, rather it serves as a crucial building block within a more extensive security system to address a security problem. For example, securing a blockchain ecosystem requires many different cryptographic primitives, such as hash functions, symmetric key cryptography, digital signatures, and public key cryptography.

In addition to a confidentiality service, cryptography also provides other security services such as integrity, authentication (entity authentication and data origin authentication), and non-repudiation. Additionally, accountability is also provided, which is a requirement in many security systems.

Before discussing cryptography further, some mathematical terms and concepts need to be explained in order to build a foundation for fully understanding the material provided later in this chapter.

The next section serves as a basic introduction to these concepts. An explanation with proofs and relevant background for all of these terms would require somewhat involved mathematics, which is beyond the scope of this book. More details on these topics can be found in any standard number theory, algebra, or cryptography-specific book. For example, *A Course in Number Theory and Cryptography* by *Neal Koblitz* provides an excellent presentation of all relevant mathematical concepts.

Mathematics

As the subject of cryptography is based on mathematics, this section will introduce some basic concepts that will help you understand the concepts presented later in the chapter.

Set

A **set** is a collection of distinct objects, for example, $X = \{1, 2, 3, 4, 5\}$.

Group

A **group** is a commutative set with one operation that combines two elements of the set. The group operation is closed and associated with a defined identity element. Additionally, each element in the set has an inverse. **Closure** (closed) means that if, for example, elements A and B are in the set, then the resultant element after performing an operation on the elements is also in the set. **Associative** means that the grouping of elements does not affect the result of the operation.

Field

A **field** is a set that contains both additive and multiplicative groups. More precisely, all elements in the set form an additive and multiplicative group. It satisfies specific axioms for addition and multiplication. For all group operations, the **distributive law** is also applied. The law dictates that the same sum or product will be produced even if any of the terms or factors are reordered.

A finite field

A **finite field** is one with a finite set of elements. Also known as *Galois fields*, these structures are of particular importance in cryptography as they can be used to produce accurate and error-free results of arithmetic operations. For example, prime finite fields are used in **Elliptic Curve Cryptography** (**ECC**) to construct discrete logarithm problems.

Order

The **order** is the number of elements in a field. It is also known as the *cardinality* of the field.

An abelian group

An **abelian group** is formed when the operation on the elements of a set is commutative. The commutative law means that changing the order of the elements does not affect the result of the operation, for example, $A \times B = B \times A$.

Prime fields

A **prime field** is a finite one with a prime number of elements. It has specific rules for addition and multiplication, and each nonzero element in the field has an inverse. Addition and multiplication operations are performed modulo p, that is, prime.

Ring

If more than one operation can be defined over an abelian group, that group becomes a **ring**. There are also specific properties that need to be satisfied. A ring must have closure and associative and distributive properties.

A cyclic group

A **cyclic group** is a type of group that can be generated by a single element called the *group generator*.

Modular arithmetic

Also known as clock arithmetic, numbers in modular arithmetic wrap around when they reach a certain fixed number. This fixed number is a positive number called **modulus**, and all operations are performed concerning this fixed number. Analogous to a clock, there are numbers from 1 to 12. When it reaches 12, the number 1 starts again. In other words, this type of arithmetic deals with the remainders after the division operation. For example, 50 mod 11 is 6 because 50 / 11 leaves a remainder of 6.

This completes a basic introduction to some mathematical concepts involved in cryptography. In the next section, you will be introduced to cryptography concepts.

Cryptography

A generic cryptography model is shown in the following diagram:

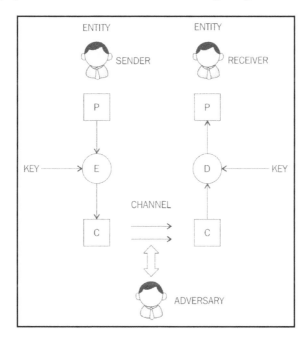

A model of the generic encryption and decryption model

In the preceding diagram, **P**, **E**, **C**, and **D** represent plaintext, encryption, ciphertext, and decryption, respectively. Also based on this model, explanations of concepts such as entity, sender, receiver, adversary, key, and channel follow:

- **Entity**: Either a person or system that sends, receives, or performs operations on data
- **Sender**: This is an entity that transmits the data
- **Receiver**: This is an entity that takes delivery of the data
- **Adversary**: This is an entity that tries to circumvent the security service
- **Key**: A key is data that is used to encrypt or decrypt other data
- **Channel**: Channel provides a medium of communication between entities

Next, we will describe the cryptography services mentioned earlier in the chapter in greater detail.

Confidentiality

Confidentiality is the assurance that information is only available to authorized entities.

Integrity

Integrity is the assurance that information is modifiable only by authorized entities.

Authentication

Authentication provides assurance about the identity of an entity or the validity of a message.

There are two types of authentication mechanisms, namely entity authentication and data origin authentication, which are discussed in the following section.

Entity authentication

Entity authentication is the assurance that an entity is currently involved and active in a communication session. Traditionally, users are issued a username and password that is used to gain access to the various platforms with which they are working. This practice is known as **single-factor authentication**, as there is only one factor involved, namely, *something you know*, that is, the password and username. This type of authentication is not very secure for a variety of reasons, for example, password leakage; therefore, additional factors are now commonly used to provide better security. The use of additional techniques for user identification is known as **multifactor authentication** (or two-factor authentication if only two methods are used).

Various authentication factors are described here:

- The first factor is *something you have*, such as a hardware token or a smart card. In this case, a user can use a hardware token in addition to login credentials to gain access to a system. This mechanism protects the user by requiring two factors of authentication. A user who has access to the hardware token and knows the login credentials will be able to access the system. Both factors should be available to gain access to the system, thus making this method a two-factor authentication mechanism. In case if the hardware token is lost, on its own it won't be of any use unless, *something you know*, the login password is also used in conjunction with the hardware token.
- The second factor is *something you are*, which uses biometric features to identify the user. With this method, a user's fingerprint, retina, iris, or hand geometry is used to provide an additional factor for authentication. This way, it can be ensured that the user was indeed present during the authentication process, as biometric features are unique to every individual. However, careful implementation is required to guarantee a high level of security, as some research has suggested that biometric systems can be circumvented under specific conditions.

Data origin authentication

Also known as *message authentication*, **data origin authentication** is an assurance that the source of the information is indeed verified. Data origin authentication guarantees data integrity because if a source is corroborated, then the data must not have been altered. Various methods, such as **Message Authentication Codes** (**MACs**) and digital signatures are most commonly used. These terms will be explained in detail later in the chapter.

Non-repudiation

Non-repudiation is the assurance that an entity cannot deny a previous commitment or action by providing incontrovertible evidence. It is a security service that offers definitive proof that a particular activity has occurred. This property is essential in debatable situations whereby an entity has denied the actions performed, for example, placement of an order on an e-commerce system. This service produces cryptographic evidence in electronic transactions so that in case of disputes, it can be used as a confirmation of an action.

Non-repudiation has been an active research area for many years. Disputes in electronic transactions are a common issue, and there is a need to address them to increase the confidence level of consumers in such services.

The non-repudiation protocol usually runs in a communication network, and it is used to provide evidence that an action has been taken by an entity (originator or recipient) on the network. In this context, there are two communications models that can be used to transfer messages from originator A to recipient B:

- A message is sent directly from originator A to recipient B.
- A message is sent to a delivery agent from originator A, which then delivers the message to recipient B.

The primary requirements of a non-repudiation protocol are fairness, effectiveness, and timeliness. In many scenarios, there are multiple participants involved in a transaction, as opposed to only two parties. For example, in electronic trading systems, there can be many entities, such as clearing agents, brokers, and traders that can be involved in a single transaction. In this case, two-party non-repudiation protocols are not appropriate. To address this problem, **Multi-Party Non-Repudiation** (**MPNR**) protocols have been developed.

Accountability

Accountability is the assurance which states that actions affecting security can be traced back to the responsible party. This is usually provided by logging and audit mechanisms in systems where a detailed audit is required due to the nature of the business, for example, in electronic trading systems. Detailed logs are vital to trace an entity's actions, such as when a trade is placed in an audit record with the date and timestamp and the entity's identity is generated and saved in the log file. This log file can optionally be encrypted and be part of the database or a standalone ASCII text log file on a system.

In order to provide all of the services discussed earlier, different cryptographic primitives are used that are presented in the next section.

Cryptographic primitives

Cryptographic primitives are the basic building blocks of a security protocol or system. In the following section, you are introduced to cryptographic algorithms that are essential for building secure protocols and systems. A **security protocol** is a set of steps taken to achieve the required security goals by utilizing appropriate security mechanisms. Various types of security protocols are in use, such as authentication protocols, non-repudiation protocols, and key management protocols.

The taxonomy of cryptographic primitives can be visualized as shown here:

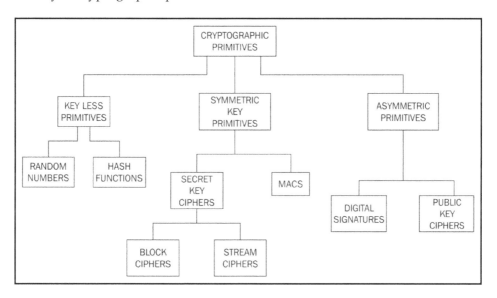

Cryptographic primitives

As shown in the cryptographic primitives taxonomy diagram, cryptography is mainly divided into two categories: *symmetric cryptography* and *asymmetric cryptography*.

These primitives are discussed further in the next section.

Symmetric cryptography

Symmetric cryptography refers to a type of cryptography where the key that is used to encrypt the data is the same one that is used for decrypting the data. Thus, it is also known as **shared key cryptography**. The key must be established or agreed upon before the data exchange occurs between the communicating parties. This is the reason it is also called **secret key cryptography**.

There are two types of symmetric ciphers: *stream ciphers* and *block ciphers*. **Data Encryption Standard** (**DES**) and **Advanced Encryption Standard** (**AES**) are typical examples of block ciphers, whereas RC4 and A5 are commonly used stream ciphers.

Stream ciphers

Stream ciphers are encryption algorithms that apply encryption algorithms on a bit-by-bit basis (one bit at a time) to plaintext using a keystream. There are two types of stream ciphers: *synchronous stream ciphers* and *asynchronous stream ciphers*:

- **Synchronous stream ciphers** are those where the keystream is dependent only on the key
- **Asynchronous stream ciphers** have a keystream that is also dependent on the encrypted data

In stream ciphers, encryption and decryption are the same function because they are simple modulo-2 additions or XOR operations. The fundamental requirement in stream ciphers is the security and randomness of keystreams. Various techniques ranging from pseudorandom number generators to true random number generators implemented in hardware have been developed to generate random numbers, and it is vital that all key generators be cryptographically secure:

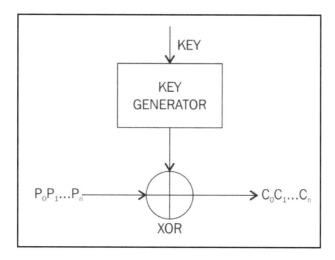

Operation of a stream cipher

Block ciphers

Block ciphers are encryption algorithms that break up the text to be encrypted (plaintext) into blocks of a fixed length and apply the encryption block-by-block. Block ciphers are generally built using a design strategy known as a **Feistel cipher**. Recent block ciphers, such as AES (Rijndael) have been built using a combination of substitution and permutation called a **Substitution-Permutation Network** (**SPN**).

Feistel ciphers are based on the Feistel network, which is a structure developed by Horst Feistel. This structure is based on the idea of combining multiple rounds of repeated operations to achieve desirable cryptographic properties known as *confusion* and *diffusion*. Feistel networks operate by dividing data into two blocks (left and right) and processing these blocks via keyed *round functions* in iterations to provide sufficient pseudorandom permutation.

Confusion makes the relationship between the encrypted text and plaintext complex. This is achieved by substitution. In practice, *A* in plaintext is replaced by *X* in encrypted text. In modern cryptographic algorithms, substitution is performed using lookup tables called *S-boxes*. The diffusion property spreads the plaintext statistically over the encrypted data. This ensures that even if a single bit is changed in the input text, it results in changing at least half (on average) of the bits in the ciphertext. Confusion is required to make finding the encryption key very difficult, even if many encrypted and decrypted data pairs are created using the same key. In practice, this is achieved by transposition or permutation.

A key advantage of using a Feistel cipher is that encryption and decryption operations are almost identical and only require a reversal of the encryption process to achieve decryption. DES is a prime example of Feistel-based ciphers:

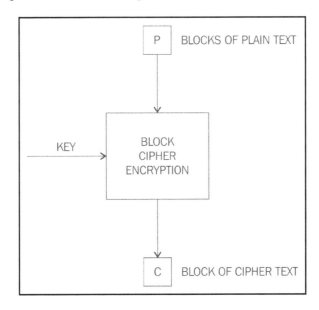

Simplified operation of a block cipher

Various modes of operation for block ciphers are **Electronic Code Book** (**ECB**), **Cipher Block Chaining** (**CBC**), **Output Feedback** (**OFB**) mode, and **Counter** (**CTR**) mode. These modes are used to specify the way in which an encryption function is applied to the plaintext. Some of these modes of block cipher encryption are introduced here.

Block encryption mode

In **block encryption mode**, the plaintext is divided into blocks of fixed length depending on the type of cipher used. Then the encryption function is applied to each block.

The most common block encryption modes are briefly discussed in the following subsections.

Electronic Code Book

Electronic Code Book (**ECB**) is a basic mode of operation in which the encrypted data is produced as a result of applying the encryption algorithm one-by-one to each block of plaintext. This is the most straightforward mode, but it should not be used in practice as it is insecure and can reveal information:

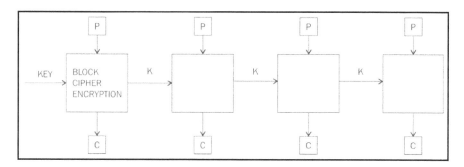

Electronic Code Book mode for block ciphers

The preceding diagram shows that we have plaintext **P** provided as an input to the block cipher encryption function, along with a key **KEY** and ciphertext **C** is produced as output.

Cipher Block Chaining

In **Cipher Block Chaining** (**CBC**) mode, each block of plaintext is XOR'd with the previously-encrypted block. CBC mode uses the **Initialization Vector** (**IV**) to encrypt the first block. It is recommended that the IV be randomly chosen:

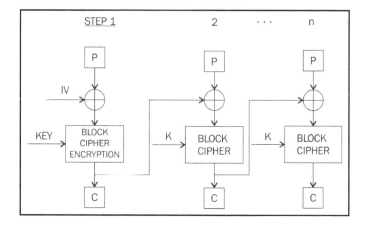

Cipher block chaining mode

Counter mode

The **Counter** (**CTR**) mode effectively uses a block cipher as a stream cipher. In this case, a unique nonce is supplied that is concatenated with the counter value to produce a **keystream**:

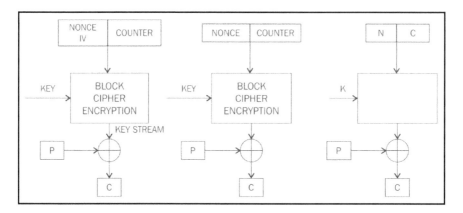

Counter mode

There are other modes, such as **Cipher Feedback** (**CFB**) mode, **Galois Counter** (**GCM**) mode, and **Output Feedback** (**OFB**) mode, which are also used in various scenarios.

Keystream generation mode

In **keystream generation mode**, the encryption function generates a keystream that is then XOR'd with the plaintext stream to achieve encryption.

Message authentication mode

In **message authentication mode**, a **Message Authentication Code** (**MAC**) results from an encryption function. The MAC is a cryptographic checksum that provides an integrity service. The most common method to generate a MAC using block ciphers is CBC-MAC, where a part of the last block of the chain is used as a MAC. For example, a MAC can be used to ensure that if a message is modified by an unauthorized entity. This can be achieved by encrypting the message with a key using the MAC function. The resultant message and MAC of the message once received by the receiver can be checked by encrypting the message received again by the key and comparing it with the MAC received from the sender. If they both match, then the message has not modified by unauthorized user thus integrity service is provided. If they both don't match, then it means that message is modified by unauthorized entity during the transmission.

Cryptographic hash mode

Hash functions are primarily used to compress a message to a fixed-length digest. In **cryptographic hash mode**, block ciphers are used as a compression function to produce a hash of plaintext.

With this, we have now concluded the introduction to block ciphers. In the following section, you will be introduced to the design and mechanism of a currently market-dominant block cipher known as AES.

Before discussing AES, however, some history is presented about the **Data Encryption Standard** (**DES**) that led to the development of the new AES standard.

Data Encryption Standard

The **Data Encryption Standard** (**DES**) was introduced by the U.S. **National Institute of Standards and Technology** (**NIST**) as a standard algorithm for encryption, and it was in widespread use during the 1980s and 1990s. However, it did not prove to be very resistant to brute force attacks, due to advances in technology and cryptography research. In July 1998, for example, the **Electronic Frontier Foundation** (**EFF**) broke DES using a special-purpose machine called EFF DES cracker (or *Deep Crack*).

DES uses a key of only 56 bits, which raised some concerns. This problem was addressed with the introduction of **Triple DES** (**3DES**), which proposed the use of a 168-bit key by means of three 56-bit keys and the same number of executions of the DES algorithm, thus making brute force attacks almost impossible. However, other limitations, such as slow performance and 64-bit block size, were not desirable.

Advanced Encryption Standard

In 2001, after an open competition, an encryption algorithm named Rijndael invented by cryptographers Joan Daemen and Vincent Rijmen was standardized as **Advanced Encryption Standard** (**AES**) with minor modifications by NIST. So far, no attack has been found against AES that is more effective than the brute-force method. The original version of Rijndael permits different key and block sizes of 128-bit, 192-bit, and 256-bits. In the AES standard, however, only a 128-bit block size is allowed. However, key sizes of 128-bit, 192-bit, and 256-bit are permissible.

How AES works

During AES algorithm processing, a 4 x 4 array of bytes known as the **state** is modified using multiple rounds. Full encryption requires 10 to 14 rounds, depending on the size of the key. The following table shows the key sizes and the required number of rounds:

Key size	Number of rounds required
128-bit	10 rounds
192-bit	12 rounds
256-bit	14 rounds

Once the state is initialized with the input to the cipher, four operations are performed in four stages to encrypt the input. These stages are: AddRoundKey, SubBytes, ShiftRows, and MixColumns:

1. In the AddRoundKey step, the state array is XOR'd with a subkey, which is derived from the master key
2. SubBytes is the substitution step where a lookup table (S-box) is used to replace all bytes of the state array
3. The ShiftRows step is used to shift each row to the left, except for the first one, in the state array to the left in a cyclic and incremental manner
4. Finally, all bytes are mixed in the MixColumns step in a linear fashion, column-wise

The preceding steps describe one round of AES.

In the final round (either 10, 12, or 14, depending on the key size), stage 4 is replaced with AddRoundKey to ensure that the first three steps cannot be simply reversed:

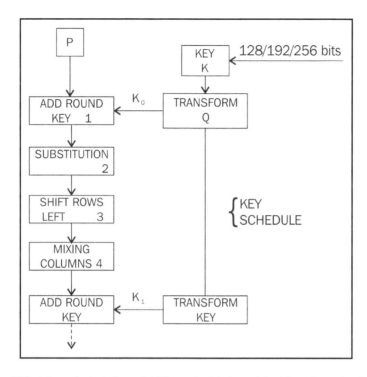

AES block diagram, showing the first round of AES encryption. In the last round, the mixing step is not performed

Various cryptocurrency wallets use AES encryption to encrypt locally-stored data. Especially in Bitcoin wallet, AES-256 in the CBC mode is used.

Here's an OpenSSL example of how to encrypt and decrypt using AES:

```
$ openssl enc -aes-256-cbc -in message.txt -out message.bin
enter aes-256-cbc encryption password:
Verifying - enter aes-256-cbc encryption password:
$ ls -ltr
-rw-rw-r-- 1 drequinox drequinox 14 Sep 21 05:54 message.txt
-rw-rw-r-- 1 drequinox drequinox 32 Sep 21 05:57 message.bin
$ cat message.bin
```

The following are the contents of the message.bin file:

```
Salted__w     s_ỹ  h~     :~/Crypt$
:~/Crypt$
```

Note that `message.bin` is a binary file. Sometimes, it is desirable to encode this binary file in a text format for compatibility/interoperability reasons. The following command can be used to do just that:

```
$ openssl enc -base64 -in message.bin -out message.b64
$ ls -ltr
-rw-rw-r-- 1 drequinox drequinox 14 Sep 21 05:54 message.txt
-rw-rw-r-- 1 drequinox drequinox 32 Sep 21 05:57 message.bin
-rw-rw-r-- 1 drequinox drequinox 45 Sep 21 06:00 message.b64
$  cat message.b64
U2FsdGVkX193uByIcwZf0Z7J1at+4L+Fj8/uzeDAtJE=
```

In order to decrypt an AES-encrypted file, the following commands can be used. An example of `message.bin` from a previous example is used:

```
$ openssl enc -d -aes-256-cbc -in message.bin -out message.dec
enter aes-256-cbc decryption password:
$ ls -ltr
-rw-rw-r-- 1 drequinox drequinox 14 Sep 21 05:54 message.txt
-rw-rw-r-- 1 drequinox drequinox 32 Sep 21 05:57 message.bin
-rw-rw-r-- 1 drequinox drequinox 45 Sep 21 06:00 message.b64
-rw-rw-r-- 1 drequinox drequinox 14 Sep 21 06:06 message.dec
$ cat message.dec
Datatoencrypt
```

Astute readers will have noticed that no IV has been provided, even though it's required in all block encryption modes of operation except ECB. The reason for this is that OpenSSL automatically derives the IV from the given password. Users can specify the IV using the following switch:

```
-K/-iv       , (Initialization Vector) should be provided in Hex.
```

In order to decode from base64, the following commands are used. Follow the `message.b64` file from the previous example:

```
$ openssl enc -d -base64 -in message.b64 -out message.ptx
$ ls -ltr
-rw-rw-r-- 1 drequinox drequinox 14 Sep 21 05:54 message.txt
-rw-rw-r-- 1 drequinox drequinox 32 Sep 21 05:57 message.bin
-rw-rw-r-- 1 drequinox drequinox 45 Sep 21 06:00 message.b64
-rw-rw-r-- 1 drequinox drequinox 14 Sep 21 06:06 message.dec
-rw-rw-r-- 1 drequinox drequinox 32 Sep 21 06:16 message.ptx
$ cat message.ptx
```

The following are the contents of the `message.ptx` file:

```
:~/Crypt$ cat message.ptx
Salted__w    s_ÿ h~         :~/Crypt$
```

There are many types of ciphers that are supported in OpenSSL. You can explore these options based on the preceding examples. A list of supported cipher types is shown in the following screenshot:

```
Cipher Types
-aes-128-cbc              -aes-128-ccm              -aes-128-cfb
-aes-128-cfb1             -aes-128-cfb8             -aes-128-ctr
-aes-128-ecb              -aes-128-ofb              -aes-192-cbc
-aes-192-ccm              -aes-192-cfb              -aes-192-cfb1
-aes-192-cfb8             -aes-192-ctr              -aes-192-ecb
-aes-192-ofb              -aes-256-cbc              -aes-256-ccm
-aes-256-cfb              -aes-256-cfb1             -aes-256-cfb8
-aes-256-ctr              -aes-256-ecb              -aes-256-ofb
-aes128                   -aes192                   -aes256
-bf                       -bf-cbc                   -bf-cfb
-bf-ecb                   -bf-ofb                   -blowfish
-camellia-128-cbc         -camellia-128-cfb         -camellia-128-cfb1
-camellia-128-cfb8        -camellia-128-ecb         -camellia-128-ofb
-camellia-192-cbc         -camellia-192-cfb         -camellia-192-cfb1
-camellia-192-cfb8        -camellia-192-ecb         -camellia-192-ofb
-camellia-256-cbc         -camellia-256-cfb         -camellia-256-cfb1
-camellia-256-cfb8        -camellia-256-ecb         -camellia-256-ofb
-camellia128              -camellia192              -camellia256
-cast                     -cast-cbc                 -cast5-cbc
-cast5-cfb                -cast5-ecb                -cast5-ofb
-des                      -des-cbc                  -des-cfb
-des-cfb1                 -des-cfb8                 -des-ecb
-des-ede                  -des-ede-cbc              -des-ede-cfb
-des-ede-ofb              -des-ede3                 -des-ede3-cbc
-des-ede3-cfb             -des-ede3-cfb1            -des-ede3-cfb8
-des-ede3-ofb             -des-ofb                  -des3
-desx                     -desx-cbc                 -id-aes128-CCM
-id-aes128-wrap           -id-aes192-CCM            -id-aes192-wrap
-id-aes256-CCM            -id-aes256-wrap           -id-smime-alg-CMS3DESwrap
-idea                     -idea-cbc                 -idea-cfb
-idea-ecb                 -idea-ofb                 -rc2
-rc2-40-cbc               -rc2-64-cbc               -rc2-cbc
-rc2-cfb                  -rc2-ecb                  -rc2-ofb
-rc4                      -rc4-40                   -seed
-seed-cbc                 -seed-cfb                 -seed-ecb
-seed-ofb
```

Screenshot displaying rich library options available in OpenSSL

OpenSSL tool can be used to experiment with all the ciphers shown in the screenshot.

Summary

In this chapter, we introduced you to symmetric key cryptography. We started with basic mathematical definitions and cryptographic primitives. After this, we introduced you to the concepts of stream and block ciphers along with working modes of block ciphers. Moreover, we introduced you to the practical exercises using OpenSSL to complement the theoretical concepts.

In the next chapter, we will present public key cryptography, which is used extensively in blockchain technology and has very interesting properties.

Public Key Cryptography 4

In this chapter, you will be introduced to the concepts and practical aspects of public key cryptography, also called asymmetric cryptography or asymmetric key cryptography. We will continue to use OpenSSL, as we did in the previous chapter, to experiment with some applications of cryptographic algorithms so that you can gain hands-on experience. We will start with the theoretical foundations of public key cryptography and will gradually build on the concepts with relevant practical exercises. In addition, we will also examine hash functions, which are another cryptographic primitive used extensively in blockchains. After this, we will introduce some new and advanced cryptography constructs.

Asymmetric cryptography

Asymmetric cryptography refers to a type of cryptography where the key that is used to encrypt the data is different from the key that is used to decrypt the data. This is also known as **public key cryptography**. It uses both public and private keys to encrypt and decrypt data, respectively. Various asymmetric cryptography schemes are in use, including RSA, DSA, and ElGammal.

An overview of public key cryptography is shown in the following diagram:

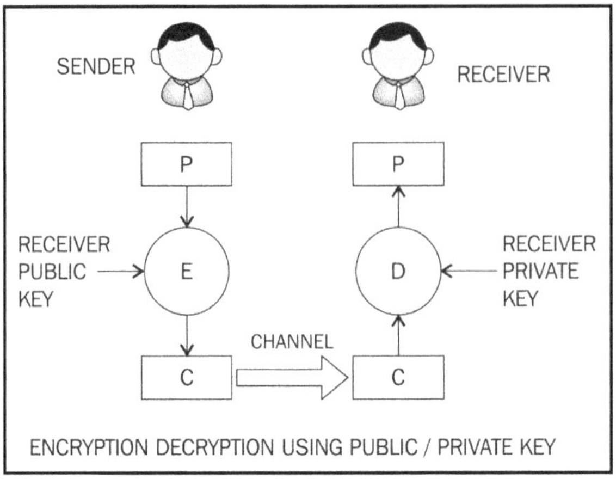

Encryption/decryption using public/private keys

The preceding diagram illustrates how a sender encrypts data **P** using the recipient's public key and encryption function **E** and producing an output encrypted data **C** which is then transmitted over the network to the receiver. Once it reaches the receiver, it can be decrypted using the receiver's private key by feeding the **C** encrypted data into function **D**, which will output plaintext **P**. This way, the private key remains on the receiver's side, and there is no need to share keys in order to perform encryption and decryption, which is the case with symmetric encryption.

The following diagram shows how the receiver uses public key cryptography to verify the integrity of the received message. In this model, the sender signs the data using their private key and transmits the message across to the receiver. Once the message is received, it is verified for integrity by the sender's public key.

It's worth noting that there is no encryption being performed in this model. It is simply presented here to help you understand thoroughly the sections covering message authentication and validation later in this chapter:

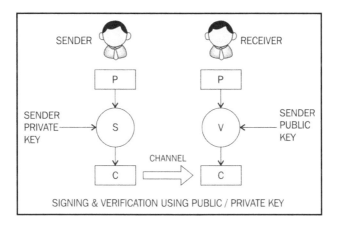

Model of a public-key cryptography signature scheme

The preceding diagram shows that sender digitally signs the plaintext **P** with his private key using signing function **S** and produces data **C** which is sent to the receiver who verifies **C** using sender public key and function **V** to ensure the message has indeed come from the sender.

Security mechanisms offered by public key cryptosystems include key establishment, digital signatures, identification, encryption, and decryption.

Key establishment mechanisms are concerned with the design of protocols that allow the setting up of keys over an insecure channel. Non-repudiation services, a very desirable property in many scenarios, can be provided using **digital signatures**. Sometimes, it is important not only to authenticate a user but also to identify the entity involved in a transaction. This can also be achieved by a combination of digital signatures and **challenge-response protocols**. Finally, the encryption mechanism to provide confidentiality can also be obtained using public key cryptosystems, such as RSA, ECC, and ElGammal.

Public key algorithms are slower in terms of computation than symmetric key algorithms. Therefore, they are not commonly used in the encryption of large files or the actual data that requires encryption. They are usually used to exchange keys for symmetric algorithm. Once the keys are established securely, symmetric key algorithms can be used to encrypt the data.

Public key cryptography algorithms are based on various underlying mathematical functions. The three main categories of asymmetric algorithms are described here.

Integer factorization

Integer factorization schemes are based on the fact that large integers are very hard to factor. RSA is the prime example of this type of algorithm.

Discrete logarithm

A **discrete logarithm scheme** is based on a problem in modular arithmetic. It is easy to calculate the result of modulo function, but it is computationally impractical to find the exponent of the generator. In other words, it is extremely difficult to find the input from the result. This is a one-way function.

For example, consider the following equation:

$$3^2 \ mod \ 10 = 9$$

Now, given 9, the result of the preceding equation finding 2 which is the exponent of the generator 3 in the preceding question, is extremely hard to determine. This difficult problem is commonly used in the Diffie-Hellman key exchange and digital signature algorithms.

Elliptic curves

The **elliptic curves algorithm** is based on the discrete logarithm problem discussed earlier but in the context of elliptic curves. An **elliptic curve** is an algebraic cubic curve over a field, which can be defined by the following equation. The curve is non-singular, which means that it has no cusps or self-intersections. It has two variables a and b, as well as a point of infinity.

$$y^2 = x^3 + ax + b$$

Here, a and b are integers whose values are elements of the field on which the elliptic curve is defined. Elliptic curves can be defined over real numbers, rational numbers, complex numbers, or finite fields. For cryptographic purposes, an elliptic curve over prime finite fields is used instead of real numbers. Additionally, the prime should be greater than 3. Different curves can be generated by varying the value of a and/or b.

The most prominently used cryptosystems based on elliptic curves are the **Elliptic Curve Digital Signature Algorithm** (**ECDSA**) and the **Elliptic Curve Diffie-Hellman** (**ECDH**) key exchange.

To understand public key cryptography, the key concept that needs to be explored is the concept of public and private keys.

Public and private keys

A **private key**, as the name suggests, is a randomly generated number that is kept secret and held privately by its users. Private keys need to be protected and no unauthorized access should be granted to that key; otherwise, the whole scheme of public key cryptography is jeopardized, as this is the key that is used to decrypt messages. Private keys can be of various lengths depending on the type and class of algorithms used. For example, in RSA, typically a key of 1024-bits or 2048-bits is used. The 1024-bit key size is no longer considered secure, and at least a 2048-bit key size is recommended.

A **public key** is freely available and published by the private key owner. Anyone who would then like to send the publisher of the public key an encrypted message can do so by encrypting the message using the published public key and sending it to the holder of the private key. No one else is able to decrypt the message because the corresponding private key is held securely by the intended recipient. Once the public key encrypted message is received, the recipient can decrypt the message using the private key. There are a few concerns, however, regarding public keys. These include authenticity and identification of the publisher of the public keys.

In the following section, we will introduce two examples of asymmetric key cryptography: RSA and ECC. RSA is the first implementation of public key cryptography whereas ECC is used extensively in blockchain technology.

RSA

RSA was invented in 1977 by Ron Rivest, Adi Shamir, and Leonard Adelman, hence the name **Rivest–Shamir–Adleman** (**RSA**). This type of public key cryptography is based on the integer factorization problem, where the multiplication of two large prime numbers is easy, but it is difficult to factor it (the result of multiplication, product) back to the two original numbers.

The crux of the work involved with the RSA algorithm is during the key generation process. An RSA key pair is generated by performing the following steps:

1. **Modulus generation**:

    *   Select *p* and *q*, which are very large prime numbers
    *   Multiply *p* and *q*, *n=p.q* to generate modulus *n*

2. **Generate co-prime**:

    *   Assume a number called *e*.
    *   *e* should satisfy a certain condition; that is, it should be greater than 1 and less than *(p-1) (q-1)*. In other words, *e* must be a number such that no number other than 1 can divide *e* and *(p-1) (q-1)*. This is called **co-prime**, that is, *e* is the co-prime of *(p-1) (q-1)*.

3. **Generate the public key**:

    The modulus generated in step 1 and co-prime *e* generated in step 2 is a pair together that is a public key. This part is the public part that can be shared with anyone; however, *p* and *q* need to be kept secret.

4. **Generate the private key**:

    The private key, called *d* here, is calculated from *p*, *q*, and *e*. The private key is basically the inverse of *e modulo (p-1) (q-1)*. In the equation form, it is this as follows:

$$ed = 1 \ mod \ (p\text{-}1) \ (q\text{-}1)$$

Usually, the extended Euclidean algorithm is used to calculate *d*. This algorithm takes *p*, *q*, and *e* and calculates *d*. The key idea in this scheme is that anyone who knows *p* and *q* can easily calculate private key *d* by applying the extended Euclidean algorithm. However, someone who does not know the value of *p* and *q* cannot generate *d*. This also implies that *p* and *q* should be large enough for the modulus *n* to become extremely difficult (computationally impractical) to factor.

Encryption and decryption using RSA

RSA uses the following equation to produce ciphertext:

$$C = P^e \bmod n$$

This means that plaintext P is raised to e number of times and then reduced to modulo n. Decryption in RSA is provided in the following equation:

$$P = C^d \bmod n$$

This means that the receiver who has a public key pair (n, e) can decipher the data by raising C to the value of the private key d and reducing to modulo n.

Elliptic Curve Cryptography

Elliptic Curve Cryptography (**ECC**) is based on the discrete logarithm problem founded upon elliptic curves over finite fields (Galois fields). The main benefit of ECC over other types of public key algorithms is that it requires a smaller key size while providing the same level of security as, for example, RSA. Two notable schemes that originate from ECC are ECDH for key exchange and ECDSA for digital signatures.

ECC can also be used for encryption, but it is not usually used for this purpose in practice. Instead, it is used for key exchange and digital signatures commonly. As ECC needs less space to operate, it is becoming very popular on embedded platforms and in systems where storage resources are limited. By comparison, the same level of security can be achieved with ECC only using 256-bit operands as compared to 3072-bits in RSA.

Mathematics behind ECC

To understand ECC, a basic introduction to the underlying mathematics is necessary. An elliptic curve is basically a type of polynomial equation known as the **Weierstrass equation**, which generates a curve over a finite field. The most commonly-used field is where all the arithmetic operations are performed modulo a prime p. Elliptic curve groups consist of points on the curve over a finite field.

An elliptic curve is defined in the following equation:

$$y^2 = x^3 + Ax + B \; mod \; P$$

Here, A and B belong to a finite field Zp or Fp (prime finite field) along with a special value called the **point of infinity**. The point of infinity (∞) is used to provide identity operations for points on the curve.

Furthermore, a condition also needs to be met that ensures that the equation mentioned earlier has no repeated roots. This means that the curve is non-singular.

The condition is described in the following equation, which is a standard requirement that needs to be met. More precisely, this ensures that the curve is non-singular:

$$4a^3 + 27b^2 \neq 0 \; mod \; p$$

To construct the discrete logarithm problem based on elliptic curves, a large enough cyclic group is required. First, the group elements are identified as a set of points that satisfy the previous equation. After this, group operations need to be defined on these points.

Group operations on elliptic curves are point addition and point doubling. **Point addition** is a process where two different points are added, and **point doubling** means that the same point is added to itself.

Point addition

Point addition is shown in the following diagram. This is a geometric representation of point addition on elliptic curves. In this method, a diagonal line is drawn through the curve that intersects the curve at two points **P** and **Q**, as shown in the diagram, which yields a third point between the curve and the line. This point is mirrored as **P+Q**, which represents the result of the addition as **R**.

This is shown as **P+Q** in the following diagram:

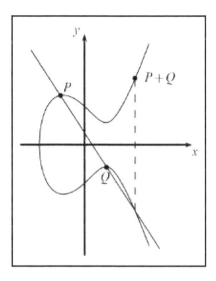

Point addition over R

The group operation denoted by the + sign for addition yields the following equation:

$$P + Q = R$$

In this case, two points are added to compute the coordinates of the third point on the curve:

$$P + Q = R$$

More precisely, this means that coordinates are added, as shown in the following equation:

$$(x_1, y_1) + (x_2, y_2) = (x_3, y_3)$$

The equation of point addition is as follows:

$$X_3 = s^2 - x_1 - x_2 \bmod p$$

$$y_3 = s (x_1 - x_3) - y_1 \bmod p$$

Here, we see the result of the preceding equation:

$$S = \frac{(y_2 - y_1)}{(x_2 - x_1)} \, mod \; p$$

S in the preceding equation depicts the line going through *P* and *Q*.

An example of point addition is shown in the following diagram. It was produced using Certicom's online calculator. This example shows the addition and solutions for the equation over finite field $\mathbf{F}_{23}$. This is in contrast to the example shown earlier, which is over real numbers and only shows the curve but provides no solutions to the equation:

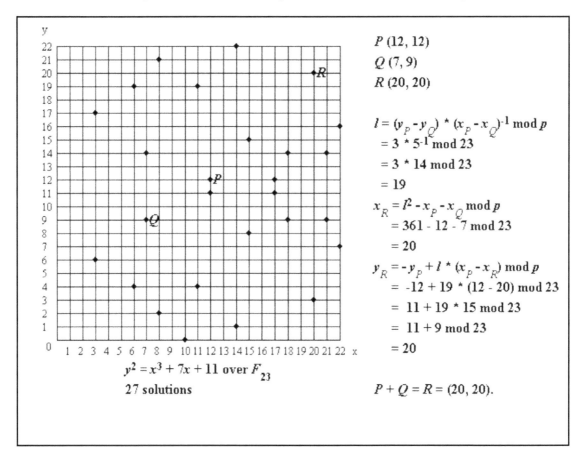

Example of point addition

In the preceding example, the graph on the left side shows the points that satisfy this equation:

$$y^2 = x^3 + 7x + 11$$

There are 27 solutions to the equation shown earlier over finite field F_{23}. P and Q are chosen to be added to produce point R. Calculations are shown on the right side, which calculates the third point R. Note that here, l is used to depict the line going through P and Q.

As an example, to show how the equation is satisfied by the points shown in the graph, a point (x, y) is picked up where $x = 3$ and $y = 6$.

Using these values shows that the equation is indeed satisfied:

$$y^2 \bmod 23 = x^3 + 7x + 11 \bmod 23$$

$$6^2 \bmod 23 = 3^3 + 7(3) + 11 \bmod 23$$

$$36 \bmod 23 = 59 \bmod 23$$

$$13 = 13$$

The next subsection introduces the concept of point doubling, which is another operation that can be performed on elliptic curves.

Point doubling

The other group operation on elliptic curves is called **point doubling**. This is a process where **P** is added to itself. In this method, a tangent line is drawn through the curve, as shown in the following graph. The second point is obtained, which is at the intersection of the tangent line drawn and the curve.

This point is then mirrored to yield the result, which is shown as *2P = P + P*:

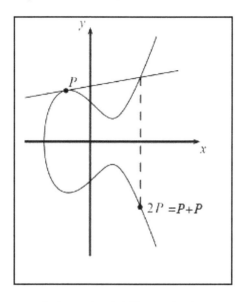

Graph representing point doubling over real numbers

In the case of point doubling, the equation becomes:

$$x_3 = s^2 - x_1 - x_2 \; mod \; p$$

$$y_3 = s(x_1 - x_3) - y_1 \; mod \; p$$

$$S = \frac{3x_1^2 + a}{2y_1}$$

Here, *S* is the slope of tangent (tangent line) going through *P*. It is the line shown on top in the preceding diagram. In the preceding example, the curve is plotted over real numbers as a simple example, and no solution to the equation is shown.

The following example shows the solutions and point doubling of elliptic curves over finite field $\mathbf{F}_{23}$. The graph on the left side shows the points that satisfy the equation:

$$y^2 = x^3 + 7x + 11$$

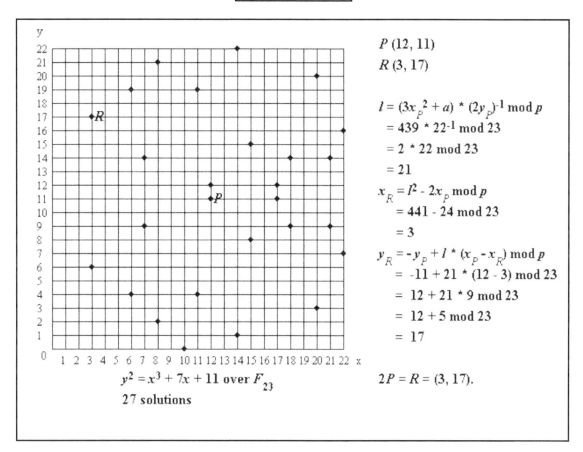

$P\ (12, 11)$

$R\ (3, 17)$

$l = (3x_p^2 + a) * (2y_p)^{-1} \bmod p$

$\quad = 439 * 22^{-1} \bmod 23$

$\quad = 2 * 22 \bmod 23$

$\quad = 21$

$x_R = l^2 - 2x_p \bmod p$

$\quad = 441 - 24 \bmod 23$

$\quad = 3$

$y_R = -y_p + l * (x_p - x_R) \bmod p$

$\quad = -11 + 21 * (12 - 3) \bmod 23$

$\quad = 12 + 21 * 9 \bmod 23$

$\quad = 12 + 5 \bmod 23$

$\quad = 17$

$y^2 = x^3 + 7x + 11$ over F_{23}

27 solutions

$2P = R = (3, 17)$.

Example of point doubling

As shown on the right side in the preceding graph, the calculation that finds the R after P is added into itself (point doubling). There is no Q as shown here, and the same point P is used for doubling. Note that in the calculation, l is used to depict the tangent line going through P.

In the next section, an introduction to the discrete logarithm problem will be presented.

Discrete logarithm problem in ECC

The discrete logarithm problem in ECC is based on the idea that, under certain conditions, all points on an elliptic curve form a cyclic group.

On an elliptic curve, the public key is a random multiple of the generator point, whereas the private key is a randomly chosen integer used to generate the multiple. In other words, a private key is a randomly selected integer, whereas the public key is a point on the curve. The discrete logarithm problem is used to find the private key (an integer) where that integer falls within all points on the elliptic curve. The following equation shows this concept more precisely.

Consider an elliptic curve E, with two elements P and T. The discrete logarithmic problem is to find the integer d, where $1 <= d <= \#E$, such that:

$$\boxed{P + P + \cdots + P = d\,P = T}$$

Here, T is the public key (a point on the curve), and d is the private key. In other words, the public key is a random multiple of the generator, whereas the private key is the integer that is used to generate the multiple. $\#E$ represents the order of the elliptic curve, which means the number of points that are present in the cyclic group of the elliptic curve. A **cyclic group** is formed by a combination of points on the elliptic curve and point of infinity.

A key pair is linked with the specific domain parameters of an elliptic curve. Domain parameters include field size, field representation, two elements from the field a and b, two field elements Xg and Yg, order n of point G that is calculated as $G = (Xg, Yg)$, and the cofactor $h = \#E(Fq)/n$. A practical example using OpenSSL will be described later in this section.

Various parameters are recommended and standardized to use as curves with ECC. An example of `secp256k1` specifications is shown here. This is the specification that is used in Bitcoin:

The elliptic curve domain parameters over $\mathbb{F}_p$ associated with a Koblitz curve `secp256k1` are specified by the sextuple $T = (p, a, b, G, n, h)$ where the finite field $\mathbb{F}_p$ is defined by:

p = FFFFFFFF FFFFFFFF FFFFFFFF FFFFFFFF FFFFFFFF FFFFFFFF FFFFFFFE FFFFFC2F

= $2^{256} - 2^{32} - 2^9 - 2^8 - 2^7 - 2^6 - 2^4 - 1$

The curve $E: y^2 = x^3 + ax + b$ over $\mathbb{F}_p$ is defined by:

a = 00000000 00000000 00000000 00000000 00000000 00000000 00000000 00000000

b = 00000000 00000000 00000000 00000000 00000000 00000000 00000000 00000007

The base point G in compressed form is:

G = 02 79BE667E F9DCBBAC 55A06295 CE870B07 029BFCDB 2DCE28D9 59F2815B 16F81798

and in uncompressed form is:

G = 04 79BE667E F9DCBBAC 55A06295 CE870B07 029BFCDB 2DCE28D9 59F2815B 16F81798 483ADA77 26A3C465 5DA4FBFC 0E1108A8 FD17B448 A6855419 9C47D08F FB10D4B8

Finally the order n of G and the cofactor are:

n = FFFFFFFF FFFFFFFF FFFFFFFF FFFFFFFE BAAEDCE6 AF48A03B BFD25E8C D0364141

h = 01

Specification of secp256k1 taken from http://www.secg.org/sec2-v2.pdf

An explanation of all of these values in the sextuple is as follows:

- *P* is the prime *p* that specifies the size of the finite field.
- *a* and *b* are the coefficients of the elliptic curve equation.
- *G* is the base point that generates the required subgroup, also known as the *generator*. The base point can be represented in either compressed or uncompressed form. There is no need to store all points on the curve in a practical implementation. The compressed generator works because the points on the curve can be identified using only the *x* coordinate and the least significant bit of the *y* coordinate.
- *n* is the order of the subgroup.
- *h* is the cofactor of the subgroup.

In the following section, two examples of using OpenSSL are shown to help you understand the practical aspects of RSA and ECC cryptography.

RSA using OpenSSL

The following example illustrates how RSA public and private key pairs can be generated using the OpenSSL command line.

RSA public and private key pair

First, how the RSA private key can be generated using OpenSSL is shown in the following subsection.

Private key

Execute the following command to generate the private key:

```
$ openssl genpkey -algorithm RSA -out privatekey.pem -pkeyopt \
rsa_keygen_bits:1024
.............................++++++
...................++++++
```

 The backslash (\) used in the commands are for continuation

After executing the command, a file named `privatekey.pem` is produced, which contains the generated private key as follows:

```
$ cat privatekey.pem
-----BEGIN PRIVATE KEY-----
MIICdgIBADANBgkqhkiG9w0BAQEFAASCAmAwggJcAgEAAoGBAKJOFBzPy2vOd6em
Bk/UGrzDy7TvgDYnYxBfiEJId/r+EyMt/F14k2fDTOVwxXaXTxiQgD+BKuiey/69
9itnrqW/xy/pocDMvobj8QCngEntOdNoVSaN+t0f9nRM3iVM94mz3/C/v4vXvoac
PyPkr/0jhIV0woCurXGTghgqIbHRAgMBAAECgYEAlB3s/N4lJh0l1TkOSYunWtzT
6isnNkR7g1WrY9H+rG9xx4kP5b1DyE3SvxBLJA6xgBle8JVQMzm3sKJrJPFZzzT5
NNNnugCxairxcF1mPzJAP3aqpcSjxKpTv4qgqYevwgW1A0R3xKQZzBKU+bTO2hXV
D1oHxu75mDY3xCwqSAECQQDUYV04wNSEjEy9tYJ0zaryDAcvd/VG2/U/6qiQGajB
eSpSqoEESigbusKku+wVtRYgWWEomL/X58t+K01eMMZZAkEAw6PUR9YLebsm/Sji
iOShV4AKuFdi7t7DYWE5Ulb1uqP/i28zN/ytt4BXKIs/KcFykQGeAC6LDHZyycyc
ntDIOQJAVqrE1/wYvV5jkqcXbYLgV5YA+KYDOb9Y/ZRM5UETVKCVXNanf5CjfW1h
MMhfNxyGwvy2YVK0Nu8oY3xYPi+5QQJAUGcmORe4w6Cs12JUJ5p+zG0s+rG/URhw
B7djTXm7p6b6wR1EWYAZDM9MArenj8uXAA1AGCcIsmiDqHfU7lgz0QJAe9mOdNGW
7qRppgmOE5nuEbxkDSQI7OqHYbOLuwfCjHzJBrSgqyi6pj9/9CbXJrZPgNDwdLEb
GgpDKtZs9gLv3A==
-----END PRIVATE KEY-----
```

Public key

As the private key is mathematically linked to the public key, it is also possible to generate or derive the public key from the private key. Using the example of the preceding private key, the public key can be generated as shown here:

```
$ openssl rsa -pubout -in privatekey.pem -out publickey.pem

writing RSA key
```

The public key can be viewed using a file reader or any text viewer:

```
$ cat publickey.pem
-----BEGIN PUBLIC KEY-----
MIGfMA0GCSqGSIb3DQEBAQUAA4GNADCBiQKBgQCiThQcz8trznenpgZP1Bq8w8u0
74A2J2MQX4hCSHf6/hMjLfxdeJNnw0zlcMV2l08YkIA/gSronsv+vfYrZ66lv8cv
6aHAzL6G4/EAp4BJ7TnTaFUmjfrdH/Z0TN4lTPeJs9/wv7+L176GnD8j5K/9I4SF
dMKArq1xk4IYKiGx0QIDAQAB
-----END PUBLIC KEY-----
```

In order to see more details of the various components, such as the modulus, prime numbers that are used in the encryption process, or exponents and coefficients of the generated private key, the following command can be used (only partial output is shown here as the actual output is very long):

```
$ openssl rsa -text -in privatekey.pem
Private-Key: (1024 bit)
modulus:
    00:a2:4e:14:1c:cf:cb:6b:ce:77:a7:a6:06:4f:d4:
    1a:bc:c3:cb:b4:ef:80:36:27:63:10:5f:88:42:48:
    77:fa:fe:13:23:2d:fc:5d:78:93:67:c3:4c:e5:70:
    c5:76:97:4f:18:90:80:3f:81:2a:e8:9e:cb:fe:bd:
    f6:2b:67:ae:a5:bf:c7:2f:e9:a1:c0:cc:be:86:e3:
    f1:00:a7:80:49:ed:39:d3:68:55:26:8d:fa:dd:1f:
    f6:74:4c:de:25:4c:f7:89:b3:df:f0:bf:bf:8b:d7:
    be:86:9c:3f:23:e4:af:fd:23:84:85:74:c2:80:ae:
    ad:71:93:82:18:2a:21:b1:d1
publicExponent: 65537 (0x10001)
privateExponent:
    00:94:1d:ec:fc:de:25:26:1d:25:d5:39:0e:49:8b:
    a7:5a:dc:d3:ea:2b:27:36:44:7b:83:55:ab:63:d1:
    fe:ac:6f:71:c7:89:0f:e5:bd:43:c8:4d:d2:bf:10:
    4b:24:0e:b1:80:19:5e:f0:95:50:33:39:b7:b0:a2:
    6b:24:f1:59:cf:34:f9:34:d3:67:ba:00:b1:6a:2a:
    f1:70:5d:66:3f:32:40:3f:76:aa:a5:c4:a3:c4:aa:
    53:bf:8a:a0:a9:87:af:c2:05:b5:03:44:77:c4:a4:
    19:cc:12:94:f9:b4:ce:da:15:d5:0f:5a:07:c6:ee:
    f9:98:36:37:c4:2c:2a:48:01
prime1:
    00:d4:61:5d:38:c0:d4:84:8c:4c:bd:b5:82:74:cd:
    aa:f2:0c:07:2f:77:f5:46:db:f5:3f:ea:a8:90:19:
    a8:c1:79:2a:52:aa:81:04:4a:28:1b:ba:c2:a4:bb:
    ec:15:b5:16:20:59:61:28:98:bf:d7:e7:cb:7e:2b:
    4d:5e:30:c6:59
prime2:
    00:c3:a3:d4:47:d6:0b:79:bb:26:fd:28:e2:88:e4:
    a1:57:80:0a:b8:57:62:ee:de:c3:61:61:39:52:56:
    f5:ba:a3:ff:8b:6f:33:37:fc:ad:b7:80:57:28:8b:
    3f:29:c1:72:91:01:9e:00:2e:8b:0c:76:72:c9:cc:
    9c:9e:d0:c8:39
```

Exploring the public key

Similarly, the public key can be explored using the following commands. Public and private keys are base64-encoded:

```
$ openssl pkey -in publickey.pem -pubin -text
-----BEGIN PUBLIC KEY-----
MIGfMA0GCSqGSIb3DQEBAQUAA4GNADCBiQKBgQCiThQcz8trznenpgZP1Bq8w8u0
74A2J2MQX4hCSHf6/hMjLfxdeJNnw0zlcMV2108YkIA/gSronsv+vfYrZ66lv8cv
6aHAzL6G4/EAp4BJ7TnTaFUmjfrdH/Z0TN4lTPeJs9/wv7+L176GnD8j5K/9I4SF
dMKArq1xk4IYKiGx0QIDAQAB
-----END PUBLIC KEY-----
Public-Key: (1024 bit)
Modulus:
    00:a2:4e:14:1c:cf:cb:6b:ce:77:a7:a6:06:4f:d4:
    1a:bc:c3:cb:b4:ef:80:36:27:63:10:5f:88:42:48:
    77:fa:fe:13:23:2d:fc:5d:78:93:67:c3:4c:e5:70:
    c5:76:97:4f:18:90:80:3f:81:2a:e8:9e:cb:fe:bd:
    f6:2b:67:ae:a5:bf:c7:2f:e9:a1:c0:cc:be:86:e3:
    f1:00:a7:80:49:ed:39:d3:68:55:26:8d:fa:dd:1f:
    f6:74:4c:de:25:4c:f7:89:b3:df:f0:bf:bf:8b:d7:
    be:86:9c:3f:23:e4:af:fd:23:84:85:74:c2:80:ae:
    ad:71:93:82:18:2a:21:b1:d1
Exponent: 65537 (0x10001)
```

Now the public key can be shared openly, and anyone who wants to send you a message can use the public key to encrypt the message and send it to you. You can then use the corresponding private key to decrypt the file.

Encryption and decryption

In this section, an example will be presented that demonstrates how encryption and decryption operations can be performed using RSA with OpenSSL.

Encryption

Taking the private key generated in the previous example, the command to encrypt a text file message.txt can be constructed as shown here:

```
$ echo datatoencrypt > message.txt
$ openssl rsautl -encrypt -inkey publickey.pem -pubin -in message.txt \
  -out message.rsa
```

This will produce a file named `message.rsa`, which is in a binary format. If you open `message.rsa` in the nano editor or any other text editor of your choice, it will show some garbage as shown in the following screenshot:

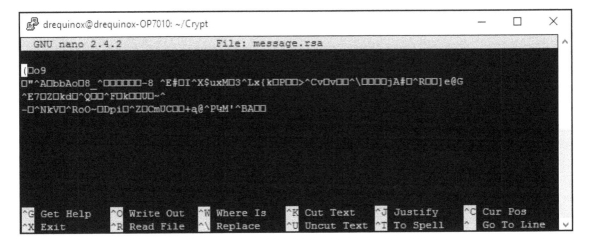

message.rsa showing garbage (encrypted) data

Decryption

In order to decrypt the RSA-encrypted file, the following command can be used:

```
$ openssl rsautl -decrypt -inkey privatekey.pem -in message.rsa \
  -out message.dec
```

Now, if the file is read using `cat`, decrypted plaintext can be seen as shown here:

```
$ cat message.dec
datatoencrypt
```

ECC using OpenSSL

OpenSSL provides a very rich library of functions to perform ECC. The following subsection shows how to use ECC functions in a practical manner in OpenSSL.

ECC private and public key pair

In this subsection, first an example is presented that demonstrates the creation of a private key using ECC functions available in the OpenSSL library.

Private key

ECC is based on domain parameters defined by various standards. You can see the list of all available standards defined and recommended curves available in OpenSSL using the following command. (Once again, only partial output is shown here, and it is truncated in the middle.):

```
$ openssl ecparam -list_curves
secp112r1 : SECG/WTLS curve over a 112 bit prime field
secp112r2 : SECG curve over a 112 bit prime field
secp128r1 : SECG curve over a 128 bit prime field
secp128r2 : SECG curve over a 128 bit prime field
secp160k1 : SECG curve over a 160 bit prime field
secp160r1 : SECG curve over a 160 bit prime field
secp160r2 : SECG/WTLS curve over a 160 bit prime field
secp192k1 : SECG curve over a 192 bit prime field
secp224k1 : SECG curve over a 224 bit prime field
secp224r1 : NIST/SECG curve over a 224 bit prime field
secp256k1 : SECG curve over a 256 bit prime field
secp384r1 : NIST/SECG curve over a 384 bit prime field
secp521r1 : NIST/SECG curve over a 521 bit prime field
prime192v1: NIST/X9.62/SECG curve over a 192 bit prime field
   .
   .
   .
   .
brainpoolP384r1: RFC 5639 curve over a 384 bit prime field
brainpoolP384t1: RFC 5639 curve over a 384 bit prime field
brainpoolP512r1: RFC 5639 curve over a 512 bit prime field
brainpoolP512t1: RFC 5639 curve over a 512 bit prime field
```

In the following example, `secp256k1` is employed to demonstrate ECC usage.

Private key generation

To generate the private key, execute the following command:

```
$ openssl ecparam -name secp256k1 -genkey -noout -out ec-privatekey.pem
$ cat ec-privatekey.pem
-----BEGIN EC PRIVATE KEY-----
MHQCAQEEIJHUIm9NZAgfpUrSxUk/iINq1ghM/ewn/RLNreuR52h/oAcGBSuBBAAK
oUQDQgAE0G33mCZ4PKbg5EtwQjk6ucv9Qc9DTr8JdcGXYGxHdzr0Jt1NInaYE0GG
ChFMT5pK+wfvSLkY15ul0oczwWKjng==
-----END EC PRIVATE KEY-----
```

The file named `ec-privatekey.pem` now contains the **Elliptic Curve** (**EC**) private key that is generated based on the `secp256k1` curve. In order to generate a public key from a private key, issue the following command:

```
$ openssl ec -in ec-privatekey.pem -pubout -out ec-pubkey.pem
read EC key
writing EC key
```

Reading the file produces the following output, displaying the generated public key:

```
$ cat ec-pubkey.pem
-----BEGIN PUBLIC KEY-----
MFYwEAYHKoZIzj0CAQYFK4EEAAoDQgAE0G33mCZ4PKbg5EtwQjk6ucv9Qc9DTr8J
dcGXYGxHdzr0Jt1NInaYE0GGChFMT5pK+wfvSLkYl5ul0oczwWKjng==
-----END PUBLIC KEY-----
```

Now the `ec-pubkey.pem` file contains the public key derived from `ec-privatekey.pem`. The private key can be further explored using the following command:

```
$ openssl ec -in ec-privatekey.pem -text -noout
read EC key
Private-Key: (256 bit)
priv:
    00:91:d4:22:6f:4d:64:08:1f:a5:4a:d2:c5:49:3f:
    88:83:6a:d6:08:4c:fd:ec:27:fd:12:cd:ad:eb:91:
    e7:68:7f
pub:
    04:d0:6d:f7:98:26:78:3c:a6:e0:e4:4b:70:42:39:
    3a:b9:cb:fd:41:cf:43:4e:bf:09:75:c1:97:60:6c:
    47:77:3a:f4:26:dd:4d:22:76:98:13:41:86:0a:11:
    4c:4f:9a:4a:fb:07:ef:48:b9:18:97:9b:a5:d2:87:
    33:c1:62:a3:9e
ASN1 OID: secp256k1
```

Similarly, the public key can be further explored with the following command:

```
$ openssl ec -in ec-pubkey.pem -pubin -text -noout
read EC key
Private-Key: (256 bit)
pub:
    04:d0:6d:f7:98:26:78:3c:a6:e0:e4:4b:70:42:39:
    3a:b9:cb:fd:41:cf:43:4e:bf:09:75:c1:97:60:6c:
    47:77:3a:f4:26:dd:4d:22:76:98:13:41:86:0a:11:
    4c:4f:9a:4a:fb:07:ef:48:b9:18:97:9b:a5:d2:87:
    33:c1:62:a3:9e
ASN1 OID: secp256k1
```

It is also possible to generate a file with the required parameters, in this case, `secp256k1`, and then explore it further to understand the underlying parameters:

```
$ openssl ecparam -name secp256k1 -out secp256k1.pem
$ cat secp256k1.pem
-----BEGIN EC PARAMETERS-----
BgUrgQQACg==
-----END EC PARAMETERS-----
```

The file now contains all the `secp256k1` parameters, and it can be analyzed using the following command:

```
$ openssl ecparam -in secp256k1.pem -text -param_enc explicit -noout
```

This command will produce the output similar to the one shown here:

```
Field Type: prime-field
Prime:
    00:ff:ff:ff:ff:ff:ff:ff:ff:ff:ff:ff:ff:ff:ff:
    ff:ff:ff:ff:ff:ff:ff:ff:ff:ff:ff:ff:ff:fe:ff:
    ff:fc:2f
A:    0
B:    7 (0x7)
Generator (uncompressed):
    04:79:be:66:7e:f9:dc:bb:ac:55:a0:62:95:ce:87:
    0b:07:02:9b:fc:db:2d:ce:28:d9:59:f2:81:5b:16:
    f8:17:98:48:3a:da:77:26:a3:c4:65:5d:a4:fb:fc:
    0e:11:08:a8:fd:17:b4:48:a6:85:54:19:9c:47:d0:
    8f:fb:10:d4:b8
Order:
    00:ff:ff:ff:ff:ff:ff:ff:ff:ff:ff:ff:ff:ff:ff:
    ff:fe:ba:ae:dc:e6:af:48:a0:3b:bf:d2:5e:8c:d0:
    36:41:41
Cofactor:  1 (0x1)
```

The preceding example shows the prime number used and values of A and B, with the generator, order, and cofactor of the `secp256k1` curve domain parameters.

With the preceding example, our introduction to public key cryptography from encryption and decryption perspective is complete. Other relevant constructs like digital signatures will be discussed later in the chapter.

In the next section, we will look at another category of cryptographic primitives, hash functions. Hash functions are not used to encrypt data; instead, they produce a fixed-length digest of the data that is provided as input to the hash function.

Hash functions

Hash functions are used to create fixed-length digests of arbitrarily-long input strings. Hash functions are keyless, and they provide the data integrity service. They are usually built using iterated and dedicated hash function construction techniques.

Various families of hash functions are available, such as MD, SHA-1, SHA-2, SHA-3, RIPEMD, and Whirlpool. Hash functions are commonly used for digital signatures and **Message Authentication Codes** (**MACs**), such as HMACs. They have three security properties, namely preimage resistance, second preimage resistance, and collision resistance. These properties are explained later in this section.

Hash functions are also typically used to provide data integrity services. These can be used both as one-way functions and to construct other cryptographic primitives, such as MACs and digital signatures. Some applications use hash functions as a means for generating **Pseudo-random Numbers Generator** (**PRNGs**). There are two practical and three security properties of hash functions that must be met depending on the level of integrity required. These properties are discussed in the following subsections.

Compression of arbitrary messages into fixed-length digest

This property relates to the fact that a hash function must be able to take an input text of any length and output a fixed-length compressed message. Hash functions produce a compressed output in various bit sizes, usually between 128-bits and 512-bits.

Easy to compute

Hash functions are efficient and fast one-way functions. It is required that hash functions be very quick to compute regardless of the message size. The efficiency may decrease if the message is too big, but the function should still be fast enough for practical use.

In the following section, security properties of hash functions are discussed.

Preimage resistance

This property can be explained by using the simple equation shown as follows:

$$h(x) = y$$

Here, *h* is the hash function, *x* is the input, and *y* is the hash. The first security property requires that *y* cannot be reverse-computed to *x*. *x* is considered a preimage of *y*, hence the name **preimage resistance**. This is also called a one-way property.

Second preimage resistance

The **second preimage resistance** property requires that given *x* and *h(x)*, it is almost impossible to find any other message *m*, where *m != x* and *hash of m = hash of x* or *h(m) = h(x)*. This property is also known as **weak collision resistance**.

Collision resistance

The **collision resistance** property requires that two different input messages should not hash to the same output. In other words, *h(x) != h(z)*. This property is also known as **strong collision resistance**.

All these properties are shown in the following diagram:

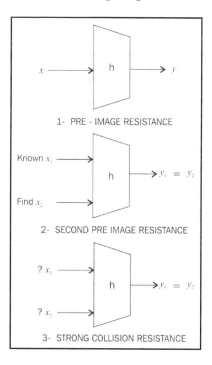

Three security properties of hash functions

Due to their very nature, hash functions will always have some collisions. This is where two different messages hash to the same output. However, they should be computationally impractical to find. A concept known as the **avalanche effect** is desirable in all hash functions. The avalanche effect specifies that a small change, even a single character change in the input text, will result in an entirely different hash output.

Hash functions are usually designed by following an iterated hash functions approach. With this method, the input message is compressed in multiple rounds on a block-by-block basis in order to produce the compressed output. A popular type of iterated hash function is **Merkle-Damgard construction**. This construction is based on the idea of dividing the input data into equal block sizes and then feeding them through the compression functions in an iterative manner. The collision resistance of the property of compression functions ensures that the hash output is also collision-resistant. Compression functions can be built using block ciphers. In addition to Merkle-Damgard, there are various other constructions of compression functions proposed by researchers, for example, Miyaguchi-Preneel and Davies-Meyer.

Multiple categories of hash function are introduced in the following subsections.

Message Digest

Message Digest (**MD**) functions were prevalent in the early 1990s. MD4 and MD5 fall into this category. Both MD functions were found to be insecure and are not recommended for use anymore. MD5 is a 128-bit hash function that was commonly used for file integrity checks.

Secure Hash Algorithms

The following list describes the most common **Secure Hash Algorithms** (**SHAs**):

- **SHA-0**: This is a 160-bit function introduced by NIST in 1993.
- **SHA-1**: SHA-1 was introduced in 1995 by NIST as a replacement for SHA-0. This is also a 160-bit hash function. SHA-1 is used commonly in SSL and TLS implementations. It should be noted that SHA-1 is now considered insecure, and it is being deprecated by certificate authorities. Its usage is discouraged in any new implementations.
- **SHA-2**: This category includes four functions defined by the number of bits of the hash: SHA-224, SHA-256, SHA-384, and SHA-512.

- **SHA-3**: This is the latest family of SHA functions. SHA-3-224, SHA-3-256, SHA-3-384, and SHA-3-512 are members of this family. SHA-3 is a NIST-standardized version of Keccak. Keccak uses a new approach called **sponge construction** instead of the commonly used Merkle-Damgard transformation.
- **RIPEMD**: RIPEMD is the acronym for **RACE Integrity Primitives Evaluation Message Digest**. It is based on the design ideas used to build MD4. There are multiple versions of RIPEMD, including 128-bit, 160-bit, 256-bit, and 320-bit.
- **Whirlpool**: This is based on a modified version of the Rijndael cipher known as *W*. It uses the Miyaguchi-Preneel compression function, which is a type of one-way function used for the compression of two fixed-length inputs into a single fixed-length output. It is a single block length compression function.

Hash functions have many practical applications ranging from simple file integrity checks and password storage to use in cryptographic protocols and algorithms. They are used in hash tables, distributed hash tables, bloom filters, virus fingerprinting, peer-to-peer file sharing, and many other applications.

Hash functions play a vital role in blockchain. Especially, The PoW function in particular uses SHA-256 twice in order to verify the computational effort spent by miners. RIPEMD 160 is used to produce Bitcoin addresses. This will be discussed further in later chapters.

In the next section, the design of the SHA algorithm is introduced.

Design of Secure Hash Algorithms

In the following section, you will be introduced to the design of SHA-256 and SHA-3. Both of these are used in Bitcoin and Ethereum, respectively. Ethereum does not use NIST Standard SHA-3, but Keccak, which is the original algorithm presented to NIST. NIST, after some modifications, such as an increase in the number of rounds and simpler message padding, standardized Keccak as SHA-3.

Design of SHA-256

SHA-256 has the input message size < 2^{64}-bits. Block size is 512-bits, and it has a word size of 32-bits. The output is a 256-bit digest.

The compression function processes a 512-bit message block and a 256-bit intermediate hash value. There arc two main components of this function: the compression function and a message schedule.

The algorithm works as follows, in eight steps:

1. **Preprocessing**:

    1. Padding of the message is used to adjust the length of a block to 512-bits if it is smaller than the required block size of 512-bits.
    2. Parsing the message into message blocks, which ensures that the message and its padding is divided into equal blocks of 512-bits.
    3. Setting up the initial hash value, which consists of the eight 32-bit words obtained by taking the first 32-bits of the fractional parts of the square roots of the first eight prime numbers. These initial values are randomly chosen to initialize the process, and they provide a level of confidence that no backdoor exists in the algorithm.

2. **Hash computation**:

    4. Each message block is then processed in a sequence, and it requires 64 rounds to compute the full hash output. Each round uses slightly different constants to ensure that no two rounds are the same.
    5. The message schedule is prepared.
    6. Eight working variables are initialized.
    7. The intermediate hash value is calculated.
    8. Finally, the message is processed, and the output hash is produced:

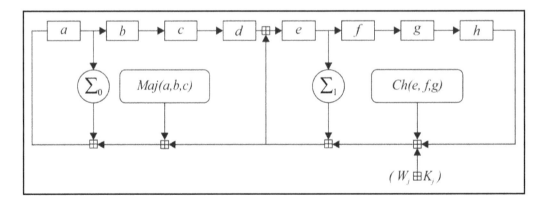

One round of a SHA-256 compression function

In the preceding diagram, **a**, **b**, **c**, **d**, **e**, **f**, **g**, and **h** are the registers. *Maj* and *Ch* are applied bitwise. Σ_0 and Σ_1 performs bitwise rotation. Round constants are W_j and K_j, which are added, *mod 2^{32}*.

Design of SHA-3 (Keccak)

The structure of SHA-3 is very different from that of SHA-1 and SHA-2. The key idea behind SHA-3 is based on unkeyed permutations, as opposed to other typical hash function constructions that used keyed permutations. Keccak also does not make use of the Merkle-Damgard transformation that is commonly used to handle arbitrary-length input messages in hash functions. A newer approach called **sponge and squeeze construction** is used in Keccak. It is a random permutation model. Different variants of SHA-3 have been standardized, such as SHA-3-224, SHA-3-256, SHA-3-384, SHA-3-512, SHAKE-128, and SHAKE-256. SHAKE-128 and SHAKE-256 are **Extendable Output Functions** (**XOFs**), which are also standardized by NIST. XOFs allow the output to be extended to any desired length.

The following diagram shows the sponge and squeeze model, which is the basis of SHA-3 or Keccak. Analogous to a sponge, the data is first absorbed into the sponge after applying padding. There it is then changed into a subset of permutation state using XOR, and then the output is squeezed out of the sponge function that represents the transformed state. The rate is the input block size of a sponge function, while capacity determines the general security level:

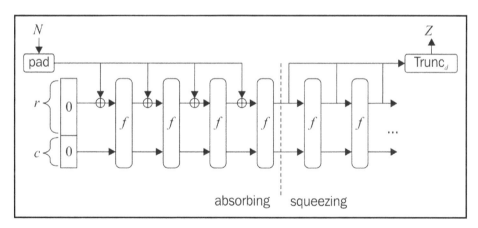

SHA-3 absorbing and squeezing function

OpenSSL example of hash functions

The following command will produce a hash of 256-bits of the `Hello` messages using the SHA-256 algorithm:

```
$ echo -n 'Hello' | openssl dgst -sha256
(stdin)= 185f8db32271fe25f561a6fc938b2e264306ec304eda518007d1764826381969
```

Note that even a small change in the text, such as changing the case of the letter `H`, results in a big change in the output hash. This is known as the avalanche effect, as discussed earlier:

```
$ echo -n 'hello' | openssl dgst -sha256
(stdin)= 2cf24dba5fb0a30e26e83b2ac5b9e29e1b161e5c1fa7425e73043362938b9824
```

Note that both outputs are completely different:

```
Hello:
18:5f:8d:b3:22:71:fe:25:f5:61:a6:fc:93:8b:2e:26:43:06:ec:30:4e:da:51:80:07:
d1:76:48:26:38:19:69
hello:
2c:f2:4d:ba:5f:b0:a3:0e:26:e8:3b:2a:c5:b9:e2:9e:1b:16:1e:5c:1f:a7:42:5e:73:
04:33:62:93:8b:98:24
```

Usually, hash functions do not use a key. Nevertheless, if they *are* used with a key, then they can be used to create another cryptographic construct called MACs.

Message Authentication Codes

MACs are sometimes called **keyed hash functions**, and they can be used to provide message integrity and authentication. More specifically, they are used to provide data origin authentication. These are symmetric cryptographic primitives that use a shared key between the sender and the receiver. MACs can be constructed using block ciphers or hash functions.

MACs using block ciphers

With this approach, block ciphers are used in the **Cipher Block Chaining** (**CBC**) mode in order to generate a MAC. Any block cipher, for example AES in the CBC mode, can be used. The MAC of the message is, in fact, the output of the last round of the CBC operation. The length of the MAC output is the same as the block length of the block cipher used to generate the MAC.

MACs are verified simply by computing the MAC of the message and comparing it to the received MAC. If they are the same, then the message integrity is confirmed; otherwise, the message is considered altered. It should also be noted that MACs work like digital signatures, however they cannot provide non-repudiation service due to their symmetric nature.

Hash-based MACs

Similar to the hash function, **Hash-based MACs** (**HMACs**) produce a fixed-length output and take an arbitrarily long message as the input. In this scheme, the sender signs a message using the MAC and the receiver verifies it using the shared key. The key is hashed with the message using either of the two methods known as **secret prefix** or the **secret suffix**. With the secret prefix method, the key is concatenated with the message; that is, the key comes first and the message comes afterwards, whereas with the secret suffix method, the key comes after the message, as shown in the following equations:

Secret prefix: $M = MACk(x) = h(k||x)$

Secret suffix: $M=MACk(x) = h(x||k)$

There are pros and cons to both methods. Some attacks on both schemes have occurred. There are HMAC constructions schemes that use various techniques, such as **ipad** and **opad** (inner padding and outer padding) that have been proposed by cryptographic researchers. These are considered secure with some assumptions:

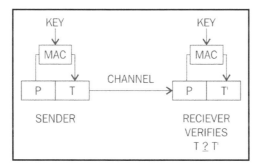

Operation of a MAC function

There are various powerful applications of hash functions used in peer-to-peer networks and blockchain technology. Some noticeable examples, such as Merkle trees, Patricia trees, and **Distributed Hash Table** (**DHT**), are discussed in the following subsections.

Merkle trees

The concept of Merkle tree was introduced by Ralph Merkle. A diagram of Merkle tree is shown here. **Merkle trees** enable secure and efficient verification of large datasets.

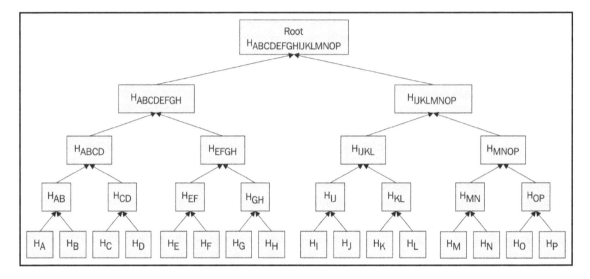

A Merkle tree

A Merkle tree is a binary tree in which the inputs are first placed at the leaves (node with no children), and then the values of pairs of child nodes are hashed together to produce a value for the parent node (internal node) until a single hash value known as **Merkle root** is achieved.

Patricia trees

To understand Patricia trees, you will first be introduced to the concept of a **trie**. A trie, or a digital tree, is an ordered tree data structure used to store a dataset.

Practical Algorithm to Retrieve Information Coded in Alphanumeric (**Patricia**), also known as *Radix tree*, is a compact representation of a trie in which a node that is the only child of a parent is merged with its parent.

A **Merkle-Patricia tree**, based on the definitions of Patricia and Merkle, is a tree that has a root node which contains the hash value of the entire data structure.

Distributed Hash Tables

A hash table is a data structure that is used to map keys to values. Internally, a hash function is used to calculate an index into an array of buckets from which the required value can be found. Buckets have records stored in them using a hash key and are organized into a particular order.

With the definition provided earlier in mind, one can think of a DHT as a data structure where data is spread across various nodes, and nodes are equivalent to buckets in a peer-to-peer network.

The following diagram shows how a DHT works. Data is passed through a hash function, which then generates a compact key. This key is then linked with the data (values) on the peer-to-peer network. When users on the network request the data (via the filename), the filename can be hashed again to produce the same key, and any node on the network can then be requested to find the corresponding data. DHT provides decentralization, fault tolerance, and scalability:

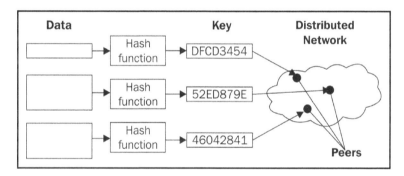

Distributed hash tables

Another application of hash functions is in digital signatures, where they can be used in combination with asymmetric cryptography. This concept is discussed in detail in the examples provided in the following subsections.

Digital signatures

Digital signatures provide a means of associating a message with an entity from which the message has originated. Digital signatures are used to provide data origin authentication and non-repudiation.

Digital signatures are used in blockchain where the transactions are digitally signed by senders using their private key before broadcasting the transaction to the network. This digital signing, proves they are the rightful owner of the asset, for example, bitcoins. These transactions are verified again by other nodes on the network to ensure that the funds indeed belong to the node (user) who claims to be the owner. We will discuss these concepts in more detail in chapters dedicated to Bitcoin and Ethereum in this book.

Digital signatures are calculated in two steps. As an example, the high-level steps of an RSA digital signature scheme follow.

RSA digital signature algorithm

The following is the RSA digital signature algorithm:

1. **Calculate the hash value of the data packet**: This will provide the data integrity guarantee as the hash can be computed at the receiver's end again and matched with the original hash to check whether the data has been modified in transit. Technically, message signing can work without hashing the data first, but is not considered secure.
2. **Signs the hash value with the signer's private key**: As only the signer has the private key, the authenticity of the signature and the signed data is ensured.

Digital signatures have some important properties, such as authenticity, unforgeability, and nonreusability. **Authenticity** means that the digital signatures are verifiable by a receiving party. The **unforgeability** property ensures that only the sender of the message can use the signing functionality using the private key. In other words, no one else can produce the signed message produced by a legitimate sender. **Nonreusability** means that the digital signature cannot be separated from a message and used again for another message.

The operation of a generic digital signature function is shown in the following diagram:

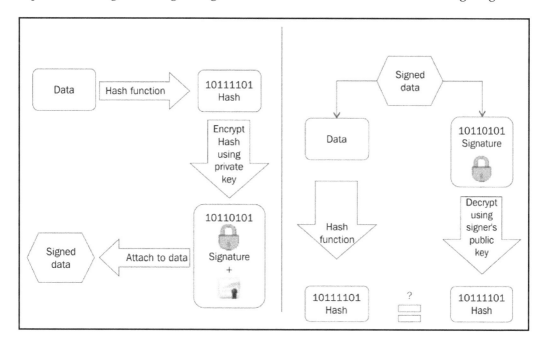

Digital signing (left) and verification process (right) (Example of RSA digital signatures)

If a sender wants to send an authenticated message to a receiver, there are two methods that can be used: sign then encrypt and encrypt then sign. These two approaches to using digital signatures with encryption are as follows.

Sign then encrypt

With this approach, the sender digitally signs the data using the private key, appends the signature to the data, and then encrypts the data and the digital signature using the receiver's public key. This is considered a more secure scheme as compared to the *encrypt then sign* scheme described next.

Encrypt then sign

With this method, the sender encrypts the data using the receiver's public key and then digitally signs the encrypted data.

 In practice, a digital certificate that contains the digital signature is issued by a **Certificate Authority** (**CA**) that associates a public key with an identity.

Various schemes, such as RSA, **Digital Signature Algorithm** (**DSA**), and ECDSA-based digital signature schemes are used in practice. RSA is the most commonly used; however, with the traction of ECC, ECDSA-based schemes are also becoming quite popular. This is beneficial in blockchains because ECC provides same level of security that RSA does, but it uses less space. Also, generation of keys is much faster in ECC as compared to RSA, therefore it helps with overall performance of the system. The following table shows that ECC is able to provide the same level of cryptographic strength as an RSA based system with smaller key sizes:

RSA key sizes (bits)	Elliptic curve key sizes (bits)
1024	160
2048	224
3072	256
7680	384
15360	521

Comparison of RSA and Elliptic curve key sizes providing the same level of security

The ECDSA scheme is described in detail in following subsection.

Elliptic Curve Digital Signature Algorithm

In order to sign and verify using the ECDSA scheme, first key pair needs to be generated:

1. First, define an elliptic curve E:

   - With modulus P
   - Coefficients a and b

- Generator point *A* that forms a cyclic group of prime order *q*

2. An integer *d* is chosen randomly so that $0 < d < q$.
3. Calculate public key *B* so that $B = d\,A$.

The public key is the sextuple in the form shown here:

$$Kpb = (p,a,b,q,A,B)$$

The private key, *d* is randomly chosen in step 2:

$$Kpr = d$$

Now the signature can be generated using the private and public key.

4. First, an ephemeral key K_e is chosen, where $0 < K_e < q$. It should be ensured that K_e is truly random and that no two signatures have the same key; otherwise, the private key can be calculated.
5. Another value *R* is calculated using $R = K_e\,A$; that is, by multiplying *A* (the generator point) and the random ephemeral key.
6. Initialize a variable *r* with the *x* coordinate value of point *R* so that $r = xR$.
7. The signature can be calculated as follows:

$$S = \left(h(m) + dr\right)K_e^{-1} \bmod q$$

Here, *m* is the message for which the signature is being computed, and *h(m)* is the hash of the message *m*.

Signature verification is carried out by following this process:

1. Auxiliary value *w* is calculated as $w = s{-}1 \bmod q$.
2. Auxiliary value $u1 = w.\,h(m) \bmod q$.
3. Auxiliary value $u2 = w.\,r \bmod q$.
4. Calculate point *P*, $P = u1A + u2B$.

5. Verification is carried out as follows:

r, *s* is accepted as a valid signature if the *x* coordinate of point *P* calculated in step 4 has the same value as the signature parameter *r mod q*; that is:

$$Xp = r \ mod \ q \ means \ valid \ signature$$

$$Xp \ != r \ mod \ q \ means \ invalid \ signature$$

Various practical examples are shown in the following subsections, which demonstrate how the RSA digital signature can be generated, used, and verified using OpenSSL.

How to generate a digital signature using OpenSSL

The first step is to generate a hash of the message file:

```
$ openssl dgst -sha256 message.txt
SHA256(message.txt)=
eb96d1f89812bf4967d9fb4ead128c3b787272b7be21dd2529278db1128d559c
```

Both hash generation and signing can be done in a single step, as shown here. Note that `privatekey.pem` is generated in the steps provided previously:

```
$ openssl dgst -sha256 -sign privatekey.pem -out signature.bin message.txt
```

Now, let's display the directory showing the relevant files:

```
$ ls -ltr
total 36
-rw-rw-r-- 1 drequinox drequinox 14 Sep 21 05:54 message.txt
-rw-rw-r-- 1 drequinox drequinox 32 Sep 21 05:57 message.bin
-rw-rw-r-- 1 drequinox drequinox 45 Sep 21 06:00 message.b64
-rw-rw-r-- 1 drequinox drequinox 32 Sep 21 06:16 message.ptx
-rw-rw-r-- 1 drequinox drequinox 916 Sep 21 06:28 privatekey.pem
-rw-rw-r-- 1 drequinox drequinox 272 Sep 21 06:30 publickey.pem
-rw-rw-r-- 1 drequinox drequinox 128 Sep 21 06:43 message.rsa
-rw-rw-r-- 1 drequinox drequinox 14 Sep 21 06:49 message.dec
-rw-rw-r-- 1 drequinox drequinox  128 Sep 21 07:05 signature.bin
```

Let's look at the contents of `signature.bin` by executing the following command:

```
$ cat signature.bin
```

Executing this command will give the following output:

```
V _[ h] h t  + T~O1  s {  Cǫ"# A Q U, uf   p* ⊏ ⋆7    T'  u eAy
$ x <$ a  `  :L qWh uG   = $  :~/Crypt$
```

In order to verify the signature, the following operation can be performed:

```
$ openssl dgst -sha256 -verify publickey.pem -signature \
  signature.bin message.txt
Verified OK
```

Similarly, if some other signature file which is not valid is used, the verification will fail, as shown here:

```
$ openssl dgst -sha256 -verify publickey.pem -signature
someothersignature.bin message.txt
Verification Failure
```

Next, an example is presented that shows how OpenSSL can be used to perform ECDSA-related operations.

ECDSA using OpenSSL

First, the private key is generated using the following commands:

```
$ openssl ecparam -genkey -name secp256k1 -noout -out eccprivatekey.pem
$ cat eccprivatekey.pem
-----BEGIN EC PRIVATE KEY-----
MHQCAQEEIMVmyrnEDOs7SYxS/AbXoIwqZqJ+gND9Z2/nQyzcpaPBoAcGBSuBBAAK
oUQDQgAEEKKS4E4+TATIeBX8o2J6PxKkjcoWrXPwNRo/k4Y/CZA4pXvlyTgH5LYm
QbU0qUtPM7dAEzOsaoXmetqB+6cM+Q==
-----END EC PRIVATE KEY-----
```

Next, the public key is generated from the private key:

```
$ openssl ec -in eccprivatekey.pem -pubout -out eccpublickey.pem
read EC key
writing EC key
$ cat eccpublickey.pem
-----BEGIN PUBLIC KEY-----
MFYwEAYHKoZIzj0CAQYFK4EEAAoDQgAEEKKS4E4+TATIeBX8o2J6PxKkjcoWrXPw
NRo/k4Y/CZA4pXvlyTgH5LYmQbU0qUtPM7dAEzOsaoXmetqB+6cM+Q==
-----END PUBLIC KEY-----
```

Now, suppose a file named `testsign.txt` needs to be signed and verified. This can be achieved as follows:

1. Create a test file:

```
$ echo testing > testsign.txt
$ cat testsign.txt
testing
```

2. Run the following command to generate a signature using a private key for the `testsign.txt` file:

```
$ openssl dgst -ecdsa-with-SHA1 -sign eccprivatekey.pem \
    testsign.txt > ecsign.bin
```

3. Finally, the command for verification can be run as shown here:

```
$ openssl dgst -ecdsa-with-SHA1 -verify eccpublickey.pem \
    -signature ecsign.bin testsign.txt
Verified OK
```

A certificate can also be produced by using the private key generated earlier by using the following command:

```
$ openssl req -new -key eccprivatekey.pem -x509 -nodes -days 365 \
    -out ecccertificate.pem
```

This command will produce the output similar to the one shown here. Enter the appropriate parameters to generate the certificate:

```
You are about to be asked to enter information that will be incorporated
into your certificate request.
What you are about to enter is what is called a Distinguished Name or a DN.
There are quite a few fields but you can leave some blank
For some fields there will be a default value,
If you enter '.', the field will be left blank.
-----
Country Name (2 letter code) [AU]:GB
State or Province Name (full name) [Some-State]:Cambridge
Locality Name (eg, city) []:Cambridge
Organization Name (eg, company) [Internet Widgits Pty Ltd]:Dr.Equinox!
Organizational Unit Name (eg, section) []:NA
Common Name (e.g. server FQDN or YOUR name) []:drequinox
Email Address []:drequinox@drequinox.com
```

The certificate can be explored using the following command:

```
$ openssl x509 -in ecccertificate.pem -text -noout
```

The following output shows the certificate:

X509 certificate that uses ECDSA algorithm with SHA-256

There following topics in cryptography are presented because of their relevance to blockchain, or their potential use in future blockchain ecosystems.

Homomorphic encryption

Usually, public key cryptosystems, such as RSA, are multiplicative homomorphic or additive homomorphic, such as the Paillier cryptosystem, and are called **Partially Homomorphic Encryption** (**PHE**) systems. Additive PHEs are suitable for e-voting and banking applications.

Until recently, there has been no system that supported both operations, but in 2009, a **Fully Homomorphic Encryption** (**FHE**) system was discovered by Craig Gentry. As these schemes enable the processing of encrypted data without the need for decryption, they have many different potential applications, especially in scenarios where maintaining privacy is required, but data is also mandated to be processed by potentially untrusted parties, for example, cloud computing and online search engines. Recent development in homomorphic encryption have been very promising, and researchers are actively working to make it efficient and more practical. This is of particular interest in blockchain technology, as described later in this book, as it can solve the problem of confidentiality and privacy in the blockchain.

Signcryption

Signcryption is a public key cryptography primitive that provides all of the functions of a digital signature and encryption. Yuliang Zheng invented signcryption, and it is now an ISO standard, ISO/IEC 29150:2011. Traditionally, sign then encrypt or encrypt then sign schemes are used to provide unforgeability, authentication, and non-repudiation, but with signcryption, all services of digital signatures and encryption are provided at a cost that is less than that of the sign then encrypt scheme.

Signcryption enables *Cost (signature & encryption) << Cost (signature) + Cost (Encryption)* in a single logical step.

Zero-Knowledge Proofs

Zero-Knowledge Proofs (**ZKPs**) were introduced by Goldwasser, Micali, and Rackoff in 1985. These proofs are used to prove the validity of an assertion without revealing any information whatsoever about the assertion. There are three properties of ZKPs that are required: completeness, soundness, and zero-knowledge property.

Completeness ensures that if a certain assertion is true, then the verifier will be convinced of this claim by the prover. The **soundness** property makes sure that if an assertion is false, then no dishonest prover can convince the verifier otherwise. The **zero-knowledge property**, as the name implies, is the key property of ZKPs whereby it is ensured that absolutely nothing is revealed about the assertion except whether it is true or false.

ZKPs have sparked a special interest among researchers in the blockchain space due to their privacy properties, which are very much desirable in financial and many other fields, including law and medicine. A recent example of the successful implementation of a ZKP mechanism is the Zcash cryptocurrency. In Zcash, a specific type of ZKP, known as **Zero-Knowledge Succinct Non-Interactive Argument of Knowledge (ZK-SNARK)**, is implemented. This will be discussed in detail in `Chapter 8`, *Alternative Coins*.

Blind signatures

Blind signatures were introduced by David Chaum in 1982. They are based on public key digital signature schemes, such as RSA. The key idea behind blind signatures is to get the message signed by the signer without actually revealing the message. This is achieved by disguising or blinding the message before signing it, hence the name *blind signatures*. This blind signature can then be verified against the original message just like a normal digital signature. Blind signatures were introduced as a mechanism to allow the development of digital cash schemes.

Encoding schemes

Other than cryptographic primitives, binary-to-text **encoding schemes** are also used in various scenarios. The most common use is to convert binary data into text so that it can either be processed, saved, or transmitted via a protocol that does not support the processing of binary data. For example, sometimes, images are stored in the database as base64 encoding, which allows a text field to be able to store a picture. A commonly-used encoding scheme is base64. Another encoding named base58 was popularized by its use in Bitcoin.

Cryptography is a vast field, and this section has merely introduced the basic concepts that are essential to understanding cryptography in general and specifically from the blockchain and cryptocurrency point of view. In the next section, basic financial market concepts will be presented.

The section describes general terminology related to trading, exchanges, and the trade life cycle. More detailed information will be provided in later chapters, where specific use cases are discussed.

Financial markets and trading

Financial markets enable trading of financial securities such as bonds, equities, derivatives and currencies. There are broadly three types of markets: money markets, credit markets, and capital markets:

- **Money markets**: These are short-term markets where money is lent to companies or banks to do interbank lending. Foreign exchange or FX is another category of money markets where currencies are traded.
- **Credit markets**: These consist mostly of retail banks where they borrow money from central banks and loan it to companies or households in the form of mortgages or loans.
- **Capital markets**: These facilitate the buying and selling of financial instruments, mainly stocks and bonds. Capital markets can be divided into two types: primary and secondary markets. Stocks are issued directly by the companies to investors in primary markets, whereas in secondary markets, investors resell their securities to other investors via stock exchanges. Various electronic trading systems are used by exchanges today to facilitate the trading of financial instruments.

Trading

A market is a place where parties engage in exchange. It can be either a physical location or an electronic or virtual location. Various financial instruments, including equities, stocks, foreign exchange, commodities, and various types of derivatives are traded at these marketplaces. Recently, many financial institutions have introduced software platforms to trade various types of instruments from different asset classes.

Trading can be defined as an activity in which traders buy or sell various financial instruments to generate profit and hedge risk. Investors, borrowers, hedgers, asset exchangers, and gamblers are a few types of traders. Traders have a short position when they owe something, in other words, if they have sold a contract they have a short position and have a long position when they buy a contract. There are various ways to transact trades, such as through brokers or directly on an exchange or **Over-The-Counter** (**OTC**) where buyers and sellers trade directly with each other instead of using an exchange. **Brokers** are agents who arrange trades for their customers. Brokers act on a client's behalf to deal at a given price or the best possible price.

Exchanges

Exchanges are usually considered to be a very safe, regulated, and reliable place for trading. During the last decade, electronic trading has gained more popularity as compared to traditional floor-based trading. Now traders send orders to a central electronic order book from which the orders, prices, and related attributes are published to all associated systems using communications networks, thus in essence creating a virtual marketplace. Exchange trades can be performed only by members of the exchange. To trade without these limitations, the counterparties can participate in OTC trading directly.

Orders and order properties

Orders are instructions to trade, and they are the main building blocks of a trading system. They have the following general attributes:

- The instrument name
- Quantity to be traded
- Direction (buy or sell)
- The type of the order that represents various conditions, for example, limit orders and stop orders are orders to buy or sell once the price hits the price specified in the order, for example, Google shares for 200 GBP. Limit order allows selling or buying of stock at a specific price or better than the specified price in the order. For example, sell Microsoft shares if price is 100 USD or better.

Orders are traded by bid prices and offer prices. Traders show their intention to buy or sell by attaching bid and offer prices to their orders. The price at which a trader will buy is known as the **bid price**. The price at which a trader is willing to sell is known as the **offer price**.

Order management and routing systems

Order routing systems routes and delivers orders to various destinations depending on the business logic. Customers use them to send orders to their brokers, who then send these orders to dealers, clearing houses, and exchanges.

There are different types of orders. The two most common ones are markets orders and limit order.

A **market order** is an instruction to trade at the best price currently available in the market. These orders get filled immediately at spot prices. On the other hand, a **limit order** is an instruction to trade at the best price available, but only if it is not lower than the limit price set by the trader. This can also be higher depending on the direction of the order: either to sell or buy. All of these orders are managed in an **order book**, which is a list of orders maintained by exchange, and it records the intention of buying or selling by the traders.

A **position** is a commitment to sell or buy a number of financial instruments, including securities, currencies, or commodities for a given price. The contracts, securities, commodities, and currencies that traders buy or sell are commonly known as **trading instruments**, and they come under the broad umbrella of **asset classes**. The most common classes are real assets, financial assets, derivative contracts, and insurance contracts.

Components of a trade

A **trade ticket** is the combination of all of the details related to a trade. However, there is some variation depending on the type of the instrument and the asset class. These elements are described in the following subsections.

The underlying instrument

The **underlying instrument** is the basis of the trade. It can be a currency, a bond, interest rate, commodity, or equities.

The attributes of financial instruments are discussed in the following subsection.

General attributes

This includes the general identification information and essential features associated with every trade. Typical attributes include a unique ID, instrument name, type, status, trade date, and time.

Economics

Economics are features related to the value of the trade, for example, buy or sell value, ticker, exchange, price, and quantity.

Sales

Sales refer to the sales-characteristic related details, such as the name of the salesperson. It is just an informational field, usually without any impact on the trade life cycle.

Counterparty

The **counterparty** is an essential component of a trade as it shows the other side (the other party involved in the trade) of the trade, and it is required to settle the trade successfully. The normal attributes include counterparty name, address, payment type, any reference IDs, settlement date, and delivery type.

Trade life cycle

A general **trade life cycle** includes the various stages from order placement to execution and settlement. This life cycle is described step-by-step as follows:

- **Pre-execution**: An order is placed at this stage.
- **Execution and booking**: When the order is matched and executed, it converts it into a trade. At this stage, the contract between counterparties is matured.
- **Confirmation**: This is where both counterparties agree to the particulars of the trade.
- **Post booking**: This stage is concerned with various scrutiny and verification processes required to ascertain the correctness of the trade.
- **Settlement**: This is the most vital part of trade life cycle. At this stage, the trade is final.
- **Overnight (end-of-day processing)**: End-of-day processes include report generation, profit and loss calculations, and various risk calculations.

This life cycle is also shown in the following screenshot:

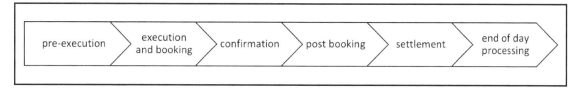

Trade life cycle

In all the aforementioned processes, many people and business functions are involved. Most commonly, these functions are divided into functions such as front office, middle office, and back office.

In the following section, you are introduced to some concepts that are essential to understanding the strict and necessary rules and regulations that govern the financial industry. Some concepts are described here and then again in later chapters when specific use cases are discussed. These ideas will help you understand the scenarios described.

Order anticipators

Order anticipators try to make a profit before other traders can carry out trading. This is based on the anticipation of a trader who knows how trading activities of other trades will affect prices. Frontrunners, sentiment-oriented technical traders, and squeezers are some examples of order anticipators.

Market manipulation

Market manipulation is strictly illegal in many countries. Fraudulent traders can spread false information in the market, which can then result in price movements thus enabling illegal profiteering. Usually, manipulative market conduct is trade-based, and it includes generalized and time-specific manipulations. Actions that can create an artificial shortage of stock, an impression of false activity, and price manipulation to gain criminal benefits are included in this category.

Both of the terms discussed here are relevant to the financial crime. However, there is a possibility of developing blockchain-based systems that can thwart market abuse due to its transparency and security properties.

Summary

We started this chapter with the introduction of asymmetric key cryptography. We discussed various constructs such as RSA and ECC. We also performed some experiments using OpenSSL to see that how theoretical concepts can be implemented practically. After this, we discussed hash functions in detail along with its properties and usage. Next, we covered concepts such as Merkle trees, which are used extensively in blockchain and, in fact, are at its core. We also presented other concepts such as Patricia trees and hash tables.

In the next chapter, we will present Bitcoin, which is the first blockchain invented in 2009 with the introduction of Bitcoin cryptocurrency.

Introducing Bitcoin

5

Bitcoin is the first application of blockchain technology. In this chapter, you will be introduced to Bitcoin technology in detail.

Bitcoin has started a revolution with the introduction of the very first fully decentralized digital currency, and the one that has proven to be extremely secure and stable from a network and protocol point of view. As a currency bitcoin is quite unstable and highly volatile, albeit valuable. We will explain this later in the chapter. This has also sparked a great interest in academic and industrial research and introduced many new research areas.

Since its introduction in 2008 by Satoshi Nakamoto, Bitcoin has gained massive popularity, and it is currently the most successful digital currency in the world with billions of dollars invested in it. The current market cap, at the time of writing, for this currency is $149, 984, 293, 122. Its popularity is also evident from the high number of users and investors, increasing bitcoin price, everyday news related to Bitcoin, and the number of start-ups and companies that are offering bitcoin-based online exchanges, and it's now also traded as *Bitcoin Futures* on **Chicago Mercantile Exchange** (**CME**).

 Interested readers can read more about *Bitcoin Futures* at `http://www.cmegroup.com/trading/bitcoin-futures.html`.

The name of the Bitcoin inventor *Satoshi Nakamoto* is believed to be a pseudonym, as the true identity of Bitcoin inventor is unknown. It is built on decades of research in the field of cryptography, digital cash, and distributed computing. In the following section, a brief history is presented in order to provide the background required to understand the foundations behind the invention of Bitcoin.

Digital currencies have always been an active area of research for many decades. Early proposals to create digital cash go as far back as the early 1980s. In 1982, David Chaum, a computer scientist, and cryptographer proposed a scheme that used blind signatures to build untraceable digital currency. This research was published in a research paper, *Blind Signatures for Untraceable Payments*.

 Interested readers can read the original research paper which David Chaum describes his invention of the cryptographic primitive of blind signatures at `http://www.hit.bme.hu/~buttyan/courses/BMEVIHIM219/2009/Chaum.Bl indSigForPayment.1982.PDF`.

In this scheme, a bank would issue digital money by signing a blind and random serial number presented to it by the user. The user could then use the digital token signed by the bank as currency. The limitation of this scheme was that the bank had to keep track of all used serial numbers. This was a central system by design and required to be trusted by the users.

Later on, in 1988, David Chaum and others proposed a refined version named e-cash that not only used a blinded signature, but also some private identification data to craft a message that was then sent to the bank.

 Original research paper for this is available at `http://citeseerx.ist.psu.edu/viewdoc/summary?doi=10.1.1.26.5759`.

This scheme allowed the detection of double spending but did not prevent it. If the same token was used at two different locations, then the identity of the double spender would be revealed. e-cash could only represent a fixed amount of money.

Adam Back, a cryptographer and now CEO of Blockstream, who is involved in blockchain development, introduced *hashcash* in 1997. It was originally proposed to thwart email spam. The idea behind hashcash was to solve a computational puzzle that was easy to verify but comparatively difficult to compute. The idea was that for a single user and a single email, the extra computational effort was negligible, but someone sending a large number of spam emails would be discouraged as the time and resources required to run the spam campaign would increase substantially.

In 1998, B-money was proposed by Wei Dai, a computer engineer who used to work for Microsoft, which introduced the idea of using **Proof of Work** (**PoW**) to create money. The term *Proof of Work* emerged and got popular later with Bitcoin, but in Wei Dai's B-money a scheme of creating money was introduced by providing a solution to a previously unsolved computational problem. It was referred in the paper as *solution to a previously unsolved computational problem*. This concept is similar to PoW, where money is created by broadcasting a solution to a previously unsolved computational problem.

 The original paper is available at `http://www.weidai.com/bmoney.txt`.

A major weakness in the system was that an adversary with higher computational power could generate unsolicited money without allowing the network to adjust to an appropriate difficulty level. The system lacked details on the consensus mechanism between nodes and some security issues such as Sybil attacks were also not addressed. At the same time, Nick Szabo, a computer scientist introduced the concept of BitGold, which was also based on the PoW mechanism but had the same problems as B-money with the exception that the network difficulty level was adjustable. Tomas Sander and Amnon Ta-Shma from the **International Computer Science Institute** (**ICSI**), Berkley introduced an e-cash scheme under a research paper named *Auditable, Anonymous Electronic Cash* in 1999. This scheme, for the first time, used Merkle trees to represent coins and **Zero-Knowledge Proofs** (**ZKPs**) to prove the possession of coins.

 The original research paper called *Auditable, Anonymous Electronic Cash* is available at: `http://www.cs.tau.ac.il/~amnon/Papers/ST.crypto99.pdf`.

In this scheme, a central bank was required that kept a record of all used serial numbers. This scheme allowed users to be fully anonymous. This was a theoretical design which was not practical to implement due to inefficient proof mechanisms.

Reusable Proof of Work (**RPoW**) was introduced in 2004 by Hal Finney, a computer scientist, developer and first person to receive Bitcoin from Satoshi Nakamoto. It used the hashcash scheme by Adam Back as a proof of computational resources spent to create the money. This was also a central system that kept a central database to keep track of all used PoW tokens. This was an online system that used remote attestation made possible by a trusted computing platform (TPM hardware).

All the previously mentioned schemes are intelligently designed but were weak from one aspect or another. Specifically, all these schemes rely on a central server that is required to be trusted by the users.

Bitcoin

In 2008, Bitcoin was introduced through a paper called, *Bitcoin: A Peer-to-Peer Electronic Cash System*.

 This paper is available at `https://bitcoin.org/bitcoin.pdf`.

It was written by Satoshi Nakamoto, which is believed to be a pseudonym, as the true identity of Bitcoin inventor is unknown and subject of much speculation. The first key idea introduced in the paper was of a purely peer-to-peer electronic cash that does need an intermediary bank to transfer payments between peers.

Bitcoin is built on decades of cryptographic research such as the research in Merkle trees, hash functions, public key cryptography, and digital signatures. Moreover, ideas such as BitGold, B-money, hashcash, and cryptographic time stamping provided the foundations for bitcoin invention. All these technologies are cleverly combined in Bitcoin to create the world's first decentralized currency. The key issue that has been addressed in Bitcoin is an elegant solution to the Byzantine Generals' Problem along with a practical solution of the double-spend problem. Recall, that both of these concepts are explained in Chapter 1, *Blockchain 101*.

The value of bitcoin has increased significantly since 2011, and then since March 2017 as shown in the following graph:

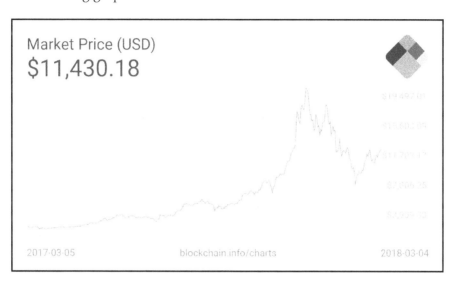

Bitcoin price since March 2017

The regulation of Bitcoin is a controversial subject and as much as it is a libertarian's dream, law enforcement agencies, governments and banks are proposing various regulations to control it, such as BitLicense issued by New York's state department of financial services. This is a license issued to businesses that perform activities related to virtual currencies. Due to high cost and very strict regulatory requirements pertaining to BitLicense many companies have withdrawn their services from New York.

For people with a libertarian ideology, Bitcoin is a platform which can be used instead of banks for business but they think that because of regulations, Bitcoin may become another institution which is not trusted. The original idea behind Bitcoin was to develop an e-cash system which requires no trusted third party and users can be anonymous. If regulations require **Know Your Customer** (**KYC**) checks and detailed information about business transactions to facilitate regulatory process then it might be too much information to share and as a result Bitcoin may not be attractive anymore to some.

There are now many initiatives being taken to regulate Bitcoin, cryptocurrencies and related activities such as ICOs. **Securities and Exchange Commission** (**SEC**) has recently announced that digital tokens, coins and relevant activities such as **Initial Coin Offerings** (**ICOs**) fall under the category of securities. This means that any digital currency trading platforms will need to be registered with SEC and will have all relevant securities laws and regulations applicable to them. This impacted the Bitcoin price directly and it fell almost 10% on the day this announcement was made.

Interested readers can read more about the regulation of Bitcoin and other relevant activities at `https://www.coindesk.com/category/regulation/`.

The growth of Bitcoin is also due to so-called **network effect**. Also called demand-side economies of scale, it is a concept that basically means more users who use the network, the more valuable it becomes. Over time, an exponential increase has been seen in the Bitcoin network growth. This increase in the number of users is largely financial gain driven. Also, the scarcity of Bitcoin and built-in inflation control mechanism gives it value as there are only 21 million bitcoins that can ever be mined and in addition the miner reward halves every four years. Even though the price of bitcoin fluctuates a lot, it has increased significantly over the last few years. Currently (at the time of writing this), bitcoin price is 9,250 U.S Dollars (USD).

Bitcoin definition

Bitcoin can be defined in various ways; it's a protocol, a digital currency, and a platform. It is a combination of peer-to-peer network, protocols, software that facilitate the creation and usage of the digital currency named bitcoin. Nodes in this peer-to-peer network talk to each other using the Bitcoin protocol.

Note that Bitcoin with a capital B is used to refer to the Bitcoin protocol, whereas bitcoin with a lowercase b is used to refer to bitcoin, the currency.

Decentralization of currency was made possible for the first time with the invention of bitcoin. Moreover, the double spending problem was solved in an elegant and ingenious way in bitcoin. Double spending problem arises when, for example, a user sends coins to two different users at the same time and they are verified independently as valid transactions. The double spending problem is resolved in Bitcoin by using a distributed ledger (blockchain) where every transaction is recorded permanently and by implementing transaction validation and confirmation mechanism. This process will be explained later in the chapter where we introduce the concept of *mining*.

Bitcoin – a bird's-eye view

In this section, we will see how the Bitcoin network looks from a user's point of view. How a transaction is made, how it propagates from a user to the network, how transactions are verified, and finally accumulated in blocks. We will look at what are the various actors and components of the Bitcoin network. Finally, some discussion on how all actors and components interact with each other to form the Bitcoin network will also be provided.

First, let us see that what the main components of a Bitcoin network are. Bitcoin is composed of the elements listed here. We will further expand on these elements as we progress through the chapter.

- Digital keys
- Addresses
- Transactions
- Blockchain
- Miners
- The Bitcoin network
- Wallets (client software)

Now, we will see that how a user will use the Bitcoin network. The following example will help you understand that how the Bitcoin network looks like from an end user's perspective. We will see that what actors and components are involved in a Bitcoin transaction. One of the most common transactions is sending money to someone else, therefore in the following example we will see that how a payment can be sent from one user to another on the Bitcoin network.

Sending a payment to someone

This example will demonstrate that how money can be sent using Bitcoin network from one user to another. There are several steps that are involved in this process. As an example, we are using Blockchain wallet for mobile devices.

The steps are described here:

1. First, either the payment is requested from a user by sending his Bitcoin address to the sender via email or some other means such as SMS, chat applications or in fact any appropriate communication mechanism. The sender can also initiate a transfer to send money to another user. In both cases, the address of beneficiary is required. As an example, the Blockchain wallet is shown here where a payment request is created:

bitcoin payment request (using Blockchain wallet)

2. The sender either enters the receiver's address or scans the QR code that has the Bitcoin address, amount and optional description encoded in it. The wallet application recognizes this QR code and decodes it into something like `Please send <Amount> BTC to the Bitcoin address <receiver's Bitcoin address>`.

3. This will look like as shown here with values: `Please send 0.00033324 BTC to the Bitcoin address 1JzouJCVmMQBmTcd8K4Y5BP36gEFNn1ZJ3`.

4. This is also shown in the screenshot presented here:

Please send 0.00033324 BTC to
the Bitcoin address
1JzouJCVmMQBmTcd8K4Y5BP36g
EFNn1ZJ3.

bitcoin://
1JzouJCVmMQBmTcd8K4Y5BP36g
EFNn1ZJ3?amount=0.00033324

Bitcoin payment QR code

 The QR code shown in the preceding screenshot is decoded to `bitcoin://1JzouJCVmMQBmTcd8K4Y5BP36gEFNn1ZJ3?amount=0.000 33324` which can be opened as a URL in Bitcoin wallet.

5. In the wallet application of the sender, this transaction is constructed by following some rules and broadcasted to the Bitcoin network. This transaction is digitally signed using the private key of the sender before broadcasting it. How the transaction is created, digitally signed, broadcasted, validated and added to the block will become clear in the following sections. From a user's point of view, once the QR code is decoded the transaction will appear similar to what is shown in the following screenshot:

Send BTC using Blockchain wallet

Note that in the preceding screenshot there are a number of fields such as **From**, **To**, **BTC**, and **Fee**. While other fields are self-explanatory, it's worth noting that **Fee** is calculated based on the size of the transaction and a fee rate is a value that depends on the volume of the transaction in the network. This is represented in Satoshis/byte. Fee in Bitcoin network ensures that your transaction will be included by miners in the block.

Recently the Bitcoin fees were so high that even for smaller transactions a high amount of fee was charged. This was due to the fact that miners are free to choose which transactions they pick to verify and add in a block, and they select the ones with higher fees. The high number of users creating thousands of transactions also played a role in causing this situation of high fees because transactions were competing with each other to be picked up first and miners picked up the ones with highest fees. This fee is also usually estimated and calculated by the Bitcoin wallet software automatically before sending the transactions. The higher the transaction fee the more chances are that your transaction will be picked up at priority and included in the block. This task is performed by the miners. Mining and miners is a concept that we will look at a bit later in this chapter in the context of Bitcoin mining.

Once the transaction is sent it will appear as shown here in the Blockchain wallet software:

Transaction sent

4. At this stage, the transaction has been constructed, signed and sent out to the Bitcoin network. This transaction will be picked up by miners to be verified and included in the block. Also note that in the preceding screenshot, confirmation is pending for this transaction. These confirmations will start to appear as soon as the transaction is verified, included in the block, and mined. Also, the appropriate fee will be deducted from the original value to be transferred and will be paid to the miner who has included it in the block for mining.

This flow is shown in the following diagram, where a payment of 0.001267 BTC (approximately 11 USD) is originated from the sender's address and been paid to receiver's address (starting with 1Jz). The fee of 0.00010622 (approximately 95 cents) is also deducted from the transaction as mining fee.

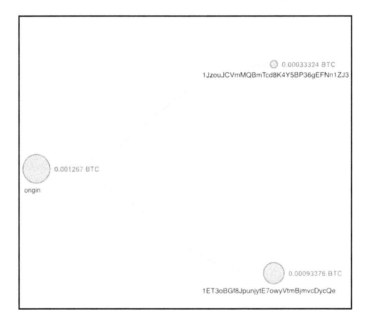

Transaction flow visualization (Blockchain.info)

The preceding screenshot visually shows how the transaction flowed on the network from origin (sender) to receivers on the right-hand side.

A summary view of various attributes of the transaction is shown here:

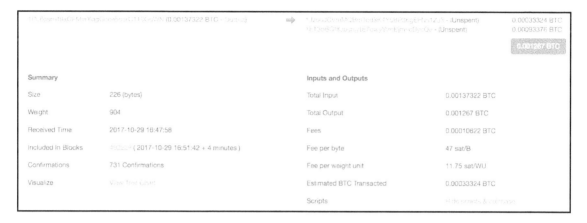

Looking at the preceding screenshot there are a number of fields that contain various values. Important fields are listed here with their purpose and explanation:

- **Size**: This is the size of the transaction in bytes.
- **Weight**: This is the new metric given for block and transaction size since the introduction of **Segregated Witness** (**SegWit**) version of Bitcoin.
- **Received Time**: This is the time when the transaction is received.
- **Included In Blocks**: This shows the block number on the blockchain in which the transaction is included.
- **Confirmations**: This is the number of confirmations by miners for this transaction.
- **Total Input**: This is the number of total inputs in the transaction.
- **Total Output**: This is the number of total outputs in the transaction.
- **Fees**: This is the total fees charged.
- **Fee per byte**: This field represents the total fee divided by the number of bytes in a transaction. For example 10 Satoshis per byte.
- **Fee per weight unit**: For legacy transaction it is calculated using *total number of bytes * 4*. For SegWit transactions it is calculated by combining SegWit marker, flag, and witness field as one weight unit and each byte of other fields as four weight units.

Transaction ID of this transaction on the Bitcoin network is
`d28ca5a59b2239864eac1c96d3fd1c23b747f0ded8f5af0161bae8a616b56a1d` and can
be further explored using the `https://blockchain.info/tx/`
`d28ca5a59b2239864eac1c96d3fd1c23b747f0ded8f5af0161bae8a616b56a1d` link via services
provided by `https://blockchain.info/`. This transaction ID is available in the wallet
software after transaction is sent to the network. From there it can be further explored using
one of many Bitcoin blockchain explorers available online. We are using `https://`
`blockchain.info/` as an example.

Bitcoin transactions are serialized for transmission over the network and encoded in
hexadecimal format. As an example, the preceding transaction, is also shown here. We will
see later in the *Transactions* section that how this hexadecimal encoded transaction can be
decoded and what fields make up a transaction.

```
01000000017d3876b14a7ac16d8d550abc78345b6571134ff173918a096ef90ff0430e12408
b0000006b483045022100de6fd8120d9f142a82d5da9389e271caa3a757b01757c8e4fa7afb
f92e74257c02202a78d4fbd52ae9f3a0083760d76f84643cf8ab80f5ef971e3f98ccba2c717
58d012102c16942555f5e633645895c9affcb994ea7910097b7734a6c2d25468622f25e12ff
ffffff022c820000000000001976a914c568ffeb46c6a9362e44a5a49deaa6eab05a619a88a
cc06c0100000000001976a9149386c8c880488e80a6ce8f186f788f3585f74aee88ac000000
00
```

In summary, the payment transaction in the Bitcoin network can be divided into the
following steps:

1. Transaction starts with a sender signing the transaction with their private key
2. Transaction is serialized so that it can be transmitted over the network
3. Transaction is broadcasted to the network
4. Miners listening for the transactions picks up the transaction
5. Transaction are verified for their validity by the miners
6. Transaction are added to the candidate/proposed block for mining
7. Once mined, the result is broadcasted to all nodes on the Bitcoin network

Mining, transaction and other relevant concepts will become clearer in the following
sections in the chapter. Now in the next section various denominations of bitcoin are
presented.

The bitcoin currency, being digital has various denominations which are shown in the following table. A sender or receiver can request any amount. The smallest bitcoin denomination is the Satoshi. The bitcoin currency units are described as follows:

DENOMINATION	ABBREVIATION	FAMILIAR NAME	VALUE IN BTC
Satoshi	SAT	Satoshi	0.00000001 BTC
Microbit	µBTC (uBTC)	Microbitcoin or Bit	0.000001 BTC
Millibit	mBTC	Millibitcoin	0.001 BTC
Centibit	cBTC	Centibitcoin	0.01 BTC
Decibit	dBTC	Decibitcoin	0.1 BTC
Bitcoin	BTC	Bitcoin	1 BTC
DecaBit	daBTC	Decabitcoin	10 BTC
Hectobit	hBTC	Hectobitcoin	100 BTC
Kilobit	kBTC	Kilobitcoin	1000 BTC
Megabit	MBTC	Megabitcoin	1000000 BTC

bitcoin denominations

Now you will be introduced to the building blocks of Bitcoin one by one. First, we will look at the keys and addresses which are used to represent the ownership and transfer of value on the Bitcoin network.

Digital keys and addresses

On the Bitcoin network, possession of bitcoins and transfer of value via transactions is reliant upon private keys, public keys, and addresses. In `Chapter 4`, *Public Key Cryptography*, we have already covered these concepts, and here we will see that how private and public keys are used in the Bitcoin network.

Elliptic Curve Cryptography (**ECC**) is used to generate public and private key pairs in the Bitcoin network.

Private keys in Bitcoin

Private keys are required to be kept safe and normally resides only on the owner's side. Private keys are used to digitally sign the transactions proving the ownership of the bitcoins.

Private keys are fundamentally 256-bit numbers randomly chosen in the range specified by the `secp256k1` ECDSA curve recommendation. Any randomly chosen 256-bit number from `0x1` to `0xFFFF FFFF FFFF FFFF FFFF FFFF FFFF FFFE BAAE DCE6 AF48 A03B BFD2 5E8C D036 4140` is a valid private key.

Private keys are usually encoded using **Wallet Import Format** (**WIF**) in order to make them easier to copy and use. It is a way to represent the full size private key in a different format. WIF can be converted into a private key and vice versa. The steps are described here.

The following is an example of a private key:

`A3ED7EC8A03667180D01FB4251A546C2B9F2FE33507C68B7D9D4E1FA5714195201`

When it is converted into WIF format it looks like this:

`L2iN7umV7kbr6LuCmgM27rBnptGbDVc8g4ZBm6EbgTPQXnj1RCZP`

Interested readers can do some experimentation using the tool available at the following website:
`http://gobittest.appspot.com/PrivateKey`

Also, **mini private key format** is sometimes used to create the private key with a maximum of up to 30 characters in order to allow storage where physical space is limited, for example, etching on physical coins or encoding in damage-resistant QR codes. The QR code becomes more damage resistant because more dots can be used for error correction and less for encoding the private key. The private key encoded using mini private key format is also sometimes called **minikey**. The first character of mini private key is always uppercase letter S. A mini private key can be converted into a normal size private key but an existing normal size private key cannot be converted into a mini private key. This format was used in Casascius physical bitcoins.

Interested readers can find more information here
`https://en.bitcoin.it/wiki/Casascius_physical_bitcoins.`

A Casascius physical bitcoin's security hologram paper with minikey and QR code

The Bitcoin core client also allows the encryption of the wallet that contains the private keys.

Public keys in Bitcoin

Public keys exist on the blockchain and all network participants can see it. Public keys are derived from private keys due to their special mathematical relationship with the private keys. Once a transaction signed with the private key is broadcasted on the Bitcoin network, public keys are used by the nodes to verify that the transaction has indeed been signed with the corresponding private key. This process of verification proves the ownership of the bitcoin.

Bitcoin uses ECC based on the `secp256k1` standard. More specifically it makes use of ECDSA to ensure that funds remain secure and can only be spent by the legitimate owner. If you need to refresh the relevant cryptography concepts, you can refer to `Chapter 4`, *Public Key Cryptography* where ECC was explained. A public key is 256-bits in length. Public keys can be represented in an uncompressed or compressed format. Public keys are fundamentally x and y coordinates on an elliptic curve. In an uncompressed format public keys are presented with a prefix of `0x4` in a hexadecimal format. The x and y coordinates are both 32-bit in length. In total, the compressed public key is 33-bytes long as compared to 65-bytes in the uncompressed format. The compressed version of public keys includes only the x part, since the y part can be derived from it.

The reason why the compressed version of public keys works is that if the ECC graph is visualized, it reveals that the y coordinate can be either below the x axis or above the x axis and as the curve is symmetric, only the location in the prime field is required to be stored. If y is even then it is above the x axis and if it is odd then it is below the x axis. This means that instead of storing both x and y as the public key only x can be stored with the information that if y is even or odd.

Initially, Bitcoin client used uncompressed keys, but starting from Bitcoin core client 0.6, compressed keys are used as standard. This resulted in almost 50% reduction of space used to store public keys in the blockchain.

Keys are identified by various prefixes, described as follows:

- Uncompressed public keys use `0x04` as the prefix
- Compressed public key starts with `0x03` if the y 32-bit part of the public key is odd
- Compressed public key starts with `0x02` if the y 32-bit part of the public key is even

Addresses in Bitcoin

A bitcoin address is created by taking the corresponding public key of a private key and hashing it twice, first with the SHA-256 algorithm and then with RIPEMD-160. The resultant 160-bit hash is then prefixed with a version number and finally encoded with a Base58Check encoding scheme. The bitcoin addresses are 26-35 characters long and begin with digit `1` or `3`.

A typical bitcoin address looks like a string shown here:

`1ANAguGG8bikEv2fYsTBnRUmx7QUcK58wt`

This is also commonly encoded in a QR code for easy distribution. The QR code of the preceding bitcoin address is shown in the following screenshot:

QR code of a bitcoin address 1ANAguGG8bikEv2fYsTBnRUmx7QUcK58wt

Currently, there are two types of addresses, the commonly used P2PKH and another P2SH type, starting with number 1 and 3, respectively. In the early days, Bitcoin used direct Pay to Pubkey, which is now superseded by P2PKH. These types will be explained later in the chapter. However, direct Pay to Pubkey is still used in Bitcoin for coinbase addresses. Addresses should not be used more than once; otherwise, privacy and security issues can arise. Avoiding address reuse circumvents anonymity issues to an extent, Bitcoin has some other security issues as well, such as transaction malleability, Sybil attacks, race attacks and selfish mining which require different approaches to resolve.

Transaction malleability has been resolved with so-called *Segregated Witness* soft fork upgrade of the Bitcoin protocol. This concept will be explained later in the chapter.

From bitaddress.org, private key and bitcoin address in a paper wallet

Base58Check encoding

Bitcoin addresses are encoded using the Base58Check encoding. This encoding is used to limit the confusion between various characters, such as 0OIl as they can look the same in different fonts. The encoding basically takes the binary byte arrays and converts them into human-readable strings. This string is composed by utilizing a set of 58 alphanumeric symbols. More explanation and logic can be found in the `base58.h` source file (`https://github.com/bitcoin/bitcoin/blob/master/src/base58.h`) in the bitcoin source code:

```
/**
 * Why base-58 instead of standard base-64 encoding?
 * - Don't want 0OIl characters that look the same in some fonts and
 * could be used to create visually identical looking data.
 * - A string with non-alphanumeric characters is not as easily accepted as
 input.
 * - E-mail usually won't line-break if there's no punctuation to break at.
 * - Double-clicking selects the whole string as one word if it's all
 alphanumeric.
 */
```

Vanity addresses

As bitcoin addresses are based on base-58 encoding, it is possible to generate addresses that contain human-readable messages. An example is shown as follows:

1BasHiry2VoCQCdX6X
64oxvKRuf7fW6qGr

Vanity public address encoded in QR

Vanity addresses are generated using a purely brute-force method. An example of a paper wallet with vanity address is shown in the following screenshot:

Vanity address generated from https://bitcoinvanitygen.com/

In the preceding screenshot, on the right-hand bottom corner the public vanity address with QR code is displayed. The paper wallets can be stored physically as an alternative to electronic storage of private keys.

Multisignature addresses

As the name implies, these addresses require multiple private keys. In practical terms, it means that in order to release the coins a certain set of signatures is required. This is also known as **M-of-N MultiSig**. Here *M* represents threshold or the minimum number of signatures required from *N* number of keys to release the bitcoins.

Transactions

Transactions are at the core of the bitcoin ecosystem. Transactions can be as simple as just sending some bitcoins to a bitcoin address, or it can be quite complex depending on the requirements. Each transaction is composed of at least one input and output. Inputs can be thought of as coins being spent that have been created in a previous transaction and outputs as coins being created. If a transaction is minting new coins, then there is no input and therefore no signature is needed. If a transaction is to send coins to some other user (a bitcoin address), then it needs to be signed by the sender with their private key and a reference is also required to the previous transaction in order to show the origin of the coins. Coins are, in fact, unspent transaction outputs represented in Satoshis.

Transactions are not encrypted and are publicly visible in the blockchain. Blocks are made up of transactions and these can be viewed using any online blockchain explorer.

The transaction life cycle

The following steps describe the transaction life cycle:

1. A user/sender sends a transaction using wallet software or some other interface.
2. The wallet software signs the transaction using the sender's private key.
3. The transaction is broadcasted to the Bitcoin network using a flooding algorithm.
4. Mining nodes (miners) who are listening for the transactions verify and include this transaction in the next block to be mined. Just before the transaction are placed in the block they are placed in a special memory buffer called **transaction pool**. The purpose of the transaction pool is explained in the next section.
5. Mining starts, which is a process by which the blockchain is secured and new coins are generated as a reward for the miners who spend appropriate computational resources. This concept is explained in more detail later in this chapter.
6. Once a miner solves the PoW problem it broadcasts the newly mined block to the network. PoW is explained in detail later in this chapter.
7. The nodes verify the block and propagate the block further, and confirmations start to generate.

8. Finally, the confirmations start to appear in the receiver's wallet and after approximately three confirmations, the transaction is considered finalized and confirmed. However, three to six is just a recommended number; the transaction can be considered final even after the first confirmation. The key idea behind waiting for six confirmations is that the probability of double spending is virtually eliminated after three confirmations.

Transaction fee

Transaction fees are charged by the miners. The fee charged is dependent upon the size and weight of the transaction. Transaction fees are calculated by subtracting the sum of the inputs and the sum of the outputs.

A simple formula can be used:

$$fee = sum(inputs) - sum(outputs)$$

The fees are used as an incentive for miners to encourage them to include a user transaction in the block the miners are creating. All transactions end up in the memory pool, from where miners pick up transactions based on their priority to include them in the proposed block. The calculation of priority is introduced later in this chapter; however, from a transaction fee point of view, a transaction with a higher fee will be picked up sooner by the miners.

There are different rules based on which fee is calculated for various types of actions, such as sending transactions, inclusion in blocks, and relaying by nodes. Fees are not fixed by the Bitcoin protocol and are not mandatory; even a transaction with no fee will be processed in due course but may take a very long time. This is however no longer practical due to the high volume of transactions and competing investors on the Bitcoin network, therefore it is advisable to provide a fee always. The time for transaction confirmation usually ranges from 10 minutes to over 12 hours in some cases. Transaction time is dependent on transaction fees and network activity. If the network is very busy then naturally transactions will take longer to process and if you pay a higher fee then your transaction is more likely to be picked by miners first due to additional incentive of the higher fee.

Transaction pools

Also known as memory pools, these pools are basically created in local memory (computer RAM) by nodes in order to maintain a temporary list of transactions that are not yet confirmed in a block. Transactions are included in a block after passing verification and based on their priority.

The transaction data structure

A transaction at a high level contains metadata, inputs, and outputs. Transactions are combined to create a block.

The transaction data structure is shown in the following table:

Field	Size	Description
Version number	4 bytes	Used to specify rules to be used by the miners and nodes for transaction processing.
Input counter	1-9 bytes	The number (positive integer) of inputs included in the transaction.
List of inputs	Variable	Each input is composed of several fields, including `Previous Tx hash`, `Previous Txout-index`, `Txin-script length`, `Txin-script`, and optional sequence number. The first transaction in a block is also called a coinbase transaction. It specifies one or more transaction inputs.
Output counter	1-9 bytes	A positive integer representing the number of outputs.
List of outputs	Variable	Outputs included in the transaction.
Lock time	4 bytes	This field defines the earliest time when a transaction becomes valid. It is either a Unix timestamp or block height.

A sample transaction is shown as follows. This is the decoded transaction from the first example of a payment transaction provided at the start of this chapter.

```
{
    "lock_time":0,
    "size":226,
    "inputs":[
        {
```

```
                "prev_out":{
                    "index":139,
   "hash":"40120e43f00ff96e098a9173f14f1371655b3478bc0a558d6dc17a4ab176387d"
                },
    "script":"483045022100de6fd8120d9f142a82d5da9389e271caa3a757b01757c8e4fa7af
bf92e74257c02202a78d4fbd52ae9f3a0083760d76f84643cf8ab80f5ef971e3f98ccba2c71
758d012102c16942555f5e633645895c9affcb994ea7910097b7734a6c2d25468622f25e12"
            }
    ],
    "version":1,
    "vin_sz":1,
   "hash":"d28ca5a59b2239864eac1c96d3fd1c23b747f0ded8f5af0161bae8a616b56a1d",
    "vout_sz":2,
    "out":[
        {
            "script_string":"OP_DUP OP_HASH160
c568ffeb46c6a9362e44a5a49deaa6eab05a619a OP_EQUALVERIFY OP_CHECKSIG",
            "address":"1JzouJCVmMQBmTcd8K4Y5BP36gEFNn1ZJ3",
            "value":33324,
            "script":"76a914c568ffeb46c6a9362e44a5a49deaa6eab05a619a88ac"
        },
        {
            "script_string":"OP_DUP OP_HASH160
9386c8c880488e80a6ce8f186f788f3585f74aee OP_EQUALVERIFY OP_CHECKSIG",
            "address":"1ET3oBGf8JpunjytE7owyVtmBjmvcDycQe",
            "value":93376,
            "script":"76a9149386c8c880488e80a6ce8f186f788f3585f74aee88ac"
        }
    ]
}
```

As shown in the preceding code, there are a number of structures that make up the transaction. All these elements are described in the following subsections.

Metadata

This part of the transaction contains some values such as the size of the transaction, the number of inputs and outputs, the hash of the transaction, and a lock_time field. Every transaction has a prefix specifying the version number. These fields are shown in the preceding example: lock_time, size, and version.

Inputs

Generally, each input spends a previous output. Each output is considered as **Unspent Transaction Output** (**UTXO**) until an input consumes it. UTXO is an unspent transaction output that can be spent as an input to a new transaction.

Transaction input data structure is shown in the following table:

Field	Size	Description
Transaction hash	32 bytes	This is the hash of the previous transaction with UTXO.
Output index	4 bytes	This is the previous transactions output index, that is, UTXO to be spent.
Script length	1-9 bytes	This is the size of the unlocking script.
Unlocking script	Variable	Input script (`ScriptSig`) which satisfies the requirements of the locking script.
Sequence number	4 bytes	Usually disabled or contains lock time. Disabled is represented by `'0xFFFFFFFF'`.

In the preceding example the inputs are defined under `"inputs"` : [section.

Outputs

Outputs have three fields, and they contain instructions for sending bitcoins. The first field contains the amount of Satoshis whereas the second field contains the size of the locking script. Finally, the third field contains a locking script that holds the conditions that need to be met in order for the output to be spent. More information on transaction spending using locking and unlocking scripts and producing outputs is discussed later in this section.

Transaction output data structure is shown here:

Field	Size	Description
Value	8 bytes	Total number in positive integers of Satoshis to be transferred
Script size	1-9 bytes	Size of the locking script
Locking script	Variable	Output script (`ScriptPubKey`)

In the preceding example two outputs are shown under `"OUT"`: [section.

Verification

Verification is performed using Bitcoin's scripting language which is described in the next section in detail.

The script language

Bitcoin uses a simple stack-based language called **script** to describe how bitcoins can be spent and transferred. It is not Turing complete and has no loops to avoid any undesirable effects of long-running/hung scripts on the Bitcoin network. This scripting language is based on a Forth programming language like syntax and uses a reverse polish notation in which every operand is followed by its operators. It is evaluated from the left to the right using a **Last In, First Out** (**LIFO**) stack.

Scripts use various opcodes or instructions to define their operation. Opcodes are also known as words, commands, or functions. Earlier versions of the Bitcoin node had a few opcodes that are no longer used due to bugs discovered in their design.

The various categories of the scripting opcodes are constants, flow control, stack, bitwise logic, splice, arithmetic, cryptography, and lock time.

A transaction script is evaluated by combining `ScriptSig` and `ScriptPubKey`. `ScriptSig` is the unlocking script, whereas `ScriptPubKey` is the locking script. This is how a transaction to be spent is evaluated:

1. First, it is unlocked and then it is spent
2. `ScriptSig` is provided by the user who wishes to unlock the transaction
3. `ScriptPubkey` is part of the transaction output and specifies the conditions that need to be fulfilled in order to spend the output
4. In other words, outputs are locked by `ScriptPubKey` that contains the conditions, when met will unlock the output, and coins can then be redeemed

Commonly used opcodes

All opcodes are declared in the `script.h` file in the Bitcoin reference client source code.

 This can be accessed from the link at
`https://github.com/bitcoin/bitcoin/blob/master/src/script/script`
`.h` under the following comment:
`/** Script opcodes */`

A description of the most commonly used opcodes is listed here. This table is taken from the Bitcoin developer's guide:

Opcode	Description
OP_CHECKSIG	This takes a public key and signature and validates the signature of the hash of the transaction. If it matches, then TRUE is pushed onto the stack; otherwise, FALSE is pushed.
OP_EQUAL	This returns 1 if the inputs are exactly equal; otherwise, 0 is returned.
OP_DUP	This duplicates the top item in the stack.
OP_HASH160	The input is hashed twice, first with SHA-256 and then with RIPEMD-160.
OP_VERIFY	This marks the transaction as invalid if the top stack value is not true.
OP_EQUALVERIFY	This is the same as OP_EQUAL, but it runs OP_VERIFY afterwards.
OP_CHECKMULTISIG	This takes the first signature and compares it against each public key until a match is found and repeats this process until all signatures are checked. If all signatures turn out to be valid, then a value of 1 is returned as a result; otherwise, 0 is returned.

Types of transactions

There are various scripts available in Bitcoin to handle the value transfer from the source to the destination. These scripts range from very simple to quite complex depending upon the requirements of the transaction. Standard transaction types are discussed here. Standard transactions are evaluated using IsStandard() and IsStandardTx() tests and only standard transactions that pass the test are generally allowed to be mined or broadcasted on the Bitcoin network. However, nonstandard transactions are valid and allowed on the network.

The following are the standard transaction types:

- **Pay to Public Key Hash** (**P2PKH**): P2PKH is the most commonly used transaction type and is used to send transactions to the bitcoin addresses. The format of the transaction is shown as follows:

    ```
    ScriptPubKey: OP_DUP OP_HASH160 <pubKeyHash> OP_EQUALVERIFY
    OP_CHECKSIG
        ScriptSig: <sig> <pubKey>
    ```

    The `ScriptPubKey` and `ScriptSig` parameters are concatenated together and executed. An example will follow shortly in this section, where this is explained in more detail.

- **Pay to Script Hash** (**P2SH**): P2SH is used in order to send transactions to a script hash (that is, the addresses starting with 3) and was standardized in BIP16. In addition to passing the script, the redeem script is also evaluated and must be valid. The template is shown as follows:

    ```
    ScriptPubKey: OP_HASH160 <redeemScriptHash> OP_EQUAL
    ScriptSig: [<sig>...<sign>] <redeemScript>
    ```

- **MultiSig** (**Pay to MultiSig**): M-of-N MultiSig transaction script is a complex type of script where it is possible to construct a script that required multiple signatures to be valid in order to redeem a transaction. Various complex transactions such as escrow and deposits can be built using this script. The template is shown here:

    ```
    ScriptPubKey: <m> <pubKey> [<pubKey> . . . ] <n> OP_CHECKMULTISIG
    ScriptSig: 0 [<sig > . . . <sign>]
    ```

    Raw multisig is obsolete, and multisig is usually part of the P2SH redeem script, mentioned in the previous bullet point.

- **Pay to Pubkey**: This script is a very simple script that is commonly used in coinbase transactions. It is now obsolete and was used in an old version of bitcoin. The public key is stored within the script in this case, and the unlocking script is required to sign the transaction with the private key.

    The template is shown as follows:

    ```
    <PubKey> OP_CHECKSIG
    ```

- **Null data/OP_RETURN**: This script is used to store arbitrary data on the blockchain for a fee. The limit of the message is 40 bytes. The output of this script is unredeemable because `OP_RETURN` will fail the validation in any case. `ScriptSig` is not required in this case.

  The template is very simple and is shown as follows:

  ```
  OP_RETURN <data>
  ```

A P2PKH script execution is shown in the following diagram:

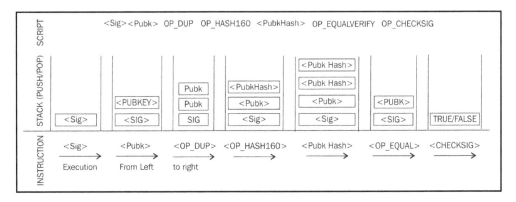

P2PKH script execution

All transactions are eventually encoded into the hexadecimal format before transmitting over the Bitcoin network. A sample transaction is shown here in hexadecimal format that is retrieved using `bitcoin-cli` on the Bitcoin node running on mainnet:

```
$ bitcoin-cli getrawtransaction
"d28ca5a59b2239864eac1c96d3fd1c23b747f0ded8f5af0161bae8a616b56a1d"
{
  "result":
"01000000017d3876b14a7ac16d8d550abc78345b6571134ff173918a096ef90ff0430e1240
8b0000006b483045022100de6fd8120d9f142a82d5da9389e271caa3a757b01757c8e4fa7af
bf92e74257c02202a78d4fbd52ae9f3a0083760d76f84643cf8ab80f5ef971e3f98ccba2c71
758d012102c16942555f5e633645895c9affcb994ea7910097b7734a6c2d25468622f25e12f
ffffffff022c820000000000001976a914c568ffeb46c6a9362e44a5a49deaa6eab05a619a88
acc06c0100000000001976a9149386c8c880488e80a6ce8f186f788f3585f74aee88ac00000
000",
  "error": null,
  "id": null
}
```

Note that this is the same transaction that was presented as an example at the start of this chapter.

Coinbase transactions

A coinbase transaction or generation transaction is always created by a miner and is the first transaction in a block. It is used to create new coins. It includes a special field, also called `coinbase`, which acts as an input to the coinbase transaction. This transaction also allows up to 100 bytes of arbitrary data that can be used to store arbitrary data. In the genesis block, this transaction included the most famous comment taken from *The Times* newspaper:

> *"The Times 03/Jan/2009 Chancellor on brink of second bailout for banks."*

This message is a proof that the genesis block was not mined earlier than January 3, 2009. This is because first Bitcoin block (genesis block) was created on January 3, 2009 and this news excerpt was taken from that day's newspaper.

A coinbase transaction input has the same number of fields as usual transaction input, but the structure contains coinbase data size and coinbase data fields instead of unlocking script size and unlocking script fields. Also, it does not have a reference pointer to the previous transaction. This structure is shown in the following table:

Field	Size	Description
Transaction hash	32 bytes	Set to all zeroes as no hash reference is used
Output index	4 bytes	Set to `0xFFFFFFFF`
Coinbase data length	1-9 bytes	2 bytes-100 bytes
Data	Variable	Any data
Sequence number	4 bytes	Set to `0xFFFFFFFF`

Contracts

As defined in the Bitcoin core developer guide, contracts are basically transactions that use the Bitcoin system to enforce a financial agreement. This is a simple definition but has far-reaching consequences as it allows users to design complex contracts that can be used in many real-world scenarios. Contracts allow the development of a completely decentralized, independent, and reduced risk platform.

Various contracts, such as escrow, arbitration, and micropayment channels, can be built using the Bitcoin scripting language. The current implementation of a script is very limited, but various types of contracts are still possible to develop. For example, the release of funds only if multiple parties sign the transaction or perhaps the release of funds only after a certain time has elapsed. Both of these scenarios can be realized using multisig and transaction lock time options.

Transaction verification

This verification process is performed by Bitcoin nodes. The following is described in the Bitcoin developer guide:

1. Check the syntax and ensure that the syntax and data structure of the transaction conforms to the rules provided by the protocol.
2. Verify that no transaction inputs and outputs are empty.
3. Check whether the size in bytes is less than the maximum block size.
4. The output value must be in the allowed money range (0 to 21 million BTC).
5. All inputs must have a specified previous output, except for coinbase transactions, which should not be relayed.
6. Verify that `nLockTime` must not exceed 31-bits. (`nLockTime` specifies the time before which transaction will not be included in the block.)
7. For a transaction to be valid, it should not be less than 100 bytes.
8. The number of signature operations in a standard transaction should be less than or not more than two.
9. Reject nonstandard transactions; for example, `ScriptSig` is allowed to only push numbers on the stack. `ScriptPubkey` not passing the `isStandard()` checks. The `isStandard()` checks specify that only standard transactions are allowed.
10. A transaction is rejected if there is already a matching transaction in the pool or in a block in the main branch.
11. The transaction will be rejected if the referenced output for each input exists in any other transaction in the pool.
12. For each input, there must exist a referenced output unspent transaction.
13. For each input, if the referenced output transaction is the coinbase, it must have at least 100 confirmations; otherwise, the transaction will be rejected.
14. For each input, if the referenced output does not exist or has been spent already, the transaction will be rejected.

15. Using the referenced output transactions to get input values, verify that each input value, as well as the sum, is in the allowed range of 0-21 million BTC. Reject the transaction if the sum of input values is less than the sum of output values.

16. Reject the transaction if the transaction fee would be too low to get into an empty block.

17. Each input unlocking script must have corresponding valid output scripts.

Transaction malleability

Transaction malleability in Bitcoin was introduced due to a bug in the bitcoin implementation. Due to this bug, it became possible for an adversary to change the transaction ID of a transaction, thus resulting in a scenario where it would appear that a certain transaction has not been executed. This can allow scenarios where double deposits or withdrawals can occur. In other words, this bug allows the changing of the unique ID of a Bitcoin transaction before it is confirmed. If the ID is changed before confirmation, it would seem that the transaction did not occur at all which can then allow these attacks.

Blockchain

Blockchain is a public ledger of a timestamped, ordered, and immutable list of all transactions on the Bitcoin network. Each block is identified by a hash in the chain and is linked to its previous block by referencing the previous block's hash.

In the following table structure of a block is presented, followed by a detailed diagram that provides a detailed view of the blockchain structure.

The structure of a block

The following table shows the structure of a block:

Field	Size	Description
Block size	4 bytes	This is the size of the block.
Block header	80 bytes	This includes fields from the block header described in the next section.

| Transaction counter | Variable | This field contains the total number of transactions in the block, including the coinbase transaction. Size ranges from 1-9 bytes |
| Transactions | Variable | All transactions in the block. |

The structure of a block header

The following table depicts the structure of a block header:

Field	Size	Description
Version	4 bytes	The block version number that dictates the block validation rules to follow.
Previous block's header hash	32 bytes	This is a double SHA-256 hash of the previous block's header.
Merkle root hash	32 bytes	This is a double SHA-256 hash of the Merkle tree of all transactions included in the block.
Timestamp	4 bytes	This field contains the approximate creation time of the block in the Unix epoch time format. More precisely, this is the time when the miner has started hashing the header. (The time from the miner's point of view.)
Difficulty target	4 bytes	This is the current difficulty target of the network/block.
Nonce	4 bytes	This is an arbitrary number that miners change repeatedly to produce a hash that is lower than the difficulty target.

As shown in the following diagram, blockchain is a chain of blocks where each block is linked to its previous block by referencing the previous block header's hash. This linking makes sure that no transaction can be modified unless the block that records it and all blocks that follow it are also modified. The first block is not linked to any previous block and is known as the genesis block.

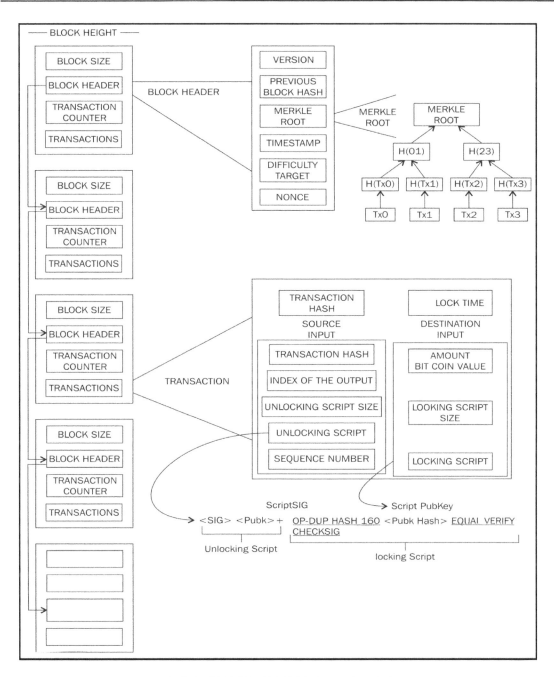

A visualization of the blockchain, block, block header, transactions and scripts

The preceding diagram shows a high-level overview of the Bitcoin blockchain. On the left-hand side blocks are shown starting from top to bottom. Each block contains transactions and block headers which are further magnified on the right-hand side. On the top, first, block header is expanded to show various elements within the block header. Then on the right-hand side the Merkle root element of the block header is shown in magnified view which shows that how Merkle root is calculated. We have discussed Merkle trees in detail previously, you can refer to Chapter 3, *Symmetric Cryptography* if you need to revise the concept. Further down transactions are also magnified to show the structure of a transaction and the elements that it contains. Also, note that transactions are then further elaborated by showing that what locking and unlocking scripts look like. This diagram shows a lot of components, we will discuss all these in this chapter.

The genesis block

This is the first block in the Bitcoin blockchain. The genesis block was hardcoded in the bitcoin core software. It is in the chainparams.cpp file (https://github.com/bitcoin/bitcoin/blob/master/src/chainparams.cpp):

```
static CBlock CreateGenesisBlock(uint32_t nTime, uint32_t nNonce, uint32_t nBits, int32_t nVersion, const CAmount& genesisReward)
{
    const char* pszTimestamp = "The Times 03/Jan/2009 Chancellor on brink of second bailout for banks";
    const CScript genesisOutputScript = CScript() << ParseHex("04678afdb0fe5548271967f1a67130b7105cd6a828e03909a67962e0ea1f61deb649f6bc3f4cef38c4f35504e51ec112de5c384df7ba0b8d578a4c702b6bf11d5f") << OP_CHECKSIG;
    return CreateGenesisBlock(pszTimestamp, genesisOutputScript, nTime, nNonce,
    nBits, nVersion, genesisReward);
}
```

Bitcoin provides protection against double spending by enforcing strict rules on transaction verification and via mining. Transactions and blocks are added in the blockchain only after strict rule checking explained earlier in the *Transaction verification* section and successful PoW solution. Block height is the number of blocks before a particular block in the blockchain. The current height (as of March 6, 2018) of the blockchain is 512,328 blocks. PoW is used to secure the blockchain. Each block contains one or more transactions, out of which the first transaction is a coinbase transaction. There is a special condition for coinbase transactions that prevent them from being spent until at least 100 blocks in order to avoid a situation where the block may be declared stale later on.

Stale blocks are created when a block is solved and every other miner who is still working to find a solution to the hash puzzle is working on that block. Mining and hash puzzles will be discussed later in the chapter in detail. As the block is no longer required to be worked on, this is considered a stale block.

Orphan blocks are also called detached blocks and were accepted at one point in time by the network as valid blocks but were rejected when a proven longer chain was created that did not include this initially accepted block. They are not part of the main chain and can occur at times when two miners manage to produce the blocks at the same time.

The latest block version is version 4, which was proposed with BIP65 and has been used since bitcoin core client 0.11.2 since the implementation of BIP9 bits in the `nVersion` field are being used to indicate soft fork changes.

Because of the distributed nature of bitcoin, network forks can occur naturally. In cases where two nodes simultaneously announce a valid block can result in a situation where there are two blockchains with different transactions. This is an undesirable situation but can be addressed by the Bitcoin network only by accepting the longest chain. In this case, the smaller chain will be considered orphaned. If an adversary manages to gain 51% control of the network hash rate (computational power), then they can impose their own version of transaction history.

Forks in blockchain can also occur with the introduction of changes in the Bitcoin protocol. In case of a *soft fork*, a client which chooses not to upgrade to the latest version supporting the updated protocol will still be able to work and operate normally. In this case, previous and new blocks are both acceptable, thus making soft fork backwards compatible.

In case of a soft fork, only miners are required to upgrade to the new client software in order to make use of the new protocol rules. Planned upgrades do not necessarily create forks because all users should have updated already. A hard fork, on the other hand, invalidates previously valid blocks and requires all users to upgrade. New transaction types are sometimes added as a soft fork, and any changes such as block structure change or major protocol changes results in a hard fork. The current size of the bitcoin blockchain as of October 29, 2017, stands at approximately 139 GB.

The following diagram shows the size increase of blockchain as a function of time:

Current size of blockchain as of 29/10/2017

New blocks are added to the blockchain approximately every 10 minutes and network difficulty is adjusted dynamically every 2016 blocks in order to maintain a steady addition of new blocks to the network.

Network difficulty is calculated using the following equation:

$$Target = Previous\ target * Time/2016 * 10\ minutes$$

Difficulty and target are interchangeable and represent the same thing. Previous target represents the old target value, and time is the time spent to generate previous 2016 blocks. Network difficulty basically means how hard it is for miners to find a new block, that is, how difficult the hashing puzzle is now.

In the next section, mining is discussed, which will explain how the hashing puzzle is solved.

Mining

Mining is a process by which new blocks are added to the blockchain. Blocks contain transactions that are validated via the mining process by mining nodes on the Bitcoin network. Blocks, once mined and verified are added to the blockchain which keeps the blockchain growing. This process is resource-intensive due to the requirements of PoW where miners compete in order to find a number which is less than the difficulty target of the network. This difficulty in finding the correct value (also called sometimes the mathematical puzzle) is there to ensure that the required resources have been spent by miners before a new proposed block can be accepted. New coins are minted by the miners by solving the PoW problem, also known as partial hash inversion problem. This process consumes a high amount of resources including computing power and electricity. This process also secures the system against frauds and double spending attacks while adding more virtual currency to the Bitcoin ecosystem.

Roughly one new block is created (mined) every 10 minutes to control the frequency of generation of bitcoins. This frequency needs to be maintained by the Bitcoin network and is encoded in the bitcoin core clients in order to control the *money supply*. Miners are rewarded with new coins if and when they discover new blocks by solving PoW. Miners are paid transaction fees in return for including transactions in their proposed blocks. New blocks are created at an approximate fixed rate of every 10 minutes. The rate of creation of new bitcoins decreases by 50%, every 210,000 blocks, roughly every 4 years. When bitcoin was initially introduced, the block reward was 50 bitcoins; then in 2012, this was reduced to 25 bitcoins. In July 2016, this was further reduced to 12.5 coins (12 coins) and the next reduction is estimated to be on July 4, 2020. This will reduce the coin reward further down to approximately six coins.

Approximately 144 blocks, that is, 1,728 bitcoins are generated per day. The number of actual coins can vary per day; however, the number of blocks remains at 144 per day. Bitcoin supply is also limited and in 2140, almost 21 million bitcoins will be finally created and no new bitcoins can be created after that. Bitcoin miners, however, will still be able to profit from the ecosystem by charging transaction fees.

Tasks of the miners

Once a node connects to the bitcoin network, there are several tasks that a bitcoin miner performs:

1. **Synching up with the network**: Once a new node joins the bitcoin network, it downloads the blockchain by requesting historical blocks from other nodes. This is mentioned here in the context of the bitcoin miner; however, this not necessarily a task only for a miner.

2. **Transaction validation**: Transactions broadcasted on the network are validated by full nodes by verifying and validating signatures and outputs.

3. **Block validation**: Miners and full nodes can start validating blocks received by them by evaluating them against certain rules. This includes the verification of each transaction in the block along with verification of the nonce value.

4. **Create a new block**: Miners propose a new block by combining transactions broadcasted on the network after validating them.

5. **Perform Proof of Work**: This task is the core of the mining process and this is where miners find a valid block by solving a computational puzzle. The block header contains a 32-bit nonce field and miners are required to repeatedly vary the nonce until the resultant hash is less than a predetermined target.

6. **Fetch reward**: Once a node solves the hash puzzle (PoW), it immediately broadcasts the results, and other nodes verify it and accept the block. There is a slight chance that the newly minted block will not be accepted by other miners on the network due to a clash with another block found at roughly the same time, but once accepted, the miner is rewarded with 12.5 bitcoins and any associated transaction fees.

Mining rewards

When Bitcoin started in 2009 the mining reward used to be 50 bitcoins. After every 210,000 blocks, the block reward halves. In November 2012 it halved down to 25 bitcoins. Currently, it is 12.5 BTC per block since July 2016. Next halving is on Friday, 12 June 2020 after which the block reward will be reduced down to 6.25 BTC per block. This mechanism is hardcoded in Bitcoin to regulate, control inflation and limit the supply of bitcoins.

Proof of Work (PoW)

This is a proof that enough computational resources have been spent in order to build a valid block. PoW is based on the idea that a random node is selected every time to create a new block. In this model, nodes compete with each other in order to be selected in proportion to their computing capacity. The following equation sums up the PoW requirement in bitcoin:

$$H (N \parallel P\_hash \parallel Tx \parallel Tx \parallel \ldots Tx) < Target$$

Where N is a nonce, P_hash is a hash of the previous block, Tx represents transactions in the block, and $Target$ is the target network difficulty value. This means that the hash of the previously mentioned concatenated fields should be less than the target hash value.

The only way to find this nonce is the brute force method. Once a certain pattern of a certain number of zeroes is met by a miner, the block is immediately broadcasted and accepted by other miners.

The mining algorithm

The mining algorithm consists of the following steps.

1. The previous block's header is retrieved from the bitcoin network.
2. Assemble a set of transactions broadcasted on the network into a block to be proposed.
3. Compute the double hash of the previous block's header combined with a nonce and the newly proposed block using the SHA-256 algorithm.
4. Check if the resultant hash is lower than the current difficulty level (target) then PoW is solved. As a result of successful PoW the discovered block is broadcasted to the network and miners fetch the reward.
5. If the resultant hash is not less than the current difficulty level (target), then repeat the process after incrementing the nonce.

    As the hash rate of the bitcoin network increased, the total amount of 32-bit nonce was exhausted too quickly. In order to address this issue, the extra nonce solution was implemented, whereby the coinbase transaction is used as a source of extra nonce to provide a larger range of nonce to be searched by the miners.

This process can be visualized by using the following flowchart:

Mining process

Mining difficulty increased over time and bitcoins that could be mined by single CPU laptop computers now require dedicated mining centers to solve the hash puzzle. The current difficulty level can be queried using the Bitcoin command-line interface using the following command:

```
$ bitcoin-cli getdifficulty
1452839779145
```

This number represents the difficulty level of the Bitcoin network. Recall from previous sections that miners compete to find a solution to a problem. This number, in fact shows, that how difficult it is to find a hash which is lower than the network difficulty target. All successfully mined blocks must contain a hash that is less than this target number. This number is updated every 2 weeks or 2016 blocks to ensure that on average 10-minute block generation time is maintained.

Bitcoin network difficulty has increased exponentially, the following graph shows this difficulty level over a period of one year:

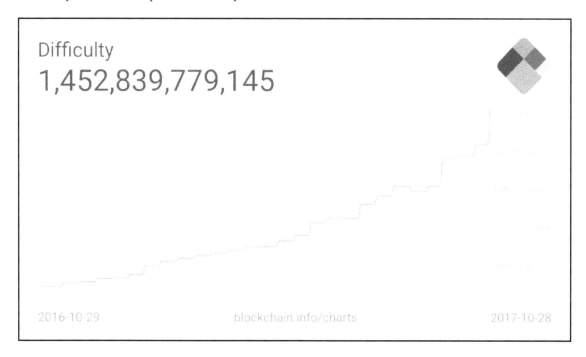

Mining difficulty over the last year

The preceding graph shows the difficulty of the Bitcoin network over a period of last year and it has increased quite significantly. The reason why mining difficulty increases is because in Bitcoin, the block generation time has to be always around 10 minutes. This means that if blocks are being mined too quickly by fast hardware then the difficulty increases so that the block generation time can remain at roughly 10 minutes per block. This is also true in reverse if blocks are not mined every 10 minutes than the difficulty is decreased. Difficulty, is calculated every 2016 blocks (in two weeks) and adjusted accordingly. If the previous set of 2016 blocks were mined in less than a period of two weeks then difficulty will be increased. Similarly, if 2016 blocks were found in more than two weeks (If blocks are mined every 10 minutes then 2016 blocks take 2 weeks to be mined) then the difficulty is decreased.

The hash rate

The hashing rate basically represents the rate of calculating hashes per second. In other words, this is the speed at which miners in the Bitcoin network are calculating hashes to find a block. In early days of bitcoin, it used to be quite small as CPUs were used. However, with dedicated mining pools and ASICs now, this has gone up exponentially in the last few years. This has resulted in increased difficulty of the Bitcoin network. The following hash rate graph shows the hash rate increase over time and is currently measured in Exa hashes. This means that in 1 second, the Bitcoin network miners are computing more than 24,000,000,000,000,000,000 hashes per second.

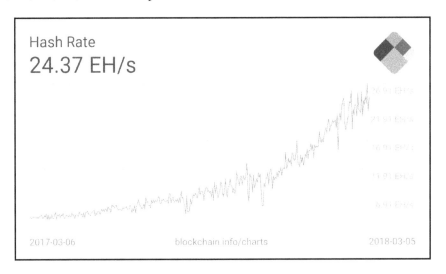

Hashing rate (measured in Exa-hashes) as of March 2018, shown over a period of 1 year

Mining systems

Over time, bitcoin miners have used various methods to mine bitcoins. As the core principle behind mining is based on the double SHA-256 algorithm, overtime experts have developed sophisticated systems to calculate the hash faster and faster. The following is a review of the different types of mining methods used in bitcoin and how they evolved with time.

CPU

CPU mining was the first type of mining available in the original bitcoin client. Users could even use laptop or desktop computers to mine bitcoins. CPU mining is no longer profitable and now more advanced mining methods such as ASIC-based mining is used. CPU mining only lasted for around just over a year since the introduction of Bitcoin and soon other methods were explored and tried by the miners.

GPU

Due to the increased difficulty of the bitcoin network and the general tendency of finding faster methods to mine, miners started to use GPUs or graphics cards available in PCs to perform mining. GPUs support faster and parallelized calculations that are usually programmed using the OpenCL language. This turned out to be a faster option as compared to CPUs. Users also used techniques such as overclocking to gain maximum benefit of the GPU power. Also, the possibility of using multiple graphics cards increased the popularity of graphics cards' usage for bitcoin mining. GPU mining, however, has some limitations, such as overheating and the requirement for specialized motherboards and extra hardware to house multiple graphics cards. From another angle, graphics cards have become quite expensive due to increased demand and this has impacted gamers and graphic software users.

FPGA

Even GPU mining did not last long, and soon miners found another way to perform mining using FPGAs. **Field Programmable Gate Array** (**FPGA**) is basically an integrated circuit that can be programmed to perform specific operations. FPGAs are usually programmed in **Hardware Description Languages** (**HDLs**), such as Verilog and VHDL. Double SHA-256 quickly became an attractive programming task for FPGA programmers and several open source projects started too. FPGA offered much better performance as compared to GPUs; however, issues such as accessibility, programming difficulty, and the requirement for specialized knowledge to program and configure FPGAs resulted in a short life of the FPGA era for bitcoin mining.

The arrival of ASICs resulted in quickly phased out FPGA- based systems for mining. Mining hardware such as X6500 miner, Ztex, and Icarus were developed during the time when FPGA mining was profitable. Various FPGA manufacturers, such as Xilinx and Altera, produce FPGA hardware and development boards that can be used to program mining algorithms. It should be noted that GPU mining is still profitable for some other cryptocurrencies to some extent such as Zcoin (`https://zcoin.io/guide-on-how-to-mine-zcoin-xzc/`), but not Bitcoin, because network difficulty of Bitcoin is so high that only ASICs (specialized hardware) running in parallel can produce some reasonable profit.

ASICs

Application Specific Integrated Circuit (**ASIC**) was designed to perform the SHA-256 operation. These special chips were sold by various manufacturers and offered a very high hashing rate. This worked for some time, but due to the quickly increasing mining difficulty level, single-unit ASICs are no longer profitable.

Currently, mining is out of the reach of individuals as vast amounts of energy and money is needed to be spent in order to build a profitable mining platform. Now professional mining centers using thousands of ASIC units in parallel are offering mining contracts to users to perform mining on their behalf. There is no technical limitation, a single user can run thousands of ASICs in parallel but it will require dedicated data centers and hardware, therefore, cost for a single individual can become prohibitive. The following are the four types of mining hardware:

CPU

GPU

FPGA

ASIC

Mining pools

A mining pool forms when group of miners work together to mine a block. The pool manager receives the coinbase transaction if the block is successfully mined, which is then responsible for distributing the reward to the group of miners who invested resources to mine the block. This is profitable as compared to solo mining, where only one sole miner is trying to solve the partial hash inversion function (hash puzzle) because, in mining pools, the reward is paid to each member of the pool regardless of whether they (more specifically, their individual node) solved the puzzle or not.

There are various models that a mining pool manager can use to pay to the miners, such as the **Pay Per Share** (**PPS**) model and the proportional model. In the PPS model, the mining pool manager pays a flat fee to all miners who participated in the mining exercise, whereas in the proportional model, the share is calculated based on the amount of computing resources spent to solve the hash puzzle.

Many commercial pools now exist and provide mining service contracts via the cloud and easy-to-use web interfaces. The most commonly used ones are AntPool (`https://www.antpool.com`), BTC (`https://btc.com`), and BTC TOP (`http://www.btc.top`). A comparison of hashing power for all major mining pools is shown in the following diagram:

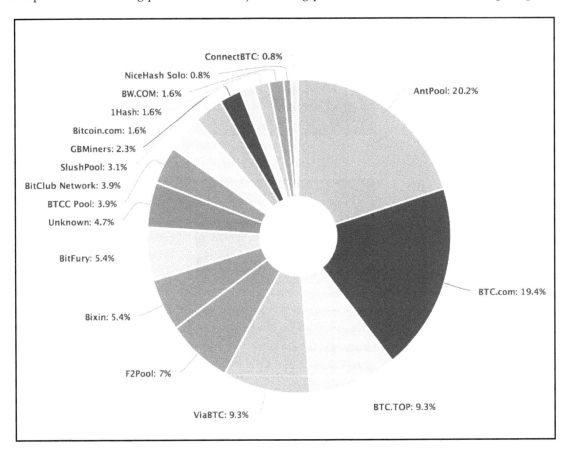

Mining pools and their hashing power (hash rate) as of 28/10/2017

Source: https://blockchain.info/pools

Mining centralization can occur if a pool manages to control more than 51% of the network by generating more than 51% hash rate of the Bitcoin network.

As discussed earlier in the introduction section, a 51% attack can result in successful double-spending attacks, and it can impact consensus and in fact impose another version of transaction history on the Bitcoin network.

This event has happened once in the Bitcoin history when GHash.IO, a large mining pool, managed to acquire more than 51% of the network capacity. Theoretical solutions, such as two-phase PoW (`http://hackingdistributed.com/2014/06/18/how-to-disincentivize-large-bitcoin-mining-pools/`), have been proposed in academia to disincentivize large mining pools. This scheme introduces a second cryptographic puzzle that results in mining pools to either reveal their private keys or provide a considerable portion of the hash rate of their mining pool, thus reducing the overall hash rate of the pool.

Various types of hardware are commercially available for mining purposes. Currently, the most profitable one is ASIC mining, and specialized hardware is available from a number of vendors such as Antminer, AvalonMiner and Whatsminer. Solo mining is not much profitable now unless a vast amount of money and energy is spent to build your own mining rig or even a data center. With the current difficulty factor (March 2018), if a user manages to produce a hash rate of 12 TH/s, they can hope to make 0.0009170 BTC (around $6) per day, which is very low as compared to the investment required to source the equipment that can produce 12 TH. Including running costs such as electricity, this turns out to be not very profitable. ˙

For example, Antminer S9, is an efficient ASIC miner which produces hash power of 13.5 TH/s and it seems that it can produce some profit per day, which is true but a single Antminer S9 costs around 1700 GBP and combining it with electricity cost the return on investment is almost after a year's mining when it produces around 0.3 BTC. It may seem still OK, to invest but also think about the fact that the Bitcoin network difficulty keeps going up with time and during a year it will become more difficult to mine and the mining hardware will run out its utility in a few months.

Summary

We started this chapter by introducing Bitcoin and how a transaction works from a user's point of view. Then, we presented an introduction to transactions from a technical point of view. Later we discussed public and private keys that are used in Bitcoin.

In the following section, we presented addresses and its different types, following it with a discussion on transactions, its types, and usage. Next, we looked at blockchain with a detailed explanation regarding how blockchain works and what various components are included in the Bitcoin blockchain.

In the last few sections of the chapter, we presented the mining process and relevant concepts.

In the next chapter, we will examine concepts related to the Bitcoin network, its elements, and client software tools.

Bitcoin Network and Payments

6

In this chapter, we will present the Bitcoin network, relevant network protocols, and wallets. We will explore different types of wallets that are available for bitcoin. Moreover, we will examine how the Bitcoin protocol works and the types of messages exchanged on the network between nodes, during various node and network operations. Also, we will explore various advanced and modern Bitcoin protocols that have been developed to address limitations in the original Bitcoin. Finally, we'll give you an introduction to bitcoin trading and investment.

We will start with the detailed introduction of the Bitcoin network.

The Bitcoin network

The Bitcoin network is a peer-to-peer network where nodes exchange transactions and blocks. There are different types of nodes on the network. There are two main types of nodes, full nodes and SPV nodes. **Full nodes**, as the name implies, are implementations of Bitcoin core clients performing the wallet, miner, full blockchain storage, and network routing functions. However, it is not necessary to perform all these functions. **Simple Payment Verification** (**SPV**) nodes or lightweight clients perform only wallet and network routing functionality. The latest version of Bitcoin protocol is 70015 and was introduced with Bitcoin core client 0.13.2.

Some nodes prefer to be full blockchain nodes with complete blockchain as they are more secure and play a vital role in block propagation while some nodes perform network routing functions only but do not perform mining or store private keys (the wallet function). Another type is solo miner nodes that can perform mining, store full blockchain, and act as a Bitcoin network routing node.

There are a few nonstandard but heavily used nodes that are called **pool protocol servers**. These nodes make use of alternative protocols, such as the stratum protocol. These nodes are used in mining pools. Nodes that only compute hashes use the stratum protocol to submit their solutions to the mining pool. Some nodes perform only mining functions and are called mining nodes. It is possible to run an SPV client which runs a wallet and network routing function without a blockchain. SPV clients only download the headers of the blocks while syncing with the network and when required they can request transactions from full nodes. The verification of transactions is possible by using Merkle root in the block header with Merkle branch to prove that the transaction is present in a block in the blockchain.

Most protocols on the internet are line-based, which means that each line is delimited by a carriage return (\r) and newline (\n) character. Stratum is also a line-based protocol that makes use of plain TCP sockets and human-readable JSON-RPC to operate and communicate between nodes. Stratum is commonly used to connect to mining pools.

The Bitcoin network is identified by its different magic values. A list is shown as follows:

Network	Magic value	Hex
main	0xD9B4BEF9	F9 BE B4 D9
testnet3	0x0709110B	0B 11 09 07

Bitcoin network magic values

Magic values are used to indicate the message origin network.

A full node performs four functions: wallet, miner, blockchain, and the network routing node.

Before we examine that how Bitcoin discovery protocol and block synchronization works, we need to understand that what are the different types of messages that Bitcoin protocol uses. The list of message types is provided here.

There are 27 types of protocol messages in total, but they're likely to increase over time as the protocol grows. The most commonly used protocol messages and their explanation are listed as follows:

- `version`: This is the first message that a node sends out to the network, advertising its version and block count. The remote node then replies with the same information and the connection is then established.

- `verack`: This is the response of the version message accepting the connection request.
- `inv`: This is used by nodes to advertise their knowledge of blocks and transactions.
- `getdata`: This is a response to `inv`, requesting a single block or transaction identified by its hash.
- `getblocks`: This returns an `inv` packet containing the list of all blocks starting after the last known hash or 500 blocks.
- `getheaders`: This is used to request block headers in a specified range.
- `tx`: This is used to send a transaction as a response to the `getdata` protocol message.
- `block`: This sends a block in response to the `getdata` protocol message.
- `headers`: This packet returns up to 2,000 block headers as a reply to the `getheaders` request.
- `getaddr`: This is sent as a request to get information about known peers.
- `addr`: This provides information about nodes on the network. It contains the number of addresses and address list in the form of IP address and port number.

When a Bitcoin core node starts up, first, it initiates the discovery of all peers. This is achieved by querying DNS seeds that are hardcoded into the Bitcoin core client and are maintained by Bitcoin community members. This lookup returns a number of DNS A records. The Bitcoin protocol works on TCP port 8333 by default for the main network and TCP 18333 for testnet. The following code shows an example of DNS seeds in `chainparams.cpp`:

```
// Pieter Wuille, only supports x1, x5, x9, and xd
vSeeds.emplace_back("seed.bitcoin.sipa.be");
// Matt Corallo, only supports x9
vSeeds.emplace_back("dnsseed.bluematt.me");
// Luke Dashjr
vSeeds.emplace_back("dnsseed.bitcoin.dashjr.org");
// Christian Decker, supports x1 - xf
vSeeds.emplace_back("seed.bitcoinstats.com");
// Jonas Schnelli, only supports x1, x5, x9, and xd
vSeeds.emplace_back("seed.bitcoin.jonasschnelli.ch");
// Peter Todd, only supports x1, x5, x9, and xd
vSeeds.emplace_back("seed.btc.petertodd.org");
```

First, the client sends a protocol message `version` that contains various fields, such as version, services, timestamp, network address, nonce, and some other fields. The remote node responds with its own `version` message followed by the `verack` message exchange between both nodes, indicating that the connection has been established.

After this, `getaddr` and `addr` messages are exchanged to find the peers that the client does not know. Meanwhile, either of the nodes can send a `ping` message to see whether the connection is still active. The `getaddr` and `addr` messages are the types defined in the Bitcoin protocol. This process is shown in the following protocol diagram:

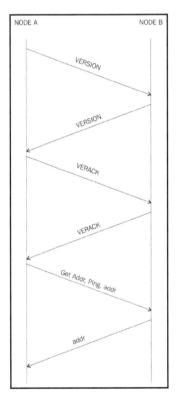

Visualization of node discovery protocol

The preceding network protocol sequence diagram shows communication between two Bitcoin nodes during initial connectivity. **NODE A** is shown on the left side and **NODE B** on the right. First, **NODE A** starts the connection by sending the `version` message which contains version number and current time to the remote peer **NODE B**. **NODE B** then responds with its own `version` message containing the version number and current time. **NODE A** and **NODE B** then exchange a `verack` message indicating that the connection has been successfully established. After the connection is successful the peers can exchange `getaddr` and `addr` messages to discover other peers on the network.

Now the block download can begin. If the node already has all the blocks fully synchronized, then it listens for new blocks using the `inv` protocol message; otherwise, it first checks whether it has a response to `inv` messages and have inventories already. If yes, then it requests the blocks using the `getdata` protocol message; if not, then it requests inventories using the `getblocks` message. This method was used until version 0.9.3. This was a slower process known as **blocks-first approach** and was replaced with **headers-first approach** in 0.10.0.

Initial block download can use blocks-first or the headers-first method to synchronize blocks depending on the version of the Bitcoin core client. The blocks-first method is very slow and was discontinued since February 16, 2015 with the release of version 0.10.0.

Since version 0.10.0, the initial block download method named headers-first was introduced. This resulted in major performance improvement and the blockchain synchronization that used to take days to complete started taking only a few hours. The core idea is that the new node first asks peers for block headers and validates them. Once this is completed, blocks are requested in parallel from all available peers as the blueprint of the complete chain is already downloaded in the form of the block header chain.

In this method, when the client starts up, it checks whether the blockchain is fully synchronized already if the header chain is already synchronized; if not, which is the case the first time the client starts up, it requests headers from other peers using the `getheaders` message. If the blockchain is fully synchronized, it listens for new blocks via `inv` messages, and if it already has a fully synchronized header chain, then it requests blocks using the `getdata` protocol messages. The node also checks whether the header chain has more headers than blocks and then it requests blocks by issuing the `getdata` protocol message.

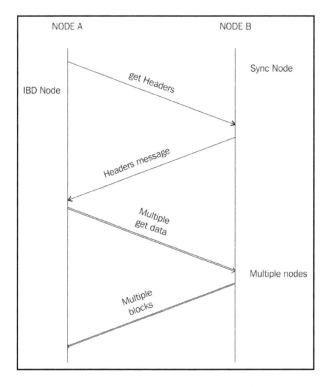

Bitcoin core client >= 0.10.0 header and block synchronization

The preceding diagram shows the Bitcoin block synchronization process between two nodes on the Bitcoin network. **NODE A**, shown on the left side is called **Initial Block Download Node** (**IBD Node**) and **NODE B**, shown on the right is called **Sync Node**.

IBD Node means that this is the node that is requesting the blocks and **Sync Node** means the node from where the blocks are being requested. The process starts by **NODE A** first sending the `getheaders` message which is responded with the `headers` message from the **Sync Node**. The payload of the `getheaders` message is one or more header hashes. If it's a new node then there is only the first genesis block's header hash. The **Sync Node** replies with sending up to 2,000 block headers to the **IBD Node**. After this, the **IBD Node** starts to download more headers from the **Sync Node** and in parallel, downloads blocks from multiple nodes. In other words, **IBD Node** makes requests to multiple nodes and as a result multiple blocks are sent to **IBD Node** from **Sync Node** and other nodes. If the **Sync Node** does not have more headers than 2,000, when **IBD Node** makes a `getheaders` request then **IBD Node** sends `getheaders` message to other nodes. This process continues in parallel until the blockchain synchronization is complete.

The `getblockchaininfo` and `getpeerinfo` RPCs were updated with a new functionality to cater for this change. A **Remote Procedure Call** (**RPC**), `getchaintips`, is used to list all known branches of the blockchain. This also includes headers only blocks. The `getblockchaininfo` RPC is used to provide the information about the current state of the blockchain. The `getpeerinfo` RPC is used to list both the number of blocks and the headers that are in common between peers.

Wireshark can also be used to visualize message exchange between peers and can serve as an invaluable tool to learn about the Bitcoin protocol. A sample is shown here. This is a basic example showing the `version`, `verack`, `getaddr`, `ping`, `addr`, and `inv` messages.

In the details, valuable information such as the packet type, command name, and results of the protocol messages can be seen:

```
Filter:  ip.dst == 52.1.165.219 and bitcoin          ▼  Expression...  Clear  Apply  Save

No.      Time            Source           Destination         Protocol Length Info
     131 98.598526000    192.168.0.13     52.1.165.219        Bitcoin      192 version
     150 99.180294000    192.168.0.13     52.1.165.219        Bitcoin       90 verack
     151 99.180421000    192.168.0.13     52.1.165.219        Bitcoin      122 getaddr, ping
     152 99.180715000    192.168.0.13     52.1.165.219        Bitcoin     1288 addr, getheaders[Malformed Packet]
     486 112.053746000   192.168.0.13     52.1.165.219        Bitcoin      127 inv
     818 143.630367000   192.168.0.13     52.1.165.219        Bitcoin      127 inv
    1004 178.729768000   192.168.0.13     52.1.165.219        Bitcoin      127 inv

▶ Transmission Control Protocol, Src Port: 52864 (52864), Dst Port: 18333 (18333), Seq: 207, Ack: 1291, Len: 1222
▼ Bitcoin protocol
    Packet magic: 0x0b110907
    Command name: addr
    Payload Length: 31
    Payload checksum: 0xa03fc07d
  ▼ Address message
      Count: 1
    ▼ Address: afbd0258000000000000000000000000000000000000ffff...
      ▼ Node services: 0x0000000000000000
        .... .... .... .... .... .... .... ...0 = Network node: Not set
        Node address: ::ffff:86.15.44.209 (::ffff:86.15.44.209)
        Node port: 18333
        Address timestamp: Oct 16, 2016 00:37:19.000000000 BST
▼ Bitcoin protocol
    Packet magic: 0x0b110907
    Command name: getheaders
    Payload Length: 1029
    Payload checksum: 0x4e54961d
  ▼ Getheaders message
      Count: 126
      Starting hash: 1101001f152142abccc039503abc56b149bd56c2b3925b65...
      Starting hash: 000000001980703bd53b0c7bf0ac995bccfeeffd5cddc780...
      Starting hash: 000000007ad1fed813d20301b1762895a2e5b08c8a58b3ea...
      Starting hash: 000000003624c451f726a3e983d02279d9c7cf672d36f1d5...
```

A sample block message in Wireshark

A protocol graph showing the flow of data between the two peers is shown in the preceding diagram. This can help you understand when a node starts up and what type of messages are used.

In the following example, the Bitcoin dissector is used to analyze the traffic and identify the Bitcoin protocol commands.

Exchange of messages such as version, getaddr, and getdata can be seen in the following example along with the appropriate comment describing the message name.

This exercise can be very useful in order to learn Bitcoin protocol and it is recommended that the experiments be carried out on the Bitcoin testnet (`https://en.bitcoin.it/wiki/Testnet`), where various messages and transactions can be sent over the network and then be analyzed by Wireshark.

 Wireshark is a network analysis tool available at `https://www.wireshark.org`.

The analysis performed by Wireshark in the following screenshot shows the exchange of messages between two nodes. If you look closely, you'll notice that top three messages show the node discovery protocol that we have discussed before:

Time	192.168.0.13 → 136.243.139.96	Comment
97.734135000	(57868) version (18333)	Bitcoin: version
98.025045000	(57868) verack (18333)	Bitcoin: verack
98.025177000	(57868) getaddr, pin... (18333)	Bitcoin: getaddr, ping, addr
98.025468000	(57868) getheaders... (18333)	Bitcoin: getheaders, [unknown command], [unknown command], [unknown command], headers
98.160419000	(57868) [TCP Retran... (18333)	Bitcoin: [TCP Retransmission] , getheaders, [unknown command], [unknown command], [unknown command]
98.598399000	(57868) getdata (18333)	Bitcoin: getdata
144.343544000	(57868) inv (18333)	Bitcoin: inv
176.152240000	(57868) getdata (18333)	Bitcoin: getdata
179.493755000	(57868) getdata (18333)	Bitcoin: getdata
218.101646000	(57868) ping (18333)	Bitcoin: ping
218.192004000	(57868) [unknown co... (18333)	Bitcoin: [unknown command]
218.444431000	(57868) [TCP Retran... (18333)	Bitcoin: [TCP Retransmission] , [unknown command]
336.234936000	(57868) getdata (18333)	Bitcoin: getdata
337.843423000	(57868) [unknown co... (18333)	Bitcoin: [unknown command]
338.143885000	(57868) ping (18333)	Bitcoin: ping
448.764093000	(57868) getdata (18333)	Bitcoin: getdata
457.894823000	(57868) [unknown co... (18333)	Bitcoin: [unknown command]
458.195265000	(57868) ping (18333)	Bitcoin: ping
578.011774000	(57868) [unknown co... (18333)	Bitcoin: [unknown command]
578.212044000	(57868) ping (18333)	Bitcoin: ping
585.587671000	(57868) inv (18333)	Bitcoin: inv
647.169633000	(57868) inv (18333)	Bitcoin: inv
671.962545000	(57868) getdata (18333)	Bitcoin: getdata
698.037067000	(57868) [unknown co... (18333)	Bitcoin: [unknown command]
698.237350000	(57868) ping (18333)	Bitcoin: ping
701.563581000	(57868) inv (18333)	Bitcoin: inv
701.986269000	(57868) inv (18333)	Bitcoin: inv
705.022173000	(57868) inv (18333)	Bitcoin: inv
812.115878000	(57868) inv (18323)	Bitcoin: inv
818.198570000	(57868) [unknown co... (18333)	Bitcoin: [unknown command]
818.298733000	(57868) ping (18333)	Bitcoin: ping

Node discovery protocol in Wireshark

Full clients are thick clients or full nodes that download the entire blockchain; this is the most secure method of validating the blockchain as a client. Bitcoin network nodes can operate in two fundamental modes: full client or lightweight SPV client. SPV clients are used to verify payments without requiring the download of a full blockchain. SPV nodes only keep a copy of block headers of the current valid longest blockchain. Verification is performed by looking at the Merkle branch that links the transactions to the original block the transaction was accepted in. This is not very practical and requires a more practical approach, which was implemented with BIP 37 (`https://github.com/bitcoin/bips/blob/master/bip-0037.mediawiki`), where bloom filters were used to filter out relevant transactions only.

Bloom filter is basically a data structure (a bit vector with indexes) that is used to test the membership of an element in a probabilistic manner. It basically provides probabilistic lookup with false positives but no false negatives. It means that this filter can produce an output where an element that is not a member of the set being tested is wrongly considered to be in the set, but it can never produce an output where an element does exist in the set, but it asserts that it does not.

Elements are added to the bloom filter after hashing them several times and then set the corresponding bits in the bit vector to 1 via the corresponding index. In order to check the presence of the element in the bloom filter, the same hash functions are applied and compared with the bits in the bit vector to see whether the same bits are set to 1. Not every hash function (such as SHA-1) is suitable for bloom filters as they need to be fast, independent, and uniformly distributed. The most commonly used hash functions for bloom filters are FNV, Murmur, and Jenkins.

These filters are mainly used by SPV clients to request transactions and the Merkle blocks they are interested in. A Merkle block is a lightweight version of the block, which includes a block header, some hashes, a list of 1-bit flags, and a transaction count. This information can then be used to build a Merkle tree. This is achieved by creating a filter that matches only those transaction and blocks that have been requested by the SPV client. Once the `version` messages have been exchanged and connection has been established between peers, the nodes can set filters according to their requirements.

These probabilistic filters offer a varying degree of privacy or precision depending upon how accurately or loosely they have been set. A strict bloom filter will only filter transactions that have been requested by the node but at the expense of the possibility of revealing the user addresses to adversaries who can correlate transactions with their IP addresses, thus compromising privacy. On the other hand, a loosely set filter can result in retrieving more unrelated transactions but will offer more privacy. Also, for SPV clients, bloom filters allow them to use low bandwidth as opposed to downloading all transactions for verification.

BIP 37 proposed the Bitcoin implementation of bloom filters and introduced three new messages to the Bitcoin protocol:

- `filterload`: This is used to set the bloom filter on the connection
- `filteradd`: This adds a new data element to the current filter
- `filterclear`: This deletes the currently loaded filter

 More details can be found in the BIP 37 specification. This is available at `https://github.com/bitcoin/bips/blob/master/bip-0037.mediawiki`.

Wallets

The wallet software is used to store private or public keys and Bitcoin address. It performs various functions, such as receiving and sending bitcoins. Nowadays, software usually offers both functionalities: Bitcoin client and wallet. On the disk, the Bitcoin core client wallets are stored as the Berkeley DB file:

```
$ file wallet.dat
wallet.dat: Berkeley DB (B-tree, version 9, native byte-order)
```

Private keys are generated by randomly choosing a 256-bit number by wallet software. The rules of generation are predefined and were discussed in Chapter 4, *Public Key Cryptography*. Private keys are used by wallets to sign the outgoing transactions. Wallets do not store any coins, and there is no concept of wallets storing balance or coins for a user. In fact, in the Bitcoin network, coins do not exist; instead, only transaction information is stored on the blockchain (more precisely, UTXO, unspent outputs), which are then used to calculate the number of bitcoins.

In Bitcoin, there are different types of wallets that can be used to store private keys. As a software program, they also provide some functions to the users to manage and carry out transactions on the Bitcoin network.

Non-deterministic wallets

These wallets contain randomly generated private keys and are also called *just a bunch of key wallets*. The Bitcoin core client generates some keys when first started and generates keys as and when required. Managing a large number of keys is very difficult and an error-prone process can lead to theft and loss of coins. Moreover, there is a need to create regular backups of the keys and protect them appropriately, for example, by encrypting them in order to prevent theft or loss.

Deterministic wallets

In this type of wallet, keys are derived out of a seed value via hash functions. This seed number is generated randomly and is commonly represented by human-readable *mnemonic code* words. Mnemonic code words are defined in BIP 39, a Bitcoin improvement proposal for mnemonic code for generating deterministic keys. This BIP is available at `https://github.com/bitcoin/bips/blob/master/bip-0039.mediawiki`. This phrase can be used to recover all keys and makes private key management comparatively easier.

Hierarchical Deterministic wallets

Defined in BIP32 and BIP44, **Hierarchical Deterministic** (**HD**) wallets store keys in a tree structure derived from a seed. The seed generates the parent key (master key), which is used to generate child keys and, subsequently, grandchild keys. Key generation in HD wallets does not generate keys directly; instead, it produces some information (private key generation information) that can be used to generate a sequence of private keys. The complete hierarchy of private keys in an HD wallet is easily recoverable if the master private key is known. It is because of this property that HD wallets are very easy to maintain and are highly portable. There are many free and commercially available HD wallets available. For example, Trezor (`https://trezor.io`), Jaxx (`https://jaxx.io/`) and Electrum (`https://electrum.org/`).

Brain wallets

The master private key can also be derived from the hash of passwords that are memorized. The key idea is that this passphrase is used to derive the private key and if used in HD wallets, this can result in a full HD wallet that is derived from a single memorized password. This is known as a brain wallet. This method is prone to password guessing and brute force attacks but techniques such as key stretching can be used to slow down the progress made by the attacker.

Paper wallets

As the name implies, this is a paper-based wallet with the required key material printed on it. It requires physical security to be stored.

 Paper wallets can be generated online from various service providers, such as https://bitcoinpaperwallet.com/ or https://www.bitaddress.org/.

Hardware wallets

Another method is to use a tamper-resistant device to store keys. This tamper-resistant device can be custom-built or with the advent of NFC-enabled phones, this can also be a **Secure Element** (**SE**) in NFC phones. Trezor and Ledger wallets (various types) are the most commonly used Bitcoin hardware wallets. The following is the photo of a Trezor wallet:

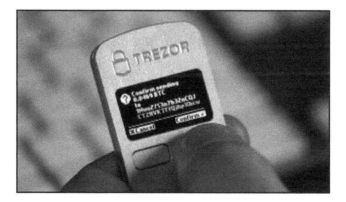

Trezor wallet

Online wallets

Online wallets, as the name implies, are stored entirely online and are provided as a service usually via the cloud. They provide a web interface to the users to manage their wallets and perform various functions such as making and receiving payments. They are easy to use but imply that the user trusts the online wallet service provider. An example of online wallet is GreenAddress, which is available at `https://greenaddress.it/en/`.

Mobile wallets

Mobile wallets, as the name suggests, are installed on mobile devices. They can provide various methods to make payments, most notably the ability to use smartphone cameras to scan QR codes quickly and make payments. Mobile wallets are available for the Android platform and iOS, for example, Blockchain, breadwallet, Copay, and Jaxx.

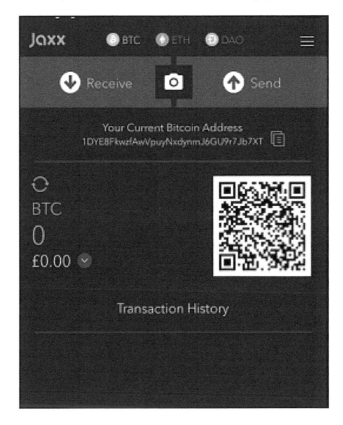

Jaxx mobile wallet

The choice of Bitcoin wallet depends on several factors such as security, ease of use, and available features. Out of all these attributes, security of course comes first and when making a decision about which wallet to use, security should be of paramount importance. Hardware wallets tend to be more secure as compared to web wallets because of their tamper resistant design. Web wallets by nature are hosted on websites, which may not be as secure as a tamper resistant hardware device. Generally, mobile wallets for smartphone devices are quite popular due to a balanced combination of features and security. There are many companies offering these wallets on the iOS App Store and Android Play. It is however quite difficult to suggest that which type of wallet should be used, it also depends on personal preferences and features available in a wallet. It is advisable that security should be kept in mind while making decision on which wallet to choose.

Bitcoin payments

Bitcoins can be accepted as payments using various techniques. Bitcoin is not recognized as a legal currency in many jurisdictions, but it is increasingly being accepted as a payment method by many online merchants and e-commerce websites. There are a number of ways in which buyers can pay the business that accepts bitcoins. For example, in an online shop, Bitcoin merchant solutions can be used, whereas in traditional, physical shops, point of sale terminals and other specialized hardware can be used. Customers can simply scan the QR code with the seller's payment URI in it and pay using their mobile devices. Bitcoin URIs allow users to make payments by simply clicking on links or scanning QR codes. **Uniform Resource Identifier** (**URI**) is basically a string that represents the transaction information. It is defined in BIP 21. The QR code can be displayed near the point of the sale terminal. Nearly all Bitcoin wallets support this feature.

Businesses can use the following logo to advertise that they accept bitcoins as payment from customers.

bitcoin accepted here logo

Various payment solutions, such as XBTerminal and 34 Bytes bitcoin **Point of Sale** (**POS**) terminal are available commercially.

Generally, these solutions work by following these steps:

1. The sales person enters the amount of money to be charged in Fiat currency, for example, US Dollars

2. Once the value is entered in the system the terminal prints a receipt with QR code on it and other relevant information such as amount

3. The customer can then scan this QR code using their mobile Bitcoin wallet to send the payment to the Bitcoin address of the seller embedded within the QR code

4. Once the payment is received on the designated Bitcoin address, a receipt is printed out as a physical evidence of sale

A Bitcoin POS device from 34 Bytes is shown here:

34 Bytes POS solution

The bitcoin payment processor, offered by many online service providers, allows integration with e-commerce websites. There are many options available. These payment processors can be used to accept bitcoins as payments. Some service providers also allow secure storage of bitcoins. For example, bitpay, `https://bitpay.com`. Another example is Bitcoin Merchant Solutions available at `https://www.bitcoin.com/merchant-solutions`.

Various **Bitcoin Improvement Proposals** (**BIPs**) have been proposed and finalized in order to introduce and standardize bitcoin payments. Most notably, BIP 70 (*Payment Protocol*) describes the protocol for secure communication between a merchant and customers. This protocol uses X.509 certificates for authentication and runs over HTTP and HTTPS. There are three messages in this protocol: `PaymentRequest`, `Payment`, and `PaymentACK`. The key features of this proposal are defense against man-in-the-middle attacks and secure proof of payment. Man-in-the-middle attacks can result in a scenario where the attacker is sitting between the merchant and the buyer and it would seem to the buyer that they are talking to the merchant, but in fact, the man in the middle is interacting with the buyer instead of the merchant. This can result in manipulation of the merchant's Bitcoin address to defraud the buyer.

Several other BIPs, such as BIP 71 (*Payment Protocol MIME types*) and BIP 72 (*URI extensions for Payment Protocol*), have also been implemented to standardize payment scheme to support BIP 70 (*Payment Protocol*).

Bitcoin lightning network, is a solution for scalable off-chain instant payments. It was introduced in early 2016, which allows off-blockchain payments. This network makes use of payments channels that run off the blockchain which allows greater speed and scalability of Bitcoin.

 This paper is available at `https://lightning.network` and interested readers are encouraged to read the paper in order to understand the theory and rationale behind this invention.

Innovation in Bitcoin

Bitcoin has undergone many changes and still evolving into a more and more robust and better system by addressing various weaknesses in the system. Especially, performance has been a topic of hot debate among Bitcoin experts and enthusiasts for many years. As such, various proposals have been made in the last few years to improve Bitcoin performance resulting in greater transaction speed, increased security, payment standardization and overall performance improvement at the protocol level.

These improvement proposals are usually made in the form of BIPs or fundamentally new versions of Bitcoin protocols resulting in a new network altogether. Some of the changes proposed are implementable via a soft fork but few need a hard fork and as a result, give birth to a new currency.

In the following sections, we will see what are the various BIPs that can be proposed for improvement in Bitcoin and then we will discuss some advanced protocols that have been proposed and implemented to address various weaknesses in the Bitcoin.

Bitcoin Improvement Proposals (BIPs)

These documents are used to propose or inform the Bitcoin community about the improvements suggested, the design issues, or information about some aspects of the bitcoin ecosystem. There are three types of Bitcoin improvement proposals, abbreviated as BIPs:

- **Standard BIP**: Used to describe the major changes that have a major impact on the Bitcoin system, for example, block size changes, network protocol changes, or transaction verification changes.
- **Process BIP**: A major difference between standard and process BIPs is that standard BIPs cover protocol changes, whereas process BIPs usually deal with proposing a change in a process that is outside the core Bitcoin protocol. These are implemented only after a consensus among bitcoin users.
- **Informational BIP**: These are usually used to just advise or record some information about the Bitcoin ecosystem, such as design issues.

Advanced protocols

In this section, we will see that what are the various advanced protocols that have been suggested or implemented for improving the Bitcoin protocol.

Transaction throughput is one of the critical issues that need to be addressed. Inherently, the Bitcoin network can only process from approximately 3 to 7 transactions per second which is a tiny number as compared to other financial networks, such as Visa which can process approximately, on average, 24,000 transactions per second. PayPal can process approximately 200 transactions per second whereas Ethereum can process up to on average 20. As Bitcoin Network grew exponentially over the last few years, these issues started to grow even further. The difference of processing speed is also shown below in a graph which shows the scale of difference between Bitcoin and other networks' transaction speeds.

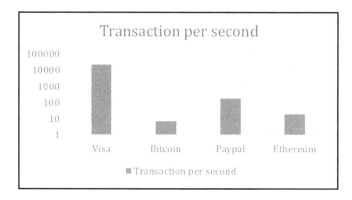

Bitcoin transaction speed as compared to other networks (on logarithmic scale)

Also, security issues such as transaction malleability are of real concern which can result in denial of service. Various proposals have been made to improve the Bitcoin proposal to address various weaknesses. A selection of these proposals is presented in the following subsections.

Segregated Witness (SegWit)

The SegWit or Segregated Witness is a soft fork based update to the Bitcoin protocol which addresses some weaknesses such as throughput and security in the Bitcoin protocol. SegWit offers a number of improvements as listed here:

- Fix for transaction malleability due to the separation of signature data from transactional data. In this case, it is no longer possible to modify transaction ID because it is no longer calculated based on the signature data present within the transaction.
- Reduction in transaction size results in cheaper transaction fees.
- Reduction in transaction signing and verification times, which results in faster transactions.
- Script versioning, which allows version number to be prefixed to locking scripts. This change can result in improvements in the scripting language without requiring a hard fork and by just increasing the version number of the script.
- Reduction in input verification time.

SegWit was proposed in BIP 141, BIP 143, BIP 144 and BIP 145. It has been activated on Bitcoin main network on August 24, 2017. The key idea behind SegWit is the separation of signature data from transaction data, which results in reduced size of the transaction. This results in block size increase up to 4 MB. However, the practical limit is between 1.6 MB to 2 MB. Instead of hard size limit of 1 MB blocks, SegWit has introduced a new concept of block weight limit.

To spend an **Unspent Transaction Output** (**UTXO**) in Bitcoin, it needs a valid signature to be provided. In the pre-SegWit scenario, this signature is provided within the locking script whereas in SegWit this signature is not part of the transaction and is provided separately.

There are two types of transaction that can now be constructed using SegWit wallets but note that these are not new transaction types as such, these are just new ways by which UTXOs can be spent. These types are:

- **Pay to Witness public key hash** (**P2WPKH**)
- **Pay to Witness Script hash** (**P2WSH**)

Bitcoin Cash

Bitcoin Cash increases the block limit to 8 MB. This immediately increases the number of transactions that can be processed in one block to a much larger number as compared to 1 MB limit in original Bitcoin protocol. It uses PoW as consensus algorithm, and mining hardware is still ASIC based. The block interval is changed from 10 minutes to 10 seconds and up to 2 hours. It also provides replay protection and wipe-out protection.

Bitcoin Unlimited

In this proposal, the size of the block is increased but not set to a hard limit. Instead, miners come to a consensus on the block size cap over a period of time. Other concepts such as *parallel validation* and *extreme thin blocks* have also been proposed in Bitcoin Unlimited.

 Its client is available for download at
`https://www.bitcoinunlimited.info`.

Extreme thin blocks allow for a faster block propagation between Bitcoin nodes. In this scheme the node requesting blocks sends a `getdata` request along with a bloom filter to another node. Purpose of this bloom filter is to filter out the transactions that already exists in the **mempool** (short for **memory pool**) of the requesting node. The node then sends back a *thin block* only containing the missing transactions. This fixes an inefficiency in Bitcoin where by transaction are regularly received twice, once at the time of broadcast by the sender and then again when a mined block is broadcasted with the confirmed transaction.

Parallel validation allows nodes to validate more than one block along with new incoming transactions in parallel. This mechanism is in contrast to Bitcoin where a node during its validation period after receiving a new block cannot relay new transactions or validate any blocks until it has accepted or rejected the block.

Bitcoin Gold

This proposal has been implemented as a hard fork since block 49,1407 of the original Bitcoin blockchain. Being a hard fork, it resulted in a new blockchain, named **Bitcoin Gold** (**BTG**). The core idea behind this concept is to address the issue of mining centralization which has hurt the original Bitcoin idea of decentralized digital cash whereby more hash power has resulted in a power shift towards miners with more hashing power. BTG uses the Equihash algorithm as its mining algorithm instead of PoW; hence it is inherently ASIC resistant and uses GPUs for mining.

There are other proposals like Bitcoin Next Generation, Solidus, Spectre, and SegWit2x which will be discussed later in this book in `Chapter 18`, *Scalability and Other Challenges*, in the context of performance improvement in blockchain networks.

Bitcoin investment and buying and selling bitcoins

There are many online exchanges where users can buy and sell bitcoins. This is a big business on the internet now and it offers bitcoin trading, CFDs, spread betting, margin trading, and various other choices. Traders can buy bitcoins or trade by opening long or short positions to make a profit when bitcoin's price goes up or down. Several other features, such as exchanging bitcoins for other virtual currencies, are also possible, and many online bitcoin exchanges provide this function. Advanced market data, trading strategies, charts, and relevant data to support traders is also available. An example is shown from CEX (`https://cex.io`) here. Other exchanges offer similar types of services.

Example of bitcoin exchange cex.io

The following screenshot shows the order book at the exchange where all buy and sell orders are listed:

Sell Orders			Buy Orders		
Price per BTC	BTC Amount	Total: (USD)	Price per BTC	BTC Amount	Total: (USD)
642.4085	฿0.20450000	$ 131.38	641.6210	฿0.01390000	$ 8.92
642.4915	฿0.20910000	$ 134.35	641.6201	฿0.23162780	$ 148.62
643.4470	฿0.05000000	$ 32.18	641.6200	฿0.12050000	$ 77.32
643.4900	฿0.11844972	$ 76.67	641.6117	฿1.83477084	$ 1177.22
643.5000	฿1.85749652	$ 1195.00	641.5584	฿0.30000000	$ 192.47
643.6500	฿3.00000000	$ 1930.95	641.5217	฿0.18190000	$ 116.63
643.6999	฿0.13844181	$ 89.12	641.0217	฿0.10000000	$ 64.11
643.7000	฿45.80000000	$ 29481.46	640.5300	฿0.67323160	$ 431.23
643.7487	฿1.22995638	$ 791.79	640.5000	฿0.40815400	$ 261.43

Example of bitcoin order book at exchange cex.io

The order book shown in the preceding screenshot displays sell and buy orders. Sell orders are also called ask and buy orders are also called bid orders. This means that ask price is at what seller is willing to sell the bitcoin whereas bid price is what the buyer is willing to pay. If bid and ask prices match then a trade can occur. Most common order types are market orders and limit orders. Market orders mean that as soon as the prices match the order will be filled immediately. Limit orders allow buying and selling of set number of bitcoins at a specified price or better. Also, a period of time can be set during which the order can be left open, if not executed then it will be cancelled. We have introduced trading concepts in more detail in `Chapter 4`, *Public Key Cryptography*, under *Financial markets* section, interested readers can refer to this section for more details.

Summary

We started this chapter with the introduction to Bitcoin network, following it with a discussion on Bitcoin node discovery and block synchronization protocols. Moreover, we presented different types of network messages. Then we examined different types of Bitcoin wallets and discussed various attributes and features of each type. Following this, we looked at Bitcoin payments and payment processors. In the last section, we discussed Bitcoin innovations, which included topics such as Bitcoin Improvement Proposals, and advanced Bitcoin protocols. Finally, we presented a basic introduction to Bitcoin buying and selling.

In the next chapter, we will discuss Bitcoin clients, such as Bitcoin Core client, which can be used to interact with the Bitcoin blockchain and also acts as a wallet. In addition, we will explore some of the APIs that are available for programming Bitcoin applications.

Bitcoin Clients and APIs

7

In this chapter, we provides you with an introduction to Bitcoin client installation and a basic introduction to various APIs and tools that are available for developing Bitcoin applications. We will examine how to set up a Bitcoin node in live and test networks. Also, we will discuss various commands and utilities that are used to perform various functions in Bitcoin system.

Bitcoin installation

The Bitcoin Core client can be installed from `https://bitcoin.org/en/download`. This is available for different architectures and platforms ranging from x86 Windows to ARM Linux, as shown in the following screenshot:

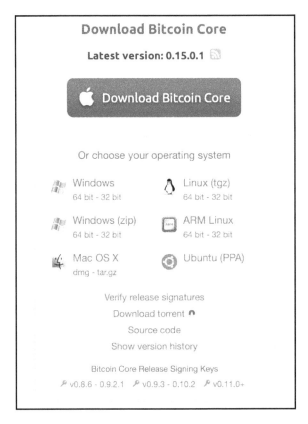

Download Bitcoin Core

Types of Bitcoin Core clients

Let's explore the different types of Bitcoin Core clients.

Bitcoind

This is the core client software that can be run as a daemon, and it provides the JSON RPC interface.

Bitcoin-cli

This is the command line feature-rich tool to interact with the daemon; the daemon then interacts with the blockchain and performs various functions. Bitcoin-cli calls only JSON-RPC functions and does not perform any actions on its own on the blockchain.

Bitcoin-qt

This is the Bitcoin Core client GUI. When the wallet software starts up first, it verifies the blocks on the disk and then starts up and shows the following GUI:

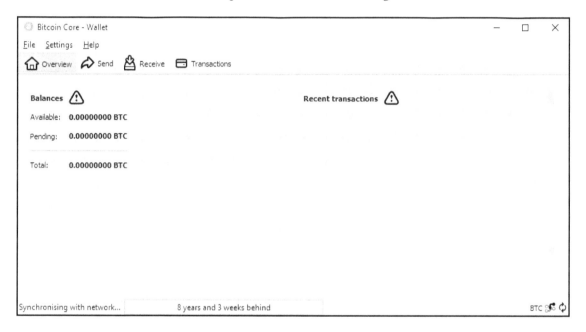

Bitcoin Core QT client, just after installation, showing that blockchain is not in sync

The verification process is not specific to the Bitcoin-qt client; it is performed by the Bitcoind client as well.

Setting up a Bitcoin node

A sample run of the Bitcoin Core installation on Ubuntu is shown here; for other platforms, you can get details from `https://bitcoin.org/en/`:

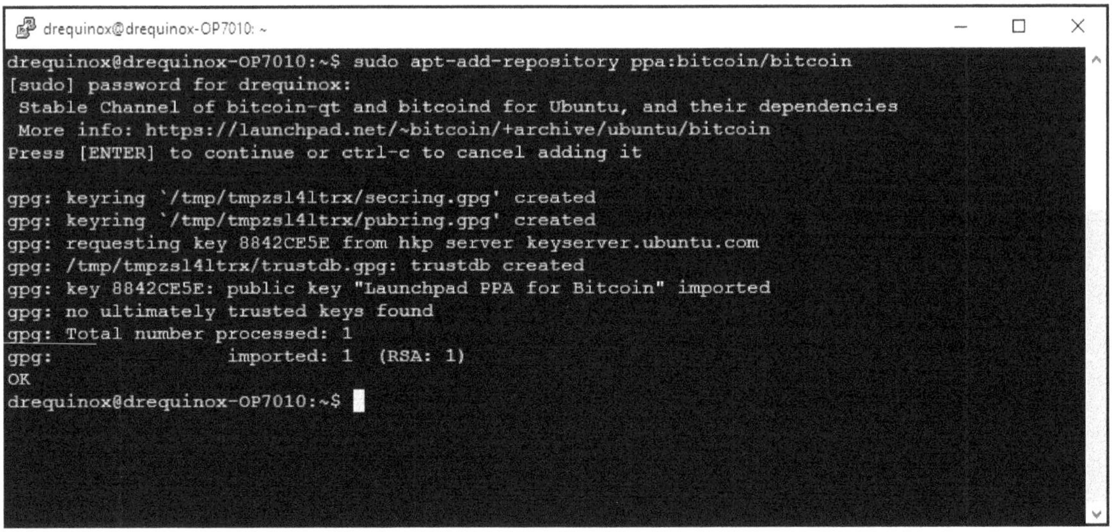

```
drequinox@drequinox-OP7010: ~                                    —    □    ✕

drequinox@drequinox-OP7010:~$ sudo apt-add-repository ppa:bitcoin/bitcoin
[sudo] password for drequinox:
 Stable Channel of bitcoin-qt and bitcoind for Ubuntu, and their dependencies
 More info: https://launchpad.net/~bitcoin/+archive/ubuntu/bitcoin
Press [ENTER] to continue or ctrl-c to cancel adding it

gpg: keyring `/tmp/tmpzsl4ltrx/secring.gpg' created
gpg: keyring `/tmp/tmpzsl4ltrx/pubring.gpg' created
gpg: requesting key 8842CE5E from hkp server keyserver.ubuntu.com
gpg: /tmp/tmpzsl4ltrx/trustdb.gpg: trustdb created
gpg: key 8842CE5E: public key "Launchpad PPA for Bitcoin" imported
gpg: no ultimately trusted keys found
gpg: Total number processed: 1
gpg:               imported: 1  (RSA: 1)
OK
drequinox@drequinox-OP7010:~$ █
```

Bitcoin setup

1. Run the following command:

   ```
   $ sudo apt-get update
   ```

2. Depending on the client required to be installed, users can use either of the following commands, or they can issue both commands at once:

   ```
   $ sudo apt-get install bitcoind
   $ sudo apt-get install bitcoin-qt
   $ sudo apt-get install bitcoin-qt bitcoind
   Reading package lists... Done
   Building dependency tree
   Reading state information... Done
   .......
   ```

Setting up the source code

The Bitcoin source code can be downloaded and compiled if users wish to participate in the Bitcoin code or for learning purpose. The `git` command can be used to download the Bitcoin source code:

```
$ sudo apt-get install git
$ mkdir bcsource
$ cd bcsource
$ git clone https://github.com/bitcoin/bitcoin.git
Cloning into 'bitcoin'...
remote: Counting objects: 78960, done.
remote: Compressing objects: 100% (3/3), done.
remote: Total 78960 (delta 0), reused 0 (delta 0), pack-reused 78957
Receiving objects: 100% (78960/78960), 72.53 MiB | 1.85 MiB/s, done.
Resolving deltas: 100% (57908/57908), done.
Checking connectivity... done.
```

Change the directory to `bitcoin`:

```
$ cd bitcoin
```

After the preceding steps are completed, the code can be compiled:

```
$ ./autogen.sh
$ ./configure.sh
$ make
$ sudo make install
```

Setting up bitcoin.conf

The `bitcoin.conf` file is a configuration file that is used by the Bitcoin Core client to save configuration settings. All command-line options for the `bitcoind` client with the exception of the `-conf` switch can be set up in the configuration file, and when Bitcoin-qt or Bitcoind will start up, it will take the configuration information from that file.

In Linux systems, this is usually found in `$HOME/.bitcoin/`, or it can also specified in the command line using the `-conf=<file>` switch to Bitcoind core client software.

Starting up a node in testnet

The bitcoin node can be started in the testnet mode if you want to test the Bitcoin network and run an experiment. This is a faster network as compared to the live network and has relaxed rules for mining and transactions.

Various faucet services are available for the bitcoin test network. One example is Bitcoin TestNet sandbox, where users can request bitcoins to be paid to their testnet bitcoin address.

 This can be accessed via `https://testnet.manu.backend.hamburg/`.

This is very useful for experimentation with transactions on testnet.

The command line to start up testnet is as follows:

```
bitcoind --testnet -daemon
bitcoin-cli --testnet <command>
bitcoin-qt --testnet
```

Starting up a node in regtest

The regtest mode (regression testing mode) can be used to create a local blockchain for testing purposes.

The following commands can be used to start up a node in the regtest mode:

```
$ bitcoind -regtest -daemon
Bitcoin server starting
```

Blocks can be generated using the following command:

```
$ bitcoin-cli -regtest generate 200
```

Relevant log messages can be viewed in the `.bitcoin/regtest` directory on a Linux system under `debug.log`:

Messages in Bitcoin debug log

After block generation, the balance can be viewed as follows:

```
$ bitcoin-cli -regtest getbalance
8750.00000000
```

The node can be stopped using this:

```
$ bitcoin-cli -regtest stop
Bitcoin server stopping
```

Experimenting with Bitcoin-cli

Bitcoin-cli is the command-line interface available with the Bitcoin Core client and can be used to perform various functions using the RPC interface provided by the Bitcoin Core client:

A sample run of bitcoin-cli getinfo; the same format can be used to invoke other commands

A list of all commands can be shown via the command shown in the following screenshot:

```
drequinox@drequinox-OP7010:~$ bitcoin-cli -testnet help | more
== Blockchain ==
getbestblockhash
getblock "hash" ( verbose )
getblockchaininfo
getblockcount
getblockhash index
getblockheader "hash" ( verbose )
getchaintips
getdifficulty
getmempoolancestors txid (verbose)
getmempooldescendants txid (verbose)
getmempoolentry txid
getmempoolinfo
getrawmempool ( verbose )
gettxout "txid" n ( includemempool )
gettxoutproof ["txid",...] ( blockhash )
gettxoutsetinfo
verifychain ( checklevel numblocks )
verifytxoutproof "proof"

== Control ==
getinfo
help ( "command" )
stop
```

Testnet bitcoin-cli' this is just the first few lines of the output, actual output has many commands

The preceding screenshot shows a list of various command-line options available in Bitcoin-cli, the Bitcoin command-line interface. These commands can be used to query the blockchain and control the local node.

> Starting from Bitcoin Core client 0.10.0, the HTTP REST interface is also available. By default, this runs on the same TCP port 8332 as JSON-RPC.

Bitcoin programming and the command-line interface

Bitcoin programming is a very rich field now. The Bitcoin Core client exposes various JSON RPC commands that can be used to construct raw transactions and perform other functions via custom scripts or programs. Also, the command-line tool, Bitcoin-cli, is available, which makes use of the JSON-RPC interface and provides a rich toolset to work with Bitcoin.

These APIs are also available via many online service providers in the form of bitcoin APIs, and they provide a simple HTTP REST interface. Bitcoin APIs, such as Blockchain.info (`https://blockchain.info/api`) and BitPay (`https://bitpay.com/api`), Block.io (`https://www.block.io`), and many others, offer a myriad of options to develop Bitcoin-based solutions.

Various libraries are available for bitcoin programming. A list is shown as follows, and those of you interested can further explore the libraries.

- **Libbitcoin**: Available at `https://libbitcoin.dyne.org/` and provides powerful command-line utilities and clients
- **Pycoin**: Available at `https://github.com/richardkiss/pycoin`, is a library for Python
- **Bitcoinj**: This library is available at `https://bitcoinj.github.io/` and is implemented in Java

There are many online bitcoin APIs available; the most commonly used APIs are listed as follows:

- `https://bitcore.io/`
- `https://bitcoinjs.org/`
- `https://blockchain.info/api`

As all APIs offer almost similar type of functionality, it can get confusing to decide which one to use. It is also difficult to recommend which API is the best because all APIs are similarly feature-rich. One thing to keep in mind, however, is, security, so whenever you evaluate an API for usage, in addition to assessing the offered features, also evaluate how secure is the design of the API.

Summary

We began this chapter with the introduction of Bitcoin installation, followed by some discussion on source code setup and setup of Bitcoin clients for various networks. After this, we examined various command-line options available in the Bitcoin client.

Finally, we also saw which APIs are available for Bitcoin programming and main points to keep in mind while evaluating APIs for usage.

In the next chapter, we will explore alternative coins that emerged after bitcoin. We will also examine in detail various properties and attributes associated with the alternative cryptocurrencies.

8
Alternative Coins

Since the initial success of Bitcoin, many alternative currency projects have been launched. Bitcoin was released in 2009, and the first alternative coin project (named Namecoin) was introduced in 2011. In 2013 and 2014, the **alternative coins** (**altcoin**) market grew exponentially, and many different types of alternative coin project were started.

A few of those became a success, whereas many were unpopular due to less interest and as a result, they did not succeed. A few were *pump and dump* scams that surfaced for some time but soon disappeared. Alternative approaches to bitcoin can be divided broadly into two categories, based on the primary purpose of their development. If the primary goal is to build a decentralized blockchain platform, they are called alternative chains; if the sole purpose of the alternative project is to introduce a new virtual currency, it is called an altcoin.

Alternative blockchains will be discussed in detail in `Chapter 16`, *Alternative Blockchains*.

This chapter is mainly dedicated to altcoins whose primary purpose is to introduce a new virtual currency (coin) although some material will also be presented on the topic of alternative protocols built on top of bitcoin to provide various services. These include concepts such as Namecoin, where the primary purpose is to provide decentralized naming and identity services instead of currency.

Currently, as of late 2018, there are hundreds of altcoins on the market, and they hold some monetary value such as Namecoin, Zcash, Primecoin, and many others. We will examine some of these later in this chapter. Zcash is a more successful altcoin introduced in 2016. On the other hand, Primecoin did not gain much popularity however it is still used. Many of these alternative projects are direct forks of Bitcoin source code although some of those have been written from scratch. Some altcoins set out to address Bitcoin limitations such as privacy. Some others offer different types of mining, changes in block times, and distribution schemes.

By definition, an altcoin is generated in the case of a hard fork. If bitcoin has a hard fork then the other, older chain is effectively considered another coin. However, there is no established rule as to which chain becomes the altcoin. This has happened with Ethereum, where a hard fork caused a new currency **Ethereum Classic** (**ETC**) to come into existence in addition to the **Ethereum** (**ETH**) currency. Ethereum classic is the old chain and Ether is the new chain after the fork. Such a contentious hard fork is not desirable for some reasons. First it is against the true spirit of decentralization as the Ethereum foundation, a central entity, decided to go ahead with the hard fork even though not everyone agreed to the proposition; second, it also splits the user community due to disagreement over the hard fork. Although a hard fork, in theory, generates an altcoin, it is limited in what it can offer because, even if the change results in a hard fork, usually there are no drastic changes around the fundamental parameters of the coin. They typically remain the same. For this reason, it is desirable to either write a new coin from scratch or fork the bitcoin (or another coin's source code) to create a new currency with the desired parameters and features.

Altcoins must be able to attract new users, trades, and miners otherwise the currency will have no value. Currency gains its value, especially in the virtual currency space, due to the network effect and its acceptability by the community. If a coin fails to attract enough users then soon it will be forgotten. Users can be attracted by providing an initial amount of coins and can be achieved by using various methods. There is, however, a risk that if the new coin does not perform well than their initial investment may be lost. Methods of providing an initial number of altcoins are discussed as follows:

- **Create a new blockchain**: Altcoins can create a new blockchain and allocate coins to initial miners, but this approach is now unpopular due to many scam schemes or *pump and dump* schemes where initial miners made a profit with the launch of a new currency and then disappeared.

- **Proof of Burn (PoB)**: Another approach to allocating initial funds to a new altcoin is PoB, also called a one-way peg or price ceiling. In this method users permanently destroy a certain quantity of bitcoins in proportion to the quantity of altcoins to be claimed. For example, if ten bitcoins were destroyed then altcoins can have a value no greater than some bitcoins destroyed. This means that bitcoins are being converted into altcoins by burning them.
- **Proof of ownership**: Instead of permanently destroying bitcoins, an alternative method is to prove that users own a certain number of bitcoins. This proof of ownership can be used to claim altcoins by tethering altcoin blocks to Bitcoin blocks. For example, this can be achieved by merged mining in which effectively bitcoin miners can mine altcoin blocks while mining for bitcoin without any extra work. Merged mining is explained later in the chapter.
- **Pegged sidechains**: Sidechains, as the name suggests, are blockchains separate from the bitcoin network but bitcoins can be transferred to them. Altcoins can also be transferred back to the bitcoin network. This concept is called a **two-way peg**.

Investing and trading these alternative coins is also a big business, albeit not as big as bitcoin but enough to attract new investors and traders and provide liquidity to the market. Combined altcoin market capitalization is shown as follows:

The graph is generated from `https://coinmarketcap.com/`.

This graph shows that at the time of writing the Combined Altcoin Market Capitalization is more than 200 billion US Dollars

Current market cap (as of March, 2018) of the top 10 coins is shown as follows:

Name	Market Cap	Price USD
Bitcoin	$151,388,873,045	$8,951.83
Ethereum	$68,472,253,587	$697.94
Ripple	$31,340,920,806	$0.801723
Bitcoin Cash	$17,182,167,856	$1,010.08
Litecoin	$9,952,905,688	$179.11
NEO	$5,638,100,000	$86.74
Cardano	$5,450,310,987	$0.210217
Stellar	$5,438,720,268	$0.294010
EOS	$4,347,501,290	$6.04
Monero	$4,211,690,257	$266.40

The data is taken from `https://coinmarketcap.com/`.

There are various factors and new concepts introduced with alternative coins. Many concepts were invented even before bitcoin but with bitcoin were not only new concepts, such as a solution to the Byzantine Generals' Problem, introduced but also previous ideas such as hashcash and **Proof of Work** (**PoW**) were used ingeniously and came into the limelight.

Since then, with the introduction of alternative coin projects, various new techniques and concepts have been developed and introduced. To appreciate the current landscape of alternative cryptocurrencies, it is essential to understand some theoretical concepts first.

Theoretical foundations

In this section, various theoretical concepts are introduced to the reader that has been developed with the introduction of different altcoins in the past few years.

Alternatives to Proof of Work

The PoW scheme in the context of cryptocurrency was first used in Bitcoin and served as a mechanism to provide assurance that a miner had completed the required amount of work to find a block. This process in return provided decentralization, security, and stability for the blockchain. This is the primary vehicle in Bitcoin for providing decentralized distributed consensus. PoW schemes are required to have a much-desired property called **progress freeness**, which means that the reward for consuming computational resources should be random and proportional to the contribution made by the miners. In this case, some chance of winning the block reward is given to even those miners who have comparatively less computational power.

The term progress freeness was introduced by Arvind Narayanan and others in the book *Bitcoin and Cryptocurrency Technologies*. Other requirements for mining computational puzzles include adjustable difficulty and quick verification. Adjustable difficulty ensures that the difficulty target for mining on the blockchain is regulated in response to increased hashing power and the number of users.

Quick verification is a property which means that mining computational puzzles should be easy and quick to verify. Another aspect of the PoW scheme, especially the one used in Bitcoin (Double SHA-256), is that since the introduction of ASICs the power is shifting towards miners or mining pools who can afford to operate large-scale ASIC farms. This power shift challenges the core philosophy of the decentralization of Bitcoin.

There are a few alternatives that have been proposed such as ASIC-resistant puzzles and are designed in such a way that building ASICs for solving this puzzle is infeasible and does not result in a major performance gain over commodity hardware. A common technique used for this purpose is to apply a class of computationally hard problems called **memory hard computational puzzles**. The core idea behind this method is that as puzzle solving requires a large amount of memory, it is not feasible to be implemented on ASIC-based systems.

This technique was initially used in Litecoin and Tenebrix where the Scrypt hash function was used as an ASIC-resistant PoW scheme. Even though this scheme was initially advertised as ASIC resistant, recently Scrypt ASICs have now become available, disproving the original claim by Litecoin. This happened because Scrypt is a memory intensive mechanism and initially it was thought that building ASICs with large memories is difficult due to technical and cost limitations. This is no longer the case, because memory is increasingly becoming cheaper and with the ability to produce nanometer scale circuits it is possible to build ASICs that can run Scrypt algorithm.

Another approach to ASIC resistance is where multiple hash functions are required to be calculated to provide PoW. This is also called a **chained hashing scheme**. The rationale behind this idea is that designing multiple hash functions on an ASIC is not very feasible. The most common example is the X11 memory hard function implemented in Dash. X11 comprises 11 SHA-3 contestants where one algorithm outputs the calculated hash to the next algorithm until all 11 algorithms are used in a sequence. These algorithms include BLAKE, BMW, Groestl, JH, Keccak, Skein, Luffa, CubeHash, SHAvite, SIMD, and ECHO.

This approach did provide some resistance to ASIC development initially, but now ASIC miners are available commercially and support mining of X11 and similar schemes. A recent example is ASIC Baikal Miner, which supports X11, X13, X14, and X15 mining. Other examples include miners such as iBeLink DM384M X11 miner and PinIdea X11 ASIC miner.

Perhaps another approach could be to design self-mutating puzzles that intelligently or randomly change the PoW scheme or its requirements as a function of time. This strategy will make it almost impossible to be implemented in ASICs as it will require multiple ASICs to be designed for each function and also randomly changing schemes would be almost impossible to handle in ASICs. At the moment, it is unclear how this can be achieved practically.

PoW does have various drawbacks, and the biggest of all is energy consumption. It is estimated that the total electricity consumed by Bitcoin miners currently is more than that of Bangladesh at 54.69 **Terawatt hash** (**TWh**). This is huge, and all that power is in a way wasted; in fact, no useful purpose is served except mining. Environmentalists have raised real concerns about this situation. In addition to electricity consumption, the carbon footprint is also very high currently estimated at around 387 kg of CO_2 per transaction.

The following graph shows the scale of Bitcoin energy consumption as compared to other countries. This is only expected to grow and it is estimated that by the end of year 2018, the energy consumption can reach approximately 125 TWh per year.

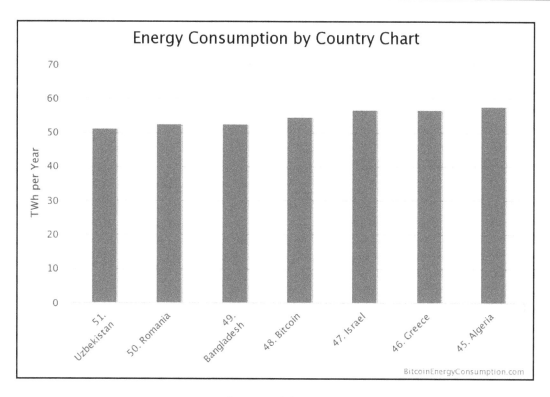

Energy consumption by country

The preceding graph shown is taken from the website which tracks this subject. It is available at `https://digiconomist.net/bitcoin-energy-consumption`.

It has been proposed that PoW puzzles can be designed in such a way that they serve two purposes. First, their primary purpose is in consensus mechanisms and second to perform some useful scientific computation. This way not only can the schemes be used in mining but they can also help to solve other scientific problems too potentially. This proof of useful work has been recently put into practice by Primecoin where the requirement is to find special prime number chains known as Cunningham chains and bi-twin chains. As the study of prime number distribution has special significance in scientific disciplines such as physics, by mining Primecoin miners not only achieve the block reward but also help in finding the special prime numbers.

Proof of Storage

Also known as proof of retrievability, this is another type of proof of useful work that requires storage of a large amount of data. Introduced by Microsoft Research, this scheme provides a useful benefit of distributed storage of archival data. Miners are required to store a pseudo, randomly-selected subset of large data to perform mining.

Proof of Stake (PoS)

This proof is also called virtual mining. This is another type of mining puzzle that has been proposed as an alternative to traditional PoW schemes. It was first proposed in Peercoin in August 2012. In this scheme, the idea is that users are required to demonstrate possession of a certain amount of currency (coins) thus proving that they have a stake in the coin. The simplest form of the stake is where mining is made comparatively easier for those users who demonstrably own larger amounts of digital currency. The benefits of this scheme are twofold; first acquiring large amounts of digital currency is relatively difficult as compared to buying high-end ASIC devices and second it results in saving computational resources. Various forms of stake have been proposed and are briefly discussed in the following subsection.

Various stake types

Different type of stakes will now be introduced in the following subsections.

Proof of coinage

The age of a coin is the time since the coins were last used or held. This is a different approach from the usual form of PoS where mining is made easier for users who have the highest stake in the altcoin. In the coin-age-based approach, the age of the coin (coinage) is reset every time a block is mined. The miner is rewarded for holding and not spending coins for a period of time. This mechanism has been implemented in Peercoin combined with PoW in a creative way.

The difficulty of mining puzzles (PoW) is inversely proportional to the coinage, meaning that if miners consume some coinage using coin-stake transactions, then the PoW requirements are relieved.

Proof of Deposit (PoD)

The core idea behind this scheme is that newly minted blocks by miners are made unspendable for a certain period. More precisely the coins get locked for a set number of blocks during the mining operation. The scheme works by allowing miners to perform mining at the cost of freezing a certain number of coins for some time. This is a type of PoS.

Proof of Burn

As an alternate expenditure to computing power, PoB, in fact, destroys a certain number of bitcoins to get equivalent altcoins. This is commonly used when starting up a new coin projects as a means to provide a fair initial distribution. This can be considered an alternative mining scheme where the value of the new coins comes from the fact that previously a certain number of coins have been destroyed.

Proof of Activity (PoA)

This scheme is a hybrid of PoW and PoS. In this scheme, blocks are initially produced using PoW, but then each block randomly assigns three stakeholders that are required to digitally sign it. The validity of subsequent blocks is dependent on the successful signing of previously randomly chosen blocks.

There is, however, a possible issue known as the nothing at stake problem where it would be trivial to create a fork of the blockchain. This is possible because in PoW appropriate computational resources are required to mine whereas in PoS there is no such requirement; as a result, an attacker can try to mine on multiple chains using the same coin.

Nonoutsourceable puzzles

The key motivation behind this puzzle is to develop resistance again the development of mining pools. Mining pools as previously discussed offer rewards to all participants in proportion to the computing power they consume. However, in this model the mining pool operator is a central authority to whom all the rewards go and who can enforce specific rules. Also, in this model, all miners only trust each other because they are working towards a common goal together in the hope of the pool manager getting the reward. Nonoutsourceable puzzles are a scheme that allows miners to claim rewards for themselves; consequently, pool formation becomes unlikely due to inherent mistrust between anonymous miners.

There are also various other alternatives to PoW, some of which have been described in Chapter 1, *Blockchain 101* and some will be explained later in this book in Chapter 15, *Hyperledger* and Chapter 18, *Scalability and Other Challenges*. As this is an ongoing area of research, new alternatives will keep emerging as blockchain technology grows.

Difficulty adjustment and retargeting algorithms

Another concept that has been introduced with the advent of bitcoin and altcoins is difficulty in retargeting algorithms. In bitcoin, a difficulty target is calculated simply by the following equation; however other coins have either developed their algorithms or implemented modified versions of the bitcoin difficulty algorithm:

$$T = Time\ previous * time\ actual\ /\ 2016 * 10\ min$$

The idea behind difficulty regulation in bitcoin is that a generation of 2016 blocks should take roughly around two weeks (inter-block time should be around 10 minutes). If it takes longer than two weeks to mine 2016 blocks, then the difficulty is decreased, and if it takes less than two weeks to mine 2016 blocks, then the difficulty is increased. When ASICs were introduced due to a high block generation rate, the difficulty increased exponentially, and that is one drawback of PoW algorithms that are not ASIC resistant. This leads to mining power centralization.

This also poses another problem; if a new coin starts now with the same PoW based on SHA-256 as bitcoin uses, then it would be easy for a malicious user to just simply use an ASIC miner and control the entire network. This attack would be more practical if there is less interest in the new altcoin and someone decides to take over the network by consuming adequately high computing resources. This may not be a possible attack if other miners with similar computing power also join the altcoin network because then miners will be competing with each other.

Also, multipools pose a more significant threat where a group of miners can automatically switch to the currency that is becoming profitable. This phenomenon is known as **pool hopping** and can adversely affect a blockchain, and consequently the growth of the altcoin. Pool hopping impacts the network adversely because pool hoppers join the network only when the difficulty is low and they can gain quick rewards; the moment difficulty goes up (or is readjusted) they hop off and then come back again when the difficulty is adjusted back.

For example, if a multipool consumes its resources in quickly mining a new coin, the difficulty will increase very quickly; when the multipool leaves the currency network; it becomes almost unusable because of the fact that now the difficulty has increased to such a level that it is no longer profitable for solo miners and can no longer be maintained. The only fix for this problem is to initiate a hard fork which is usually undesirable for the community.

There are a few algorithms that have come into existence to address this issue and are discussed later in this chapter. All these algorithms are based on the idea of readjusting various parameters in response to hash rate changes; these parameters include the number of previous blocks, the difficulty of previous blocks, the ratio of adjustment, and the number by which the difficulty can be readjusted back or up.

In the following section, readers will be introduced to the few difficulty algorithms being used in and proposed for various altcoins.

Kimoto Gravity Well

This algorithm is used in various altcoins to regulate difficulty. This method was first introduced in Megacoin and used to adjust the difficulty of the network every block adaptively. The logic of the algorithm is shown as follows:

$$KGW = 1 + (0.7084 * pow((double(PastBlocksMass)/double(144)), -1.228))$$

The algorithm runs in a loop that goes through a set of predetermined blocks (*PastBlockMass*) and calculates a new readjustment value. The core idea behind this algorithm is to develop an adaptive difficulty regulation mechanism that can readjust the difficulty in response to rapid spikes in hash rates. **Kimoto Gravity Well** (**KGW**) ensures that the time between blocks remains approximately the same. In Bitcoin, the difficulty is adjusted every 2016 blocks, but in KGW the difficulty is adjusted at every block.

This algorithm is vulnerable to time warp attacks, which, allow an attacker to enjoy less difficulty in creating new blocks temporarily. This attack allows a time window where the difficulty becomes low, and the attacker can quickly generate many coins at a fast rate.

 More information can be found at the link `https://cryptofrenzy.` `wordpress.com/2014/02/09/multipools-vs-gravity-well/`.

Dark Gravity Wave

Dark Gravity Wave (DGW) is a new algorithm designed to address certain flaws such as the time warp attack in the KGW algorithm. This concept was first introduced in Dash, previously known as Darkcoin. It makes use of multiple exponential moving averages and simple move averages to achieve a smoother readjustment mechanism. The formula is shown as follows:

$$2222222/ ((((Difficulty+2600)/9)^2)$$

This formula is implemented in Dash coin, Bitcoin SegWit2X and various other altcoins as a mechanism to readjust difficulty.

DGW version 3.0 is the latest implementation of DGW algorithm and allows improved difficulty retargeting as compared to KGW.

 More information can be found at `https://dashpay.atlassian.net/wiki/spaces/DOC/pages/1146926/Dark+Gravity+Wave`.

DigiShield

This is another difficulty retargeting algorithm that has recently been used in Zcash with slight variations and after adequate experimentation. This algorithm works by going through a fixed number of previous blocks to calculate the time they took to be generated and then readjusts the difficulty to the difficulty of the previous block by dividing the actual time span by averaging the target time. In this scheme, the retargeting is calculated much more rapidly, and also the recovery from a sudden increase or decrease in hash rate is quick. This algorithm protects against multipools, which can result in rapid hash rate increases.

The network difficulty is readjusted every block or every minute depending on the implementation. The key innovation is faster readjusting times as compared to KGW.

Zcash uses DigiShield v3.0 which uses the following formula for difficulty adjustment:

(New difficulty) = (previous difficulty) x SQRT [(150 seconds) / (last solve time)

There is detailed discussion available on it at `https://github.com/zcash/zcash/issues/147#issuecomment-245140908`.

MIDAS

Multi-Interval Difficulty Adjustment System (**MIDAS**) is an algorithm that is comparatively more complex than the algorithms discussed previously due to number of parameters it uses. This method responds much more rapidly to abrupt changes in hash rates. This algorithm also protects against time warp attacks.

The original post about this is now available via web archive at `https://web.archive.org/web/20161005171345/http://dillingers.com/blog/2015/04/21/altcoin-difficulty-adjustment-with-midas/`.

The interested readers can read more about this at the preceding location.

This concludes our introduction to various difficulty adjustment algorithms.

Many alternative cryptocurrencies and protocols have emerged as an attempt to address various limitations in Bitcoin.

Bitcoin limitations

Various limitations in Bitcoin have also sparked some interest in altcoins, which were developed specifically to address limitations in Bitcoin. The most prominent and widely discussed limitation is the lack of anonymity in Bitcoin. We will now discuss some of the limitations of Bitcoin.

Privacy and anonymity

As the blockchain is a public ledger of all transactions and is openly available, it becomes trivial to analyze it. Combined with traffic analyses, transactions can be linked back to their source IP addresses, thus possibly revealing a transaction's originator. This is a big concern from a privacy point of view.

Even though in Bitcoin it is a recommended and common practice to generate a new address for every transaction, thus allowing some level of unlinkability, this is not enough, and various techniques have been developed and successfully used to trace the flow of transactions throughout the network and link them back to their originator. These techniques analyze blockchains by using transaction graphs, address graphs and entity graphs which facilitate linking users back to the transactions, thus raising privacy concerns. The techniques mentioned earlier in the preceding analysis can be further enriched by using publicly available information about transactions and linking them to the actual users. There are open source block parsers available that can be used to extract transaction information, balances, and scripts from the blockchain database.

 A parser available at `https://github.com/mikispag/rusty-blockparser` is written in Rust language and provides advanced blockchain analysis capabilities.

Various proposals have been made to address the privacy issue in Bitcoin. These proposals fall into three categories: mixing protocols, third-party mixing networks, and inherent anonymity.

A brief discussion of each category is presented as follows.

Mixing protocols

These schemes are used to provide anonymity to bitcoin transactions. In this model, a mixing service provider (an intermediary or a shared wallet) is used. Users send coins to this shared wallet as a deposit, and then, the shared wallet can send some other coins (of the same value deposited by some other users) to the destination. Users can also receive coins that were sent by others via this intermediary. This way the link between outputs and inputs is no longer there and transaction graph analysis will not be able to reveal the actual relationship between senders and receivers.

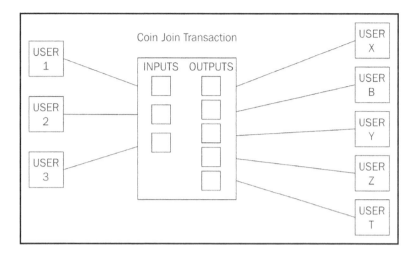

CoinJoin transaction with three users joining their transaction into a single larger CoinJoin transaction

CoinJoin is one example of mixing protocols, where two transactions are joined together to form a single transaction while keeping the inputs and outputs unchanged. The core idea behind CoinJoin is to build a shared transaction that is signed by all participants. This technique improves privacy for all participants involved in the transactions.

Third-party mixing protocols

Various third-party mixing services are available, but if the service is centralized, then it poses the threat of tracing the mapping between senders and receivers because the mixing service knows about all inputs and outputs. In addition to this, fully centralized miners even pose the risk of the administrators of the service stealing the coins.

Various services, with varying degrees of complexity, such as CoinShuffle, Coinmux, and Darksend in Dash (coin) are available that are based on the idea of CoinJoin (mixing) transactions. CoinShuffle is a decentralized alternative to traditional mixing services as it does not require a trusted third party.

CoinJoin-based schemes, however, have some weaknesses, most prominently the possibility of launching a denial of service attack by users who committed to signing the transactions initially but now are not providing their signature, thus delaying or stopping joint transaction altogether.

Inherent anonymity

This category includes coins that support privacy inherently and is built into the design of the currency. The most popular is Zcash, which uses **Zero-Knowledge Proofs** (**ZKP**) to achieve anonymity. It is discussed in detail later in the chapter. Other examples include Monero, which makes use of ring signatures to provide anonymous services.

The next section introduces various enhancements that have been made or are proposed, to extend the Bitcoin protocol.

Extended protocols on top of Bitcoin

Several protocols, discussed in the following sections, have been proposed and implemented on top of Bitcoin to enhance and extend the Bitcoin protocol and use for various other purposes instead of just as a virtual currency.

Colored coins

Colored coins are a set of methods that have been developed to represent digital assets on the Bitcoin blockchain. Coloring a bitcoin refers colloquially to updating it with some metadata representing a digital asset (smart property). The coin still works and operates as a bitcoin but additionally carries some metadata that represents some assets. This can be some information related to the asset, some calculations related to transactions or any arbitrary data. This mechanism allows issuing and tracking specific bitcoins. Metadata can be recorded using the bitcoins OP_RETURN opcode or optionally in multisignature addresses. This metadata can also be encrypted if required to address any privacy concerns. Some implementations also support storage of metadata on publicly available torrent networks which means that virtually unlimited amounts of metadata can be stored. Usually these are JSON objects representing various attributes of the colored coin. Moreover, smart contracts are also supported. One example of such implementation is Colu, which can be found at, http://colu.co/.

Colored coins can be used to represent a multitude of assets including, but not limited to commodities, certificates, shares, bonds, and voting. It should also be noted that to work with colored coins, a wallet that interprets colored coins is necessary and normal Bitcoin wallets will not work. Normal Bitcoin wallets will not work, because they cannot differentiate between *colored coins* and *not colored coins*.

Colored coin wallets can be set up online using a service available at `https://www.coinprism.com/`. By using this service, any digital asset can be created and issued via a colored coin.

The idea of colored coins is very appealing as it does not require any modification to the existing Bitcoin protocol and can make use of the already existing secure Bitcoin network. In addition to the traditional representation of digital assets, there is also the possibility of creating smart assets that behave according to the parameters and conditions defined for them. These parameters include time validation, restrictions on transferability, and fees. This opens the possibility of creating smart contracts which we will discussed in chapter 9, *Smart Contracts*.

A significant use case can be the issuance of financial instruments on the blockchain. This will ensure low transaction fees, valid and mathematically secure proof of ownership, fast transferability without requiring some intermediary, and instant dividend payouts to the investors.

 A rich API is available for colored coins at `http://coloredcoins.org/`.

Counterparty

This is another service that can be used to create custom tokens that act as a cryptocurrency and can be used for various purposes such as issuing digital assets on top of bitcoin blockchain. This is quite a robust platform and runs on bitcoin blockchains at their core but has developed its client and other components to support issuing digital assets. The architecture consists of a counterparty server, counter block, counter wallet, and `armory_utxsvr`. Counterparty works based on the same idea as colored coins by embedding data into regular bitcoin transactions but provides a much more productive library and set of powerful tools to support the handling of digital assets. This embedding is also called **embedded consensus** because the counterparty transactions are embedded within bitcoin transactions. The method of embedding the data is by using `OP_RETURN` opcode in bitcoin.

The currency produced and used by Counterparty is known as XCP and is used by smart contracts as the fee for running the contract. At the time of writing its price is 2.78 USD. XCPs were created by using the PoB method discussed previously.

Counterparty allows the development of smart contracts on Ethereum using solidity language and allows interaction with bitcoin blockchain. To achieve this, BTC Relay is used as a means to provide interoperability between Ethereum and Bitcoin. This is a clever concept where Ethereum contracts can talk to bitcoin blockchain and transactions through BTC Relay. The relayers (nodes that are running BTC Relay) fetch the bitcoin block headers and relay them to a smart contract on the Ethereum network that verifies the PoW. This process verifies that a transaction has occurred on the bitcoin network.

This is available at `http://btcrelay.org/`.

Technically, this is an Ethereum contract that is capable of storing and verifying bitcoin block headers just like bitcoin simple payment verification lightweight clients do by using bloom filters. SPV clients were discussed in detail in the previous chapter. The idea can be visualized with the following diagram:

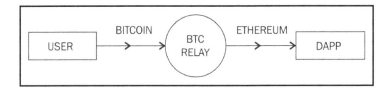

BTC relay concept

Counterparty is available at `http://counterparty.io/`.

Development of altcoins

Altcoin projects can be started very quickly from a coding point of view by simply forking the bitcoin or another coin's source code, but this probably is not enough. When a new coin project is started, several things need to be considered to ensure a successful launch and the coin's longevity. Usually, the code base is written in C++ as was the case with bitcoin, but almost any language can be used to develop coin projects, for example, Golang or Rust.

Writing code or forking the code for an existing coin is the trivial part, the challenging issue is how to start a new currency so that investors and users can be attracted to it. Generally, the following steps are taken in order to start a new coin project.

From a technical point of view, in the case of forking the code of another coin, for example, bitcoin, there are various parameters that can be changed to effectively create a new coin. These parameters are required to be tweaked or introduced in order to create a new coin. These parameters can include but are not limited to the following.

Consensus algorithms

There is a choice of consensus algorithms available, for example PoW used in Bitcoin or PoS, used in Peercoin. There are also other algorithms available such as **Proof of Capacity** (**PoC**) and few others, but PoW and PoS are the most common choices.

Hashing algorithms

This is either SHA-256, Scrypt, X11, X13, X15, or any other hashing algorithm that is adequate for use as a consensus algorithm.

Difficulty adjustment algorithms

Various options are available in this category to provide difficulty retargeting mechanisms. The most prominent examples are KGW, DGW, Nite's Gravity Wave, and DigiShield. Also, all these algorithms can be tweaked based on requirements to produce different results; therefore, many variants are possible.

Inter-block time

This is the time elapsed between the generation of each block. For bitcoin the blocks are generated every 10 minutes, for litecoin it's 2.5 minutes. Any value can be used but an appropriate value is usually between a few minutes; if the generation time is too fast it might destabilize the blockchain, if it's too slow it may not attract many users.

Block rewards

A block reward is for the miner who solves the mining puzzle and is allowed to have a coinbase transaction that contains the reward. This used to be 50 coins in bitcoin initially and now many altcoins set this parameter to a very high number; for example, in Dogecoin it is 10,000, currently.

Reward halving rate

This is another important factor; in bitcoin, it is halved every 4 years and now is set to 12.5 bitcoins. It's a variable number that can be set to any time period or none at all depending on the requirements.

Block size and transaction size

This is another important factor that determines how high or low the transaction rate can be on the network. Block sizes in bitcoin are limited to 1 MB but in altcoins, it can vary depending on the requirements.

Interest rate

This property applies only to PoS systems where the owner of the coins can earn interest at a rate defined by the network in return for some coins that are held on the network as a stake to protect the network. This interest rate keeps inflation under control. If interest rate is too low then it can cause hyperinflation.

Coinage

This parameter defines how long the coin has to remain unspent in order for it to become eligible to be considered stake worthy.

Total supply of coins

This number sets the total limit of the coins that can ever be generated. For example, in Bitcoin the limit is 21 million, whereas in Dogecoin it's unlimited. This limit is fixed by the block reward and halving schedule discussed earlier.

There are two options to create your own virtual currency: forking existing established cryptocurrency source code or writing a new one from scratch. The latter option is less popular but the first option is easier and has allowed the creation of many virtual currencies over the last few years. Fundamentally, the idea is that first a cryptocurrency source code is forked and then appropriate changes are made at different strategic locations in the source code to effectively create a new currency. NEM coin is one of the newly created coins that have their code written entirely from scratch.

In the next section, readers are introduced to some altcoin projects. It is not possible to cover all alternative currencies in this chapter, but a few selected coins are discussed in the following section. Selection is based on longevity, market cap, and innovation. Each coin is discussed from different angles such as theoretical foundations, trading, and mining.

Namecoin

Namecoin is the first fork of the Bitcoin source code. The key idea behind Namecoin is not to produce an altcoin but instead to provide improved decentralization, censorship resistance, privacy, security, and faster-decentralized naming. Decentralized naming services are intended to respond to inherent limitations such as slowness and centralized control in the traditional **Domain Name System** (**DNS**) protocols used on the internet. Namecoin is also the first solution to Zooko's triangle, which was briefly discussed in Chapter 1, *Blockchain 101*.

Namecoin is used to essentially provide a service to register a key/value pair. One major use case of Namecoin is that it can provide a decentralized **Transport Layer Security** (**TLS**) certificate validation mechanism, driven by blockchain-based distributed and decentralized consensus.

It is based on the same technology introduced with bitcoin, but with its own blockchain and wallet software.

 The source code for the Namecoin core is available at
https://github.com/namecoin/namecoin-core.

In summary, Namecoin provides the following three services:

- Secure storage and transfer of names (keys)
- Attachment of some value to the names by attaching up to 520 bytes of data
- Production of a digital currency (Namecoin)

Namecoin also for the first time introduced merged mining, which allows a miner to mine on more than one chain simultaneously. The idea is simple but very effective: miners create a Namecoin block and produce a hash of that block. Then the hash is added to a Bitcoin block and miners solve that block at equal to or greater than the Namecoin block difficulty to prove that enough work has been contributed towards solving the Namecoin block.

The coinbase transaction is used to include the hash of the transactions from Namecoin (or any other altcoin if merged mining with that coin). The mining task is to solve Bitcoin blocks whose coinbase `scriptSig` contains a hash pointer to Namecoin (or any other altcoin) block. This is shown in the following diagram:

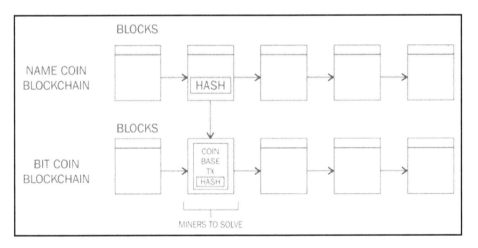

Merged mining visualization

If a miner manages to solve a hash at the bitcoin blockchain difficulty level, the bitcoin block is built and becomes part of the Bitcoin network. In this case, the Namecoin hash is ignored by the bitcoin blockchain. On the other hand, if a miner solves a block at Namecoin blockchain difficulty level a new block is created in the Namecoin blockchain. The core benefit of this scheme is that all the computational power spent by the miners contributes towards securing both Namecoin and Bitcoin.

Trading Namecoins

The current market cap of Namecoin is $29,143,884 USD as per `https://coinmarketcap.com/` in March, 2018. It can be bought and sold at various exchanges such as:

- `https://cryptonit.net/`
- `https://bisq.network`
- `https://www.evonax.com`
- `https://bter.com`

Obtaining Namecoins

Even though Namecoins can be mined independently, they are usually mined as part of bitcoin mining by utilizing the merged mining technique as explained earlier. This way Namecoin can be mined as a by-product of bitcoin mining. Solo mining is no longer profitable as is evident from the following difficulty graph; instead, it is recommended to use merged mining, use a mining pool, or even use a cryptocurrency exchange to buy Namecoin.

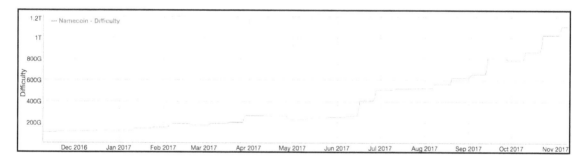

Namecoin difficulty as shown at: https://bitinfocharts.com/comparison/difficulty-nmc.html (since December, 2016)

Various mining pools such as `https://slushpool.com` also offer the option of merged mining. This allows a miner to mine primarily bitcoin but also, as a result, earn Namecoin too.

Another method that can be used to quickly get some Namecoins is to swap your existing coins with Namecoins, for example, if you already have some bitcoins or another cryptocurrency that can be used to exchange with Namecoin.

An online service, `https://shapeshift.io/`, is available that provides this service. This service allows conversion from one cryptocurrency to another, using a simple user-friendly interface.

For example, paying BTC to receive NMC is shown as follows:

1. First the deposit coin is selected, which in this case is bitcoin and coin to be received is selected, which is Namecoin in this case. In the top editbox, the Namecoin address where you want to receive the exchanged Namecoin is entered. In the second editbox, at the bottom the bitcoin refund address is entered, where the coins will be returned to in case the transaction fails for any reason.

2. The exchange rate and miner fee are calculated instantly as soon as the deposit and exchange currency are chosen. Exchange rate is driven by the market conditions whereas miner fee is calculated algorithmically based on the target currency chosen and what the target network's miner would charge.

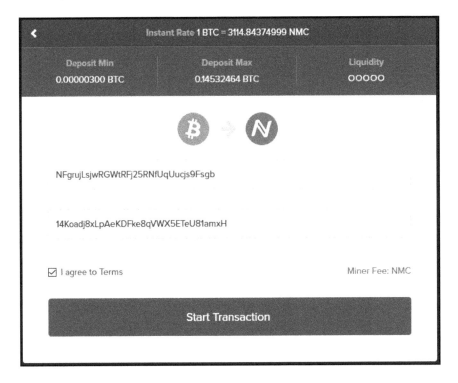

Bitcoin to Namecoin exchange

3. Once **Start Transaction** is clicked, the transaction starts and instructs the user to send the bitcoins to a specific bitcoin address. When the user sends the required amount, the conversion process starts as shown in the following screenshot. This whole process takes few minutes:

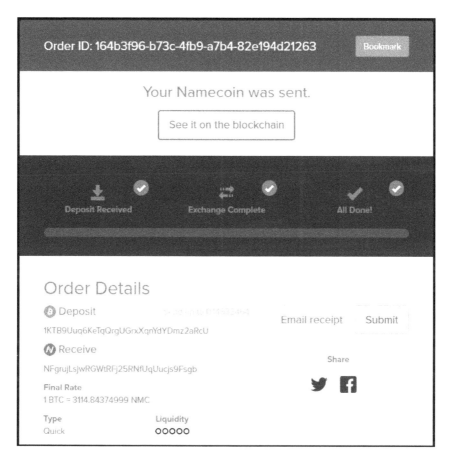

Notification of Namecoin delivery

The preceding screenshot shows that after sending the deposit the exchange occurs and finally **All Done!** message is displayed indicating that the exchange has been successful.

A few other order details are displayed on the page such as what currency was deposited and what was received after exchange. In this case it is Bitcoin to Namecoin exchange. It's also worth noting that relevant addresses are also displayed under each coin icon. There are few other option such **Email receipt** which can be invoked to receive an email receipt of the transaction.

When the process completes, the transactions can be viewed in the Namecoin wallet as shown here:

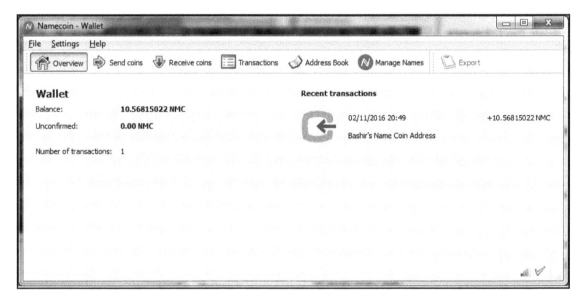

Namecoin wallet

It may take some time (usually around 1 hour) to confirm the transactions; until that time, it is not possible to use the Namecoins to manage names. Once Namecoins are available in the wallet, the **Manage Names** option can be used to generate Namecoin records.

Generating Namecoin records

Namecoin records are in the form of key and value pairs. A name is a lowercase string of the form `d/examplename` whereas a value is a case-sensitive, UTF-8 encoded JSON object with a maximum of 520 bytes. The name should be RFC1035 (`https://tools.ietf.org/html/rfc1035`)-compliant.

A general Namecoin name can be an arbitrary binary string up to 255 bytes long with, 1024-bits of associated identifying information. A record on a Namecoin chain is only valid for around 200 days or 36,000 blocks after which it needs to be renewed. Namecoin also introduced `.bit` top-level domains that can be registered using Namecoin and can be browsed using specialized Namecoin-enabled resolvers. Namecoin wallet software as shown in the following screenshot can be used to register `.bit` domain names.

The name is entered and, after the **Submit** button is pressed, it will ask for configuration information such as DNS, IP, or identity:

Namecoin wallet: domain name configuration

As shown in the following screenshot, `masteringblockchain` will register as `masteringblockchain.bit` on the Namecoin blockchain:

Namecoin wallet: showing registered name

Litecoin

Litecoin is a fork of the bitcoin source code released in 2011. It uses Scrypt as PoW, originally introduced in the Tenebrix coin. Litecoin allows for faster transactions as compared to bitcoin due to its faster block generation time of 2.5 minutes. Also, difficulty readjustment is achieved every 3.5 days roughly due to faster block generation time. The total coin supply is 84 million.

Scrypt is a sequentially memory hard function that is the first alternative to the SHA-256-based PoW algorithm. It was originally proposed as a **Password-Based Key Derivation Function** (**PBKDF**). The key idea is that if the function requires a significant amount of memory to run then custom hardware such as ASICs will require more VLSI area, which would be infeasible to build. The Scrypt algorithm requires a large array of pseudorandom bits to be held in memory and a key is derived from this in a pseudorandom fashion.

The algorithm is based on a phenomenon called **Time-Memory Trade-Off** (**TMTO**). If memory requirements are relaxed, then it results in increased computational cost. Put another way, TMTO shortens the running time of a program if more memory is given to it. This trade-off makes it unfeasible for an attacker to gain more memory because it is expensive and difficult to implement on custom hardware, or if the attacker chooses not to increase memory, then it results in the algorithm running slowly due to high processing requirements. This means that ASICs are difficult to build for this algorithm.

Scrypt uses the following parameters to generate a derived key (*Kd*):

- **Passphrase**: This is a string of characters to hash
- **Salt**: This is a random string that is provided to Scrypt functions (generally all hash functions) in order to provide a defense against brute-force dictionary attacks using rainbow tables
- **N**: This is a memory/CPU cost parameter that must be a power of $2 > 1$
- **P**: This is the parallelization parameter
- **R**: This is the block size parameter
- **dkLen**: This is the intended length of the derived key in bytes

Formally, this function can be written as follows:

$$Kd = scrypt\ (P,\ S,\ N,\ P,\ R,\ dkLen)$$

Before applying the core Scrypt function, the algorithm takes *P* and *S* as input and applies PBKDF2 and SHA-256-based HMAC. Then the output is fed to an algorithm called ROMix, which internally uses the Blockmix algorithm using the Salsa20/8 core stream cipher to fill up the memory which requires large memory to operate, thus enforcing the sequentially memory hard property.

The output from this step of the algorithm is finally fed to the PBKDF2 function again in order to produce a derived key. This process is shown in the following diagram:

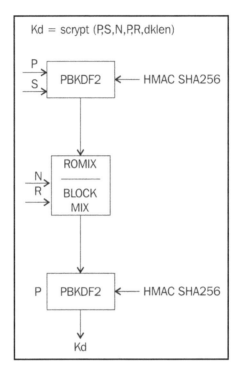

Scrypt algorithm

Scrypt is used in Litecoin mining with specific parameters where *N= 1024, R = 1, P=1*, and *S = random 80 bytes* producing a 256-bit output.

It appears that, due to the selection of these parameters, the development of ASICs for Scrypt for Litecoin mining turned out to be not very difficult. In an ASIC for Litecoin mining, a sequential logic can be developed that takes the data and nonce as input and applies the PBKDF2 algorithm with HMAC-SHA256; then the resultant bit stream is fed into the SALSA20/8 function which produces a hash that again is fed down to the PBKDF2 and HMAC-256 functions to produce a 256-bit hash output. As is the case with bitcoin PoW, in Scrypt also if the output hash is less than the target hash (already passed as input at the start, stored in memory, and checked with every iteration) then the function terminates; otherwise, the nonce is incremented and the process is repeated again until a hash is found that is lower than the difficulty target.

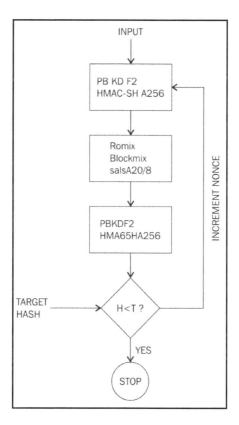

Scrypt ASIC design simplified flowchart

- **Trading litecoin**: As with other coins, trading litecoin is easily carried out on various online exchanges. The current market cap of litecoin is $10,448,974,615. The current price (as of March, 2018) of litecoin is $188.04/LTC.
- **Mining**: Litecoin mining can be carried out solo or in pools. At the moment, ASICs for Scrypt are available that are commonly used to mine Litecoin.

Litecoin mining on a CPU is no longer profitable as is the case with many other digital currencies now. There are online cloud mining providers and ASIC miners available that can be used to mine Litecoin. Litecoin mining started from the CPU, progressed through GPU mining rigs, and eventually now has reached a point where specialized ASIC miners, such as ASIC Scrypt Miner Wolf are available from Ehsminer are now required to be used in the hope of being able to make some coins. Generally, it is true that even with ASICs it is better to mine in pools instead of solo as solo mining is not as profitable as mining in pools due to the proportional rewards scheme used by mining pools. These miners are capable of producing a hashing rate of 2 Gh/s for Scrypt algorithms.

- **Software source code and wallet**: The source code for litecoin is available at `https://github.com/litecoin-project/litecoin`. The Litecoin wallet can be downloaded from `https://litecoin.org/` and can be used just like the Bitcoin core client software.

Primecoin

Primecoin is the first digital currency on the market that introduced a useful PoW, as opposed to Bitcoin's SHA256-based PoW. Primecoin uses searching prime numbers as a PoW. Not all types of prime number meet the requirements to be selected as PoW. Three types of prime numbers (known as Cunningham chain of the first kind, Cunningham chain of the second kind, and bi-twin chains) meet the requirements of a PoW algorithm to be used in cryptocurrencies.

The difficulty is dynamically adjusted via a continuous difficulty evaluation scheme in Primecoin blockchain. The efficient verification of PoW based on prime numbers is also of high importance, because if verification is slow, then PoW is not suitable. Therefore, prime chains are selected as a PoW because finding prime chains gets difficult as the chain increases in length whereas verification remains quick enough to warrant being used as an efficient PoW algorithm.

It is also important that once a PoW has been verified on a block, it must not be reusable on another block. This is accomplished in Primecoin by a combination of PoW certificates and hashing it with the header of the parent block in the child block.

The PoW certificate is produced by linking the prime chain to the block header hash. It also requires that the block header's origin be divisible by the block header hash. If it is, it is divided and after division, the quotient is used as a PoW certificate. Another property of the adjustable difficulty of PoW algorithms is met by introducing difficulty adjustment every block instead of every 2,016, as is the case with bitcoin. This is a smoother approach as compared to bitcoin and allows readjustment in the case of sudden increases in hash power. Also, the total number of coins generated is community-driven, and there is no definite limit on the number of coins Primecoin can generate.

Trading Primecoin

Primecoins can be traded on major virtual currency trading exchanges. The current market cap of Primecoin is $17,482,507 at the time of writing (March, 2018). It is not very large but, because Primecoin is based on a novel idea and there is a dedicated community behind it, this continues to hold some market share.

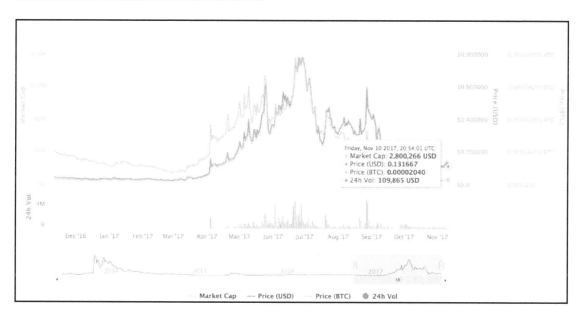

A graph, showing some statistics related to Primecoin

Data sourced from: https://coinmarketcap.com/currencies/primecoin/

Mining guide

The first step is to download a wallet. Primecoin supports native mining within the wallet, just like original Bitcoin clients, but also can be mined on the cloud via various online cloud service providers.

A quick Windows guide is presented as follows, Linux client is also available at `http://primecoin.io/downloads.php`.

1. The first step is to download the Primecoin wallet from `http://primecoin.io/index.php`.

2. Once the wallet is installed and synced with the network, mining can be started by following the next step. A debug window can be opened in the Primecoin wallet by clicking on the **Help menu** and selecting the **Debug window** menu item. Additional help can be invoked through typing `help` in the **Console** window of **Debug window** used to enable the Primecoin mining function:

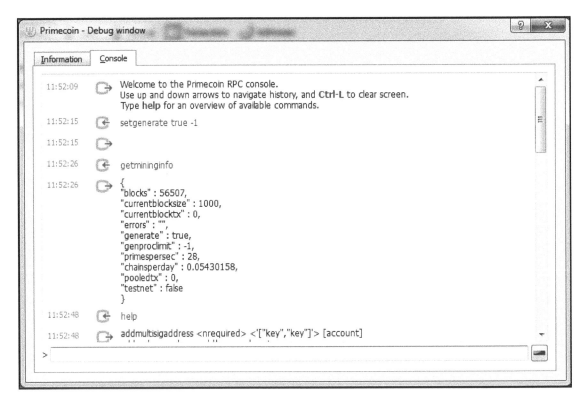

Primecoin mining

3. Once the preceding commands are successfully executed mining will start in solo mode. This may not be very fast and profitable if you have an entry level PC with slower CPU but as this is a CPU mined cryptocurrency the miner can use PCs with powerful CPUs. As an alternative cloud services can be used which host powerful server hardware:

Primecoin wallet software, synching with the network

The Primecoin source code is available at
`https://github.com/primecoin/primecoin.`

Primecoin is a novel concept and the PoW that it has introduced have great scientific significance. It is still in use with a market cap of $17,034,198 USD but it appears that no active development is being carried out to further develop Primecoin as is evident from GitHub inactivity.

Readers can further explore Primecoin by reading the Primecoin whitepaper by Sunny King (pseudonym) at:
`http://primecoin.io/bin/primecoin-paper.pdf.`

Zcash

Zcash was launched on October 28, 2016. This is the first currency that uses a specific type of ZKPs known as **Zero-Knowledge Succinct Non-Interactive Arguments of Knowledge** (**ZK-SNARKs**) to provide complete privacy to the user. These proofs are concise and easy to verify; however, setting up the initial public parameters is a complicated process. The latter include two keys: the proving key and verifying key. The process requires sampling some random numbers to construct the public parameters. The issue is that these random numbers, also called toxic waste, must be destroyed after the parameter generation in order to prevent counterfeiting of Zcash.

For this purpose, the Zcash team came up with a multi-party computation protocol to generate the required public parameters collaboratively from independent locations to ensure that toxic waste is not created. Because these public parameters are required to be created by the Zcash team, it means that the participants in the ceremony are trusted. This is the reason why the ceremony was very open and conducted by making use of a multi-party computation mechanism.

This mechanism has a property whereby all of the participants in the ceremony will have to be compromised to compromise the final parameters. When the ceremony is completed all participants physically destroyed the equipment used for private key generation. This action eliminates any trace of the participants' part of the private key on the equipment.

ZK-SNARKs must satisfy the properties for completeness, soundness, succinctness, and non- interactivity. Completeness means that there is a definite strategy for a prover to satisfy a verifier that an assertion is true. On the other hand, soundness means that no prover can convince the verifier that a false statement is true. Succinctness means that messages passed between the prover and verifier are tiny in size.

Finally, the property non-interactive means that the verification of correctness of an assertion can be carried out without any interaction or very little interaction. Also, being a ZKP, the property of zero-knowledge (discussed in `Chapter 4`, *Public Key Cryptography)* needs to be met too.

Zcash developers have introduced the concept of a **Decentralized Anonymous Payment scheme** (**DAP scheme**) that is used in the Zcash network to enable direct and private payments. The transactions reveal no information about the origin, destination, and amount of the payments. There are two types of addresses available in Zcash, Z address and T address. Z addresses are based on ZKPs and provide privacy protection whereas T addresses are similar to those of bitcoin. A snapshot of various attributes of Zcash (after an initial slow start) is shown as follows:

Attribute	Value
Name	Zcash
Launch date	28/10/16
Main purpose	Currency
Currency Code	ZEC
Maximum coins	21 million
Block time	10 minutes
Consensus facilitation algorithm	Proof of Work (equihash)
Difficulty adjustment algorithm	DigiShield V3 (modified)
Mining hardware	CPU, GPU
Difficulty adjustment period	1 block

Zcash attributes summary

Zcash uses an efficient PoW scheme named asymmetric PoW (Equihash), which is based on the *Generalized Birthday Problem*. It allows very efficient verification. It is a memory-hard and ASIC-resistant function. A novel idea (initial slow mining) has been introduced with Zcash, which means that the block reward increases gradually over a period until it reaches the 20,000th block. This allows for initial scaling of the network and experimentation by early miners, and adjustment by Zcash developers if required. The slow start did have an impact on price due to scarcity as the price of ZEC on its first day of launch reached roughly 25,000 USD. A slightly modified version of the DigiShield difficulty adjustment algorithm has been implemented in Zcash. The formula is shown as follows:

(Next difficulty) = (last difficulty) x SQRT [(150 seconds) / (last solve time)]

Trading Zcash

Zcash can be bought on major digital currency sellers and exchanges such as CryptoGo (`https://cryptogo.com`). Another exchange where Zcash can be bought or sold is Crypto Robot 365 (`https://cryptorobot365.com`). When Zcash was introduced its price was very high. As shown in the following graph, the price soared as high as approximately ten bitcoins per Zcash. Some exchanges carried out orders as high as 2,500 BTC per ZEC. Price of ZEC is around 311 USD at the time writing (March, 2018):

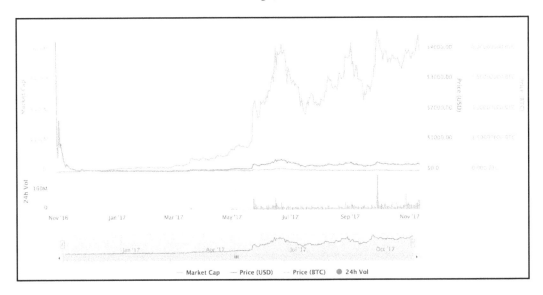

Zcash market cap and price

Mining guide

There are multiple methods to mine Zcash. Currently, CPU and GPU mining are possible. Various commercial cloud mining pools also offer contracts for mining Zcash. To perform solo mining using a CPU, the following steps can be followed on Ubuntu Linux:

1. The first step is to install prerequisites using the following command:

```
$ sudo apt-get install \
  build-essential pkg-config libc6-dev m4 g++-multilib \
  autoconf libtool ncurses-dev unzip git python \
  zlib1g-dev wget bsdmainutils automake
```

If the prerequisites are already installed, a message will display indicating that components are already the newest version. If not already installed or older than the latest package, then the installation will continue, the required packages will be downloaded, and the installation will be completed.

2. Next, run the commands to clone Zcash from Git as shown in the following screenshot:

```
$ git clone https://github.com/zcash/zcash.git
```

Note that if you are running `git` for the first time then you may have to accept a few configuration changes, which will automatically be done for you, but you may have to do this interactively.

This command will clone the Zcash Git repository locally. The output is shown in the following screenshot:

```
drequinox@drequinox-OP7010:~$ git clone https://github.com/zcash/zcash.git
Cloning into 'zcash'...
remote: Counting objects: 56593, done.
remote: Total 56593 (delta 0), reused 0 (delta 0), pack-reused 56593
Receiving objects: 100% (56593/56593), 42.78 MiB | 2.11 MiB/s, done.
Resolving deltas: 100% (43020/43020), done.
Checking connectivity... done.
drequinox@drequinox-OP7010:~$ cd zcash/
drequinox@drequinox-OP7010:~/zcash$ git checkout v1.0.0
Note: checking out 'v1.0.0'.

You are in 'detached HEAD' state. You can look around, make experimental
changes and commit them, and you can discard any commits you make in this
state without impacting any branches by performing another checkout.

If you want to create a new branch to retain commits you create, you may
do so (now or later) by using -b with the checkout command again. Example:

  git checkout -b <new-branch-name>

HEAD is now at 1feaefa... Update network magics for 1.0.0 ❤
```

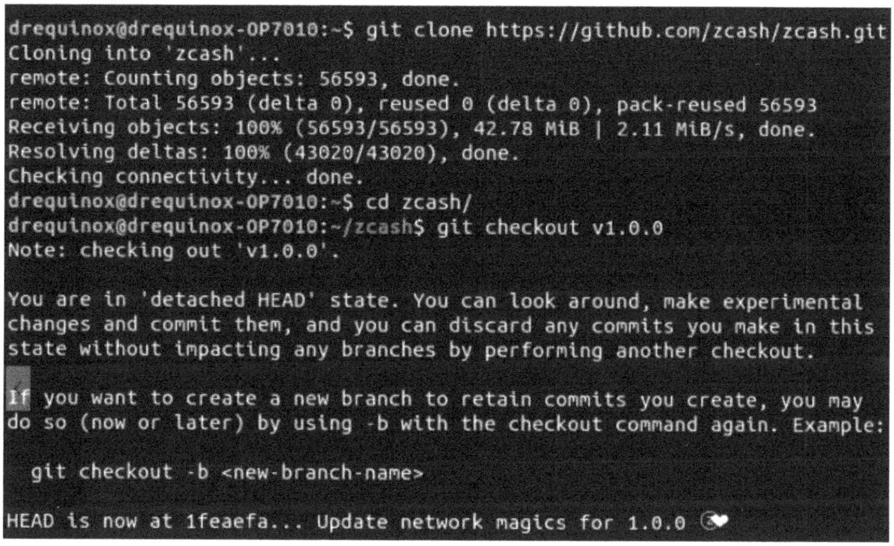

Cloning the Zcash Git repository

3. The next step is to download proving and verifying keys, by using the following commands:

```
$ ./zcutil/fetch-param.sh
```

This command will produce the output similar to the one shown here:

```
drequinox@drequinox-OP7010:~/zcash$ ./zcutil/fetch-params.sh
Zcash - fetch-params.sh

This script will fetch the Zcash zkSNARK parameters and verify their
integrity with sha256sum.

The parameters are currently just under 911MB in size, so plan accordingly
for your bandwidth constraints. If the files are already present and
have the correct sha256sum, no networking is used.

Creating params directory. For details about this directory, see:
/home/drequinox/.zcash-params/README

Retrieving: https://z.cash/downloads/sprout-proving.key
--2016-10-28 21:46:21--  https://z.cash/downloads/sprout-proving.key
Resolving z.cash (z.cash)... 104.236.171.172
Connecting to z.cash (z.cash)|104.236.171.172|:443... connected.
HTTP request sent, awaiting response... 301 Moved Permanently
Location: https://s3.amazonaws.com/zcashfinalmpc/sprout-proving.key [following]
--2016-10-28 21:46:22--  https://s3.amazonaws.com/zcashfinalmpc/sprout-proving.key
Resolving s3.amazonaws.com (s3.amazonaws.com)... 54.231.40.114
Connecting to s3.amazonaws.com (s3.amazonaws.com)|54.231.40.114|:443... connected.
HTTP request sent, awaiting response... 200 OK
Length: 910173851 (868M) [application/octet-stream]
Saving to: '/home/drequinox/.zcash-params/sprout-proving.key.dl'

     0K ........ ........ ........ ........   3% 2.71M 5m8s
 32768K ........ ........ ........ ........   7% 3.58M 4m20s
 65536K ........ ........ ........ ........  11% 2.53M 4m28s
 98304K ........ ........ .................  14% 1.75M 4m59s
131072K ........ ........ ........
```

Zcash setup fetching ZK-SNARK parameters

4. Once this command runs, it will download around 911 MBs of keys into the `~/.zcash-params/` directory. The directory contains files for proving and verifying keys:

```
$ pwd
/home/drequinox/.zcash-params
$ ls -ltr
sprout-verifying.key
sprout-proving.key
```

5. Once the preceding commands are completed successfully, the source code can be built using the following command:

```
$ ./zcutil/build.sh -j$(nproc)
```

This will produce a very long output; if everything goes well it will produce a zcashd binary file. Note that this command takes nproc as the parameter, which is basically a command that finds the number of cores or processors in the system and displays that number. If you don't have that command then replace nproc with the number of processors in your system.

6. Once the build is completed, the next step is to configure Zcash. This is achieved by creating a configuration file with the name zcash.conf in the ~/.zcash/ directory.

A sample configuration file is shown as follows:

```
addnode=mainnet.z.cash
rpcuser=drequinox
rpcpassword=xxxxxxoJNo4o5c+F6E+J4P2C1D5izlzIKPZJhTzdW5A=
gen=1
genproclimit=8
equihashsolver=tromp
```

The preceding configuration enables various features. The first line adds the mainnet node and enables mainnet connectivity. rpcuser and rpcpassword are the username and password for the RPC interface. gen = 1 is used to enable mining. genproclimit is the number of processors that can be used for mining. The last line enables a faster mining solver; this is not required if you want to use standard CPU mining.

7. Now Zcash can be started using the following command:

```
$ ./zcashd --daemon
```

Once started this will allow interaction with the RPC interface via the zcash-cli command-line interface. This is almost the same as the bitcoin command-line interface. Once the Zcash daemon is up-and-running, various commands can be run to query different attributes of Zcash. Transactions can be viewed locally by using the CLI or via a blockchain explorer.

A blockchain explorer for Zcash is available at:
`https://explorer.zcha.in/`.

Address generation

New Z addresses can be generated using the following command:

```
$ ./zcash-cli z_getnewaddress
zcPDBKuuwHJ4gqT5Q59zAMXDHhFoihyTC1aLE5Kz4GwgUXfCBWG6SDr45SFLUsZhpcdvHt7nFmC
3iQcn37rKBcVRa93DYrA
```

Running the `zcash-cli` command with the `getinfo` parameter produces the output shown in the following screenshot. It displays valuable information such as `blocks`, `difficulty`, and `balance`:

```
drequinox@drequinox-OP7010:~/zcash/src$ ./zcash-cli getinfo
{
    "version" : 1000050,
    "protocolversion" : 170002,
    "walletversion" : 60000,
    "balance" : 0.00000000,
    "blocks" : 601,
    "timeoffset" : 0,
    "connections" : 8,
    "proxy" : "",
    "difficulty" : 13748.56014152,
    "testnet" : false,
    "keypoololdest" : 1477688856,
    "keypoolsize" : 101,
    "paytxfee" : 0.00000000,
    "relayfee" : 0.00005000,
    "errors" : "WARNING: abnormally high number of blocks generated, 190 blocks received in the last 4 hours (96 expected)"
}
drequinox@drequinox-OP7010:~/zcash/src$
```

Screenshot displaying the output of getinfo

New T addresses can be generated using the following command:

```
$ ./zcash-cli getnewaddress
t1XRCGMAw36yPVCcxDUrxv2csAAuGdS8Nny
```

GPU mining

Other than CPU mining, a GPU mining option is also available. There is no official GPU miner yet; however open source developers have produced various proofs of concepts and working miners. The Zcash Company held an open competition to encourage developers to build and submit CPU and GPU miners. No winning entry has been announced as of the time of writing.

 Readers can get more information by visiting the website, `https://zcashminers.org/`.

There is another mining: using cloud mining contracts available from various online cloud mining providers. The cloud mining service providers perform mining on the customers' behalf. In addition to cloud mining contracts, miners can use their own equipment to mine via mining pools using stratum or other protocols. One key example is Zcash pool by NiceHash available at: `https://www.nicehash.com`. Using this pool, miners can sell their hash power.

An example of building and using a CPU miner on a Zcash mining pool is shown as follows.

Downloading and compiling nheqminer

The following steps can be used to download and compile `nheqminer` on an Ubuntu Linux distribution:

```
$ sudo apt-get install cmake build-essential libboost-all-dev git clone
https://github.com/nicehash/nheqminer.git
$ cd nheqminer/nheqminer
$ mkdir build
$ cd build
$ cmake .. make
```

Once all the steps are completed successfully, `nhequminer` can be run using the following command:

```
$ ./nhequminer -l eu -u <btc address> -t <number of threads>
```

`nhequminer` releases are available for Windows and Linux at the following link:
`https://github.com/nicehash/nheqminer/releases`

`nheqminer` takes several parameters such as location (`-l`), username (`-u`), and the number of threads to be used for mining (`-t`).

A sample run of Linux miner `nheqminer` for Zcash is shown as follows. In this screenshot the payout is being made to a Bitcoin address for selling hash power:

```
drequinox@drequinox-OP7010:~/nheqminer/nheqminer/build$ ./nheqminer -l eu -u 1PL6gsm49xCFMvrXqgGcee5cdrG119GoWN.worker1 -t 6 -od 0
Equihash CPU Miner for NiceHash v0.1c
Thanks to Zcash developers for providing most of the code
Special thanks to tromp for providing optimized CPU equihash solver

Setting log level to 2
[09:28:53][0x00007f51009cd700] stratum | Connecting to stratum server equihash.eu.nicehash.com:3357
[09:28:53][0x00007f51009cd700] stratum | Connected!
[09:28:53][0x00007f50fafce700] miner#1 | Starting thread #1
[09:28:53][0x00007f50fb7cf700] miner#0 | Starting thread #0
[09:28:53][0x00007f50f8fca700] miner#5 | Starting thread #5
[09:28:53][0x00007f50fa7cd700] miner#2 | Starting thread #2
[09:28:53][0x00007f50f97cb700] miner#4 | Starting thread #4
[09:28:53][0x00007f50f9fcc700] miner#3 | Starting thread #3
[09:28:54][0x00007f51009cd700] stratum | Subscribed to stratum server
[09:28:54][0x00007f51009cd700] miner | Extranonce is 5000e5b80000000000000000005000e5b9ab
[09:28:54][0x00007f51009cd700] stratum | Authorized worker 1PL6gsm49xCFMvrXqgGcee5cdrG119GoWN.worker1
[09:28:54][0x00007f51009cd700] stratum | Target set to 01e1e1e000000000000000000000000000000000000000000000000000000000
[09:28:54][0x00007f51009cd700] stratum | Received new job #000000329b82d287
[09:28:55][0x00007f50fa7cd700] stratum | Submitting share #4, nonce 02000000000000000000000000000000
[09:28:55][0x00007f51009cd700] stratum | Accepted share #4
[09:28:55][0x00007f51009cd700] stratum | Ignoring non-clean job #000000329b82d2cc
[09:28:57][0x00007f50fafce700] stratum | Submitting share #5, nonce 01000000000000000000000000000001
[09:28:57][0x00007f51009cd700] stratum | Accepted share #5
[09:28:59][0x00007f50f97cb700] stratum | Submitting share #6, nonce 04000000000000000000000000000005
```

Using the BTC address to receive payouts for selling hash power

The screenshot, shown here, shows a sample run of `nheqminer` on Windows with payouts being made to a Zcash T address for selling hash power:

Using Zcash T address to receive payouts for selling hash power

Zcash has used ZKPs in an innovative way and they pave the way for future applications that require inherent privacy, such as banking, medicine, or the law.

This section completes the introduction to Zcash; readers can explore more about Zcash online at `https://z.cash`.

Initial Coin Offerings (ICOs)

ICOs are comparable to the **Initial Public Offering** (IPO). Just as an IPO is launched to raise capital by a firm similarly, ICOs are launched to generate money for a start-up project. The critical difference is that IPOs are regulated and fall under the umbrella of securities market (shares in the company) whereas ICOs are unregulated and do not fall under any strict category of already established market structures.

However, there are few suggestions that ICOs should be treated as securities in the light of some scam ICO schemes launched in the last few months and growing concerns around investor protection. Recently the **Securities and Exchange Commission** (**SEC**) suggested that all coins, ICOS, digital assets fall under the definition of *security*. This means that same laws would be applicable to ICOs, Bitcoin and other digital coins that are in applicable to securities. Also, an introduction of formal **Know Your Customer** (**KYC**) and **Anti Money Laundering** (**AML**) is also being recommended to addresses issues related to money laundering. Experts are recommending *Howey Test* as some criteria for any ICO to be considered a security.

Another difference is that ICOs by design usually require investors to invest using cryptocurrencies and payouts are paid using cryptocurrencies, most commonly this is the new token (a new cryptocurrency) introduced by the ICO. This can also be Fiat currency, but most commonly cryptocurrency is used. For example, in the Ethereum crowdfunding campaign a new token, Ether was introduced. The name token sale for crowdfunding is also quite popular and both terms are used interchangeably. ICO are also called crowd sales.

When a new blockchain based application or organization is launched, a new token can be launched with it as a token to access and use the application and also to gain incentives that are paid in the very same token that has been introduced by the ICO. This token is released to the public in exchange of some already established cryptocurrency (for example, Bitcoin or Ethereum) or Fiat currency. The advantage is that when the usage of the application or product launched increases the value of the new token also increases with it. This way the investors who invested initially gain a good incentive.

In the year 2017, ICOs have become a leading tool for raising capital for new start-ups. The first successful ICO was that of Ethereum which raised 18 million USD in 2014. A recent success is Tezos which made 232 million USD in a few weeks' time. Another example is Filecoin which raised more than 250 million USD.

The process of creating a new token has been standardized on Ethereum blockchain thus making it relatively easy to launch an ICO and issue new tokens in exchange of Ether, Bitcoin or some other cryptocurrency. This standard is called ECR20 and is described in the next section. It's worth noting that using ECR20 is not a requirement and a completely new cryptocurrency can be invented on a new blockchain to start an ICO, but ERC20 has been used in various ICOs recently and provides a comparatively easier way to build a token for an ICO.

Recently ICOs have also been offered via platforms other than Ethereum, such as NEM (`https://nem.io`) and Stellar (`https://www.stellar.org`).

ERC20 tokens

ERC20 token is an interface which defines various functions dictating the requirements of the token. It does not, however, provide implementation details and has been left to the implementer to decide. ERC is basically an abbreviation of **Ethereum Request for Comments** which is equivalent to Bitcoin's BIPs for suggesting improvements in Ethereum blockchain.

This is defined under EIP 20, which you can read more about here `https://github.com/ethereum/EIPs/blob/master/EIPS/eip-20-token-standard.md`.

Ethereum is becoming a platform for choice for ICOs due to its ability to create new tokens and with ERC20 standard, it has become even more accessible.

ECR20 token standard defines various functions which describe various properties, rules, and attributes of the new token. These include total supply of the coins, total balance of holders, transfer function, approval and allowance functions.

There are other standards such as ERC223, ERC777 and extension of ERC20 called ERC827 are also under development.
You can refer to the followings links to learn more:

- `https://github.com/ethereum/EIPs/issues/827`
- `https://github.com/ethereum/EIPs/issues/223`
- `https://github.com/ethereum/EIPs/issues/777`

Summary

In this chapter, we introduced you to the overall cryptocurrency landscape. We discussed a number of altcoins in detail, especially Zcash and Namecoin. Cryptocurrencies are a very active area for research, especially around scalability, privacy, and security aspects. Some research has also been conducted to invent new difficulty retargeting algorithms to thwart the threat of centralization in cryptocurrencies.

Further research needs to be carried out in the areas of privacy and especially scalability of blockchain.

Now you should be able to appreciate the concept of altcoins and various motivations behind them. We also discussed few practical aspects, such as mining and starting a new currency project, which hopefully will give you a strong foundation, enabling you to explore these areas further. Altcoins are a fascinating field of research and they open many possibilities for a decentralized future.

In the next chapter, we will see what smart contracts are and discuss relevant ideas and concepts that are essential to fully understand blockchain technology.

9
Smart Contracts

This chapter provides an introduction to smart contracts. This concept is not new, but, with the advent of the blockchain, interest in this idea was revived, and this is now an active area of research in the blockchain space. Due to the cost-saving benefits that smart contracts can bring to the financial services industry by reducing the cost of transactions and simplifying complex contracts, rigorous research is being carried out by various commercial and academic institutions to formalize and make the implementation of smart contracts easy and practical, as soon as possible.

History

Smart contracts were first theorized by Nick Szabo in the late 1990s in an article named *Formalizing and Securing Relationships on Public Networks*, but it was almost 20 years before the real potential and benefits of them were indeed appreciated with the invention of Bitcoin and subsequent development in blockchain technology. Smart contracts are described by Szabo as follows:

> *"A smart contract is an electronic transaction protocol that executes the terms of a contract. The general objectives are to satisfy common contractual conditions (such as payment terms, liens, confidentiality, and even enforcement), minimize exceptions both malicious and accidental, and minimize the need for trusted intermediaries. Related economic goals include lowering fraud loss, arbitrations and enforcement costs, and other transaction costs."*

The original article written by Szabo is available at `http://firstmonday.org/ojs/index.php/fm/article/view/548`.

This idea of smart contracts was implemented in a limited fashion in Bitcoin in 2009, where Bitcoin transactions using a limited scripting language can be used to transfer value between users, over a peer-to-peer network where users do not necessarily trust each other, and there is no need for a trusted intermediary.

Definition

There is no consensus on a standard definition of smart contracts. It is essential to define what a smart contract is, and the following is my attempt to provide a generalized definition of a smart contract:

A smart contract is a secure and unstoppable computer program representing an agreement that is automatically executable and enforceable.

Dissecting this definition further reveals that a smart contract is, in fact, a computer program that is written in a language that a computer or target machine can understand. Also, it encompasses agreements between parties in the form of business logic. Another fundamental idea is that smart contracts are automatically executed when certain conditions are met. They are enforceable, which means that all contractual terms are executed as defined and expected, even in the presence of adversaries.

Enforcement is a broader term that encompasses traditional enforcement in the form of law, along with the implementation of specific measures and controls that make it possible to execute contract terms without requiring any mediation. It should be noted that true smart contracts should not rely on traditional methods of enforcement. Instead, they should work on the principle that code is law, meaning that there is no need for an arbitrator or a third party to control or influence the execution of the smart contract. Smart contracts are self-enforcing as opposed to legally enforceable. This idea might be regarded as a libertarian's dream, but it is entirely possible and is in line with the true spirit of smart contracts.

Moreover, they are secure and unstoppable, which means that these computer programs are required to be designed in such a fashion that they are fault-tolerant and executable in a reasonable amount of time. These programs should be able to execute and maintain a healthy internal state, even if external factors are unfavorable. For example, imagine a typical computer program that is encoded with some logic and executes according to the instruction coded within it. However, if the environment it is running in or external factors it relies on deviate from the normal or expected state, the program may react arbitrarily or simply abort. It is essential that smart contracts be immune to this type of issue.

Secure and unstoppable may well be considered requirements or desirable features but it will provide more significant benefits in the long run if security and unstoppable properties are included in the smart contract definition from the beginning. This will allow researchers to focus on these aspects from the start and will help to build strong foundations on which further research can then be based. There is also a suggestion by some researchers that smart contracts need not be automatically executable; instead, they can be what's called automatable, due to manual human input required in some scenarios. For example, a manual verification of a medical record might be required by a qualified medical professional. In such cases fully automated approaches may not work best. While it is true that in some cases human input and control is desirable, it is not necessary; and, for a contract to be truly smart, in the author's opinion, it has to be fully automated. Some inputs that need to be provided by people can and should also be automated via the use of Oracles. Oracles will be discussed later in this chapter in greater detail.

Smart contracts usually operate by managing their internal state using a state machine model. This allows development of an effective framework for programming smart contracts, where the state of a contract is advanced further based on some predefined criteria and conditions.

There is also on-going debate on the question of whether the code is acceptable as a contract in a court of law. A smart contract is different in presentation from traditional legal prose, albeit they do represent and enforce all contractual clauses but a court of law does not understand the code. This dilemma raises several questions about how a smart contract can be legally binding: can it be developed in such a way that it is readily acceptable and understandable in a court of law? How can dispute resolution be implemented within the code, and is it possible? Moreover, regulatory and compliance requirements is another topic that needs to be addressed before smart contracts can be used as efficiently as traditional legal documents.

Even though smart contracts are named smart, they in fact only do what they have been programmed to do, and that is fine because this very property of smart contracts ensures that smart contracts produce same output every time they are executed. This deterministic nature of smart contracts is highly desirable in blockchain platforms due to consistent consensus requirements. This means that smart contracts are not really smart, they are simply doing what they are programmed to do.

Now this gives rise to a problem whereby a large gap between real world and blockchain world emerges. In this situation, natural language is not understandable by the smart contract, and similarly, the code is not comprehensible to the natural world. So, a few questions arise, how real-life contracts can be deployed on a blockchain? How can this bridge between the real world and smart contract world be built?

The preceding questions open up various possibilities, such as making a smart contract code readable not only by machines but also by people. If humans and machines can both understand the code written in a smart contract it might be more acceptable in legal situations, as opposed to just a piece of code that no-one understands except for programmers. This desirable property is an area ripe for research, and a large research effort has been expended in this area to answer questions around semantics, meaning, and interpretation of a contract.

Some work has already been done to describe natural language contracts formally by combining both smart contract code and natural language contract through linking contract terms with machine understandable elements. This is achieved using a markup language. An example of this type of markup language is called **Legal Knowledge Interchange Format** (**LKIF**), which is an XML schema for representing theories and proofs. It was developed under the ESTRELLA Project in 2008.

 More information is available in a research paper available at `https://doi.org/10.1007/978-3-642-15402-7_30`.

Smart contracts are inherently required to be deterministic. This property will allow a smart contract to be run by any node on a network and achieve the same result. If the result differs even slightly between nodes, then consensus cannot be achieved, and a whole paradigm of distributed consensus on blockchain can fail. Moreover, it is also desirable that the contract language itself is deterministic, thus ensuring integrity and stability of the smart contracts. Deterministic in the sense that there are no non-deterministic functions used in the language, which can produce different results on various nodes.

Let's take, for example, various floating-point operations calculated by various functions in a variety of programming languages can produce different results in different runtime environments. Another example is some math functions in JavaScript, which can produce different results for the same input on different browsers, and which can, in turn, lead to various bugs. This is highly undesirable in smart contracts because if results are inconsistent between nodes, then consensus will never be achieved.

A deterministic feature ensures that smart contracts always produce the same output for a specific input. In other words, programs, when executed, produce a reliable and accurate business logic that is entirely in line with the requirements programmed in the high-level code.

In summary, a smart contract has the following four properties:

- Automatically executable
- Enforceable
- Semantically sound
- Secure and unstoppable

The first two properties are required as a minimum, whereas the latter two may not be required or implementable in some scenarios and can be relaxed. For example, a financial derivatives contract does not perhaps need to be semantically sound and unstoppable but should at least be automatically executable and enforceable at a fundamental level. On the other hand, a title deed needs to be semantically sound and complete, therefore, for it to be implemented as a smart contract, the language must be understood by both computers and people. Ian Grigg addressed this issue of interpretation with his invention of Ricardian contracts, which we will look at in more detail in the next section.

Ricardian contracts

Ricardian contracts were initially proposed in the paper, *Financial Cryptography in 7 Layers*, by *Ian Grigg* in late 1990s. These contracts were used initially in a bond trading and payment system called **Ricardo**. The fundamental idea is to write a document that is understandable and acceptable by both a court of law and computer software. Ricardian contracts address the challenge of issuance of value over the internet. It identifies the issuer and captures all the terms and clauses of the contract in a document to make it acceptable as a legally binding contract.

A Ricardian contract is a document that has several of the following properties:

- A contract offered by an issuer to holders
- A valuable right held by holders and managed by the issuer
- Easily readable by people (like a contract on paper)
- Readable by programs (parsable, like a database)
- Digitally signed
- Carries the keys and server information
- Allied with a unique and secure identifier

The preceding information is based on the original definition by Ian Grigg at `http://iang.org/papers/ricardian_contract.html`.

In practice, the contracts are implemented by producing a single document that contains the terms of the contract in legal prose and the required machine-readable tags. This document is digitally signed by the issuer using their private key. This document is then hashed using a message digest function to produce a hash by which the document can be identified. This hash is then further used and signed by parties during the performance of the contract to link each transaction, with the identifier hash thus serving as an evidence of intent. This is depicted in the next diagram, usually called a bowtie model.

The diagram shows number of elements:

- The **World of Law** on the left-hand side from where the document originates. This document is a written contract in legal prose with some machine-readable tags.
- This document is then hashed.
- The resultant message digest is used as an identifier throughout the **World of Accountancy**, shown on the right-hand side of the diagram.

The **World of Accountancy** element represents any accounting, trading, and information systems that are being used in the business to perform various business operations. The idea behind this flow is that the message digest generated by hashing the document is first used in a so-called **genesis transaction**, or first transaction, and then used in every transaction as an identifier throughout the operational execution of the contract.

This way, a secure link is created between the original written contract and every transaction in the **World of Accounting**:

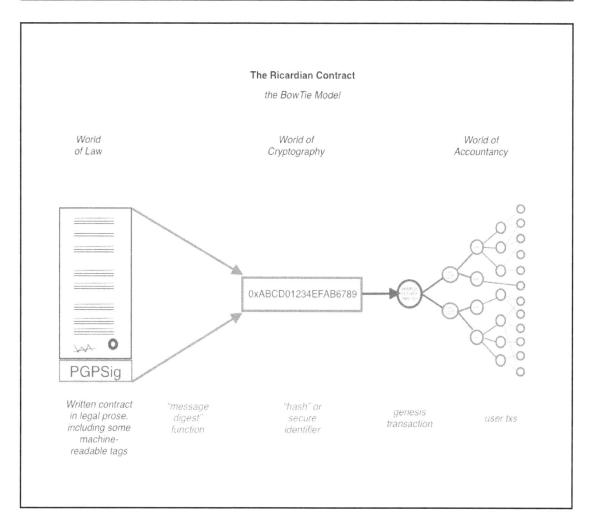

The Ricardian Contract

the BowTie Model

World of Law

World of Cryptography

World of Accountancy

0xABCD01234EFAB6789

PGPSig

Written contract in legal prose. including some machine-readable tags

"message digest" function

"hash" or secure identifier

genesis transaction

user txs

Ricardian contracts, bowtie diagram

A Ricardian contract is different from a smart contract in the sense that a smart contract does not include any contractual document and is focused purely on the execution of the contract. A Ricardian contract, on the other hand, is more concerned with the semantic richness and production of a document that contains contractual legal prose. The semantics of a contract can be divided into two types: operational semantics and denotational semantics.

The first type defines the actual execution, correctness, and safety of the contract, and the latter is concerned with the real-world meaning of the full contract. Some researchers have differentiated between smart contract code and smart legal contracts where a smart contract is only concerned with the execution of the contract. The second type encompasses both the denotational and operational semantics of a legal agreement. It perhaps makes sense to categorize smart contracts based on the difference between semantics, but it is better to consider smart contracts as a standalone entity that is capable of encoding legal prose and code (business logic) in it.

In Bitcoin, a straightforward implementation of basic smart contracts (conditional logic) can be observed, which is entirely oriented towards the execution and performance of the contract, whereas a Ricardian contract is more geared towards producing a document that is understandable by humans with some parts that a computer program can understand. This can be viewed as legal semantics versus operational performance (semantics versus performance) as shown in the following diagram. The diagram shows that Ricardian contracts are more semantically-rich, whereas smart contracts are more performance-rich. This concept was initially proposed by *Ian Grigg* in his paper, *On the intersection of Ricardian and smart contracts*.

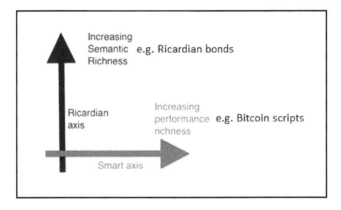

Diagram explaining performance versus semantics are orthogonal issues as described by Ian Grigg; slightly modified to show examples of different types of contracts on both axis

A smart contract is made up to have both of these elements (performance and semantics) embedded together, which completes an ideal model of a smart contract.

A Ricardian contract can be represented as a tuple of three objects, namely *Prose, parameters,* and *code.* Prose represents the legal contract in natural language; code represents the program that is a computer-understandable representation of legal prose; and parameters join the appropriate parts of the legal contract to the equivalent code.

Ricardian contracts have been implemented in many systems, such as CommonAccord, OpenBazaar, OpenAssets, and Askemos.

Smart contract templates

Smart contracts can be implemented for any industry where required, but most current use cases are related to the financial industry. This is due to the fact that blockchain found many use cases in the Finance industry first and sparked great research interest in the financial industry long before other industries. Recent work in smart contract space specific to the financial industry has proposed the idea of smart contract templates. The idea is to build standard templates that provide a framework to support legal agreements for financial instruments.

This idea was proposed by *Clack et al.* in their paper published in 2016, named *Smart Contract Templates: Foundations, design landscape and research directions*. The paper also proposed that domain-specific languages should be built to support design and implementation of smart contract templates. A language named CLACK, a common language for augmented contract knowledge has been proposed, and research has begun to develop the language. This language is intended to be very rich and provide a large variety of functions ranging from supporting legal prose to the ability to be executed on multiple platforms and cryptographic functions.

Recent work to develop smart contract templates that support legally enforceable smart contracts have been carried out by Clack et al. This proposal has been discussed in their research paper *Smart Contract Templates: essential requirements and design options*. The main aim of this paper is to investigate how legal prose can be linked with code using a markup language. It also covers that how smart legal agreements can be created, formatted, executed, and serialized for storage and transmission. This is an ongoing work and an open area for further research and development.

Contracts in the finance industry is not a new concept, and various domain-specific language DSLs are already in use in the financial industry to provide specific language for a specific domain. For example, there are DSLs available that support development of insurance products, represent energy derivatives, or are being used to build trading strategies.

 A comprehensive list of financial domain-specific languages can be found at `http://www.dslfin.org/resources.html`.

It is also important to understand the concept of domain-specific languages as this type of languages can be developed to program smart contracts. These languages are developed with limited expressiveness for a particular application or area of interest. **Domain-specific languages** (**DSLs**) are different from **general-purpose programming languages** (**GPLs**). DSLs have a small set of features that are sufficient and optimized for the domain they are intended to be used in and, unlike GPLs, are usually not used to build general purpose large application programs.

Based on the design philosophy of DSLs it can be envisaged that such languages will be developed specifically to write smart contracts. Some work has already been done, and Solidity is one such language that has been introduced with Ethereum blockchain to write smart contracts. Vyper is another language that has been recently introduced for Ethereum smart contact development.

This idea of domain-specific languages for smart contract programming can be further extended to a *graphical domain-specific language*, a smart contract modeling platform where a domain expert (not a programmer, for example, a front desk dealer) can use a graphical user interface and a canvas to define and draw the semantics and performance of a financial contract. Once the flow has been drawn and completed, it can be emulated first to test and then be deployed from the same system to the target platform, which can be a blockchain. This is also not a new concept, and a similar approach is used in the Tibco StreamBase product, which is a Java-based system used for building event-driven, high-frequency trading systems.

It is proposed that research should also be conducted in the area of developing high-level DSLs that can be used to program a smart contract in a user-friendly graphical user interface, thus allowing a non-programmer domain expert (for example, a lawyer) to design smart contracts.

Oracles

Oracles are an important component of the smart contract ecosystem. The limitation with smart contracts is that they cannot access external data, which might be required to control the execution of the business logic; for example, the stock price of a security product that is required by the contract to release the dividend payments. Oracles can be used to provide external data to smart contracts. An Oracle is an interface that delivers data from an external source to smart contracts.

Depending on the industry and requirements, Oracles can deliver different types of data ranging from weather reports, real-world news, and corporate actions to data coming from **Internet of Things** (**IoT**) devices. Oracles are trusted entities that use a secure channel to transfer data to a smart contract.

Oracles are also capable of digitally signing the data proving that the source of the data is authentic. Smart contracts can then subscribe to the Oracles, and the smart contracts can either pull the data or Oracles can push the data to the smart contracts. It is also necessary that Oracles should not be able to manipulate the data they provide and must be able to provide authentic data. Even though Oracles are trusted, it may still be possible in some cases that the data is incorrect due to manipulation. Therefore, it is necessary that Oracles are unable to change the data. This validation can be provided by using various notary schemes, discussed later in the chapter.

In this approach, an issue can already be seen which perhaps is not desirable in some cases, and that is the issue of trust. How do you trust a third party about the quality and authenticity of data they provide? This is especially true in the financial world, where market data must be accurate and reliable. It might be acceptable for a smart contract designer to accept data for an Oracle that is provided by a large, reputable, trusted third party, but the issue of centralization remains. These types of Oracles can be called standard or simple Oracles. For example, the source of the data can be from a reputable weather reporting agency or airport information system relaying the flight delays.

Another concept that can be used to ensure the credibility of data provided by third-party sources for Oracles is that data is sourced from multiple sources; even users or members of the public that have access and knowledge about some data can provide the required data. This data can then be aggregated and if a high number of same information is fed from multiple sources, then there is a high chance that the data is correct and can be trusted.

Another type of Oracle, which essentially emerged due to the decentralization requirements, is called **decentralized** Oracles. These types of Oracles can be built based on some distributed mechanism. It can also be envisaged that the Oracles can find themselves source data from another blockchain, which is driven by distributed consensus, thus ensuring the authenticity of data. For example, one institution running their private blockchain can publish their data feed via an Oracle that can then be consumed by other blockchains.

Another concept of hardware Oracles is also introduced by researchers where real-world data from physical devices is required. For example, this can be used in telemetry and IoT. However, this approach requires a mechanism in which hardware devices are tamperproof. This can be achieved by providing cryptographic evidence (non-repudiation and integrity) of IoT device's data and anti-tampering mechanism on the IoT device, which renders the device useless in case of tampering attempts.

The following diagram shows a generic model of an Oracle and smart contract ecosystem:

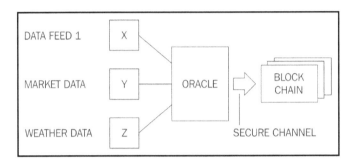

A generic model of an Oracle and smart contract ecosystem

There are platforms available now to enable a smart contract to get external data using an Oracle. There are different methods used by an Oracle to write data into the blockchain depending on the type of blockchain used. For example, in Bitcoin blockchain, an Oracle can write data to a specific transaction and a smart contract can monitor that transaction in the blockchain and read the data.

Various online services such as http://www.oraclize.it/ and https://www.realitykeys.com/ are available that provide Oracle services. Another service at https://smartcontract.com/ is also available, which provides external data and the ability to make payments using smart contracts.

All these services aim to enable the smart contract to get the data it needs to execute and make decisions. To prove the authenticity of the data retrieved by the Oracles from external sources, mechanisms like TLSnotary can be used which produce proof of communication between the data source and the Oracle. This ensures that the data fed back to the smart contract is retrieved from the source.

More details about TLSnotary can be found here: https://tlsnotary.org/.

Smart Oracles

An idea of Smart Oracle has also been proposed by *Ripple labs (codius)*. Its original whitepaper is available at `https://github.com/codius/codius/wiki/Smart-Oracles:-A-Simple,-Powerful-Approach-to-Smart-Contracts`. Smart Oracles are entities just like Oracles, but with the added capability of contract code execution. Smart Oracles proposed by Codius run using Google Native Client, which is a sandboxed environment for running untrusted x86 native code.

Deploying smart contracts on a blockchain

Smart contracts may or may not be deployed on a blockchain, but it makes sense to deploy them on a blockchain due to the distributed and decentralized consensus mechanism provided by blockchain. Ethereum is an example of a blockchain platform that natively supports the development and deployment of smart contracts. Smart contracts on Ethereum blockchain are usually part of a broader application such as **Decentralized Autonomous organization** (**DAOs**).

As a comparison, in Bitcoin blockchain, the transaction timelocks such as the `nLocktime` field and CHECKLOCKTIMEVERIFY (CLTV), CHECKSEQUENCEVERIFY script operator in the Bitcoin transaction can be seen as an enabler of a simple version of a smart contract. These timelocks enable a transaction to be locked until a specified time or until a number of blocks, thus enforcing a basic contract that a certain transaction can only be unlocked if certain conditions (elapsed time or number of blocks) are met. For example, you can implement conditions such as "Pay party X, N amount of bitcoins after 3 months". However, this is very limited and should be only viewed as an example of a basic smart contract. In addition to the example mentioned above, Bitcoin scripting language, though limited, can be used to construct basic smart contracts. One example, of a basic smart contract, is to fund a Bitcoin address that can be spent by anyone who demonstrates a "hash collision attack". This was a contest that was announced on the Bitcointalk forum where bitcoins were set as a reward for whoever manages to find hash collisions (we discussed this concept in `Chapter 4`, *Public Key Cryptography*) for hash functions. This conditional unlocking of Bitcoin only on the demonstration of a successful attack is a basic type of smart contract.

> This idea was presented on the Bitcointalk forum, and more information can be found at `https://bitcointalk.org/index.php?topic=293382.0`. This can also be considered a basic form of smart contract.

Various other blockchain platforms support smart contracts such as Monax, Lisk, Counterparty, Stellar, Hyperledger fabric, corda, and Axoni core. Smart contracts can be developed in various languages. The critical requirement, however, is determinism, which is very important because it is vital that regardless of where the smart contract code executes, it produces the same result every time and everywhere. This requirement of deterministic nature of smart contracts also implies that smart contract code is absolutely bug-free. Validation and verification of smart contracts is an active area of research and detailed discussion of this topic will be presented in Chapter 18, *Scalability and Other Challenges*. Various languages have been developed to build smart contracts such as Solidity, which runs on **Ethereum Virtual Machine** (**EVM**). It's worth noting that there are platforms which already support mainstream languages for smart contract development, such as Lisk which supports JavaScript. However, another prominent example is Hyperledger fabric which supports Golang, Java, and JavaScript for smart contract development.

The DAO

The DAO is one of the highest crowdfunded projects, and it started in April 2016. This was a set of smart contracts written to provide a platform for investment. Due to a bug in the code, this was hacked in June 2016, and an equivalent of 50 million dollars was siphoned out of the DAO into another account.

Even though the term hacked is used above, it was not really hacked, the smart contract simply did what it was asked to do. It was just an unintentional behavior that programmers of the DAO did not foresee. This incident resulted in a hard fork on Ethereum to recover from the attack. It should be noted that the notion of *code is the law* or unstoppable smart contracts should be viewed with some skepticism as the implementation of these concepts is not mature enough to merit full and unquestionable trust. This is evident from the recent events where the Ethereum foundation was able to stop and change the execution of *The DAO* by introducing a hard fork. Though this hard fork was introduced for genuine reasons, it goes against the true spirit of decentralization, and the notion of *code is law*. On the other hand, resistance against this hard fork and some miners who decided to keep mining on the original chain resulted in the creation of Ethereum Classic. This chain is the original, non-forked Ethereum blockchain where *the code is still the law*.

This attack highlights the dangers of not formally and thoroughly testing smart contracts. It also highlights the absolute need to develop a formal language for development and verification of smart contracts. The attack also highlighted the importance of thorough testing to avoid the issues that the DAO experienced. There have been various vulnerabilities discovered in Ethereum recently around the smart contract development language. Therefore, it is of utmost importance that a standard framework is developed to address all these issues. Some work has already begun, for example, an online service at `https://securify.ch`, which provides tools to formally verify smart contract. However, this area is ripe for more research to address limitations in smart contract languages.

Summary

This chapter started by introducing a history of smart contracts and was followed by a detailed discussion on the definition of a smart contract. As there is no agreement on the standard definition of a smart contract, we attempted to introduce a definition that encompasses the crux of smart contracts.

An introduction to Ricardian contracts was also provided, and the difference between Ricardian contracts and smart contracts was explained, highlighting the fact that Ricardian contracts are concerned with the definition of the contract whereas smart contracts are geared towards the actual execution of the contract.

The concept of smart contract templates was discussed, on the subject of which high-quality active research is currently being conducted in academia and industry. Some ideas about the possibility of creating high-level domain-specific languages were also discussed to create smart contracts or smart contract templates. In the later sections of the chapter, the concepts of Oracles were introduced followed by a brief discussion on the DAO, and security issues in DAO and smart contracts.

Discussion regarding formal verification and security of smart contracts will be presented later in this book in `Chapter 18`, *Scalability and Other Challenges*.

In the next chapter, we will introduce Ethereum, which is one of the most popular blockchain platforms which inherently supports smart contracts.

10
Ethereum 101

This chapter is intended to be an introduction to the Ethereum blockchain. Readers will be introduced to the fundamentals and advanced theoretical concepts behind Ethereum. A discussion on various components, protocols, and algorithms relevant to the Ethereum blockchain will be given in detail so that you can understand the theory behind this blockchain paradigm.

We will also cover both a practical and in-depth introduction to wallet software, mining, and setting up Ethereum nodes. Material on various challenges, such as security and scalability faced by Ethereum, will also be introduced. Additionally, trading and market dynamics will be discussed.

Introduction

Vitalik Buterin (`https://vitalik.ca`) conceptualized Ethereum in November, 2013. The critical idea proposed was the development of a Turing-complete language that allows the development of arbitrary programs (smart contracts) for blockchain and decentralized applications. This concept is in contrast to Bitcoin, where the scripting language is limited in nature and allows necessary operations only.

The following table shows all the releases of Ethereum starting from the first release to the planned final release:

Version	Release date
Olympic	May, 2015
Frontier	July 30, 2015
Homestead	March 14, 2016
Byzantium (first phase of Metropolis)	October 16, 2017

Metropolis	To be released
Serenity (final version of Ethereum)	To be released

The first version of Ethereum, called Olympic, was released in May, 2015. Two months later, a version of Ethereum called Frontier was released in July, 2015. After about a year of this release, another version named Homestead with various improvements was released in March, 2016. Latest Ethereum release is called Byzantium which is the first part of the development phase of Ethereum called Metropolis. This release implemented a planned hard fork at block number 4,370,000 on October 16, 2017. The second part of this release called Constantinople is expected in 2018 but there is no exact time frame available yet. The final planned release of Ethereum is called Serenity and is envisaged to introduce the final version of PoS based blockchain instead of PoW. This chapter covers Byzantium, which at the time of writing is the latest version of Ethereum.

Formal specification of Ethereum has been described in the *yellow paper* which can be used to develop Ethereum implementations. We briefly touch on this subject here.

The yellow paper

The Ethereum yellow paper available at `https://ethereum.github.io/yellowpaper/paper.pdf` has been written by *Dr. Gavin Wood, Founder, Ethereum & Parity* (`http://gavwood.com`) and serves as a formal definition of the Ethereum protocol. Anyone can implement an Ethereum client by following the protocol specifications defined in the paper.

While this paper can be somewhat challenging to read, especially for those who do not have a background in algebra or mathematics and are not familiar with mathematical notations, it contains a complete formal specification of Ethereum. This specification can be used to implement a fully compliant Ethereum client.

The list of all symbols with their meanings used in the paper is provided here with the anticipation that it will make reading the Ethereum yellow paper more accessible. Once symbol meanings are known, it becomes quite easy to understand the concepts and specifications described.

Useful mathematical symbols

The following table shows mathematical symbols with their meaning:

Symbol	Meaning	Symbol	Meaning
$\equiv$	Is defined as	$\leq$	Less than or equal to
$=$	Is equal to	σ	Sigma, World state
$\neq$	Is not equal to	μ	Mu, Machine state
$\|\ldots\|$	Length of	Υ	Upsilon, Ethereum state transition function
$\in$	Is an element of	Π	Block level state transition function
$\notin$	Is not an element of	.	Sequence concatenation
$\forall$	For all	$\exists$	There exists
$\cup$	Union	$\wedge$	Contract creation function
$\wedge$	Logical AND	Δ	Increment
:	Such that	$\lfloor \ldots \rfloor$	Floor, lowest element
{}	Set	$\lceil \ldots \rceil$	Ceiling, highest element
()	Function of tuple	$\|\ldots\|$	No of bytes
[]	Array indexing	$\oplus$	Exclusive OR
$\vee$	Logical OR	(a ,b)	Real numbers >= a and < b
>	Is greater than	$\varnothing$	Empty set, null
+	Addition		
-	Subtraction		
Σ	Summation		
{	Describing various cases of if, otherwise		

Now in the next and upcoming sections, we will introduce Ethereum blockchain and its core elements.

Ethereum blockchain

Ethereum, just like any other blockchain, can be visualized as a transaction-based state machine. This definition is mentioned in the Ethereum yellow paper written by Dr. Gavin Wood.

The core idea is that in Ethereum blockchain, a genesis state is transformed into a final state by executing transactions incrementally. The final transformation is then accepted as the absolute undisputed version of the state. In the following diagram, the Ethereum state transition function is shown, where a transaction execution has resulted in a state transition:

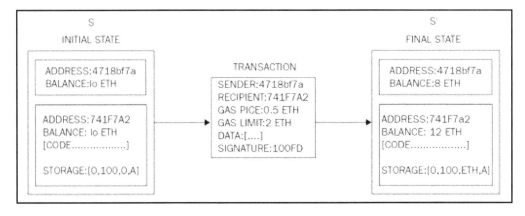

Ethereum State transition function

In the preceding example, a transfer of two Ether from address **4718bf7a** to address **741f7a2** is initiated. The initial state represents the state before the transaction execution, and the final state is what the morphed state looks like. Mining plays a central role in state transition, and we will elaborate the mining process in detail in the later sections. The state is stored on the Ethereum network as the *world state*. This is the global state of the Ethereum blockchain.

More on this will be presented later in the *Nodes and Miners* section in `Chapter 11`, Further Ethereum, in the context of state storage.

Ethereum – bird's eye view

In this section, we will see how Ethereum works from a user's point of view. For this purpose, I will present the most common use case of transferring funds. In our use case, from one user (Bashir) to another (Irshad). We will use two Ethereum clients, one for sending funds and the other for receiving. There are several steps involved in this process which are described here:

1. First either a user requests money by sending the request to the sender, or the sender decides to send money to the receiver. The request can be sent by sending the receivers Ethereum address to the sender. For example, there are two users, Bashir and Irshad. If Irshad requests money from Bashir, then she can send a request to Bashir by using QR code. Once Bashir receives this request he will either scan the QR code or manually type in Irshad's Ethereum address and send Ether to Irshad's address. This request is encoded as a QR code shown in the following screenshot which can be shared via email, text or any other communication methods. You can download Jaxx wallet from `https://jaxx.io`.

QR code as shown in the blockchain wallet application

2. Once Bashir receives this request he will either scan this QR code or copy the Ethereum address in the Ethereum wallet software and initiate a transaction. This process is shown in the following screenshot where the Jaxx Ethereum wallet software on iOS is used to send money to Irshad. The following screenshot shows that the sender has entered both the amount and destination address for sending Ether. Just before sending the Ether the final step is to confirm the transaction which is also shown here:

We have used Jaxx wallet in this example, but you can use any wallet software to achieve the same functionality. There are various wallet software available online, in the iOS App Store and the Android Play Store.

Sending of funds confirmation in Jaxx wallet from Bashir

3. Once the request (transaction) of sending money is constructed in the wallet software, it is then broadcasted to the Ethereum network. The transaction is digitally signed by the sender as proof that he is the owner of the Ether.

4. This transaction is then picked up by nodes called miners on the Ethereum network for verification and inclusion in the block. At this stage, the transaction is still unconfirmed.

5. Once it is verified and included in the block, the PoW process starts. We will explain this process in more detail later in `Chapter 11`, *Further Ethereum*.

6. Once a miner finds the answer to the PoW problem, by repeatedly hashing the block with a new nonce, this block is immediately broadcasted to the rest of the nodes which then verifies the block and PoW.

7. If all the checks pass then this block is added to the blockchain, and miners are paid rewards accordingly.

8. Finally, Irshad gets the Ether, and it is shown in her wallet software. This is shown here:

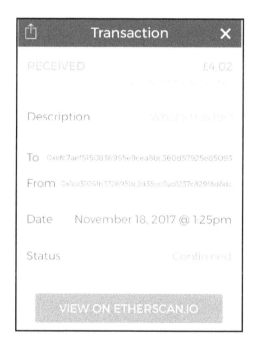

The transaction received in Irshad's blockchain wallet

On the blockchain, this transaction is identified by the following transaction hash:

`0xc63dce6747e1640abd63ee63027c3352aed8cdb92b6a02ae25225666e171009e`

Details regarding this transaction can be visualized from the block explorer at `https://etherscan.io/`, as shown in the following screenshot:

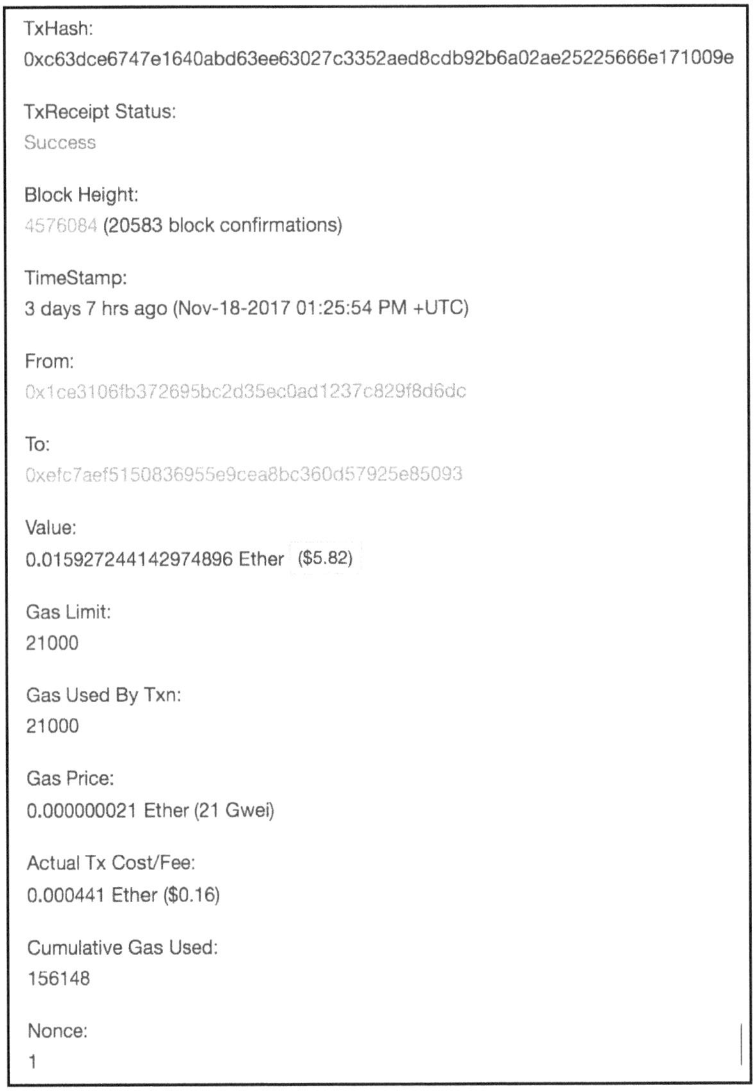

TxHash:
0xc63dce6747e1640abd63ee63027c3352aed8cdb92b6a02ae25225666e171009e

TxReceipt Status:
Success

Block Height:
4576084 (20583 block confirmations)

TimeStamp:
3 days 7 hrs ago (Nov-18-2017 01:25:54 PM +UTC)

From:
0x1ce3106fb372695bc2d35ec0ad1237c829f8d6dc

To:
0xefc7aef5150836955e9cea8bc360d57925e85093

Value:
0.015927244142974896 Ether ($5.82)

Gas Limit:
21000

Gas Used By Txn:
21000

Gas Price:
0.000000021 Ether (21 Gwei)

Actual Tx Cost/Fee:
0.000441 Ether ($0.16)

Cumulative Gas Used:
156148

Nonce:
1

Etherscan Ethereum blockchain block explorer

Note the transaction hash (`TxHash`) at the top, later in the next chapter, and we will use this hash to see that how this transaction is constructed, processed, and stored in the blockchain. This hash is the unique ID of the transaction that can be used to trace this transaction throughout the blockchain network.

With this example, we complete our discussion on the most common usage of Ethereum network of transferring Ether from a user to another. This case was just a quick overview of the transaction process in order to introduce the concept. More in-depth technical details will be explained in the upcoming sections of this chapter where we discuss various components of the Ethereum ecosystem.

In the next section, we will see that what components make up the Ethereum ecosystem. Once we have understood all the theoretical concepts, we will see in detail that how the aforementioned transaction travels through the Ethereum blockchain to reach the beneficiary's address. At this point, we will be able to correlate the technical concepts with the preceding transfer transaction example.

The Ethereum network

The Ethereum network is a peer-to-peer network where nodes participate in order to maintain the blockchain and contribute to the consensus mechanism. Networks can be divided into three types, based on requirements and usage. These types are described in the following subsections.

Mainnet

Mainnet is the current live network of Ethereum. The current version of mainnet is Byzantium (Metropolis) and its chain ID is `1`. Chain ID is used to identify the network. A block explorer which shows detailed information about blocks and other relevant metrics is available at `https://etherscan.io`. This can be used to explore the Ethereum blockchain.

Testnet

Testnet is also called Ropsten and is the widely used test network for the Ethereum blockchain. This test blockchain is used to test smart contracts and DApps before being deployed to the production live blockchain. Moreover, being a test network, it allows experimentation and research. The main testnet is called *Ropsten* which contains all features of other smaller and special purpose testnets that were created for specific releases. For example, other testnets include Kovan and Rinkeby which were developed for testing Byzantium releases. The changes that were implemented on these smaller testnets has also been implemented on Ropsten. Now the Ropsten test network contains all properties of Kovan and Rinkeby.

Private net

As the name suggests, this is the private network that can be created by generating a new genesis block. This is usually the case in private blockchain distributed ledger networks, where a private group of entities start their blockchain and use it as a permissioned blockchain.

The following table shows the list of Ethereum network with their network IDs. These network IDs are used to identify the network by Ethereum clients.

Network name	Network ID / Chain ID
Ethereum mainnet	1
Morden	2
Ropsten	3
Rinkeby	4
Kovan	42
Ethereum Classic mainnet	61

More discussion on how to connect to testnet and how to set up private nets will be discussed in `Chapter 12`, *Ethereum Development Environment*.

Components of the Ethereum ecosystem

The Ethereum blockchain stack consists of various components. At the core, there is the Ethereum blockchain running on the peer-to-peer Ethereum network. Secondly, there's an Ethereum client (usually Geth) that runs on the nodes and connects to the peer-to-peer Ethereum network from where blockchain is downloaded and stored locally. It provides various functions, such as mining and account management. The local copy of the blockchain is synchronized regularly with the network. Another component is the web3.js library that allows interaction with the geth client via the **Remote Procedure Call** (**RPC**) interface.

This architecture can be visualized in the following diagram:

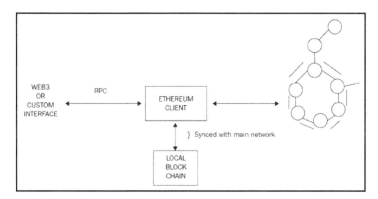

The Ethereum stack showing various components

A formal list of all high-level elements present in the Ethereum blockchain is presented here:

- Keys and addresses
- Accounts
- Transactions and messages
- Ether cryptocurrency/tokens
- The EVM
- Smart contracts

In the following section, we will discuss all of these one by one. We will also discuss relevant technical concepts related to a high-level element within that section.

Keys and addresses

Keys and addresses are used in Ethereum blockchain mainly to represent ownership and transfer of Ether. Keys are used in pairs of private and public type. The private key is generated randomly and is kept secret whereas a public key is derived from the private key. Addresses are derived from the public keys which are a 20-bytes code used to identify accounts.

The process of key generation and address derivation is described here:

1. First, a private key is randomly chosen (256 bits positive integer) under the rules defined by elliptic curve `secp256k1` specification (in the range [1, secp256k1n – 1]).
2. The public key is then derived from this private key using ECDSA recovery function. We will discuss this later in the next section, *Accounts* in the context of digital signatures.
3. An address is derived from the public key which is the right most 160 bits of the Keccak hash of the public key.

An example of how keys and addresses look like in Ethereum is shown here:

1. Private key:
   `b51928c22782e97cca95c490eb958b06fab7a70b9512c38c36974f47b954ffc4`
2. Public key:
   `3aa5b8eefd12bdc2d26f1ae348e5f383480877bda6f9e1a47f6a4afb35cf998ab847f1e3948b1173622dafc6b4ac198c97b18fe1d79f90c9093ab2ff9ad99260`
3. Address: `0x77b4b5699827c5c49f73bd16fd5ce3d828c36f32`

Accounts

Accounts are one of the main building blocks of the Ethereum blockchain. Ethereum, being a *transaction driven state machine*, the state is created or updated as a result of the interaction between accounts and transaction execution. Operations performed between and on the accounts, represent state transitions. The state transition is achieved using what's called the Ethereum state transition function, which works as follows:

1. Confirm the transaction validity by checking the syntax, signature validity, and nonce.

2. The transaction fee is calculated, and the sending address is resolved using the signature. Furthermore, sender's account balance is checked and subtracted accordingly, and nonce is incremented. An error is returned if the account balance is not enough.

3. Provide enough Ether (gas price) to cover the cost of the transaction. We will cover gas and relevant concept shortly in this chapter. This is charged per byte incrementally proportional to the size of the transaction. In this step, the actual transfer of value occurs. The flow is from the sender's account to receiver's account. The account is created automatically if the destination account specified in the transaction does not exist yet. Moreover, if the destination account is a contract, then the contract code is executed. This also depends on the amount of gas available. If enough gas is available, then the contract code will be executed fully; otherwise, it will run up to the point where it runs out of gas.

4. In cases of transaction failure due to insufficient account balance or gas, all state changes are rolled back except for fee payment, which is paid to the miners.

5. Finally, the remainder (if any) of the fee is sent back to the sender as change and fee are paid to the miners accordingly. At this point, the function returns the resulting state which is also stored on the blockchain.

Types of accounts

Two kinds of accounts exist in Ethereum:

- **Externally Owned Accounts (EOAs)**
- **Contract Accounts (CAs)**

The first type is EOAs, and the other is CAs. EOAs are similar to accounts that are controlled by a private key in Bitcoin. CAs are the accounts that have code associated with them along with the private key.

Various properties of each type of accounts are described here:

EOs:

- EOAs has ether balance
- They are capable of sending transactions
- They have no associated code
- They are controlled by private keys
- Accounts contain a key-value store
- They are associated with a human user

CAs:

- CAs have Ether balance.
- They have associated code that is kept in memory/storage on the blockchain.
- They can get triggered and execute code in response to a transaction or a message from other contracts. It is worth noting that due to the Turing-completeness property of the Ethereum blockchain, the code within contract accounts can be of any level of complexity. The code is executed by **Ethereum Virtual Machine** (**EVM**) by each mining node on the Ethereum network. EVM is discussed later in the chapter in the *The EVM* section.
- Also, CAs can maintain their permanent state and can call other contracts. It is envisaged that in the serenity release, the distinction between externally owned accounts and contract accounts may be eliminated.
- They are not intrinsically associated with any user or actor on the blockchain.
- CAs contain a key-value store.

Transactions and messages

A transaction in Ethereum is a digitally signed data packet using a private key that contains the instructions that, when completed, either result in a message call or contract creation. Transactions can be divided into two types based on the output they produce:

- **Message call transactions**: This transaction simply produces a message call that is used to pass messages from one contract account to another.
- **Contract creation transactions**: As the name suggests, these transactions result in the creation of a new contract account. This means that when this transaction is executed successfully, it creates an account with the associated code.

Both of these transactions are composed of some standard fields, which are described here.

- **Nonce**: Nonce is a number that is incremented by one every time a transaction is sent by the sender. It must be equal to the number of transactions sent and is used as a unique identifier for the transaction. A nonce value can only be used once. This is used for replay protection on the network.
- **Gas price**: The gas price field represents the amount of Wei required to execute the transaction. In other words, this is the amount of Wei you are willing to pay for this transaction. This is charged per unit of gas for all computation costs incurred as a result of the execution of this transaction

Wei is the smallest denomination of ether; therefore, it is used to count ether.

- **Gas limit**: The gas limit field contains the value that represents the maximum amount of gas that can be consumed to execute the transaction. The concept of gas and gas limit will be covered later in the chapter in more detail. For now, it is sufficient to say that this is the amount of fee in ether that a user (for example, the sender of the transaction) is willing to pay for computation.
- **To**: As the name suggests, the *to* field is a value that represents the address of the recipient of the transaction. This is a 20-byte value.
- **Value**: Value represents the total number of Wei to be transferred to the recipient; in the case of a contract account, this represents the balance that the contract will hold.
- **Signature**: Signature is composed of three fields, namely *v*, *r*, and *s*. These values represent the digital signature (*R*, *S*) and some information that can be used to recover the public key (*V*). Also, the sender of the transaction can also be determined from these values. The signature is based on ECDSA scheme and makes use of the `secp256k1` curve. The theory of **Elliptic Curve Cryptography** (**ECC**) was discussed in `Chapter 4`, *Public Key Cryptography*. In this section, ECDSA will be presented in the context of its usage in Ethereum.

V is a single byte value that depicts the size and sign of the elliptic curve point and can be either 27 or 28. *V* is used in the ECDSA recovery contract as a recovery ID. This value is used to recover (derive) the public key from the private key. In `secp256k1`, the recovery ID is expected to be either 0 or 1. In Ethereum, this is offset by 27. More details on the `ECDSARECOVER` function will be provided later in this chapter.

R is derived from a calculated point on the curve. First, a random number is picked up, which is multiplied by the generator of the curve to calculate a point on the curve. The *x* coordinate part of this point is *R*. *R* is encoded as a 32-byte sequence. *R* must be greater than 0 and less than the secp256k1n limit (`115792089237316195423570985008687907852837564279074904382605163141518161494337`).

S is calculated by multiplying *R* with the private key and adding it into the hash of the message to be signed and by finally dividing it by the random number chosen to calculate *R*. *S* is also a 32-byte sequence. *R* and *S* together represent the signature.

To sign a transaction, the `ECDSASIGN` function is used, which takes the message to be signed and the private key as an input and produces *V*, a single byte value; *R*, a 32-byte value, and *S*, another 32-byte value. The equation is as follows:

```
ECDSASIGN (Message, Private Key) = (V, R, S)
```

- **Init**: The Init field is used only in transactions that are intended to create contracts, that is, contract creation transactions. This represents a byte array of unlimited length that specifies the EVM code to be used in the account initialization process. The code contained in this field is executed only once when the account is created for the first time, it (init) gets destroyed immediately after that. Init also returns another code section called *body*, which persists and runs in response to message calls that the contract account may receive. These message calls may be sent via a transaction or an internal code execution.
- **Data**: If the transaction is a message call, then the data field is used instead of init, which represents the input data of the message call. It is also unlimited in size and is organized as a byte array.

This structure can be visualized in the following diagram, where a transaction is a tuple of the fields mentioned earlier, which is then included in a transaction **trie** (a modified Merkle-Patricia tree) composed of the transactions to be included. Finally, the root node of transaction trie is hashed using a Keccak 256-bit algorithm and is included in the block header along with a list of transactions in the block.

Transactions can be found in either transaction pools or blocks. In transaction pools, they wait for verification by a node, and in blocks, they are added after successful verification. When a mining node starts its operation of verifying blocks, it starts with the highest paying transactions in the transaction pool and executes them one by one. When the gas limit is reached, or no more transactions are left to be processed in the transaction pool, the mining starts.

In this process, the block is repeatedly hashed until a valid nonce is found such that, once hashed with the block, it results in a value less than the difficulty target. Once the block is successfully mined, it will be broadcasted immediately to the network, claiming success, and will be verified and accepted by the network. This process is similar to Bitcoin's mining process discussed in the previous chapters, `Chapter 5`, *Introducing Bitcoin* and `Chapter 6`, *Bitcoin Network and Payments*. The only difference is that Ethereum's PoW algorithm is ASIC-resistant, known as Ethash, where finding a nonce requires large memory.

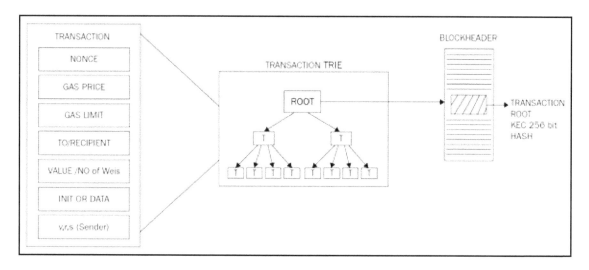

The relationship between transaction, transaction trie and block header

Contract creation transaction

There are a few essential parameters that are required when creating an account. These parameters are listed as follows:

- Sender
- Original transactor (transaction originator)
- Available gas
- Gas price
- Endowment, which is the amount of ether allocated
- A byte array of an arbitrary length
- Initialization EVM code
- Current depth of the message call/contract-creation stack (current depth means the number of items that are already there in the stack)

Addresses generated as a result of contract creation transaction are 160-bit in length. Precisely, as defined in the yellow paper, they are the rightmost 160-bits of the Keccak hash of the RLP encoding of the structure containing only the sender and the nonce. Initially, the nonce in the account is set to zero. The balance of the account is set to the value passed to the contract. Storage is also set to empty. Code hash is Keccak 256-bit hash of the empty string.

The new account is initialized when the EVM code (the Initialization EVM code, mentioned earlier) is executed. In the case of any exception during code execution, such as not having enough gas (running Out Of Gas, OOG), the state does not change. If the execution is successful, then the account is created after the payment of appropriate gas costs.

Since the Ethereum (Homestead) is the result of a contract creation transaction is either a new contract with its balance or no new contract is created with no transfer of value. This is in contrast to versions prior to Homestead, where the contract would be created regardless of the contract code deployment being successful or not due to an out-of-gas exception.

Message call transaction

A message call requires several parameters for execution, which are listed as follows:

- The sender
- The transaction originator
- Recipient
- The account whose code is to be executed (usually same as the recipient)
- Available gas
- Value
- Gas price
- Arbitrary length byte array
- Input data of the call
- Current depth of the message call/contract creation stack

Message calls result in a state transition. The message calls also produce output data, which is not used if transactions are executed. In cases where message calls are triggered by VM code, the output produced by the transaction execution is used. As defined in the yellow paper, message call is the act of passing a message from one account to another. If the destination account has an associated EVM code, then the virtual machine will start, upon the receipt of the message to perform the required operations. If the message sender is an autonomous object (external actor), then the call passes back any data returned from the EVM operation.

The state is altered by transactions. These are created by external factors and are signed and then broadcasted to the Ethereum network. Messages are passed using message calls. A description of a message is described here.

Messages

Messages, as defined in the yellow paper, are the data and value that are passed between two accounts. A **message** is a data packet passed between two accounts. This data packet contains data and value (amount of ether). It can either be sent via a smart contract (autonomous object) or from an external actor (externally owned account) in the form of a transaction that has been digitally signed by the sender.

Contracts can send messages to other contracts. Messages only exist in the execution environment and are never stored. Messages are similar to transactions; however, the main difference is that they are produced by the contracts, whereas transactions are produced by entities external (externally owned accounts) to the Ethereum environment.

A message consists of the components mentioned here:

- The sender of the message
- Recipient of the message
- Amount of Wei to transfer and message to the contract address
- Optional data field (Input data for the contract)
- The maximum amount of gas (startgas) that can be consumed

Messages are generated when CALL or DELEGATECALL opcodes are executed by the code in execution by the contracts.

In the following diagram, the segregation between two types of transaction (contract creation and Message call) is shown:

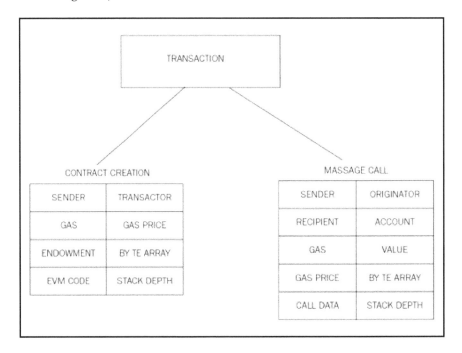

Types of transactions, required parameters for execution

The preceding diagram shows transaction types, which are divided into two types contract creation and message call. Each of these transactions have fields that are shown with each type.

Calls

A call does not broadcast anything to the blockchain; instead, it is a local call to a contract function and runs locally on the node. It is almost like a local function call. It does not consume any gas as it is a read-only operation. It is akin to a dry run or a simulated run. Calls are executed locally on a node VM and do not result in any state change because they are never mined.

Do not confuse a call this with a *message call transaction*, which in fact results in a state change. *Call* basically runs message call transactions in simulated mode and is available in the `web3.js` JavaScript API.

Transaction validation and execution

Transactions are executed after verifying the transactions for validity. Initial tests are listed as follows:

- A transaction must be well-formed and RLP-encoded without any additional trailing bytes
- The digital signature used to sign the transaction is valid
- Transaction nonce must be equal to the sender's account's current nonce gas limit must not be less than the gas used by the transaction
- The sender's account contains enough balance to cover the execution cost.

The transaction substate

A transaction substate is created during the execution of the transaction that is processed immediately after the execution completes. This transaction substate is a tuple that is composed of four items. These items are described here:

- **Suicide set or self-destruct set**: This element contains the list of accounts (if any) that are disposed of after the transaction executes.
- **Log series**: This is an indexed series of checkpoints that allow the monitoring and notification of contract calls to the entities external to the Ethereum environment, such as application frontends. It works like a trigger mechanism that is executed every time a specific function is invoked, or a specific event occurs. Logs are created in response to events occurring in the smart contract. It can also be used as a cheaper form of storage. Events will be covered with practical examples in `Chapter 14`, *Introducing Web3*.
- **Refund balance**: This is the total price of gas in the transaction that initiated the execution. Refunds are not immediately executed; instead, they are used to offset the total execution cost partially.
- **Touched accounts:** This is the set of touched accounts from which empty ones are deleted at the end of the transaction

State storage in the Ethereum blockchain

At a fundamental level, Ethereum blockchain is a transaction and consensus-driven state machine. The state needs to be stored permanently in the blockchain. For this purpose, world state, transactions, and transaction receipts are stored on the blockchain in blocks. We discuss these components next.

The world state

It is a *mapping* between Ethereum addresses and account states. The addresses are 20 bytes (160 bits) long. This mapping is a data structure that is serialized using **Recursive Length Prefix** (**RLP**).

RLP is a specially developed encoding scheme that is used in Ethereum to serialize binary data for storage or transmission over the network and also to save the state in a Patricia tree on storage media. The RLP function takes an item as an input, which can be a string or a list of items and produces raw bytes that are suitable for storage and transmission over the network. RLP does not encode data; instead, its primary purpose is to encode structures.

The account state

The account state consists of four fields: nonce, balance, storage root and code hash and is described in detail here:

- **Nonce**: This is a value that is incremented every time a transaction is sent from the address. In case of contract accounts, it represents the number of contracts created by the account. Contract accounts are one of the two types of accounts that exist in Ethereum; they will be explained later on in the chapter in more detail.
- **Balance**: This value represents the number of Weis which is the smallest unit of the currency (Ether) in Ethereum held by the address.
- **Storage root**: This field represents the root node of a Merkle Patricia tree that encodes the storage contents of the account.
- **Code hash**: This is an immutable field that contains the hash of the smart contract code that is associated with the account. In the case of normal accounts, this field contains the Keccak 256-bit hash of an empty string. This code is invoked via a message call.

The world state and its relationship with accounts trie, accounts, and block header can be visualized in the following diagram. It shows the account data structure in the middle of the diagram, which contains a storage root hash derived from the root node of the account storage trie shown on the left. The account data structure is then used in the world state trie, which is a mapping between addresses and account states.

Accounts trie is a Merkle Patricia tree used to encode the storage contents of an account. The contents are stored as a mapping between Keccak 256-bit hashes of 256-bit integer keys to the RLP-encoded 256-bit integer values.

Finally, the root node of the world state trie is hashed using the Keccak 256-bit algorithm and made part of the block header data structure, which is shown on the right-hand side of the diagram as state root hash.

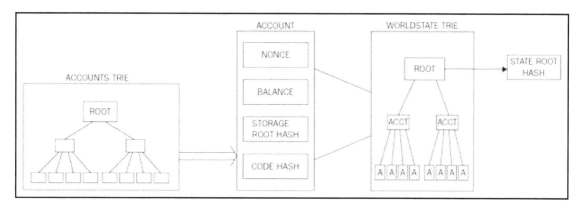

Accounts trie (storage contents of account), account tuple, world state trie, and state root hash and their relationship

Transaction receipts

Transaction receipts are used as a mechanism to store the state after a transaction has been executed. In other words, these structures are used to record the outcome of the transaction execution. It is produced after the execution of each transaction. All receipts are stored in an index-keyed trie. The hash (Keccak 256-bit) of the root of this trie is placed in the block header as the receipts root. It is composed of four elements that are described here:

- **The post-transaction state**: This item is a trie structure that holds the state after the transaction has been executed. It is encoded as a byte array.
- **Gas used**: This item represents the total amount of gas used in the block that contains the transaction receipt. The value is taken immediately after the transaction execution is completed. The total gas used is expected to be a non-negative integer.
- **Set of logs**: This field shows the set of log entries created as a result of transaction execution. Log entries contain the logger's address, a series of log topics, and the log data.

- **The bloom filter**: A bloom filter is created from the information contained in the set of logs discussed earlier. A log entry is reduced to a hash of 256 bytes, which is then embedded in the header of the block as the logs bloom. Log entry is composed of the logger's address, log topics, and log data. Log topics are encoded as a series of 32-byte data structures. Log data is made up of a few bytes of data.

With the release of Byzantium, an additional field returning the success (1) or failure (0) of the transaction is also available.

 More information about this change is available at `https://github.com/ethereum/EIPs/pull/658`.

This process of transaction receipt generation can be visualized in the following diagram:

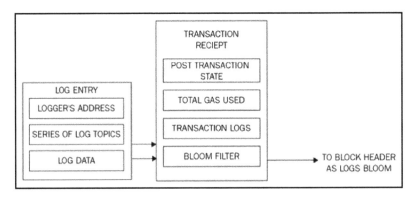

Transaction receipts and logs bloom

As the result of transaction execution process, the state morphs from an initial state to a target state. This concept was discussed briefly at the beginning of the chapter. This state needs to be stored and made available globally in the blockchain. We will see that how this process works in the next section.

Ether cryptocurrency / tokens (ETC and ETH)

As an incentive to the miners, Ethereum also rewards its own native currency called Ether, abbreviated as ETH. After the DAO hack (described later in this chapter), a hard fork was proposed in order to mitigate the issue; therefore, there are now two Ethereum blockchains: one is called Ethereum Classic, and its currency is represented by ETC, whereas the hard-forked version is ETH, which continues to grow and on which active development is being carried out. ETC, however, has its following with a dedicated community that is further developing ETC, which is the unforked original version of Ethereum.

This chapter is focused on ETH, which is the currently the most active and official Ethereum blockchain.

Ether is minted by miners as a currency reward for the computational effort they spend to secure the network by verifying and with validation transactions and blocks. Ether is used within the Ethereum blockchain to pay for the execution of contracts on the EVM. Ether is used to purchase gas as *crypto fuel*, which is required to perform computation on the Ethereum blockchain.

The denomination table is shown as follows:

Unit	Alternative name	Wei value	Number of Weis
Wei	Wei	1 Wei	1
KWei	Babbage	1^3 Wei	1,000
MWei	Lovelace	1^6 Wei	1,000,000
Gwei	Shannon	1^9 Wei	1,000,000,000
Micro Ether	Szabo	1^12 Wei	1,000,000,000,000
Milli Ether	Finney	1^15 Wei	1,000,000,000,000,000
Ether	Ether	1^18 Wei	1,000,000,000,000,000,000

Fees are charged for each computation performed by the EVM on the blockchain. A detailed fee schedule is shown in `Chapter 11`, *Further Ethereum*.

The Ethereum Virtual Machine (EVM)

EVM is a simple stack-based execution machine that runs bytecode instructions to transform the system state from one state to another. The word size of the virtual machine is set to 256-bit. The stack size is limited to 1024 elements and is based on the **Last In, First Out** (**LIFO**) queue. EVM is a Turing-complete machine but is limited by the amount of gas that is required to run any instruction. This means that infinite loops that can result in denial of service attacks are not possible due to gas requirements. EVM also supports exception handling, in case exceptions occur, such as not having enough gas or invalid instructions, in which case the machine would immediately halt and return the error to the executing agent.

EVM is an entirely isolated and sandboxed runtime environment. The code that runs on the EVM does not have access to any external resources, such as a network or filesystem. This results in increased security, deterministic execution and allows untrusted code (anyone can run code) to be run on Ethereum blockchain.

As discussed earlier, EVM is a stack-based architecture. EVM is big-endian by design, and it uses 256-bit wide words. This word size allows for Keccak 256-bit hash and ECC computations.

There are two types of storage available to contracts and EVM. The first one is called memory, which is a byte array. When a contract finishes the code execution, the memory is cleared. It is akin to the concept of RAM. The other type is called storage which is permanently stored on the blockchain. It is a key value store and can be thought of like a hard disk storage.

Memory is unlimited but constrained by gas fee requirements. The storage associated with the virtual machine is a word addressable word array that is nonvolatile and is maintained as part of the system state. Keys and value are 32 bytes in size and storage. The program code is stored in a **virtual read-only memory** (**virtual ROM**) that is accessible using the CODECOPY instruction. The CODECOPY instruction is used to copy the program code into the main memory. Initially, all storage and memory are set to zero in the EVM.

The following diagram shows the design of the EVM where the virtual ROM stores the program code that is copied into main memory using CODECOPY. The main memory is then read by the EVM by referring to the program counter and executes instructions step by step. The program counter and EVM stack are updated accordingly with each instruction execution.

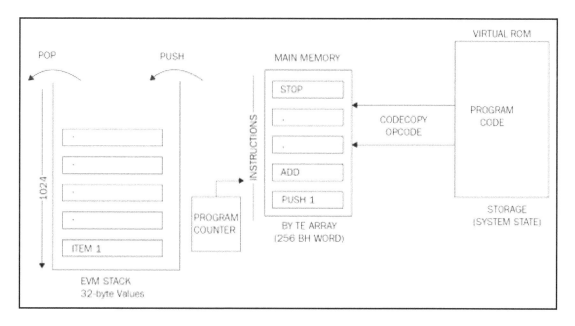

EVM operation

The preceding diagram shows an EVM stack on the left side showing that elements are pushed and popped from the stack. It also shows that a program counter is maintained which is incremented with instructions being read from main memory. Main memory gets the program code from virtual ROM / storage via the CODECOPY instruction.

EVM optimization is an active area of research, and recent research has suggested that EVM can be optimized and tuned to a very fine degree to achieve high performance. Research into the possibility of using **WebAssembly** (**WASM**) is underway already. WASM is developed by Google, Mozilla, and Microsoft and is now being designed as an open standard by the W3C community group.

WASM aims to be able to run machine code in the browser that will result in execution at native speed. Similarly, the aim of EVM 2.1 is to be able to run the EVM instruction set (opcodes) natively in CPUs, thus making it faster and efficient.

More information and GitHub repository of Ethereum flavored WebAssembly is available at https://github.com/ewasm.

Another language called **Joyfully Universal Language for (Inline) Assembly** (**JULIA**) that can compile to various backends such as EVM and eWASM is available and more information can be found here https://solidity.readthedocs.io/en/develop/julia.html#.

Execution environment

There are some key elements that are required by the execution environment to execute the code. The key parameters are provided by the execution agent, for example, a transaction. These are listed as follows:

- System state.
- Remaining gas for execution.
- The address of the account that owns the executing code.
- The address of the sender of the transaction.
- The originating address of this execution (it can be different from the sender).
- The gas price of the transaction that initiated the execution.
- Input data or transaction data depending on the type of executing agent. This is a byte array; in the case of a message call, if the execution agent is a transaction, then the transaction data is included as input data.
- The address of the account that initiated the code execution or transaction sender.
- This is the address of the sender in case the code execution is initiated by a transaction; otherwise, it is the address of the account.
- The value or transaction value. This is the amount in Wei. If the execution agent is a transaction, then it is the transaction value.
- The code to be executed presented as a byte array that the iterator function picks up in each execution cycle.
- The block header of the current block.
- The number of message calls or contract creation transactions currently in execution. In other words, this is the number of CALLs or CREATEs currently in execution.
- Permission to make modifications to the state.

The execution environment can be visualized as a tuple of ten elements, as follows:

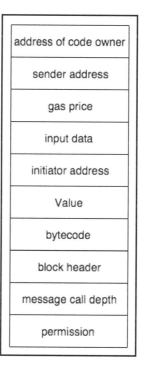

Execution environment tuple

The execution results in producing the resulting state, the gas remaining after the execution, self-destruct or suicide set (described later), log series (described later), and any gas refunds.

Machine state

Machine state is also maintained internally by the EVM. Machine state is updated after each execution cycle of EVM. An iterator function (detailed in the next section) runs in the virtual machine, which outputs the results of a single cycle of the state machine.

Machine state is a tuple that consists of the following elements:

- Available gas
- The program counter, which is a positive integer up to 256 memory contents
- Contents of the stack
- Active number of words in memory
- Contents of the stack

The EVM is designed to handle exceptions and will halt (stop execution) in case any of the following exceptions occur:

- Not having enough gas required for execution invalid instructions
- Insufficient stack items
- Invalid destination of jump opcodes
- Invalid stack size (greater than 1024)

The iterator function

The iterator function mentioned earlier performs various vital functions that are used to set the next state of the machine and eventually the world state. These functions include the following:

- It fetches the next instruction from a byte array where the machine code is stored in the execution environment.
- It adds/removes (PUSH/POP) items from the stack accordingly.
- Gas is reduced according to the gas cost of the instructions/opcodes. It increments the **Program Counter (PC)**.

Machine state can be viewed as a tuple shown in the following diagram:

Machine state tuple

The virtual machine is also able to halt in normal conditions if STOP, SUICIDE, or RETURN Opcodes are encountered during the execution cycle.

Smart contracts

We discussed smart contracts at length in the preceding Chapter 9, *Smart Contracts*. It is sufficient to say here that Ethereum supports the development of smart contracts that run on the EVM. Different languages can be used to build smart contracts, and we will discuss this in the programming section and at a deeper level in Chapter 13, *Development Tools and Frameworks* and Chapter 14, *Introducing Web3*.

There are also various contracts that are available in the precompiled format in Ethereum blockchain to support different functions. These contracts, known as **precompiled contracts** or native contracts are described in the following subsections.

These are not strictly smart contracts in the sense of user programmed solidity smart contracts, but in fact are functions that are available natively on the blockchain to support various computationally intensive tasks. They run on the local node and are coded within the Ethereum client, for example, parity or geth.

Native contracts

There are eight **precompiled contracts** in Ethereum Byzantium release. Here is the list of these contracts and details:

- **The elliptic curve public key recovery function**:

  ECDSARECOVER (Elliptic Curve DSA Recover function) is available at address 0x1. It is denoted as ECREC and requires 3,000 gas fees for execution. If the signature is invalid, then no output is returned by this function. Public key recovery is a standard mechanism by which the public key can be derived from the private key in elliptic curve cryptography.

  The ECDSA recovery function is shown as follows:

  ```
  ECDSARECOVER (H, V, R, S) = Public Key
  ```

  It takes four inputs: H, which is a 32-byte hash of the message to be signed and V, R, and S, which represent the ECDSA signature with the recovery ID and produce a 64-byte public key. V, R, and S have been discussed in detail previously in this chapter.

- **The SHA-256-bit hash function**:

  The SHA-256-bit **hash** function is a precompiled contract that is available at address 0x2 and produces a SHA256 hash of the input. The gas requirement for SHA-256 (SHA256) depends on the input data size. The output is a 32-byte value.

- **The RIPEMD-160-bit hash function**:

  The RIPEMD-160-bit hash function is used to provide **RIPEMD** 160-bit hash and is available at address 0x3. The output of this function is a 20-byte value. The **gas** requirement, similar to SHA-256, is dependent on the amount of input data.

- **The identity/datacopy function**:

  The identity function is available at address 0x4 and is denoted by the ID. It simply defines output as input; in other words, whatever input is given to the ID function, it will output the same value. The gas requirement is calculated by a simple formula: $15 + 3 \ [Id/32]$ where Id is the input data. This means that at a high level, the gas requirement is dependent on the size of the input data albeit with some calculation performed, as shown in the preceding equation.

- **Big mod exponentiation function**:

  This function implements a native **big integer exponential modular** operation. This functionality allows for **RSA** signature verification and other cryptographic operations. This is available at address 0x05.

- **Elliptic Curve (EC) point addition function**:

  We discussed elliptic curve addition in detail at a theoretical level in Chapter 4, *Public Key Cryptography*. This is the implementation of the same **EC point addition** function. This contract is available at address 0x06.

- **Elliptic Curve (EC) scalar multiplication**:

  We discussed EC multiplication (point doubling) in detail at a theoretical level in chapter 4, *Public Key Cryptography*. This is the implementation of the same EC point multiplication function. Both EC addition and doubling functions allow for ZK-SNARKS and implementation of other cryptographic constructs. This contract is available at 0x07.

- **Elliptic Curve (EC) pairing**:

  EC pairing functionality allows for performing EC pairing (bilinear maps) operations which enables ZK-SNARKS verification. This contract is available at address 0x08.

All the aforementioned precompiled contracts can potentially become native extensions and can be included in the EVM opcodes in the future.

Summary

This chapter started with a discussion on the history of Ethereum, the motivation behind Ethereum development, and Ethereum clients. Then, you were introduced to the core concepts of the Ethereum blockchain, such as state machine model, world and machine state, accounts, and types of accounts. Moreover, a detailed introduction to the core components of the EVM was also presented.

With research being carried out on topics such as scalability, optimization, throughput, capacity, and security, it is envisaged that over time, Ethereum will evolve into a more robust, user-friendly, and stable blockchain ecosystem.

In the next chapter, we will continue to explore Ethereum concepts and will look at more concepts such as programming languages, blockchain data structures, mining and various Ethereum clients.

11
Further Ethereum

This chapter is the continuation of the previous chapter. We will examine more concepts of Ethereum such as programming languages that can be used to program smart contracts on Ethereum.

We will also cover both a practical and theoretical in-depth introduction to wallet software, mining, and setting up Ethereum nodes. Material on various challenges, such as security and scalability faced by Ethereum, will also be introduced. Additionally, trading and market dynamics will be discussed. Moreover, prominent advanced supporting protocols such as Swarm and Whisper will also be introduced in this chapter.

Ethereum has several programming languages built-in to support smart contract development. We will start with programming languages and will gradually discuss other relevant topics.

This chapter includes discussion of the elements of Ethereum blockchain that we started in the previous chapter, `Chapter 10`, *Ethereum 101*. These elements include

- Programming languages
- Blocks and Blockchain
- Nodes and miners
- Wallets and client software
- APIs (Web3)
- Supporting protocols

First, we will introduce programming languages which are used to develop smart contracts on the Ethereum blockchain.

Programming languages

Code for smart contracts in Ethereum is written in a high-level language such as Serpent, LLL, Solidity, or Viper and is converted into the bytecode that EVM understands for it to be executed.

Solidity is one of the high-level languages that has been developed for Ethereum with JavaScript like syntax to write code for smart contracts. Once the code is written, it is compiled into bytecode that's understandable by the EVM using the Solidity compiler called **solc**.

Official Solidity documentation is available at
`http://solidity.readthedocs.io/en/latest/`.

Low-level Lisp-like Language (**LLL**) is another language that is used to write smart contract code. **Serpent** is a Python-like high-level language that can be used to write smart contracts for Ethereum. **Vyper** is a newer language which has been developed from scratch to achieve a secure, simple, and auditable language.

More information regarding Vyper is available at `https://github.com/ethereum/vyper`.

LLL and Serpent are no longer supported by the community and their usage has almost diminished. Most commonly used language is Solidity, which we will discuss at length in this chapter.

For example, a simple program in Solidity is shown as follows:

```
pragma solidity ^0.4.0;
contract Test1
{
    uint x=2;
    function addition1(uint x) returns (uint y)
    {
        y=x+2;
    }
}
```

This program is converted into bytecode, as shown in the following subsection. Details on how to compile Solidity code with examples will be given in `Chapter 13`, *Development Tools and Frameworks*.

Runtime bytecode

Raw hex codes:

```
606060405260e060020a6000350463989e17318114601c575b6000565b34600057602960043
5603b565b604080519182525190819003602001 90f35b600281015b91905056
```

Opcodes:

```
PUSH1 0x60 PUSH1 0x40 MSTORE PUSH1 0x2 PUSH1 0x0 SSTORE CALLVALUE PUSH1 0x0
JUMPI JUMPDEST PUSH1 0x45 DUP1 PUSH1 0x1A PUSH1 0x0 CODECOPY PUSH1 0x0
RETURN PUSH1 0x60 PUSH1 0x40 MSTORE PUSH1 0xE0 PUSH1 0x2 EXP PUSH1 0x0
CALLDATALOAD DIV PUSH4 0x989E1731 DUP2 EQ PUSH1 0x1C JUMPI JUMPDEST PUSH1
0x0 JUMP JUMPDEST CALLVALUE PUSH1 0x0 JUMPI PUSH1 0x29 PUSH1 0x4
CALLDATALOAD PUSH1 0x3B JUMP JUMPDEST PUSH1 0x40 DUP1 MLOAD SWAP2 DUP3
MSTORE MLOAD SWAP1 DUP2 SWAP1 SUB PUSH1 0x20 ADD SWAP1 RETURN JUMPDEST
PUSH1 0x2 DUP2 ADD JUMPDEST SWAP2 SWAP1 POP JUMP
```

Opcodes and their meaning

There are different opcodes that have been introduced in the EVM. Opcodes are divided into multiple categories based on the operation they perform. The list of opcodes with their meaning and usage is presented here. These tables show the mnemonic, hex value of the mnemonic, the number of items that will be removed from the stack when this mnemonic executes (`POP`), the number of items that are added to the stack (`PUSH`) when this mnemonic executes, associated gas cost with the mnemonics and purpose of the mnemonic.

Arithmetic operations

All arithmetic in EVM is modulo 2^{256}. This group of opcodes is used to perform basic arithmetic operations. The value of these operations starts from `0x00` up to `0x0b`.

Mnemonic	Value	POP	PUSH	Gas	Description
STOP	0x00	0	0	0	Halts execution
ADD	0x01	2	1	3	Adds two values

MUL	0x02	2	1	5	Multiplies two values
SUB	0x03	2	1	3	Subtraction operation
DIV	0x04	2	1	5	Integer division operation
SDIV	0x05	2	1	5	Signed integer division operation
MOD	0x06	2	1	5	Modulo remainder operation
SMOD	0x07	2	1	5	Signed modulo remainder operation
ADDMOD	0x08	3	1	8	Modulo addition operation
MULMOD	0x09	3	1	8	Module multiplication operation
EXP	0x0a	2	1	10	Exponential operation (repeated multiplication of the base)
SIGNEXTEND	0x0b	2	1	5	Extends the length of two's complement signed integer

Note that STOP is not an arithmetic operation but is categorized in this list of arithmetic operations due to the range of values (*0s*) it falls in.

Logical operations

Logical operations include operations that are used to perform comparisons and bitwise logic operations. The value of these operations is in the range of 0x10 to 0x1a.

Mnemonic	Value	POP	PUSH	Gas	Description
LT	0x10	2	1	3	Less than
GT	0x11	2	1	3	Greater than
SLT	0x12	2	1	3	Signed less than comparison
SGT	0x13	2	1	3	Signed greater than comparison
EQ	0x14	2	1	3	Equal comparison
ISZERO	0x15	1	1	3	Not operator
AND	0x16	2	1	3	Bitwise AND operation
OR	0x17	2	1	3	Bitwise OR operation
XOR	0x18	2	1	3	Bitwise exclusive OR (XOR) operation
NOT	0x19	1	1	3	Bitwise NOT operation
BYTE	0x1a	2	1	3	Retrieve single byte from word

Logical operations

Cryptographic operations

There is only one operation in this category named SHA3. It is worth noting that this is not the standard SHA-3 standardized by NIST but the original Keccak implementation.

Mnemonic	Value	POP	PUSH	Gas	Description
SHA3	0x20	2	1	30	Used to calculate Keccak 256-bit hash.

Cryptographic operation

Note that, *30* is the cost of the operation. Then *6 gas* is paid for each word. Therefore, the formula for SHA3 gas cost becomes *30 + 6 * (size of input in words)*.

Environmental information

There is a total of 13 instructions in this category. These opcodes are used to provide information related to addresses, runtime environments, and data copy operations.

Mnemonic	Value	POP	PUSH	Gas	Description
ADDRESS	0x30	0	1	2	Used to get the address of the currently executing account
BALANCE	0x31	1	1	20	Used to get the balance of the given account
ORIGIN	0x32	0	1	2	Used to get the address of the sender of the original transaction
CALLER	0x33	0	1	2	Used to get the address of the account that initiated the execution
CALLVALUE	0x34	0	1	2	Retrieves the value deposited by the instruction or transaction
CALLDATALOAD	0x35	1	1	3	Retrieves the input data that was passed a parameter with the message call
CALLDATASIZE	0x36	0	1	2	Used to retrieve the size of the input data passed with the message call
CALLDATACOPY	0x37	3	0	3	Used to copy input data passed with the message call from the current environment to the memory

CODESIZE	0x38	0	1	2	Retrieves the size of running the code in the current environment
CODECOPY	0x39	3	0	3	Copies the running code from current environment to the memory
GASPRICE	0x3a	0	1	2	Retrieves the gas price specified by the initiating transaction
EXTCODESIZE	0x3b	1	1	20	Gets the size of the specified account code
EXTCODECOPY	0x3c	4	0	20	Used to copy the account code to the memory
RETURNDATASIZE	0x3d	0	1	2	Size of data returned from the previous call
RETURNDATACOPY	0x3e	3	0	3	Copy data returned from the previous call to memory

Block information

This set of instructions is related to retrieving various attributes associated with a block. These opcodes are available in the range of 0x40 to 0x45:

Mnemonic	Value	POP	PUSH	Gas	Description
BLOCKHASH	0x40	1	1	20	Gets the hash of one of the 256 most recently completed blocks
COINBASE	0x41	0	1	2	Retrieves the address of the beneficiary set in the block
TIMESTAMP	0x42	0	1	2	Retrieves the timestamp set in the blocks
NUMBER	0x43	0	1	2	Gets the block's number
DIFFICULTY	0x44	0	1	2	Retrieves the block difficulty
GASLIMIT	0x45	0	1	2	Gets the gas limit value of the block

Stack, memory, storage, and flow operations

This set of instructions contains all mnemonics that are necessary to store items on stack and memory. Also, instructions required for controlling program flow are also included in this range.

Mnemonic	Value	POP	PUSH	Gas	Description
POP	0x50	1	0	2	Removes items from the stack
MLOAD	0x51	1	1	3	Used to load a word from the memory
MSTORE	0x52	2	0	3	Used to store a word to the memory
MSTORE8	0x53	2	0	3	Used to save a byte to the memory
SLOAD	0x54	1	1	50	Used to load a word from the storage
SSTORE	0x55	2	0	0	Saves a word to the storage
JUMP	0x56	1	0	8	Alters the program counter
JUMPI	0x57	2	0	10	Alters the program counter based on a condition
PC	0x58	0	1	2	Used to retrieve the value in the program counter before the increment
MSIZE	0x59	0	1	2	Retrieves the size of the active memory in bytes
GAS	0x5a	0	1	2	Retrieves the available gas amount
JUMPDEST	0x5b	0	0	1	Used to mark a valid destination for jumps with no effect on the machine state during the execution

Push operations

These operations include PUSH operations that are used to place items on the stack. The range of these instructions is from 0x60 to 0x7f. There are 32 PUSH operations available in total in the EVM. The PUSH operation, which reads from the byte array of the program code.

Mnemonic	Value	POP	PUSH	Gas	Description
PUSH1 . . . PUSH32	0x60 . . . 0x7f	0	1	3	Used to place N right-aligned big-endian byte item(s) on the stack. N is a value that ranges from 1 byte to 32 bytes (full word) based on the mnemonic used.

Duplication operations

As the name suggests, duplication operations are used to duplicate stack items. The range of values is from `0x80` to `0x8f`. There are 16 DUP instructions available in the EVM. Items placed on the stack or removed from the stack also change incrementally with the mnemonic used; for example, DUP1 removes one item from the stack and places two items on the stack, whereas DUP16 removes 16 items from the stack and places 17 items.

Mnemonic	Value	POP	PUSH	Gas	Description
DUP1 . . . DUP16	0x80 ...0x8f	X	Y	3	Used to duplicate the Nth stack item, where N is the number corresponding to the DUP instruction used. X and Y are the items removed and placed on the stack, respectively.

Exchange operations

The SWAP operations provide the ability to exchange stack items. There are 16 SWAP instructions available, and with each instruction, the stack items are removed and placed incrementally up to 17 items depending on the type of opcode used.

Mnemonic	Value	POP	PUSH	Gas	Description
SWAP1 . . . SWAP16	0x90 ...0x9f	X	Y	3	Used to swap the Nth stack item, where N is the number corresponding to the SWAP instruction used. X and Y are the items removed and placed on the stack, respectively.

Logging operations

Logging operations provide opcodes to append log entries on the substate tuple's log series field. There are four log operations available in total, and they range from value `0x0a` to `0xa4`.

Mnemonic	Value	POP	PUSH	Gas	Description
LOG0 . . . LOG4	0x0a ...0xa4	X	Y (0)	375, 750, 1125, 1500, 1875	Used to append log record with *N* topics, where *N* is the number corresponding to the LOG opcode used. For example, LOG0 means a log record with no topics, and LOG4 means a log record with four topics. *X* and *Y* represent the items removed and placed on the stack, respectively. *X* and *Y* change incrementally, starting from 2, 0 up to 6, 0 according to the LOG operation used.

System operations

System operations are used to perform various system-related operations, such as account creation, message calling, and execution control. There are nine opcodes available in total in this category.

Mnemonic	Value	POP	PUSH	Gas	Description
CREATE	0xf0	3	1	32,000	Used to create a new account with the associated code.
CALL	0xf1	7	1	40	Used to initiate a message call into a contract account.
CALLCODE	0xf2	7	1	40	Used to initiate a message call into this account with an alternative account's code.
RETURN	0xf3	2	0	0	Stops the execution and returns output data.
DELEGATECALL	0xf4	6	1	40	This is same as CALLCODE but does not change the current values of the sender and the value.

STATICCALL	0xfa	6	1	40	This is like the CALL instruction. The only exception is that state changing operation are not permitted.
CREATE2	0xfb	4	1	*sha3(sender + sha3(code)) % 2**160*	Create a new account with associated code.
REVERT	0xfd	2	0	0	This stop execution and revert any state changes without consuming all provided gas.
SUICIDE	0xff	1	0	0	Stops (halts) the execution and the account is registered for deletion later.

In this section, all EVM opcodes have been discussed. There are approximately 129 opcodes available in the EVM of the Byzantium release of Ethereum in total.

Blocks and blockchain

As discussed earlier in this chapter, blocks are the main building blocks of a blockchain. Ethereum blocks consist of various elements, which are described as follows:

- The block header
- The transactions list
- The list of headers of ommers or uncles

The transaction list is simply a list of all transactions included in the block. Also, the list of headers of uncles is also included in the block.

The most important and complex part of a block in Ethereum is the block header. Block header consists of various elements which are introduced here.

Block header: Block headers are the most critical and detailed components of an Ethereum block. The header contains valuable information, which is described in detail here:

- **Parent hash**: This is the Keccak 256-bit hash of the parent (previous) block's header.
- **Ommers hash**: This is the Keccak 256-bit hash of the list of ommers (uncles) blocks included in the block.

- **The beneficiary**: Beneficiary field contains the 160-bit address of the recipient that will receive the mining reward once the block is successfully mined.

- **State root**: The state root field contains the Keccak 256-bit hash of the root node of the state trie. It is calculated after all transactions have been processed and finalized.

- **Transactions root**: The transaction root is the Keccak 256-bit hash of the root node of the transaction trie. Transaction trie represents the list of transactions included in the block.

- **Receipts root**: The receipts root is the Keccak 256-bit hash of the root node of the transaction receipt trie. This trie is composed of receipts of all transactions included in the block. Transaction receipts are generated after each transaction is processed and contain useful post-transaction information. More details on transaction receipts are provided in the next section.

- **Logs bloom**: The logs bloom is a bloom filter that is composed of the logger address and log topics from the log entry of each transaction receipt of the included transaction list in the block. Logging is explained in detail in the next section.

- **Difficulty**: The difficulty level of the current block.

- **Number**: The total number of all previous blocks; the genesis block is block zero.

- **Gas limit**: The field contains the value that represents the limit set on the gas consumption per block.

- **Gas used**: The field contains the total gas consumed by the transactions included in the block.

- **Timestamp**: Timestamp is the epoch Unix time of the time of block initialization.

- **Extra data**: Extra data field can be used to store arbitrary data related to the block. Only up to 32 bytes are allowed in this field.

- **Mixhash**: Mixhash field contains a 256-bit hash that once combined with the nonce is used to prove that adequate computational effort (PoW) has been spent in order to create this block.

- **Nonce:** Nonce is a 64-bit hash (a number) that is used to prove, in combination with the *mixhash* field, that adequate computational effort (PoW) has been spent in order to create this block.

The following figure shows the detailed structure of the block and block header:

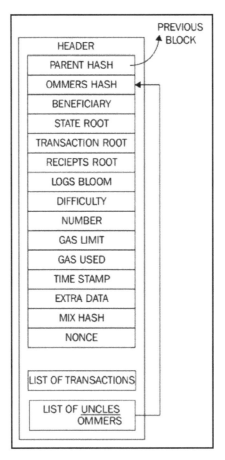

A detailed diagram of block structure with block header

The genesis block

The genesis block varies slightly from normal blocks due to the data it contains and the way it has been created. It contains 15 items that are described here.

From `https://etherscan.io/`, the actual version is shown as follows:

Element	Description
Timestamp	(Jul-30-2015 03:26:13 PM +UTC)
Transactions	8893 transactions and 0 contract internal transactions in this block
Hash	0xd4e56740f876aef8c010b86a40d5f56745a118d0906a34e69aec8c0db1cb8fa3
Parent hash	0x0000000000000000000000000000000000000000000000000000000000000000
SHA3 uncles	0x1dcc4de8dec75d7aab85b567b6ccd41ad312451b948a7413f0a142fd40d49347
Mined by	0x0000000000000000000000000000000000000000 IN 15 secs
Difficulty	17,179,869,184
Total difficulty	17,179,869,184
Size	540 bytes
Gas used	0
Nonce	0x0000000000000042
Block reward	5 Ether
Uncles reward	0
Extra data	
Gas limit	5,000

The block validation mechanism

An Ethereum block is considered valid if it passes the following checks:

- Consistent with uncles and transactions, this means that all ommers (uncles) satisfy the property that they are indeed uncles and also if the PoW for uncles is valid.
- If the previous block (parent) exists and is valid.
- If the timestamp of the block is valid. This means that the current block's timestamp must be higher than the parent block's timestamp. Also, it should be less than 15 minutes into the future. All block times are calculated in epoch time (Unix time).

- If any of these checks fails, the block will be rejected.

Block finalization

Block finalization is a process that is run by miners to validate the contents of the block and apply rewards. It results in four steps being executed. These steps are described here in detail:

1. **Ommers validation**: Validate ommers (stale blocks also called uncles). In the case of mining, determine ommers. The validation process of the headers of stale blocks checks whether the header is valid and the relationship of the Uncle with the current block satisfies the maximum depth of six blocks. A block can contain a maximum of two uncles.

2. **Transaction validation**: Validate transactions. In the case of mining, determine transactions. The process involves checking whether the total gas used in the block is equal to the final gas consumption after the final transaction i.e. cumulative gas used by the transactions included in the block.

3. **Reward application**: Apply rewards, which means updating the beneficiary's account with a reward balance. In Ethereum, a reward is also given to miners for stale blocks, which is 1/32 of the block reward. Uncles that are included in the blocks also receive 7/8 of the total block reward. The current block reward is 3 Ether. It was reduced from 5 with Byzantium release of Ethereum. A block can have a maximum of two uncles.

4. **State and nonce validation**: Verify the state and block nonce. In the case of mining, compute a valid state and block nonce.

Block difficulty

Block difficulty is increased if the time between two blocks decreases, whereas it increases if the block time between two blocks decreases. This is required to maintain a roughly consistent block generation time. The difficulty adjustment algorithm in Ethereum's Homestead release is shown as follows:

$$block\_diff = parent\_diff + parent\_diff // 2048 *$$

$$max(1 - (block\_timestamp - parent\_timestamp) // 10, -99) +$$

$$int(2**((block.number // 100000) - 2))$$

The preceding algorithm means that, if the time difference between the generation of the parent block and the current block is less than 10 seconds, the difficulty goes up. If the time difference is between 10 to 19 seconds, the difficulty level remains the same. Finally, if the time difference is 20 seconds or more, the difficulty level decreases. This decrease is proportional to the time difference.

In addition to timestamp-difference-based difficulty adjustment, there is also another part (shown in the last line of the preceding algorithm) that increases the difficulty exponentially after every 100,000 blocks. This is the so-called **Difficulty Time Bomb** or **Ice Age** introduced in the Ethereum network, which will make it very hard to mine on the Ethereum blockchain at some point in the future. This will encourage users to switch to **Proof of Stake** (**PoS**) as mining on the POW chain will eventually become prohibitively difficult.

 This change was delayed via EIP-649 (`https://github.com/ethereum/EIPs/pull/669`) for around year and a half and no clear time frame have been suggested yet.

According to the original estimates based on the algorithm, the block generation time would have become significantly higher during the second half of the year 2017, and in 2021, it would become so high that it will be virtually impossible to mine on the POW chain, even for dedicated mining centers. This way, miners will have no choice but to switch to the PoS scheme proposed by Ethereum called **Casper**.

 More information about Casper is available here `https://github.com/ethereum/research/blob/master/papers/casper-basics/casper_basics.pdf`.

This Ice Age proposal has been postponed with the release of Byzantium. Instead, the mining reward has been reduced from 5 Ethers to 3 Ethers. This is in preparation for PoS implementation in Serenity.

In the Byzantium release, the difficulty adjustment formula has been changed to take uncles into account for difficulty calculation. This new formula is shown here:

adj_factor = max((2 if len(parent.uncles) else 1) - ((timestamp - parent.timestamp) // 9), -99)

Gas

Gas is required to be paid for every operation performed on the Ethereum blockchain. This is a mechanism that ensures that infinite loops cannot cause the whole blockchain to stall due to the Turing-complete nature of the EVM. A transaction fee is charged as some amount of Ether and is taken from the account balance of the transaction originator.

A fee is paid for transactions to be included by miners for mining. If this fee is too low, the transaction may never be picked up; the more the fee, the higher are the chances that the transactions will be picked up by the miners for inclusion in the block. Conversely, if the transaction that has an appropriate fee paid is included in the block by miners but has too many complex operations to perform, it can result in an out-of-gas exception if the gas cost is not enough. In this case, the transaction will fail but will still be made part of the block, and the transaction originator will not get any refund.

Transaction cost can be estimated using the following formula:

$$Total\ cost = gasUsed * gasPrice$$

Here, *gasUsed* is the total gas that is supposed to be used by the transaction during the execution and *gasPrice* is specified by the transaction originator as an incentive to the miners to include the transaction in the next block. This is specified in Ether. Each EVM opcode has a fee assigned to it. It is an estimate because the gas used can be more or less than the value specified by the transaction originator originally. For example, if computation takes too long or the behavior of the smart contract changes in response to some other factors, then the transaction execution may perform more or fewer operations than intended initially and can result in consuming more or fewer gas. If the execution runs out of gas, everything is immediately rolled back; otherwise, if the execution is successful and there is some remaining gas, then it is returned to the transaction originator.

 A website that keeps track of latest gas price and provides other valuable statistics and calculators is available at `https://ethgasstation.info/index.php`.

Each operation costs some gas; a high-level fee schedule of a few operations is shown as an example here:

Operation Name	Gas Cost
step	1
stop	0
suicide	0
sha3	30
sload	20
txdata	5
transaction	500
contract creation	53000

Based on the preceding fee schedule and the formula discussed earlier, an example calculation of the SHA-3 operation can be calculated as follows:

- SHA-3 costs 30 gas.
- Assume that current gas price is 25 GWei, convert it into ether, which is 0.000000025 Ether. After multiplying both: *0.000000025 * 30*, we get 0.00000075 Ether.
- In total, 0.00000075 Ether is the total gas that will be charged.

Fee schedule

Gas is charged in three scenarios as a prerequisite to the execution of an operation:

- The computation of an operation
- For contract creation or message call
- Increase in the usage of memory

A list of instructions and various operations with the gas values has been provided previously in the chapter.

Forks in the blockchain

Forks are the splitting of the blockchain into two. This can be intentional or non-intentional. Usually, as a result of major protocol upgrade, a hard fork is created, and unintentional fork can be created due to bugs in the software.

With the release of Homestead, due to major protocol upgrades, it resulted in a hard fork. The protocol was upgraded at block number 1,150,000, resulting in the migration from the first version of Ethereum known as Frontier to the second version of Ethereum called Homestead. The latest version is called Byzantium which is the first part of the Metropolis release. This was released as a hard fork at block number 4,370,000.

An unintentional fork, which occurred on November 24, 2016, at 14:12:07 UTC was due to a bug in the Geth client's journaling mechanism. As a result, a network fork occurred at block number 2,686,351. This bug resulted in Geth failing to prevent empty account deletions in the case of the empty out-of-gas exception. This was not an issue in Parity (another popular Ethereum client). This means that from block number 2,686,351, the Ethereum blockchain is split into two, one running with the Parity clients and the other with Geth. This issue was resolved with the release of Geth version 1.5.3.

As a result of the DAO hack, the Ethereum blockchain was also forked to recover from the attack. This was discussed in chapter 9, *Smart Contracts*.

Nodes and miners

Ethereum network contains different nodes. Some nodes act only as wallets, some are light clients, and few are full clients running the full blockchain. One of the most important type of nodes are mining nodes. We will see what is mining in this section.

 Mining is the process by which new blocks are elected via a consensus mechanism and added to the blockchain.

As a result, currency (Ether) is rewarded to the nodes which perform mining operations. These mining nodes are known as **miners**. Miners are paid in Ether as an incentive for them to validate and verify blocks made up of transactions. The mining process helps secure the network by verifying computations.

At a theoretical level, a miner node performs the following functions:

1. Listens for the transactions broadcasted on the Ethereum network and determines the transactions to be processed
2. Determines stale blocks called uncles or ommers and includes them in the block
3. Updates the account balance with the reward earned from successfully mining the block
4. Finally, a valid state is computed, and the block is finalized, which defines the result of all state transitions

The current method of mining is based on PoW, which is similar to that of bitcoin. When a block is deemed valid, it has to satisfy not only the general consistency requirements, but it must also contain the PoW for a given difficulty.

The PoW algorithm is due to be replaced with the PoS algorithm with the release of Serenity. There is no set date for the release of Serenity, as this will be the final version of Ethereum. Considerable research work has been carried out to build the PoS algorithm which is suitable for the Ethereum network. More information on PoS research work is available at `https://ethresear.ch/t/initial-explorations-on-full-pos-proposal-mechanisms/925`.

An algorithm named Casper has been developed, which will replace the existing PoW algorithm in Ethereum. More information about Casper can be found here `https://github.com/ethereum/research/tree/master/casper4`.

This is a security deposit based on the economic protocol where nodes are required to place a security deposit before they can produce blocks. Nodes have been named *bonded validators* in Casper, whereas the act of placing the security deposit is *named bonding*.

Miners play a vital role in reaching a consensus about the canonical state of the blockchain. Consensus mechanism is explained in the next subsection.

The consensus mechanism

The consensus mechanism in Ethereum is based on the **Greedy Heaviest Observed Subtree** (**GHOST**) protocol proposed initially by Zohar and Sompolinsky in December 2013.

 Readers interested in it can explore the detailed original paper at `http://eprint.iacr.org/2013/881.pdf`.

Ethereum uses a simpler version of this protocol, where the chain that has most computational effort spent on it to build it is identified as the definite version. Another way of looking at it is to find the longest chain, as the longest chain must have been built by consuming adequate mining effort. GHOST protocol was first introduced as a mechanism to alleviate the issues arising out of fast block generation times that led to stale or orphan blocks.

In GHOST, stale blocks are added in calculations to figure out the longest and heaviest chain of blocks. Stale blocks are called uncles or ommers in Ethereum.

The following diagram shows a quick comparison between the longest and heaviest chain:

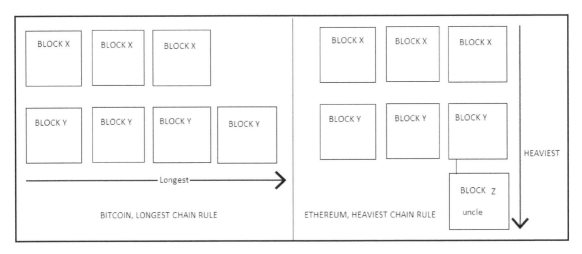

Longest versus heaviest chain

The preceding diagram shows two rules of figuring out which blockchain is the canonical version of *truth*. In case of Bitcoin, shown on the left-hand side in the diagram, the longest chain rule is applied which means that the active chain (true chain) is the one that has the most amount of PoW done. In case of Ethereum, the concept is similar from the longest chain point of view but it also includes **ommers** (also called uncles), the *orphan* blocks which means that it rewards those blocks too that were competing with other blocks during mining to be selected and performed significant PoW or were mined exactly at the same time as others but did not make it to the main chain. This makes the chain *heaviest* instead of *longest* because it also contains the *orphaned* blocks. This is shown on the right-hand side of the diagram.

To facilitate consensus PoW algorithm is used. In Ethereum the algorithm used for this purpose is called **Ethash** which is described in the next subsection.

Ethash

Ethash is the name of the PoW algorithm used in Ethereum. Originally, this was proposed as the Dagger-Hashimoto algorithm, but much has changed since the first implementation, and the PoW algorithm has now evolved into what's known as Ethash now.

Similar to Bitcoin, the core idea behind mining is to find a **nonce** (a random arbitrary number) which once concatenated with the block header and hashed, results in a number that is lower than the current network difficulty level. Initially, the difficulty was low when Ethereum was new, and even CPU and single GPU mining was profitable to a certain extent, but that is no longer the case. Now either pooled mining is profitable, or large GPU mining farms are used for mining purposes.

Ethash is a memory-hard algorithm, which makes it difficult to be implemented on specialized hardware. As in Bitcoin, ASICs have been developed, which have resulted in mining centralization over the years, but memory-hard PoW algorithms are one way of thwarting this threat, and Ethereum implements **Ethash** to discourage ASIC development for mining. Ethash is a **memory hard** algorithm and developing ASICs with large and fast memories is not feasible. This algorithm requires choosing subsets of a fixed resource called **Directed Acyclic Graph** (**DAG**) depending on the nonce and block headers.

DAG is around 2 GB in size and changes every 30,000 blocks. Mining can only start when DAG is completely generated the first time a mining node starts. The time between every 30,000 blocks is around 5.2 days and is called **epoch**. This DAG is used as a seed by the PoW algorithm called Ethash. According to current specifications, the epoch time is defined as 30,000 blocks.

The current reward scheme is 3 Ethers for successfully finding a valid nonce. In addition to receiving 3 Ethers, the successful miner also receives the cost of the gas consumed within the block and an additional reward for including stale blocks (uncles) in the block. A maximum of two uncles are allowed per block and are rewarded 7/8 of the normal block reward. In order to achieve a 12 second block time, block difficulty is adjusted at every block. The rewards are proportional to the miner's hash rate, which means how fast a miner can hash. You can use Ether mining calculator to calculate that how much hash rate is required to generate profit.

 One example of such calculator is available at: `https://etherscan.io/ether-mining-calculator`.

Mining can be performed by simply joining the Ethereum network and running an appropriate client. The key requirement is that the node should be fully synced with the main network before mining can start.

In the next section, various methods of mining are mentioned.

CPU mining

Even though not profitable on the mainnet, CPU mining is still valuable on the test network or even a private network to experiment with mining and contract deployment. Private and test networks will be discussed with practical examples in the next chapter, Chapter 12, *Ethereum Development Environment*. A Geth example is shown on how to start CPU mining here. Geth can be started with mine switch in order to start mining:

```
geth --mine --minerthreads <n>
```

CPU mining can also be started using the Web3 Geth console. Geth console can be started by issuing the following command:

```
$ geth attach
```

After this, the miner can be started by issuing the following command, which will return True if successful, or False otherwise. Take a look at the following command:

```
miner.start(4)
True
```

Number 4 here represents the number of threads that will run for mining. It can be any number depending on the number of CPUs you have.

The preceding command will start the miner with four threads. Take a look at the following command:

```
miner.stop()
True
```

The preceding command will stop the miner. The command will return True if successful.

GPU mining

At a basic level, GPU mining can be performed easily by running two commands:

```
geth --rpc
```

Once `geth` is up and running, and the blockchain is fully downloaded, Ethminer can be run in order to start mining. Ethminer is a standalone miner that can also be used in the farm mode to contribute to mining pools.

 You can download it from GitHub here `https://github.com/Genoil/` `cpp-ethereum/tree/117/releases`.

```
$ ethminer -G
```

Running with the `G` switch assumes that the appropriate graphics card is installed and configured correctly. If no appropriate graphics cards are found, `ethminer` will return an error, as shown in the following screenshot:

```
drequinox@drequinox-OP7010:~$ ethminer -G
[OPENCL]:No OpenCL platforms found
No GPU device with sufficient memory was found. Can't GPU mine. Remove the -G argument
drequinox@drequinox-OP7010:~$ 
```

Error in case no appropriate GPUs can be found

GPU mining requires an AMD or NVIDIA graphics card and an applicable OpenCL SDK.

 For NVIDIA chipset, it can be downloaded from `https://developer.nvidia.com/cuda-downloads`. For AMD chipsets, it is available at `http://developer.amd.com/tools-and-sdks/opencl-zone/amd-accelerated-parallel-processing-app-sdk`.

Once the graphics cards are installed and configured correctly, the process can be started by issuing the `ethminer -G` command.

Benchmarking

Ethminer can also be used to run benchmarking, as shown in the following screenshot. Two modes can be invoked for benchmarking. It can either be CPU or GPU. The commands are shown here:

- CPU benchmarking:

  ```
  $ ethminer -M -C
  ```

- GPU benchmarking:

  ```
  $ ethminer -M -G
  ```

The following screenshot example is shown for CPU mining benchmarking:

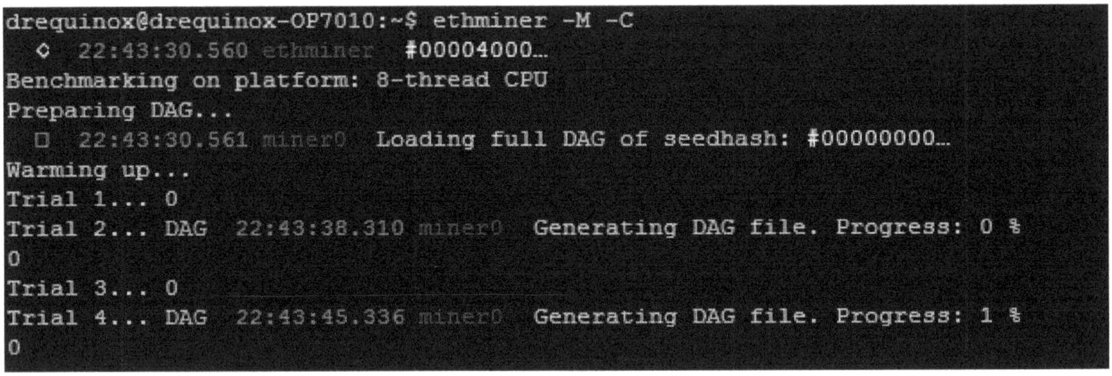

```
drequinox@drequinox-OP7010:~$ ethminer -M -C
  ◊  22:43:30.560 ethminer    #00004000…
Benchmarking on platform: 8-thread CPU
Preparing DAG...
  □  22:43:30.561 miner0   Loading full DAG of seedhash: #00000000…
Warming up...
Trial 1... 0
Trial 2... DAG  22:43:38.310 miner0   Generating DAG file. Progress: 0 %
0
Trial 3... 0
Trial 4... DAG  22:43:45.336 miner0   Generating DAG file. Progress: 1 %
0
```

CPU benchmarking

The GPU device to be used can also be specified in the command line:

```
$ ethminer -M -G --opencl-device 1
```

As GPU mining is implemented using OpenCL AMD, chipset-based GPUs tend to work faster as compared to NVIDIA GPUs. Due to the high memory requirements (DAG creation), FPGAs and ASICs will not provide any major advantage over GPUs. This is done on purpose to discourage the development of specialized hardware for mining.

Mining rigs

As difficulty increased over time for mining Ether, **mining rigs** with multiple GPUs were starting to be built by the miners. A mining rig usually contains around five GPU cards with all of them working in parallel for mining, thus improving the chances of finding valid nonces for mining.

Mining rigs can be built with some effort and are also available commercially from various vendors. A typical mining rig configuration includes the components discussed here:

- **Motherboard**: A specialized motherboard with multiple PCI-E x1 or x16 slots, for example, BIOSTAR Hi-Fi or ASRock H81, is required.
- **SSD hard drive**: An SSD hard drive is required. The SSD drive is recommended because of its much faster performance over the analog equivalent. This will be mainly used to store the blockchain. It is recommended that you have roughly 250 GB of free space on the hard disk.
- **GPU**: The GPU is the most critical component of the rig as it is the primary workhorse that will be used for mining. For example, it can be a Sapphire AMD Radeon R9 380 with 4 GB RAM. A website that maintains these benchmark metrics is available at `https://www.miningbenchmark.net`.
- **Operating system**: Linux Ubuntu's latest version is usually chosen as the operating system for the rig because it is more reliable and gives better performance as compared to Windows. Also, it allows you to run a bare minimum operating system required for mining, and essential operations as compared to heavy graphical interfaces that another operating system may have. There is also another variant of Linux available, called EthOS (available at `http://ethosdistro.com/`) that is specially built for Ethereum mining and supports mining operations natively.
- **Mining software**: Finally, mining software such as Ethminer and Geth are installed. Additionally, some remote monitoring and administration software are also installed so that rigs can be monitored and managed remotely if required. It is also important to put proper air conditioning or cooling mechanisms in place as running multiple GPUs can generate a large amount of heat. This also necessitates the need for using an appropriate monitoring software that can alert users if there are any problems with the hardware, for example, if the GPUs are overheating.

- **Power Supply Units (PSUs)**: In a mining rig there are multiple GPUs running in parallel, therefore there is a need for a constant powerful supply of electricity. There is a need to use PSUs that can take the load and can provide enough power to the GPUs to operate. Usually, 1,000 watts of power is required to be produced by PSUs. An excellent comparison of PSUs is available at `https://www.thegeekpub.com/11488/best-power-supply-mining-cryptocurrency/`.

A mining rig for Ethereum for sale at eBay

Mining pools

Many online mining pools offer Ethereum mining. Ethminer can be used to connect to a mining pool using the following command. Each pool publishes its instructions, but generally, the process of connecting to a pool is similar. An example from `http://ethereumpool.co` is shown here:

```
ethminer -C -F
http://ethereumpool.co/?miner=0.1@0x024a20cc5feba7f3dc3776075b3e61234eb1459
c@DrEquinox
```

This command will produce output similar to the one shown here:

```
miner 23:50:53.046 ethminer Getting work package . . .
```

```
drequinox@drequinox-OP7010:~$ ethminer -C -F http://ethereumpool.co/?miner=0.1@0x024a20cc5feba7f3dc3776075b3e60c20eb1459c@DrEquinox
miner  23:50:52.046 ethminer  Getting work package...
```

Screenshot of ethminer

Wallets and client software

As Ethereum is under heavy development and evolution, there are many components, clients, and tools that have been developed and introduced over the last few years.

The following is a list of all main components, client software, and tools that are available with Ethereum. This list is provided to reduce the ambiguity around many tools and clients available for Ethereum. The list provided here also explains the usage and significance of various components.

Geth

This is the Go implementation of the Ethereum client.

The latest version is available at the link here
`https://geth.ethereum.org/downloads/`.

Eth

This is the C++ implementation of the Ethereum client.

Pyethapp

This is the Python implementation of the Ethereum client

Parity

This implementation is built using Rust and developed by EthCore. EthCore is a company that works on the development of the parity client.

Parity can be downloaded from `https://www.parity.io/`.

Light clients

Simple Payment Verification (**SPV**) clients download only a small subset of the blockchain. This allows low resource devices, such as mobile phones, embedded devices, or tablets, to be able to verify the transactions.

A complete Ethereum blockchain and node are not required in this case, and SPV clients can still validate the execution of transactions. SPV clients are also called light clients. This idea is similar to Bitcoin SPV clients.

 There is a wallet available from Jaxx (`https://jaxx.io/`), which can be installed on iOS and Android, which provides the SPV functionality.

Installation

The following installation procedure describes the installation of various Ethereum clients on Ubuntu systems. Instructions for other operating systems are available on Ethereum Wiki. As Ubuntu systems will be used in examples, later on, only the installation on Ubuntu has been described here.

Geth client can be installed by using the following command on an Ubuntu system:

```
> sudo apt-get install -y software-properties-common
> sudo add-apt-repository -y ppa:ethereum/ethereum
> sudo apt-get update
> sudo apt-get install -y ethereum
```

After installation is completed Geth can be launched simply by issuing the `geth` command at Terminal, as it comes preconfigured with all the required parameters to connect to the live Ethereum network (mainnet):

```
> geth
```

Eth installation

Eth is the C++ implementation of the Ethereum client and can be installed using the following command on Ubuntu:

```
> sudo apt-get install cpp-ethereum
```

Mist browser

The Mist browser is a user-friendly interface for end users with a feature-rich graphical user interface that is used to browse **Decentralized Applications** (**DApps**) and for account management and contract management. Mist installation is covered in the next chapter.

When Mist is launched for the first time, it will initialize Geth in the background and will sync with the network. It can take from a few hours to a few days depending on the speed and type of the network to fully synchronize with the network. If testnet is used, then syncing completes relatively faster as the size of testnet (Ropsten) is not as big as mainnet. More information on how to connect to testnet will be provided in the next chapter, `Chapter 12`, *Ethereum Development Environment*.

Mist browser starting up and syncing with the main network

Mist browser is not a wallet; in fact, it is a browser of DApps and provides a user-friendly user interface for the creation and management of contracts, accounts, and browsing decentralized applications. Ethereum wallet is a DApp that is released with Mist.

A wallet is a generic program that can store private keys and based on the addresses stored within it, it can compute the existing balance of Ether associated with the addresses by querying the blockchain. It can also be used to deploy smart contracts.

 Latest version of Mist is available at `https://github.com/ethereum/mist`.

Other wallets include but are not limited to MyEtherWallet, which is an open source Ether wallet developed in JavaScript. MyEtherWallet runs in the client browser.

 This software is available at `https://www.myetherwallet.com`.

Icebox is developed by ConsenSys. This is a cold storage browser that provides secure storage of Ether. It depends on whether the computer on which Icebox is run is connected to the internet or not.

Various wallets are available for Ethereum for desktop, mobile, and web platforms. A popular Ethereum iOS wallet is named Jaxx which we used as an example earlier in this chapter.

Once the blockchain is synchronized, Mist will launch and show the following interface. In this example, two accounts are displayed with no balance:

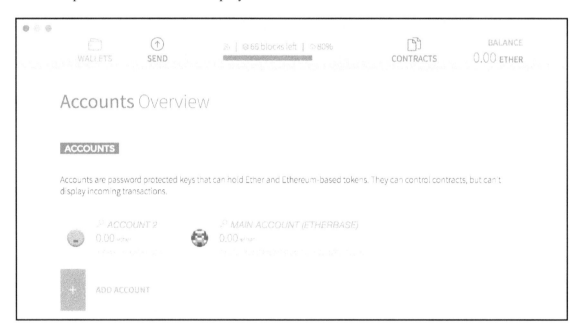

Mist browser

A new account can be created in a number of ways. In the Mist browser, it can be created by clicking on the **ACCOUNTS** menu and selecting **New account** or by clicking on the **ADD ACCOUNT** option in the Mist **Accounts Overview** screen:

Add new account

The account will need a password to be set, as shown in the preceding screenshot; once the account is set up, it will be displayed in the **Accounts Overview** section of the Mist browser.

Accounts can also be added via the command line using the Geth or Parity command-line interface. This process is shown in the next section.

Geth

Execute the following command to add a new account:

```
$ geth account new
Your new account is locked with a password. Please give a password. Do not
forget this password.
Passphrase:
Repeat passphrase:
Address: {21c2b52e18353a2cc8223322b33559c1d900c85d}
```

The list of accounts can be displayed using the `geth` client by issuing the following command:

```
$ geth account list
Account #0: {11bcc1d0b56c57aefc3b52d37e7d6c2c90b8ec35}
/home/drequinox/.ethereum/keystore/UTC--2016-05-07T13-04-15.175558799Z-
-11bcc1d0b56c57aefc3b52d37e7d6c2c90b8ec35
Account #1: {e49668b7ffbf031bbbdab7a222bdb38e7e3e1b63}
/home/drequinox/.ethereum/keystore/UTC--2016-05-10T19-16-11.952722205Z--
e49668b7ffbf031bbbdab7a222bdb38e7e3e1b63
Account #2: {21c2b52e18353a2cc8223322b33559c1d900c85d}
/home/drequinox/.ethereum/keystore/UTC--2016-11-29T22-48-09.825971090Z-
-21c2b52e18353a2cc8223322b33559c1d900c85d
```

Note that you will see different addresses when you run this on your computer

The geth console

The Geth JavaScript console can be used to perform various functions. For example, an account can be created by attaching Geth.

Geth can be attached with the running daemon, as shown in the following screenshot:

```
drequinox@drequinox-OP7010:~$ geth attach
Welcome to the Geth JavaScript console!

instance: Parity//v1.4.4-beta-a68d52c-20161118/x86_64-linux-gnu/rustc1.13.0
coinbase: 0x0000000000000000000000000000000000000000
at block: 2718377 (Tue, 29 Nov 2016 22:52:52 GMT)
 modules: eth:1.0 net:1.0 parity:1.0 parity_accounts:1.0 personal:1.0 rpc:1.0 traces:1.0 web3:1.0

>
```

Geth client

Once Geth is successfully attached with the running instance of the Ethereum client (in this case, Parity), it will display command prompt >, which provides an interactive command-line interface to interact with the Ethereum client using JavaScript notations.

For example, a new account can be added using the following command in the Geth console:

```
> personal.newAccount()
Passphrase:
Repeat passphrase: "0xc64a728a67ba67048b9c160ec39bacc5626761ce"
>
```

The list of accounts can also be displayed similarly:

```
> eth.accounts
["0x024a20cc5feba7f3dc3776075b3e60c20eb1459c",
"0x11bcc1d0b56c57aefc3b52d37e7d6c2c90b8ec35",
"0xdf482f11e3fbb7716e2868786b3afede1c1fb37f",
"0xe49668b7ffbf031bbbdab7a222bdb38e7e3e1b63",
"0xf9834defb35d24c5a61a5fe745149e9470282495"]
```

Funding the account with bitcoin

This option is available with the Mist browser by clicking on the account and then selecting the option to fund the account. The backend engine used for this operation is https:// shapeshift.io/ and can be used to fund the account from bitcoin or other currencies, including the fiat currency option as well.

Once the exchange is completed, the transferred Ether will be available in the account.

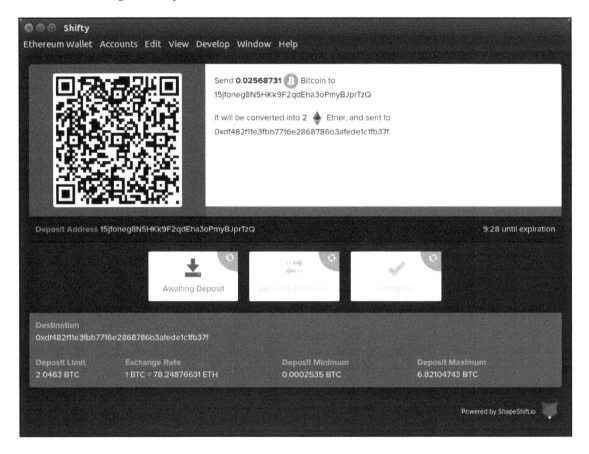

Exchange of Bitcoin to Ethereum

The preceding screenshot shows the **Shifty** interface available in Mist browser that can be used to fund your Ethereum accounts by exchanging bitcoins for Ether.

Parity installation

Parity is another implementation of the Ethereum client. It has been written using the Rust programming language. The main aim behind the development of Parity is high performance, small footprint, and reliability. Parity can be installed using the following commands on an Ubuntu or Mac system:

```
bash <(curl https://get.parity.io -Lk)
```

This will initiate the download and installation of the Parity client. After the installation of Parity is completed, the installer will also offer the installation of the Netstats client. The Netstats client is a daemon that runs in the background and collects essential statistics and displays them on `https://ethstats.net/`.

After running the preceding command, you will see the output similar to the following:

```
⊗ ⊜ ⊚   drequinox@drequinox-OP7010: /opt
drequinox@drequinox-OP7010:/opt$ bash <(curl https://get.parity.io -Lk)
  % Total    % Received % Xferd  Average Speed   Time    Time     Time  Current
                                 Dload  Upload   Total   Spent    Left  Speed
100   154  100   154    0     0    429      0 --:--:-- --:--:-- --:--:--   430
100   154  100   154    0     0    211      0 --:--:-- --:--:-- --:--:--  9625
100 12876  100 12876    0     0  11824      0  0:00:01  0:00:01 --:--:-- 11824
==> Checking OS dependencies
 ✓      Ubuntu, but version not supported
 ✓      curl
 ✓      apt-get
 ✓      sudo

Found all dependencies (3/3)
==> OK, let's install Parity now!
==> Last chance! Sure you want to install this software? [Y/n] Y

==> Installing Parity build dependencies
==> Verifying installation
 ✓      apt-get
==> Installing parity
  % Total    % Received % Xferd  Average Speed   Time    Time     Time  Current
                                 Dload  Upload   Total   Spent    Left  Speed
100 5449k  100 5449k    0     0   648k      0  0:00:08  0:00:08 --:--:--  812k
(Reading database ... 227048 files and directories currently installed.)
Preparing to unpack /tmp/parity.deb ...
Unpacking parity (1.4.4) over (1.4.4) ...
Setting up parity (1.4.4) ...
==> Parity has been installed


    Netstats Would you like to download, install and configure a Netstats client?
WARNING: this will need a secret and reconfigure any existing node/NEM installation you have.  [Y/n] Y
Installing netstats
Please enter the netstats secret: a38e1e50b1b82fa
Please enter your instance name: Ðr.Ξquinox!
Please enter your contact details (optional):

## Installing the NodeSource Node.js v0.12 repo...
```

Parity installation

Once the installation is completed successfully, the following message is displayed. Ethereum Parity node can then be started using `parity -j`. If compatibility with Geth is required to use Ethereum wallet (Mist browser) with Parity, then the `parity - geth` command should be used to run Parity. This will run Parity in compatibility mode with the Geth client and will consequently allow Mist to run on top of Parity.

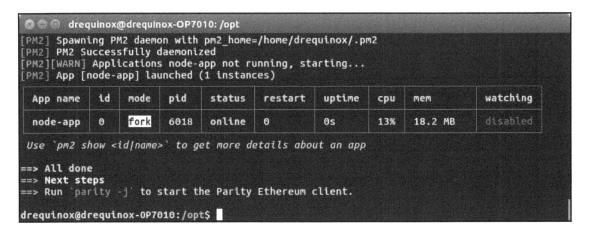

Parity startup

The client can optionally be listed on `https://ethstats.net/`. This site provides a valuable statistic about the Ethereum network such as latest block information, block times, difficulty, gas price and other valuable information. An example is shown as follows:

Ethstats.net Ethereum network statistics

All connected clients are listed on the ethstats.net, as shown in the following screenshot. These clients are listed with relevant attributes, such as the node name, node type, latency, mining status, number of peers, number of pending transactions, last block, difficultly, block transactions, and number of uncles.

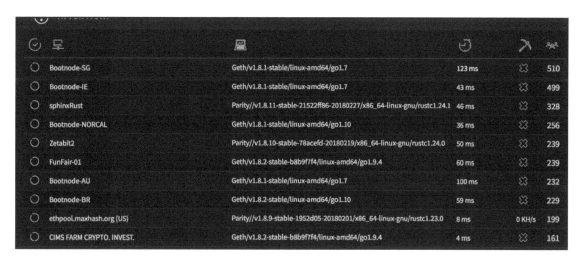

Client listed on https://ethstats.net/

Parity also offers a user-friendly web interface from where various tasks, such as account management, address book management, DApp management, contract management, and status and signer operations, can be managed.

This is accessible by issuing the following command:

```
$ parity ui
```

This will bring up the interface shown as follows:

Parity user interface

If parity is running in the Geth compatibility mode, the Parity UI is disabled. To enable the UI along with Geth compatibility, the following command can be used:

```
$ parity --geth --force-ui
```

The preceding command will start Parity in the Geth compatibility mode and also enable the web user interface.

Creating accounts using the parity command line

The following command can be used to create a new account using parity:

```
$ parity account new
Please note that password is NOT RECOVERABLE. Type password:
Repeat password:
26-11-30  2:18:55 UTC c8c92a910cfbce2e655c88d37a89b6657d1498fb
```

APIs, tools, and DApps

Web3 JavaScript API provides an interface to the Ethereum blockchain via JavaScript. It provides an object called `web3` which contains other objects that expose different methods to support interaction with the blockchain. This API covers methods related to administration of the blockchain, debugging, account-related operations, supporting protocols methods for Whisper, storage, and other network related operations.

This API will be discussed in detail in the next chapter, `Chapter 12`, *Ethereum Development Environment* where we will see how to interact with the Ethereum blockchain.

Applications (DApps and DAOs) developed on Ethereum

There are various implementations of DAOs and smart contracts in Ethereum, most notably, the DAO, which was recently misused due to a weakness in the code and required a hard fork for funds to be recovered that have been syphoned out by the attackers. The DAO was created to serve as a decentralized platform to collect and distribute investments.

Augur is another DApp that has been implemented on Ethereum, which is a decentralized prediction market.

Many other decentralized applications are listed on
`https://www.stateofthedapps.com/`.

Tools

Various frameworks and tools have been developed to support decentralized application development such as Truffle, MetaMask, Ganache, TestRPC and many more. We will talk about these in `Chapter 13`, *Development Tools and Frameworks*.

Supporting protocols

Various supporting protocols are available to assist the complete decentralized ecosystem. This includes Whisper and Swarm protocols. In addition to the contracts layer, which is the core blockchain layer, there are additional layers that need to be decentralized in order to achieve a complete decentralized ecosystem. This includes decentralized storage and decentralized messaging.

Whisper, which is being developed for Ethereum, is a decentralized messaging protocol, whereas Swarm is a decentralized storage protocol. Both of these technologies provide the basis for a fully decentralized web. Both the technologies are described in the following sections.

Whisper

Whisper provides decentralized peer-to-peer messaging capabilities to the Ethereum network. In essence, Whisper is a communication protocol that DApps use to communicate with each other. The data and routing of messages are encrypted within Whisper communications. Whisper makes use of DEVp2p wire protocol for exchanging messages between nodes on the network. Moreover, it is designed to be used for smaller data transfers and in scenarios where real-time communication is not required. Whisper is also designed to provide a communication layer that cannot be traced and provides *dark communication* between parties. Blockchain can be used for communication, but that is expensive, and a consensus is not really required for messages exchanged between nodes. Therefore, Whisper can be used as a protocol that allows censor resistant communication. Whisper messages are ephemeral and have an associated time to live TTL. Whisper is already available with Geth and can be enabled using the `--shh` option while running the Geth Ethereum client. Official Whisper documentation is available at `https://github.com/ethereum/wiki/wiki/Whisper`.

Swarm

Swarm has been developed as a distributed file storage platform. It is a decentralized, distributed, and peer-to-peer storage network. Files in this network are addressed by the hash of their content. This is in contrast to the traditional centralized services, where storage is available at a central location only. This is developed as a native base layer service for the Ethereum Web 3 stack. Swarm is integrated with DEVp2p, which is the multiprotocol network layer of Ethereum. Swarm is envisaged to provide a **Distributed Denial of Service** (**DDOS**)-resistant and fault-tolerant distributed storage layer for Ethereum Web 3.0. Similar to shh in Whisper, Swarm has a protocol called bzz which is used by each Swarm node to perform various Swarm protocol operations.

 Official Swarm documentation is available at https://swarm-guide.readthedocs.io/en/latest/.

The following diagram gives a high-level overview of how Swarm and Whisper fit together and work with the Ethereum blockchain:

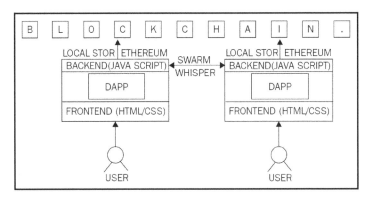

The diagram shows blockchain, Whisper, and Swarm

With the development of Whisper and Swarm a complete decentralized ecosystem emerges, where Ethereum is considered a decentralized computer (state), Whisper as decentralized communication, and Swarm as decentralized storage.

If you recall, in Chapter 2, *Decentralization* we mentioned that decentralization of the whole ecosystem is highly desirable as opposed to only decentralization of the core computation element. Development of Whisper and Swarm is a step towards decentralization of the complete blockchain ecosystem.

Scalability, security, and other challenges

Scalability in any blockchain is a fundamental issue. Security is also of paramount importance. Issues such as privacy and confidentiality have caused some adaptability issues, especially in the financial sector. However, a great deal of research is being conducted in these areas. A more detailed discussion regarding all blockchain-related issues will be carried out in Chapter 18, *Scalability and Other Challenges*.

Trading and investment

Ether is available at various exchanges for buying and selling. The current market cap of Ethereum is $67,765,787,333 USD at the time of writing (March, 2018), and an Ether is worth approximately $690.29 USD.

The following chart shows the historical market capitalization details:

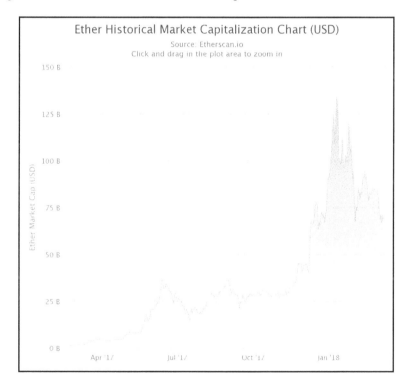

Ether historical market capitalization (source Etherscan.io)

Ether can either be purchased on various online exchanges, or it can be mined. There are online services available, such as `https://shapeshift.io`, that allow conversion from one currency to another.

Various online exchanges, such as Kraken, coinbase, and many more, offer Ether to be purchased for Fiat currency using credit cards or another virtual currency, such as bitcoin.

Summary

This chapter started with the introduction of programming languages for programming smart contracts in Ethereum. After this, other concepts such as blocks, block structure, gas, and messages were also introduced and discussed in detail. The later sections of the chapter introduced the practical installation and management of Ethereum clients. Two most famous clients, Geth and Parity, were discussed.

Finally, supporting protocols and topics related to challenges faced by Ethereum were presented. Ethereum is under continuous development, and new improvements are being made by a dedicated community of developers regularly. Ethereum improvement proposals, available at `https://github.com/ethereum/EIPs`, are also an indication of the magnitude of research and keen interest by the community in this technology. Moreover, a recently launched initiative, **Enterprise Ethereum Alliance** (**EEA**) is aiming to develop enterprise-grade Ethereum platform which will be capable of meeting enterprise-level business requirements.

In the next chapter, we will explore Ethereum smart contract development, relevant tools and frameworks.

12
Ethereum Development Environment

This chapter introduces the Ethereum development environment. Several examples will be introduced in this chapter to complement the theoretical concepts provided in earlier chapters. This chapter will mainly cover the setup of the development environment and how to use relevant tools to create and deploy smart contracts using Ethereum blockchain.

The first task is to set up a development environment. This section introduces the Ethereum setup for testnet and private net. Testnet is called Ropsten and is used by developers or users as a test platform to test smart contracts and other blockchain-related proposals. The private net option in Ethereum allows the creation of an independent private network that can be used as a shared distributed ledger between participating entities and for the development and testing of smart contracts. While there are other clients available for Ethereum, such as Parity, which was introduced in `Chapter 11`, *Further Ethereum*, Geth is the leading client for Ethereum and the common tool of choice, as such this chapter will use Geth for the examples.

There are various ways to do development for Ethereum blockchain. We will see all the mainstream options in this chapter. The topics that we will cover in this chapter are listed here:

- Test networks
- How to setup Ethereum private net

There are multiple ways to develop smart contracts on Ethereum. A usual and sensible approach is to develop and test Ethereum smart contracts either in a local private net or a simulated environment, and then it can be deployed on a public testnet. After all the relevant tests are successful on public testnet, the contracts can then be deployed to the public mainnet. There are however variations in this process, and many developers opt to only develop and test contracts on local simulated environments and then deploy on public mainnet or their private production blockchain networks. Developing first on a simulated environment and then deploying directly to a public network can lead to faster time to production, as setting up private networks may take longer as compared to setting a local development environment with a blockchain simulator. We will explore all these approaches in `Chapter 13`, *Development Tools and Frameworks* and `Chapter 14`, *Introducing Web3*.

There are new tools and frameworks available like Truffle, Ganache, and MetaMask which makes development and testing for Ethereum easier. We will look into these tools in more depth in the `Chapter 13`, *Development Tools and Frameworks*, but first, we will use a manual approach whereby we develop a smart contract and deploy it manually via command line to the private network. This will allow us to see that what actually happens in the background.

Frameworks and tools make the development easier but hide most of the finer *under the hood* details that I believe are essential for beginners to understand to build a strong foundation before they start using frameworks. It is important to understand the underlying details too. Therefore, first we will learn development using native tools available in Ethereum and once we have understood all the foundational knowledge we can start using the development frameworks like Truffle, which indeed makes development and testing very easy.

Let us start with connecting to a test network.

Test networks

The Ethereum Go client (`https://geth.ethereum.org`) Geth, can be connected to the test network using the following command:

```
$ geth --testnet
```

A sample output is shown in the following screenshot. The screenshot shows the type of the network chosen and various other pieces of information regarding the blockchain download:

```
imran@drequinox-OP7010:~$ geth --testnet
I1204 16:03:32.759308 cmd/utils/flags.go:613] WARNING: No etherbase set and no accounts found as default
I1204 16:03:32.759415 ethdb/database.go:83] Allotted 128MB cache and 1024 file handles to /home/imran/.ethereum/testnet/geth/chaindata
I1204 16:03:32.807292 ethdb/database.go:176] closed db:/home/imran/.ethereum/testnet/geth/chaindata
I1204 16:03:32.807589 node/node.go:175] instance: Geth/v1.5.2-stable-c8695209/linux/go1.7.3
I1204 16:03:32.807603 ethdb/database.go:83] Allotted 128MB cache and 1024 file handles to /home/imran/.ethereum/testnet/geth/chaindata
I1204 16:03:32.814016 eth/backend.go:280] Successfully wrote custom genesis block: 0cd786a2425d16f152c658316c423e6ce1181e15c3295826d7c99
04cba9ce303
I1204 16:03:32.814076 eth/db_upgrade.go:346] upgrading db log bloom bins
I1204 16:03:32.814112 eth/db_upgrade.go:354] upgrade completed in 36.513µs
I1204 16:03:32.814128 eth/backend.go:193] Protocol Versions: [63 62], Network Id: 2
I1204 16:03:32.814363 core/blockchain.go:214] Last header: #0 [0cd786a2…] TD=131072
I1204 16:03:32.814375 core/blockchain.go:215] Last block: #0 [0cd786a2…] TD=131072
I1204 16:03:32.814382 core/blockchain.go:216] Fast block: #0 [0cd786a2…] TD=131072
I1204 16:03:32.814840 p2p/server.go:336] Starting Server
I1204 16:03:37.983847 p2p/discover/udp.go:217] Listening, enode://faB38ec3fee8a26d75755b55f7cbdd80efacc4a98b5291acd5a23aea5465b794c84aff
e7be633524d2895768a2122a25e87cf97bd369895ace9f48f868eaef18@[::]:30303
I1204 16:03:37.983960 p2p/server.go:604] Listening on [::]:30303
I1204 16:03:37.984963 node/node.go:340] IPC endpoint opened: /home/imran/.ethereum/testnet/geth.ipc
I1204 16:04:17.984160 eth/downloader/downloader.go:326] Block synchronisation started
```

The output of the geth command connecting to Ethereum test net

A blockchain explorer for testnet is located at `https://ropsten.etherscan.io` can be used to trace transactions and blocks on the Ethereum test network.

There are other test networks available too, such as Frontier, Morden, Ropsten, and Rinkeby. Geth can be issued with a command-line flag to connect to the desired network:

`--testnet: Ropsten network: pre-configured proof-of-work test network`
`--rinkeby: Rinkeby network: pre-configured proof-of-authority test network`
`--networkid value: Network identifier (integer, 1=Frontier, 2=Morden (disused), 3=Ropsten, 4=Rinkeby) (default: 1)`

Now let us do some experiments with building a private network and then we will see how a contract can be deployed on this network using the Mist and command-line tools.

Setting up a private net

Private net allows the creation of an entirely new blockchain. This is different from testnet or mainnet in the sense that it uses its on-genesis block and network ID. In order to create private net, three components are needed:

- Network ID.
- The Genesis file.
- Data directory to store blockchain data. Even though the data directory is not strictly required to be mentioned, if there is more than one blockchain already active on the system, then the data directory should be specified so that a separate directory is used for the new blockchain.

On the mainnet, the Geth Ethereum client is capable of discovering *boot nodes* by default as they are hardcoded in the Geth client, and connects automatically, but on a private net, Geth needs to be configured by specifying appropriate flags and configuration in order for it to be discoverable by other peers or to be able to discover other peers. We will see how this is achieved shortly.

In addition to the previously mentioned three components, it is desirable that you disable **node discovery** so that other nodes on the internet cannot discover your private network and it is secure. If other networks happen to have the same genesis file and network ID, they may connect to your private net. The chance of having the same network ID and genesis block is very low, but, nevertheless, disabling node discovery is good practice, and is recommended.

In the following section, all these parameters are discussed in detail with a practical example.

Network ID

Network ID can be any positive number except 1 and 3, which are already in use by Ethereum mainnet and testnet (Ropsten), respectively. Network ID 786 has been chosen for the example private network discussed later in this section.

The genesis file

The genesis file contains the necessary fields required for a custom genesis block. This is the first block in the network and does not point to any previous block. The Ethereum protocol performs checking in order to ensure that no other node on the internet can participate in the consensus mechanism unless they have the same genesis block. Chain ID is usually used as an identification of the network.

A custom genesis file that will be used later in the example is shown here:

```
{
    "nonce": "0x0000000000000042",
    "timestamp": "0x00",
    "parentHash":
"0x0000000000000000000000000000000000000000000000000000000000000000",
    "extraData": "0x00",
    "gasLimit": "0x8000000",
    "difficulty": "0x0400",
```

```
        "mixhash":
 "0x0000000000000000000000000000000000000000000000000000000000000000",
        "coinbase": "0x3333333333333333333333333333333333333333",
        "alloc": {
        },
        "config": {
            "chainId": 786,
            "homesteadBlock": 0,
            "eip155Block": 0,
            "eip158Block": 0
        }
 }
```

This file is saved as a text file with the JSON extension; for example, `privategenesis.json`. Optionally, Ether can be pre-allocated by specifying the beneficiary's addresses and the amount of Wei, but it is usually not necessary as being on the private network, Ether can be mined very quickly.

In order to pre-allocate a section can be added to the genesis file, as shown here:

```
 "alloc": {
          "0xcf61d213faa9acadbf0d110e1397caf20445c58f ": { "balance":
 "100000" },
 }
```

Now let's see what each of these parameters mean.

- nonce: This is a 64-bit hash used to prove that PoW has been sufficiently completed. This works in combination with the mixhash parameter.
- timestamp: This is the Unix timestamp of the block. This is used to verify the sequence of the blocks and for difficulty adjustment. For example, if blocks are being generated too quickly that difficulty goes higher.
- parentHash: This is always zero being the genesis (first) block as there is no parent of the first block.
- extraData: This parameter allows a 32-bit arbitrary value to be saved with the block.
- gasLimit: This is the limit on the expenditure of gas per block.
- difficulty: This parameter is used to determine the mining target. It represents the difficulty level of the hash required to prove the PoW.

- `mixhash`: This is a 256-bit hash which works in combination with `nonce` to prove that sufficient amount of computational resources has been spent in order to complete the PoW requirements.
- `coinbase`: This is the 160-bit address where the mining reward is sent to as a result of successful mining.
- `alloc`: This parameter contains the list of pre-allocated wallets. The long hex digit is the account to which the balance is allocated.
- `config`: This section contains various configuration information defining chain ID, and blockchain hard fork block numbers. This parameter is not required to be used in private networks.

Data directory

This is the directory where the blockchain data for the private Ethereum network will be saved. For example, in the following example, it is `~/etherprivate/`.

In the Geth client, a number of parameters are specified in order to launch, further fine-tune the configuration, and launch the private network. These flags are listed here.

Flags and their meaning

The following are the flags used with the Geth client:

- `--nodiscover`: This flag ensures that the node is not automatically discoverable if it happens to have the same genesis file and network ID.
- `--maxpeers`: This flag is used to specify the number of peers allowed to be connected to the private net. If it is set to `0`, then no one will be able to connect, which might be desirable in a few scenarios, such as private testing.
- `--rpc`: This is used to enable the RPC interface in Geth.
- `--rpcapi`: This flag takes a list of APIs to be allowed as a parameter. For example, `eth`, `web3` will enable the Eth and Web3 interface over RPC.
- `--rpcport`: This sets up the TCP RPC port; for example: `9999`.
- `--rpccorsdomain`: This flag specifies the URL that is allowed to connect to the private Geth node and perform RPC operations. `cors` in `--rpccorsdomain` means cross-origin resource sharing.

- `--port`: This specifies the TCP port that will be used to listen to the incoming connections from other peers.
- `--identity`: This flag is a string that specifies the name of a private node.

Static nodes

If there is a need to connect to a specific set of peers, then these nodes can be added to a file where the `chaindata` and `keystore` files are saved.

For example, in the `~/etherprivate/` directory. The filename should be `static-nodes.json`. This is valuable in a private network because this way the nodes can be discovered on a private network. An example of the JSON file is shown as follows:

```
[
"enode://
44352ede5b9e792e437c1c0431c1578ce3676a87e1f588434aff1299d30325c233c8d426fc5
7a25380481c8a36fb3be2787375e932fb4885885f6452f6efa77f@xxx.xxx.xxx.xxx:TCP_P
ORT"
]
```

Here, xxx is the public IP address and `TCP_PORT` can be any valid and available TCP port on the system. The long hex string is the node ID.

Starting up the private network

The initial command to start the private network is shown as follows:

```
$ ./geth init ~/ethpriv/privategenesis.json --datadir ~/ethpriv/
```

It is assumed that in the home directory there is a directory named `ethereprivate` which contains the `privategenesis.json` file.

This will produce an output similar to what is shown in the following screenshot:

```
[12-13|19:19:11] No etherbase set and no accounts found as default
[12-13|19:19:11] Allocated cache and file handles          =/Users/drequinox/etherprivate/geth/chaindata       =16       =16
[12-13|19:19:11] Writing custom genesis block
[12-13|19:19:11] Successfully wrote genesis state           =chaindata                                          =6650a0…b5c158
[12-13|19:19:11] Allocated cache and file handles           =/Users/drequinox/etherprivate/geth/lightchaindata  =16       =16
[12-13|19:19:11] Writing custom genesis block
[12-13|19:19:11] Successfully wrote genesis state           =lightchaindata                                     =6650a0…b5c158
```

Private network initialization

This output indicates that a genesis block has been created successfully. In order for `geth` to start, the following command can be issued:

```
$ ./geth --datadir ~/etherprivate/ --networkid 786 --rpc --rpcapi
  'web3,eth,net,debug,personal'  --rpccorsdomain '*'
```

This will produce the following output:

```
WARN [12-13|19:20:11] No etherbase set and no accounts found as default
INFO [12-13|19:20:11] Starting peer-to-peer node            instance=Geth/v1.7.3-stable-4bb3c89d/darwin-amd64/go1.9.2
INFO [12-13|19:20:11] Allocated cache and file handles      database=/Users/drequinox/etherprivate/geth/chaindata
WARN [12-13|19:20:11] Upgrading database to use lookup entries
INFO [12-13|19:20:11] Initialised chain configuration       config="{ChainID: 786 Homestead: 0 DAO: <nil> DAOSupport:
INFO [12-13|19:20:11] Disk storage enabled for ethash caches  dir=/Users/drequinox/etherprivate/geth/ethash count=3
INFO [12-13|19:20:11] Disk storage enabled for ethash DAGs  dir=/Users/drequinox/.ethash                    count=2
INFO [12-13|19:20:11] Initialising Ethereum protocol        versions="[63 62]" network=786
INFO [12-13|19:20:11] Database deduplication successful     deduped=0
INFO [12-13|19:20:11] Loaded most recent local header       number=0 hash=6650a0…b5c158 td=1024
INFO [12-13|19:20:11] Loaded most recent local full block   number=0 hash=6650a0…b5c158 td=1024
INFO [12-13|19:20:11] Loaded most recent local fast block   number=0 hash=6650a0…b5c158 td=1024
INFO [12-13|19:20:11] Regenerated local transaction journal transactions=0 accounts=0
INFO [12-13|19:20:11] Starting P2P networking
INFO [12-13|19:20:13] UDP listener up                       self=enode://5c53ec0755806bc92432728f22a55f169a8c63df307fc
7a55d635@86.15.44.209:30303
INFO [12-13|19:20:13] RLPx listener up                      self=enode://5c53ec0755806bc92432728f22a55f169a8c63df307fc
7a55d635@86.15.44.209:30303
INFO [12-13|19:20:13] IPC endpoint opened: /Users/drequinox/etherprivate/geth.ipc
INFO [12-13|19:20:14] Mapped network port                   proto=udp extport=30303 intport=30303 interface="UPNP IGDv
INFO [12-13|19:20:14] Mapped network port                   proto=tcp extport=30303 intport=30303 interface="UPNP IGDv
```

Starting geth for a private network

Now `geth` can be attached via **Inter-Process Communications** (**IPC**) (IPC is a mechanism to allow communication between processes running on the computer locally) to the running `geth` client on a private network using the following command. This will allow you to interact with the running `geth` session on the private network:

```
$ geth attach ipc:.ethereum/privatenet/geth.ipc
```

As shown here, this will open the interactive JavaScript console for the running private net session:

```
Welcome to the Geth JavaScript console!

instance: Geth/v1.7.3-stable-4bb3c89d/darwin-amd64/go1.9.2
  modules: admin:1.0 debug:1.0 eth:1.0 miner:1.0 net:1.0 personal:1.0 rpc:1.0 txpool:1.0 web3:1.0

>
```

Starting geth to attach with private net 786

You may have noticed that a warning message appears when Geth starts up. This is shown at the top line of the *Starting geth for a private network* screenshot.

 WARNING: No etherbase set and no accounts found as default.

This message appears because there are no accounts currently available in the new test network and no account is set as etherbase to receive mining rewards. This issue can be addressed by creating a new account and setting that account as etherbase. This will also be required when mining is carried out on the test network.

This is shown in the following commands. Note that these commands are entered in the Geth JavaScript console, as shown in the preceding screenshot. The following command creates a new account. In this context, the account will be created on the private network ID 786:

```
personal.newAccount("Password123")
"0xcf61d213faa9acadbf0d110e1397caf20445c58f"
```

Once the account is created, the next step is to set it as an etherbase/coinbase account so that the mining reward goes to this account. This can be achieved using the following command:

```
> miner.setEtherbase(personal.listAccounts[0])
true
```

Currently, the etherbase account has no balance, as can be seen using the following command:

```
> eth.getBalance(eth.coinbase).toNumber();
 0
```

Finally, mining can start by simply issuing the following command. This command takes one parameter that is, number of threads. In the following example, two threads will be allocated to the mining process by specifying 2 as an argument to the start function:

```
> miner.start(2)
true
```

After mining starts, the first DAG generation is carried out and output similar to the following is produced:

```
I0211 23:58:50.380089 eth/backend.go:479] Automatic pregeneration of ethash DAG ON (ethash dir: /home/imran/.e
thash)
I0211 23:58:50.380097 miner/miner.go:136] Starting mining operation (CPU=2 TOT=3)
I0211 23:58:50.380138 eth/backend.go:486] checking DAG (ethash dir: /home/imran/.ethash)
I0211 23:58:50.380257 miner/worker.go:542] commit new work on block 1 with 0 txs & 0 uncles. Took 139.49µs
I0211 23:58:50.380292 vendor/github.com/ethereum/ethash/ethash.go:259] Generating DAG for epoch 0 (size 107373
9904) (0000000000000000000000000000000000000000000000000000000000000000)
I0211 23:58:51.166755 vendor/github.com/ethereum/ethash/ethash.go:276] Done generating DAG for epoch 0, it too
k 786.458657ms
```

DAG generation

Once DAG generation is finished and mining starts, geth will produce output similar to that shown in the following screenshot. It can be clearly seen that blocks are being mined successfully with the `Mined 5 blocks back: . . .` message.

```
I1204 22:38:02.373804 miner/worker.go:438] 🔨 ⛏ Mined 5 blocks back: block #487
I1204 22:38:02.373908 miner/worker.go:542] commit new work on block 493 with 0 txs & 0 uncles. Took 86.005µs
I1204 22:38:02.637297 miner/worker.go:344] 🔨 Mined block (#493 / 9a95245e). Wait 5 blocks for confirmation
I1204 22:38:02.637415 miner/worker.go:542] commit new work on block 494 with 0 txs & 0 uncles. Took 91.009µs
I1204 22:38:02.637436 miner/worker.go:438] 🔨 ⛏ Mined 5 blocks back: block #488
I1204 22:38:02.639064 miner/worker.go:542] commit new work on block 494 with 0 txs & 0 uncles. Took 1.609044ms
I1204 22:38:03.538525 miner/worker.go:344] 🔨 Mined block (#494 / cb89cccd). Wait 5 blocks for confirmation
I1204 22:38:03.538719 miner/worker.go:542] commit new work on block 495 with 0 txs & 0 uncles. Took 158.751µs
I1204 22:38:03.538745 miner/worker.go:438] 🔨 ⛏ Mined 5 blocks back: block #489
I1204 22:38:03.538860 miner/worker.go:542] commit new work on block 495 with 0 txs & 0 uncles. Took 95.822µs
I1204 22:38:03.548923 miner/worker.go:344] 🔨 Mined block (#495 / 539d8079). Wait 5 blocks for confirmation
I1204 22:38:03.549064 miner/worker.go:542] commit new work on block 496 with 0 txs & 0 uncles. Took 120.447µs
I1204 22:38:03.549082 miner/worker.go:438] 🔨 ⛏ Mined 5 blocks back: block #490
I1204 22:38:03.549159 miner/worker.go:542] commit new work on block 496 with 0 txs & 0 uncles. Took 64.047µs
```

Mining output

Mining can be stopped using the following command:

```
> miner.stop
true
```

In the JavaScript console, the current balance of total Ether can be queried, as shown in the following screenshot. After mining, a significant amount can be seen in the following example. Mining is extremely fast as it is a private network with no competition for solving the PoW and also in the genesis file, the network difficulty has also been set quite low:

```
> eth.getBalance(eth.coinbase).toNumber();
85000000000000000000000
```

A general tip to see the list of available objects is that if two spaces and two tabs on the keyboard are pressed in a sequence, a complete list of the available objects will be displayed. This is shown in the following screenshot:

```
>
Array          Math           TypeError        constructor        hasOwnProperty     parseFloat              toString
BigNumber      NaN            URIError         debug              inspect            parseInt               txpool
Boolean        Number         Web3             decodeURI          isFinite           personal               undefined
Date           Object         _setInterval     decodeURIComponent  isNaN              propertyIsEnumerable   unescape
Error          RangeError     _setTimeout      encodeURI          isPrototypeOf      require                valueOf
EvalError      ReferenceError admin            encodeURIComponent  jeth               rpc                    web3
Function       RegExp         clearInterval    escape             loadScript         setInterval
Infinity       String         clearTimeout     eth                miner              setTimeout
JSON           SyntaxError    console          eval               net                toLocaleString
>
```

Available objects

Furthermore, when a command is typed, it can be autocompleted by pressing *Tab* twice. If two tabs are pressed, then the list of available methods is also displayed. This is shown in the following screenshot:

```
> personal.
personal._requestManager  personal.getListAccounts  personal.lockAccount        personal.sign
personal.constructor      personal.importRawKey     personal.newAccount         personal.unlockAccount
personal.ecRecover        personal.listAccounts     personal.sendTransaction
> net.
net._requestManager  net.getListening   net.getVersion      net.peerCount
net.constructor      net.getPeerCount   net.listening       net.version
```

Available methods

In addition to the previously mentioned command, in order to get a list of available methods of an object, after typing a command, (semicolon ;) is entered. An example is shown in the next screenshot, which shows a list of all the methods available for net:

```
> net;
{
  listening: true,
  peerCount: 0,
  version: "786",
  getListening: function(callback),
  getPeerCount: function(callback),
  getVersion: function(callback)
}
>
```

List of methods

There are a few other commands that can be used to query the private network. Some examples are shown as follows:

- Get the current gas price:

```
> eth.gasPrice
18000000000
```

- Get the latest block number:

```
> eth.blockNumber
587
```

Debug can come in handy when debugging issues. A sample command is shown here; however, there are many other methods available. List of these methods can be viewed by typing debug;. The following method will return the RLP of block 0:

- Encode using RLP:

```
> debug.getBlockRlp(0)
"f901f8f901f3a0000000000000000000000000000000000000000000000000000000000000
0000a01dcc4de8dec75d7aab85b567b6ccd41ad312451b948a7413f0a142fd40d4934794333
33333333333333333333333333333333333333a056e81f171bcc55a6ff8345e692c0f86e5b48
e01b996cadc001622fb5e363b421a056e81f171bcc55a6ff8345e692c0f86e5b48e01b996ca
dc001622fb5e363b421a056e81f171bcc55a6ff8345e692c0f86e5b48e01b996cadc001622f
b5e363b421b90100000000000000000000000000000000000000000000000000000000000000
0000000000000000000000000000000000000000000000000000000000000000000000000000
0000000000000000000000000000000000000000000000000000000000000000000000000000
0000000000000000000000000000000000000000000000000000000000000000000000000000
0000000000000000000000000000000000000000000000000000000000000000000000000000
0000000000000000000000000000000000000000000000000000000000000000000000000000
0000000000000000000000000000000000000000000000000000000000000000000000000000
00082040080840800000808000a0000000000000000000000000000000000000000000000000
00000000000000000088000000000000000042c0c0"
```

- Create a new account, note that Password123 is the password chosen as an example, you can choose any:

```
personal.newAccount("Password123")
"0xcf61d213faa9acadbf0d110e1397caf20445c58f"
```

- Unlock the account before sending transactions:

```
> personal.unlockAccount
("0xcf61d213faa9acadbf0d110e1397caf20445c58f")
     Unlock account 0xcf61d213faa9acadbf0d110e1397caf20445c58f
```

- Send transactions:

```
> eth.sendTransaction({from:
"0x76f11b383dbc3becf8c5d9309219878caae265c3", to:
"0xcce6450413ac80f9ee8bd97ca02b92c065d77abc", value: 1000})
```

Note that `1000` is the amount of funds in Wei.

Another way is to use the `listAccounts[]` method, this can be done as shown here:

```
> eth.sendTransaction({from: personal.listAccounts[0], to:
personal.listAccounts[1], value: 1000})
```

Running Mist on private net

It is possible to run Mist on a private net by issuing the following command. This binary is usually available in `/opt/Ethereum` on Linux (Ubuntu) platform:

```
Under Mac OS this is usually available under /Applications/Ethereum
Wallet.app/Contents/MacOS
```

There are two methods of connectivity to `geth` from Mist, one is using **IPC** and the other is **RPC/HTTP** based. Both commands are shown here:

```
$ ./Ethereum Wallet --rpc ~/.ethereum/privatenet/geth.ipc
$./Ethereum Wallet --rpc http://127.0.0.1:8545
```

If you run Mist using `-rpc` with the HTTP option then it will display a message saying that it is a less secure method of connection, simply press **OK** as being on a private test network, as the network is local and not connected to the internet, also it will not be used publicly, therefore this is not really an issue.

The message is similar to the one shown here:

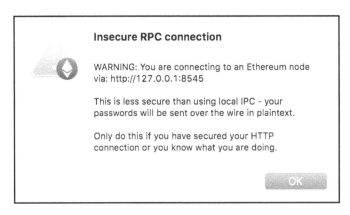

Insecure RPC connection

WARNING: You are connecting to an Ethereum node
via: http://127.0.0.1:8545

This is less secure than using local IPC - your
passwords will be sent over the wire in plaintext.

Only do this if you have secured your HTTP
connection or you know what you are doing.

OK

Insecure RPC connection

This will allow a connection to the running private net Geth session and it provides all the features, such as wallet, account management, and contract deployment on private net via Mist.

```
imran@drequinox-OP7010: /opt/Ethereum Wallet
imran@drequinox-OP7010:/opt/Ethereum Wallet$ ./Ethereum\ Wallet --rpc /home/imran/.ethereum/privatenet/geth.ipc
[2016-12-06 07:58:08.706] [INFO] main - Running in production mode: true
Secp256k1 bindings are not compiled. Pure JS implementation will be used.
[2016-12-06 07:58:08.860] [INFO] main - Starting in Wallet mode
[2016-12-06 07:58:08.932] [INFO] Db - Loading db: /home/imran/.config/Ethereum Wallet/mist.lokidb
[2016-12-06 07:58:08.947] [INFO] Windows - Creating commonly-used windows
[2016-12-06 07:58:08.948] [INFO] Windows - Create secondary window: loading, owner: notset
[2016-12-06 07:58:09.012] [INFO] updateChecker - Check for update...
[2016-12-06 07:58:11.373] [INFO] Windows - Create primary window: main, owner: notset
[2016-12-06 07:58:11.385] [INFO] Windows - Create primary window: splash, owner: notset
[2016-12-06 07:58:11.989] [INFO] ipcCommunicator - Backend language set to: en-GB
[2016-12-06 07:58:13.199] [INFO] (ui: splash) - Web3 already initialized, re-using provider.
[2016-12-06 07:58:13.362] [INFO] ClientBinaryManager - Initializing...
[2016-12-06 07:58:13.363] [INFO] ClientBinaryManager - Resolving path to Eth client binary ...
[2016-12-06 07:58:13.363] [INFO] ClientBinaryManager - Eth client binary path: /opt/Ethereum Wallet/nodes/eth/linux-x64/eth
[2016-12-06 07:58:13.663] [INFO] ClientBinaryManager - Initializing...
[2016-12-06 07:58:13.664] [INFO] ClientBinaryManager - Resolving platform...
[2016-12-06 07:58:13.664] [INFO] ClientBinaryManager - Calculating possible clients...
[2016-12-06 07:58:13.667] [INFO] ClientBinaryManager - 1 possible clients.
[2016-12-06 07:58:13.667] [INFO] ClientBinaryManager - Verifying status of all 1 possible clients...
[2016-12-06 07:58:13.669] [INFO] ClientBinaryManager - Verify Geth status ...
[2016-12-06 07:58:13.691] [INFO] ClientBinaryManager - Checking for Geth sanity check ...
[2016-12-06 07:58:13.693] [INFO] ClientBinaryManager - Checking sanity for Geth ...
[2016-12-06 07:58:13.764] [INFO] Sockets/node-ipc - Connect to {"path":"/home/imran/.ethereum/privatenet/geth.ipc"}
[2016-12-06 07:58:13.768] [INFO] Sockets/node-ipc - Connected!
[2016-12-06 07:58:13.769] [INFO] NodeSync - Ethereum node connected, re-start sync
[2016-12-06 07:58:13.770] [INFO] NodeSync - Starting sync loop
[2016-12-06 07:58:13.771] [INFO] Sockets/7 - Connect to {"path":"/home/imran/.ethereum/privatenet/geth.ipc"}
[2016-12-06 07:58:13.772] [INFO] main - Connected via IPC to node.
[2016-12-06 07:58:13.801] [INFO] Sockets/7 - Connected!
[2016-12-06 07:58:13.818] [INFO] (ui: splash) - network is privatenet
[2016-12-06 07:58:14.939] [INFO] updateChecker - App is up-to-date.
```

Running Ethereum wallet to connect to private net using IPC

Once Ethereum Mist is launched, it will show the interface shown here, indicating clearly that it's running in the **PRIVATE-NET** mode:

Mist on private net

The preceding screenshot shows various options. These options are described here:

- **WALLETS**: This will open the wallets, if any
- **SEND**: Used to send funds to other accounts
- **CONTRACTS**: used to show the contracts interface, from where new contracts can be created and deployed
- **BALANCE**: Shows the current Ether balance

Also, at the top, it shows the type of the network that we are on. In this case it is **PRIVATE-NET**.

Mist can also run over the network using RPC. This is useful if Geth is running on a different node and Mist on another. This can be achieved by running Mist with the flag shown here:

```
--rpc http://127.0.0.1:8545
```

Deploying contracts using Mist

It is very easy to deploy new contracts using Mist. Mist provides an interface where contracts can be written in solidity and then deployed on the network.

In the exercise, a simple contract that can perform various simple arithmetic calculations on the input parameter will be used. Steps on how to use Mist to deploy this contract are shown here. As we have not yet introduced Solidity, the aim here is to allow users to experience the contract deployment and interaction process.

More information on coding and Solidity will be provided later in Chapter 13, *Development Tools and Frameworks* and Chapter 14, *Introducing Web3*, after which the following code will become easy to understand. Those of you who are already familiar with JavaScript or any other similar language such as C-language will find the code almost self-explanatory.

The example contract source code is shown as follows:

```
pragma solidity ^0.4.0; A
contract SimpleContract2
{
  uint z;
  function addition(uint x) public returns (uint y)
  {
    z=x+5;
    y=z;
  }
  function difference(uint x) public returns (uint y)
  {
    z=x-5;
    y=z;
  }
  function division(uint x) public returns (uint y)
  {
    z=x/5;
    y=z;
  }

  function currValue() public view returns (uint)
  {
    return z;
  }
}
```

This code can simply be copied into Mist under the **CONTRACTS** section, as shown here. On the left-hand side, the source code is copied; once verified and when no syntax errors are detected, the option to deploy the contract will appear in the drop-down menu on the right- hand side where it says **SELECT CONTRACT TO DEPLOY**. Simply select the contract and press the **Deploy** button at the bottom of the screen.

Mist browser contract deployment

Mist will ask for the password of the account and will show a window similar to the one in the following screenshot. Enter the password and click on **SEND TRANSACTION** to deploy the contract:

Create a contract using Mist

Once deployed and mined successfully, it will appear in the list of transactions in Mist, as shown in the following screenshot:

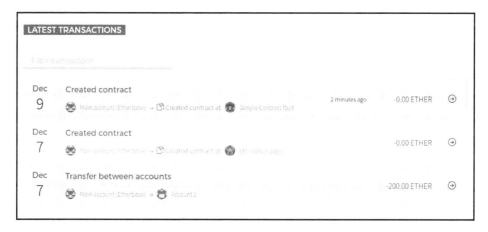

List of transactions after creation in Mist

Once the contract is available, it can be interacted with by using the available functions via Mist. This is shown in the following screenshot on the right-hand side, drop-down box, where the list of all available functions is available, from the contract:

Interaction with the contract using read and write options in Mist

In the preceding screenshot, the **READ FROM CONTRACT** and **WRITE TO CONTRACT** options are available. Also, the function that has been exposed by the contract can be seen on the right-hand side. Once the required function is selected, the appropriate value is entered for the function and the account (**Execute from**) is selected; press **EXECUTE** in order to execute the transaction, which will result in calling the selected function of the contract.

This process is shown in the following screenshot:

Contract execution in Mist

As shown in the screenshot, enter the appropriate password for the account and then press **SEND TRANSACTION** to send the transaction to the contract.

Block explorer for private net / local Ethereum block explorer

Local Ethereum block explorer is a useful tool that can be used to explore the local private net blockchain.

 There is an open source free block explorer available on GitHub at `https://github.com/etherparty/explorer`. We will use this software in our examples to visualize blocks and transactions.

This can be installed by following these steps:

1. On a Linux Ubuntu machine or macOS, run the following command in order to install the local Ethereum block explorer:

   ```
   $ git clone https://github.com/etherparty/explorer
   ```

   This will show output similar to the following:

   ```
   Cloning into 'explorer'...
   remote: Counting objects: 269, done.
   remote: Total 269 (delta 0), reused 0 (delta 0), pack-reused 269
   Receiving objects: 100% (269/269), 59.41 KiB | 134.00 KiB/s, done.
   Resolving deltas: 100% (139/139), done.
   ```

2. The next step is to change the directory to the explorer and run the following commands:

   ```
   $ cd explorer/
   $ npm start
   ```

 In case, Node.js installation is required on the computer you are using, you can check the official website for installation instructions and download node. Official website is: `https://nodejs.org/en/`.

Once the installation is finished (it may take almost 5 minutes), output similar to the following will be shown, where the HTTP server for Ethereum explorer starts up:

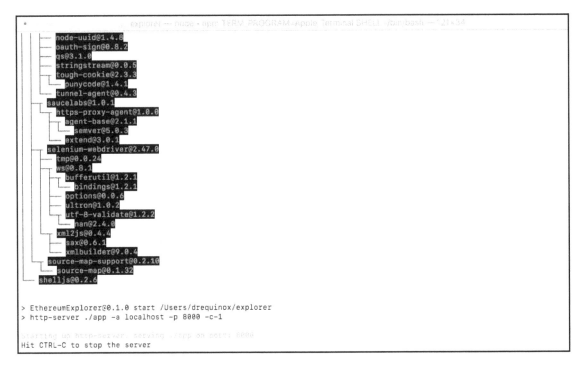

Ethereum explorer HTTP server

3. Once the web server is up, `geth` should be started up using the following command:

```
geth --datadir .ethereum/privatenet/ --networkid 786 --rpc
--rpccorsdomain 'http://localhost:8000'
```

Alternatively, you can use the following command:

```
geth --datadir .ethereum/privatenet/ --networkid 786 --rpc
--rpccorsdomain '*'
```

4. After a successful startup of `geth`, navigate to the localhost on TCP port 8000, as shown here, in order to access the local Ethereum block explorer.

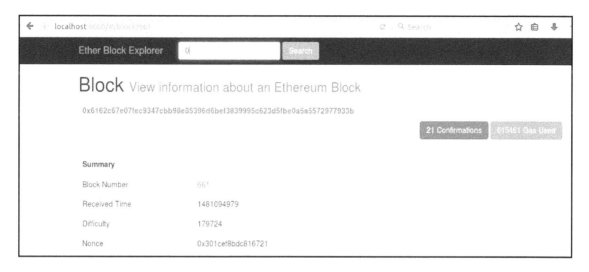

Block explorer

Alternatively, the web server can be started up using Python or any other appropriate provider. Using Python, a quick web server can be started, as shown in the following code:

```
$ python -m SimpleHTTPServer 7777
Serving HTTP on 0.0.0.0 port 7777 ...
```

The geth client will need to be started up with appropriate parameters. If not, an error like the one shown in the following screenshot can occur:

Allow Access to Geth and Refresh the Page

geth --rpc --rpccorsdomain "http://192.168.0.17:9900"

Error message

Restart `geth` to allow `rpccorsdomain`:

```
./geth --datadir ~/etherprivate/ --networkid 786 --rpc --rpcapi
'web3,eth,net,debug,personal'
--rpccorsdomain '*'
```

* means any IP can connect. You can also use your computer's local IP address.

Summary

In this chapter, we have explored Ethereum test networks and how-to setup private Ethereum networks. After the initial introduction to private network setup, we also saw that how the `geth` command-line tool can be used to perform various functions and how we can interact with the Ethereum blockchain. We also saw how Mist can be used to deploy contracts and send transactions.

In the next chapter, we will see that what tools, programming languages, and frameworks are available for development of smart contracts on Ethereum.

13
Development Tools and Frameworks

This chapter is an introduction to development tools, languages, and frameworks used for Ethereum smart contract development. We will examine different methods of developing smart contracts for the Ethereum blockchain. We will discuss various constructs of Solidity language in detail, which is currently the most popular development language for smart contract development on Ethereum.

In this chapter we will cover the following topics:

- Development tools, IDEs, and clients
    - Remix
    - Ganache
    - EthereumJS
    - TestRPC
    - MetaMask
    - Truffle
- Prerequisites
    - Node
    - Node Package Manager (NPM)
- Other tools and utilities

There are a number of tools available for Ethereum development. The following diagram shows the taxonomy of various development tools, clients, IDEs, and development frameworks for Ethereum:

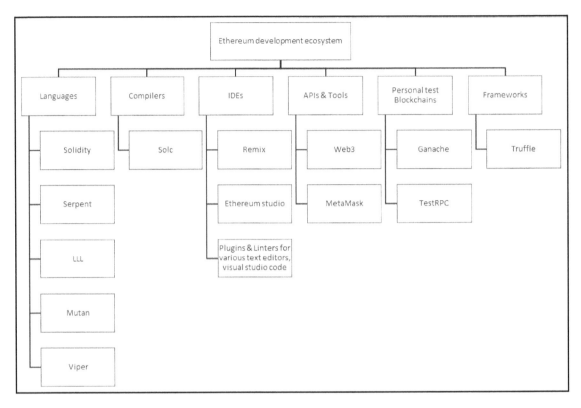

Taxonomy of Ethereum development ecosystem components

The preceding taxonomy does not include all frameworks and tools that are out there for development on Ethereum. It shows most commonly used tools and frameworks and also the ones that we will use in our examples throughout this chapter.

 There are number of resources available related to development tools for Ethereum at the address `http://ethdocs.org/en/latest/contracts-and-transactions/develope r-tools.html#developer-tools`.

In this chapter, the main focus will be on Geth, Remix IDE, Solidity, Ganache, MetaMask, solc, and Truffle. The rest of the elements such as prerequisites (Node) will also be discussed briefly.

Languages

Smart contracts can be programmed in a variety of languages for Ethereum blockchain. There are five languages that can be used in order to write contracts:

- **Mutan**: This is a Go-style language, which was deprecated in early 2015 and is no longer used.
- **LLL**: This is a **Low-level Lisp-like Language**, hence the name LLL. This is also not used anymore.
- **Serpent**: This is a simple and clean Python-like language. It is not used for contract development anymore and not supported by the community anymore.
- **Solidity**: This language has now become almost a standard for contract writing for Ethereum. This language is the focus of this chapter and is discussed in detail in later sections.
- **Vyper**: This language is a Python-like experimental language that is being developed to bring security, simplicity, and auditability to smart contract development.

Compilers

Compilers are used to convert high-level contract source code into the format that the Ethereum execution environment understands. The Solidity compiler is the most common one in use and is discussed here.

Solidity compiler (solc)

solc converts from a high-level solidity language into **Ethereum Virtual Machine** (**EVM**) bytecode so that it can be executed on the blockchain by EVM.

Installation on Linux

solc can be installed on a Linux Ubuntu operating system using the following commands:

```
$ sudo apt-get install solc
```

If PPAs are not already installed, those can be installed by running the following command:

```
$ sudo add-apt-repository ppa:ethereum/ethereum
$ sudo apt-get update
```

In order to verify the existing version of the solc and verify that it is installed, the following command can be used:

```
$ solc --version
solc, the solidity compiler commandline interface
Version: 0.4.19+commit.c4cbbb05.Darwin.appleclang
```

Installation on macOS

To install solc on macOS, execute the following commands:

```
$ brew tap ethereum/ethereum
$ brew install solidity
$ brew linkapps solidity
```

solc supports a variety of functions. A few examples are shown as follows:

- Display contract in a binary format:

  ```
  $ solc --bin Addition.sol
  ```

  This command will produce an output similar to the following. This shows the binary translation of the `Addition.sol` contract code:

```
imrans-MacBook-Pro:~ drequinox$ solc --bin Addition.sol

======= Addition.sol:Addition =======
Binary:
6060604052341561000f57600080fd5b61010b8061001e6000396000f30060606040526004361060495760003557c01000000
00000000000000000000000000000000000000000000000900463ffffffff16806336718d8014604e578063ac04e0a014
607d575b600080fd5b3415605857600080fd5b607b600480803560ff169060200190190803560ff1690602001909190505050
60a9565b005b3415608757600080fd5b608d60c9565b6040518082600ff1660ff1681526020019150506040518091039f35b
8082016000806101000a81548160ff021916908360ff1602179055550505065b6000806000905490610100a900460ff1690
50905600a165627a7a7230582037bbf1721ae442876d01fa64f7feee6baac85d550db40825cf6dea392487369e0029
imrans-MacBook-Pro:~ drequinox$ 
```

Solidity compiler binary output

- Estimate gas:

  ```
  $ solc --gas Addition.sol
  ```

This will give the following output:

```
imrans-MacBook-Pro:~ drequinox$ solc --gas Addition.sol

====== Addition.sol:Addition ======
Gas estimation:
construction:
   100 + 53400 = 53500
external:
   addx(uint8,uint8):   20475
   retrievex(): 464
imrans-MacBook-Pro:~ drequinox$
```

Gas estimation using solc

- Generate ABI:

$ solc --abi Addition.sol

The following are the contents of `Addition.abi`:

```
====== Addition.sol:Addition ======
Contract JSON ABI
[{"constant":false,"inputs":[{"name":"y","type":"uint8"},
{"name":"z","type":"uint8"}],"name":"addx","outputs":
[],"payable":false,"stateMutability":"nonpayable","type":"function"},{"constant":true,"inputs":
[],"name":"retrievex","outputs":
[{"name":"","type":"uint8"}],"payable":false,"stateMutability":"view","type":"function"}]
```

- Compilation:

Another useful command to compile and produce a binary compiled file along with an ABI is shown here:

$ solc --bin --abi --optimize -o bin Addition.sol

This command will produce two files in the output directory `bin`:

- `Addition.abi`: This contains the Application Binary Interface of the smart contract in JSON format
- `Addition.bin`: This contains the hex representation of binary of the smart contract code

The output of both files is shown in the following screenshot:

```
imrans-MacBook-Pro:bin drequinox$ cat Addition.abi
[{"constant":false,"inputs":[{"name":"y","type":"uint8"},{"name":"z","type":"uint8"}],"name":"addx","outputs":[]
,"payable":false,"stateMutability":"nonpayable","type":"function"},{"constant":true,"inputs":[],"name":"retrieve
x","outputs":[{"name":"","type":"uint8"}],"payable":false,"stateMutability":"view","type":"function"}]imrans-Mac
Book-Pro:bin drequinox$
imrans-MacBook-Pro:bin drequinox$
imrans-MacBook-Pro:bin drequinox$ cat Addition.bin
6060604052341561000f57600080fd5b60da8061001d6000396000f30060606040526004361060485763ffffffff7c010000000000000000
0000000000000000000000000000000000000006003504166336718d808114604d578063ac04e0a014606b575b600080fd5b3415605757
600080fd5b606960ff60043581169060024351660091565b005b3415607557600080fd5b607b60a5565b60405160ff9091168152602001604 0
5180910390f35b6000805460ff19169190920160ff16179055565b60005460ff16905600a165627a7a72305820f7ca91776882f1c97964c8
29324591eb96e72adb62b5548a67f4ea22e9daf2b80029imrans-MacBook-Pro:bin drequinox$
imrans-MacBook-Pro:bin drequinox$
imrans-MacBook-Pro:bin drequinox$
```

ABI and binary output of solidity compiler

ABI is the abbreviation of **Application Binary Interface**. ABI encodes information about smart contract's functions and events. It acts as an interface between EVM level bytecode and high level smart contract program code. To interact with a smart contract deployed on the Ethereum blockchain, external programs require ABI and address of the smart contract.

solc is a very powerful command and further options can be explored using `-- help` flag which will display detailed options. However, the preceding commands used for compilation, ABI generation and gas estimation should be sufficient for most development and deployment requirements.

Integrated Development Environments (IDEs)

There are various IDEs available for Solidity development. Most of the IDEs are available online and are presented via web interfaces. Remix (formerly browser Solidity) is the most commonly used IDE for building and debugging smart contracts. It is discussed here.

Remix

Remix is the web-based environment for the development and testing of contracts using Solidity. It is a feature-rich IDE which does not run on live blockchain; in fact, it is a simulated environment in which contracts can be deployed, tested, and debugged.

 It is available at `https://remix.ethereum.org`.

An example interface is shown as follows:

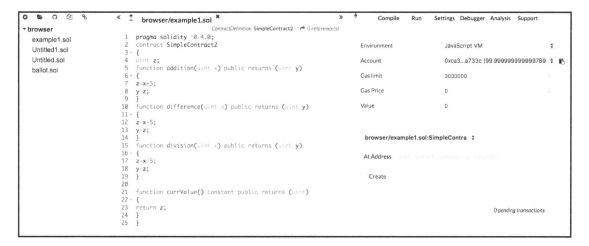

Remix IDE

On the left-hand side, there is a code editor with syntax highlighting and code formatting, and on the right-hand side, there are a number of tools available that can be used to deploy, debug, test, and interact with the contract.

Various features, such as transaction interaction, options to connect to JavaScript VM, configuration of execution environment, debugger, formal verification, and static analysis, are available. They can be configured to connect to execution environments such as JavaScript VM, injected Web3—where Mist, MetaMask, or a similar environment has provided the execution environment—or Web3 provider, which allows connection to the locally running Ethereum client (for example, `geth`) via IPC or RPC over HTTP (Web3 provider endpoint).

Remix also has a debugger for EVM which is very powerful and can be used to perform detailed level tracing and analysis of the EVM bytecode. An example is shown here:

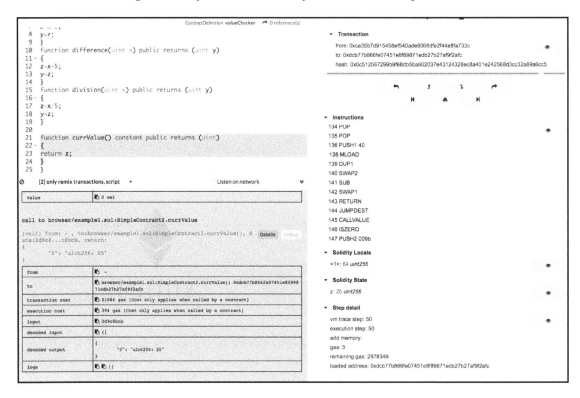

Remix IDE, debugging

The preceding screenshot shows different elements of the Remix IDE. On the top left-hand side, the source code is shown. Below that is the output log which shows informational messages and data related to compilation and execution of the contract.

The following screenshot shown shows the Remix debugger in more detail. It has the source code decoded into EVM instructions. The user can step through the instructions one by one and can examine what the source code does when executed:

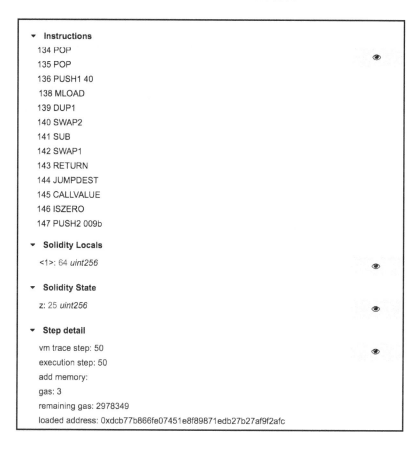

Remix Debugger

Tools and libraries

There are various tools and libraries available for Ethereum. The most common ones are discussed here.

In this section, we will first install prerequisites that are required for developing applications for Ethereum. First requirement is Node, which will see next.

Node version 7

As Node is required for most of the tools and libraries, it can be installed using the following commands:

```
$ curl -sL https://deb.nodesource.com/setup_7.x | sudo -E bash - sudo apt-get install -y nodejs
```

EthereumJS

At times, it is not possible to test on the testnet and mainnet is obviously not a place to test the contracts. Private net can be time-consuming to set up at times. EthereumJS' TestRPC comes in handy when quick testing is required and no proper testnet is available. It uses EthereumJS to simulate the Ethereum geth client behavior and allows for faster development testing. TestRPC is available via npm as a Node package.

Before installing TestRPC, Node should already have been installed and the npm package manager should also be available.

TestRPC can be installed using this command:

```
$ npm install -g ethereumjs-testrpc
```

In order to start testrpc, simply issue this command and keep it running in the background and open another Terminal to work on contracts:

```
$ testrpc
```

When TestRPC runs, it will display the output similar to the one shown in the following screenshot. It will automatically generate ten accounts and private keys, along with HD wallet. It will start to listen for incoming connection on TCP port 8545.

```
EthereumJS TestRPC v6.0.3 (ganache-core: 2.0.2)

Available Accounts
==================
(0) 0x6ca19d903eb53e00bb73622d275c965f2abad3d8
(1) 0x1f192daefa61ae050332e6a965e71fcf4621e887
(2) 0x97c0b2ea19a5b496e314e55d1e5a3a5d41b5ad21
(3) 0x3a04fbc6f8eb34b89918628a5a5fde4267e32e28
(4) 0x43e03d85a8a9328f510732be594993ac7011335c
(5) 0x6dfe1a7059df7a625c1ffaed0e97c42384b68446
(6) 0xb9992f167e68dc4bd4a1ce79c07b6193c4e72f37
(7) 0x46243dfcfb6d2d4ec60aa97ebbceac0f96aa33ab
(8) 0xe5b9c05dcb55ad987a504da7fb3dde4281d73bc4
(9) 0x37f6576fd633d95cbc29db28bbae4a272fe5594c

Private Keys
==================
(0) c82c6a860eeb57c8eedbd2e8bc59dc7c800f99118b7f1ef5540c41cdb10805dc
(1) 144271a65d21c59bd6f321659798b42e3d1a22feeb45c2c44f823db0477f330d
(2) d2a55f4406b23c8c18c55a6d30f4b4982ab17a01a6125f0d091e0d4807346905
(3) 1c16608a159b52ba84a0ae170d7642f316671251469349810960 40dccf4cae8b9
(4) b7dea27d5bd105bb3e4fbf69598b561563557d343d4c89ea2d7d689f5a160554
(5) 10d6467570c50e103ade3694ef85cf9ae0f14cf331ddcd9faaae1f752ed766c5
(6) 7571ece88840db22a09d8e6062292c1e3d106c9e9d8d634f05d4524e75bfa50a
(7) 15e215703ba63d52c870392086f3474b78b5a1b0b6f276fe48c9aae6061f478d
(8) 5dd1fd136b3ba917922b011daaf55ce2b5fd3e332a1f0d39ad5bef664190ebdb
(9) 30e1850a76ee65fcfd565caf81fa7310ff239679816be51f0b04149afe4407e1

HD Wallet
==================
Mnemonic:      prepare flavor identify liquid twice tip bullet blanket vast vivid hunt now
Base HD Path:  m/44'/60'/0'/0/{account_index}

Listening on localhost:8545
```

TestRPC

Ganache

Ganache is the latest addition to the plethora of development tools and libraries developed for Ethereum. This is, in a way a replacement of TestRPC and uses a user-friendly graphical user interface to see transaction and blocks and relevant details. This is fully working Byzantium enabled personal blockchain which is used to provide a local testing environment for blockchains.

Ganache is based on a JavaScript implementation of the Ethereum blockchain, with built-in block explorer and mining, making testing locally on the system very easy.

As shown in the following screenshot you can view transaction, blocks, and addresses in detail on the frontend:

Ganache, A personal Ethereum blockchain

Ganache can be downloaded from `http://truffleframework.com/ganache/`.

MetaMask

MetaMask allows interaction with Ethereum blockchain via Firefox and Chrome browsers. It injects a `web3` object within the running websites' JavaScript context which allows immediate interface capability for DApps. This *injection* allows DApps to interact directly with the blockchain.

It is available at `https://metamask.io/`.

MetaMask also allows account management. This acts as a verification method before any transaction is executed on the blockchain. The user is shown a secure interface to review the transaction for approval or rejection before it can reach the target blockchain.

It is available at `https://github.com/MetaMask/metamask-plugin`.

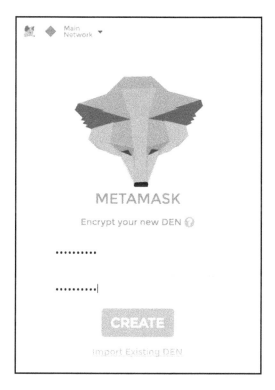

MetaMask

It allows connectivity with various Ethereum networks as shown in the following screenshot. This is the screenshot of the MetaMask, where it allows users to select the network of their choice:

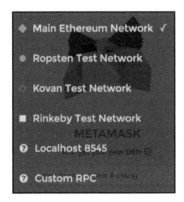

MetaMask networks as shown in the MetaMask user interface

An interesting feature to note is that MetaMask can connect to any custom RPC too which allows you to run your own blockchain, such as private nets locally or even remotely and allows your browser to connect to it. It can also be used to connect to a locally running blockchain like Ganache and TestRPC.

MetaMask allows account management and also records all transactions for these accounts. This is shown in the following screenshot:

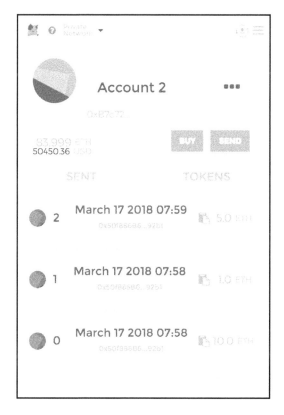

MetaMask accounts and transactions view

Truffle

Truffle (available at `http://truffleframework.com/`) is a development environment that makes it easier and simpler to test and deploy Ethereum contracts. Truffle provides contract compilation and linking along with an automated testing framework using Mocha and Chai. It also makes it easier to deploy the contracts to any private net, public, or testnet Ethereum blockchain. Also, asset pipeline is provided, which makes it easier for all JavaScript files to be processed, making them ready for use by a browser.

Installation

Before installation, it is assumed that `node` is available, which can be queried as shown here. If the `node` is not available, then the installation of `node` is required first in order to install `truffle`:

```
$ node -version
v7.2.1
```

The installation of `truffle` is very simple and can be done using the following command via **Node Package Manager** (**npm**):

```
$ sudo npm install -g truffle
```

This will take a few minutes; once it is installed, the `truffle` command can be used to display help information and verify that it is installed correctly:

```
$ sudo npm install -g truffle
Password:
/us/local/bin/truffle ->
/usr/local/lib/node_modules/truffle/build/cli.bundled.js
/usr/local/lib
└── truffle@4.0.1
```

Type `truffle` at Terminal to display usage help:

```
$ truffle
```

This will display the following output:

```
Truffle v4.0.1 - a development framework for Ethereum

Usage: truffle <command> [options]

Commands:
  init      Initialize new Ethereum project with example contracts and tests
  compile   Compile contract source files
  migrate   Run migrations to deploy contracts
  deploy    (alias for migrate)
  build     Execute build pipeline (if configuration present)
  test      Run Mocha and Solidity tests
  debug     Interactively debug any transaction on the blockchain (experimental)
  opcode    Print the compiled opcodes for a given contract
  console   Run a console with contract abstractions and commands available
  develop   Open a console with a local TestRPC
  create    Helper to create new contracts, migrations and tests
  install   Install a package from the Ethereum Package Registry
  publish   Publish a package to the Ethereum Package Registry
  networks  Show addresses for deployed contracts on each network
  watch     Watch filesystem for changes and rebuild the project automatically
  serve     Serve the build directory on localhost and watch for changes
  exec      Execute a JS module within this Truffle environment
  unbox     Unbox Truffle project
  version   Show version number and exit

See more at http://truffleframework.com/docs
```

Truffle help

Alternatively, the repository is available at `https://github.com/ConsenSys/truffle`, which can be cloned locally to install `truffle`. **Git** can be used to clone the repository using the following command:

```
$ git clone https://github.com/ConsenSys/truffle.git
```

We will use Truffle later in `Chapter 14`, *Introducing Web3* to test and deploy smart contracts on Ethereum blockchain.

Contract development and deployment

There are various steps that need to be taken in order to develop and deploy the contracts. Broadly, these can be divided into four steps: writing, testing, verification and deployment. After deployment, the next optional step is to create the user interface and present it to the end users via a web server. Web interface is sometimes not needed in the contracts where no human input or monitoring is required, but usually there is a requirement to create web interface to interact with the contract.

Writing

The writing step is concerned with writing the contract source code in Solidity. This can be done in any text editor. There are various plugins and add-ons available for Vim in Linux, Atom, and other editors that provide syntax highlighting and formatting for Solidity source code.

Visual studio code has become quite popular and is used commonly for Solidity development. There is a Solidity plugin available that allows syntax highlighting, formatting, and intelligence. It can be installed via **Extensions** option in Visual Studio Code.

Visual studio code

Testing

Testing is usually performed by automated means. Earlier in the chapter, you were introduced to Truffle, which uses the Mocha framework to test contracts. However, manual functional testing can be performed as well by using Remix and running functions manually and validating results. We will cover this in `Chapter 14`, *Introducing Web3*. Once the contract is verified, working, and tested on a simulated environment (for example, EthereumJS TestRPC, Ganache) or on private net, it can be deployed to public testnet and eventually to the live blockchain (Byzantium).

In the next section, you will be introduced to language Solidity. This is a brief introduction to Solidity, which should provide the base knowledge required in order to write the contracts. The syntax is very similar to C and JavaScript, and it is quite easy to program.

We will cover all these steps including verification, development, and creating web interface in the next chapter, `Chapter 14`, *Introducing Web3*.

Solidity language

Solidity is a domain-specific language of choice for programming contracts in Ethereum. There are, however, other languages that can be used, such as Serpent, Mutan, and LLL but Solidity is the most popular at the time of writing this. Its syntax is closer to both JavaScript and C.

Solidity has evolved into a mature language over the last few years and is quite easy to use, but it still has a long way to go before it can become advanced, standardized, and feature-rich like other well-established languages such as Java, C or C Sharp. Nevertheless, this is the most widely used language available for programming contracts currently.

It is a statically typed language, which means that variable type checking in Solidity is carried out at compile time. Each variable, either state or local, must be specified with a type at compile time. This is beneficial in the sense that any validation and checking is completed at compile time and certain types of bugs, such as interpretation of data types, can be caught earlier in the development cycle instead of at runtime, which could be costly, especially in the case of the blockchain / smart contracts paradigm. Other features of the language include inheritance, libraries, and the ability to define composite data types.

Solidity is also called a contract-oriented language. In Solidity, contracts are equivalent to the concept of classes in other object-oriented programming languages.

Types

Solidity has two categories of data types: **value types** and **reference types**.

Value types

These are explained in detail here:

Boolean

This data type has two possible values, `true` or `false`, for example:

```
bool v = true;
bool v = false;
```

This statement assigns the value `true` to v.

Integers

This data type represents integers. The following table shows various keywords used to declare integer data types:

Keyword	Types	Details
int	Signed integer	`int8` to `int256`, which means that keywords are available from `int8` up to `int256` in increments of 8, for example, `int8`, `int16`, `int24`.
uint	Unsigned integer	`uint8`, `uint16`, ... to `uint256`, unsigned integer from 8 bits to 256 bits. The usage is dependent on the requirements that how many bits are required to be stored in the variable.

For example, in this code, note that `uint` is an alias for `uint256`:

```
uint256 x;
uint y;
uint256 z;
```

These types can also be declared with the `constant` keyword, which means that no storage slot will be reserved by the compiler for these variables. In this case, each occurrence will be replaced with the actual value:

```
uint constant z=10+10;
```

State variables are declared outside the body of a function, and they remain available throughout the contract depending on the accessibility assigned to them and as long as the contract persists.

Address

This data type holds a 160-bit long (20 byte) value. This type has several members that can be used to interact with and query the contracts. These members are described here:

- **Balance**: The `balance` member returns the balance of the address in Wei.
- **Send**: This member is used to send an amount of ether to an address (Ethereum's 160-bit address) and returns `true` or `false` depending on the result of the transaction, for example, the following:

  ```
  address to = 0x6414cc08d148dce9ebf5a2d0b7c220ed2d3203da; address from
  = this;
      if (to.balance < 10 && from.balance > 50) to.send(20);
  ```

- **Call functions**: The `call`, `callcode`, and `delegatecall` calls are provided in order to interact with functions that do not have ABI. These functions should be used with caution as they are not safe to use due to the impact on type safety and security of the contracts.
- **Array value types (fixed size and dynamically sized byte arrays)**: Solidity has fixed size and dynamically sized byte arrays. Fixed size keywords range from `bytes1` to `bytes32`, whereas dynamically sized keywords include `bytes` and `string`. The `bytes` keyword is used for raw byte data and `string` is used for strings encoded in UTF-8. As these arrays are returned by the value, calling them will incur gas cost. `length` is a member of array value types and returns the length of the byte array.

  An example of a static (fixed size) array is as follows:

  ```
  bytes32[10] bankAccounts;
  ```

  An example of a dynamically sized array is as follows:

  ```
  bytes32[] trades;
  ```

Get length of trades by using the following code:

```
trades.length;
```

Literals

These used to represent a fixed value. There are different types of literals that are described in the following subsections.

Integer literals

Integer literals are a sequence of decimal numbers in the range of 0-9. An example is shown as follows:

```
uint8 x = 2;
```

String literals

String literals specify a set of characters written with double or single quotes. An example is shown as follows:

```
'packt' "packt"
```

Hexadecimal literals

Hexadecimal literals are prefixed with the keyword `hex` and specified within double or single quotation marks. An example is shown as follows:

```
(hex'AABBCC');
```

Enums

This allows the creation of user-defined types. An example is shown as follows:

```
enum Order {Filled, Placed, Expired };
Order private ord;
ord=Order.Filled;
```

Explicit conversion to and from all integer types is allowed with enums.

Function types

There are two function types: internal and external functions.

Internal functions

These can be used only within the context of the current contract.

External functions

External functions can be called via external function calls.

A **function** in solidity can be marked as a constant. Constant functions cannot change anything in the contract; they only return values when they are invoked and do not cost any gas. This is the practical implementation of the concept of *call* as discussed in the previous chapter.

The syntax to declare a function is shown as follows:

```
function <nameofthefunction> (<parameter types> <name of the variable>)
{internal|external} [constant] [payable] [returns (<return types> <name of
the variable>)]
```

Reference types

As the name suggests, these types are passed by reference and are discussed in the following section. These are also called **complex types**.

Arrays

Arrays represent a contiguous set of elements of the same size and type laid out at a memory location. The concept is the same as any other programming language. Arrays have two members named `length` and `push`:

```
uint[] OrderIds;
```

Structs

These constructs can be used to group a set of dissimilar data types under a logical group. These can be used to define new types, as shown in the following example:

```
pragma solidity ^0.4.0;
contract TestStruct {
  struct Trade
  {
    uint tradeid;
    uint quantity;
    uint price;
    string trader;
  }

  //This struct can be initialized and used as below

  Trade tStruct = Trade({tradeid:123, quantity:1, price:1,
trader:"equinox"});

}
```

Data location

Data location specifies where a particular complex data type will be stored. Depending on the default or annotation specified, the location can be storage or memory. This is applicable to arrays and structs and can be specified using the `storage` or `memory` keywords.

As copying between memory and storage can be quite expensive, specifying a location can be helpful to control the gas expenditure at times. **Calldata** is another memory location that is used to store function arguments.

Parameters of external functions use **calldata** memory. By default, parameters of functions are stored in **memory**, whereas all other local variables make use of **storage**. State variables, on the other hand, are required to use storage.

Mappings

Mappings are used for a key to value mapping. This is a way to associate a value with a key. All values in this map are already initialized with all zeroes, for example, the following:

```
mapping (address => uint) offers;
```

This example shows that offers is declared as a mapping. Another example makes this clearer:

```
mapping (string => uint) bids;
bids["packt"] = 10;
```

This is basically a dictionary or a hash table where string values are mapped to integer values. The mapping named `bids` has string `packt` mapped to value `10`.

Global variables

Solidity provides a number of global variables that are always available in the global namespace. These variables provide information about blocks and transactions. Additionally, cryptographic functions and address-related variables are available as well.

A subset of available functions and variables is shown as follows:

```
keccak256(...) returns (bytes32)
```

This function is used to compute the Keccak-256 hash of the argument provided to the function:

```
ecrecover(bytes32 hash, uint8 v, bytes32 r, bytes32 s) returns (address)
```

This function returns the associated address of the public key from the elliptic curve signature:

```
block.number
```

This returns the current block number.

Control structures

Control structures available in solidity language are `if...else`, `do`, `while`, `for`, `break`, `continue`, and `return`. They work exactly the same as other languages such as C-language or JavaScript.

Some examples are shown here:

- **if**: If x is equal to 0 then assign value 0 to y else assign 1 to z:

```
if (x == 0)
    y = 0;
else
    z = 1;
```

- **do**: Increment x while z is greater than 1:

```
do{
    x++;
} (while z>1);
```

- **while**: Increment z while x is greater than 0:

```
while(x > 0){
    z++;
}
```

- **for, break, and continue**: Perform some work until x is less than or equal to 10. This for loop will run 10 times, if z is 5 then break the for loop:

```
for(uint8 x=0; x<=10; x++)
{
    //perform some work
    z++
    if(z == 5) break;
}
```

It will continue the work similarly, but when the condition is met, the loop will start again.

- **return**: Return is used to stop the execution of a function and returns an optional value. For example:

```
return 0;
```

It will stop the execution and return value of 0.

Events

Events in Solidity can be used to log certain events in EVM logs. These are quite useful when external interfaces are required to be notified of any change or event in the contract. These logs are stored on the blockchain in transaction logs. Logs cannot be accessed from the contracts but are used as a mechanism to notify change of state or the occurrence of an event (meeting a condition) in the contract.

In a simple example here, the `valueEvent` event will return `true` if the x parameter passed to function `Matcher` is equal to or greater than `10`:

```
pragma solidity ^0.4.0;
contract valueChecker
{
    uint8 price=10;
    event valueEvent(bool returnValue);
    function Matcher(uint8 x) public returns (bool)
    {
        if (x>=price)
        {
            valueEvent(true);
            return true;
        }
    }
}
```

Inheritance

Inheritance is supported in Solidity. The `is` keyword is used to derive a contract from another contract. In the following example, `valueChecker2` is derived from the `valueChecker` contract. The derived contract has access to all non-private members of the parent contract:

```
pragma solidity ^0.4.0;
contract valueChecker
{
    uint8 price = 20;
    event valueEvent(bool returnValue);
    function Matcher(uint8 x) public returns (bool)
    {
        if (x>=price)
        {
            valueEvent(true);
            return true;
        }
    }
```

```
    }
    contract valueChecker2 is valueChecker
    {
        function Matcher2() public view returns (uint)
        {
            return price+10;
        }
    }
```

In the preceding example, if the `uint8 price = 20` is changed to `uint8 private price = 20`, then it will not be accessible by the `valueChecker2` contract. This is because now the member is declared as private, it is not allowed to be accessed by any other contract. The error message that you will see in Remix is

```
    browser/valuechecker.sol:20:8: DeclarationError: Undeclared identifier.
    return price+10;
           ^---^
```

Libraries

Libraries are deployed only once at a specific address and their code is called via CALLCODE or DELEGATECALL opcode of the EVM. The key idea behind libraries is code reusability. They are similar to contracts and act as base contracts to the calling contracts. A library can be declared as shown in the following example:

```
    library Addition
    {
        function Add(uint x,uint y) returns (uint z)
        {
            return x + y;
        }
    }
```

This library can then be called in the contract, as shown here. First, it needs to be imported and then it can be used anywhere in the code. A simple example is shown as follows:

```
    import "Addition.sol"
    function Addtwovalues() returns(uint)
    {
        return Addition.Add(100,100);
    }
```

There are a few limitations with libraries; for example, they cannot have state variables and cannot inherit or be inherited. Moreover, they cannot receive Ether either; this is in contrast to contracts that can receive Ether.

Functions

Functions in Solidity are modules of code that are associated with a contract. Functions are declared with a name, optional parameters, access modifier, optional `constant` keyword, and optional return type. This is shown in the following example:

```
function orderMatcher (uint x)
private constant returns(bool return value)
```

In the preceding example, `function` is the keyword used to declare the function. `orderMatcher` is the function name, `uint x` is an optional parameter, `private` is the **access modifier** or **specifier** that controls access to the function from external contracts, `constant` is an optional keyword used to specify that this function does not change anything in the contract but is used only to retrieve values from the contract and `returns (bool return value)` is the optional return type of the function.

- **How to define a function**: The syntax of defining a function is shown as follows:

```
    function <name of the function>(<parameters>) <visibility specifier>
returns
    (<return data type> <name of the variable>)
    {
        <function body>
    }
```

- **Function signature**: Functions in Solidity are identified by its signature, which is the first four bytes of the Keccak-256 hash of its full signature string. This is also visible in Remix IDE, as shown in the following screenshot. `f9d55e21` is the first four bytes of 32-byte Keccak-256 hash of the function named `Matcher`.

```
FUNCTIONHASHES

{
    "f9d55e21": "Matcher(uint8)"
}
```

Function hash as shown in Remix IDE

In this example function, `Matcher` has the signature hash of `d99c89cb`. This information is useful in order to build interfaces.

- **Input parameters of a function**: Input parameters of a function are declared in the form of `<data type> <parameter name>`. This example clarifies the concept where `uint x` and `uint y` are input parameters of the `checkValues` function:

```
contract myContract
{
    function checkValues(uint x, uint y)
    {
    }
}
```

- **Output parameters of a function**: Output parameters of a function are declared in the form of `<data type> <parameter name>`. This example shows a simple function returning a `uint` value:

```
contract myContract
{
    function getValue() returns (uint z)
    {
        z=x+y;
    }
}
```

A function can return multiple values. In the preceding example function, `getValue` only returns one value, but a function can return up to 14 values of different data types. The names of the unused return parameters can be omitted optionally.

- **Internal function calls**: Functions within the context of the current contract can be called internally in a direct manner. These calls are made to call the functions that exist within the same contract. These calls result in simple JUMP calls at the EVM bytecode level.
- **External function calls**: External function calls are made via message calls from a contract to another contract. In this case, all function parameters are copied to the memory. If a call to an internal function is made using the `this` keyword, it is also considered an external call. The `this` variable is a pointer that refers to the current contract. It is explicitly convertible to an address and all members for a contract are inherited from the address.

- **Fallback functions**: This is an unnamed function in a contract with no arguments and return data. This function executes every time Ether is received. It is required to be implemented within a contract if the contract is intended to receive Ether; otherwise, an exception will be thrown and Ether will be returned. This function also executes if no other function signatures match in the contract. If the contract is expected to receive Ether, then the fallback function should be declared with the payable **modifier**. The payable is required; otherwise, this function will not be able to receive any Ether. This function can be called using the `address.call()` method as, for example, in the following:

```
function ()
{
    throw;
}
```

In this case, if the fallback function is called according to the conditions described earlier; it will call `throw`, which will roll back the state to what it was before making the call. It can also be some other construct than `throw`; for example, it can log an event that can be used as an alert to feed back the outcome of the call to the calling application.

- **Modifier functions**: These functions are used to change the behavior of a function and can be called before other functions. Usually, they are used to check some conditions or verification before executing the function. _ (underscore) is used in the modifier functions that will be replaced with the actual body of the function when the modifier is called. Basically, it symbolizes the function that needs to be *guarded*. This concept is similar to guard functions in other languages.
- **Constructor function**: This is an optional function that has the same name as the contract and is executed once a contract is created. Constructor functions cannot be called later on by users, and there is only one constructor allowed in a contract. This implies that no overloading functionality is available.
- **Function visibility specifiers (access modifiers)**: Functions can be defined with four access specifiers as follows:
    - **External**: These functions are accessible from other contracts and transactions. They cannot be called internally unless the `this` keyword is used.
    - **Public**: By default, functions are public. They can be called either internally or using messages.

- **Internal**: Internal functions are visible to other derived contracts from the parent contract.
- **Private**: Private functions are only visible to the same contract they are declared in.

- **Function Modifiers:**
  - **pure**: This modifier prohibits access or modification to state
  - **view**: This modifier disables any modification to state
  - **payable**: This modifier allows payment of ether with a call
  - **constant**: This modifier disallows access or modification to state

- **Other important keywords/functions throw**: `throw` is used to stop execution. As a result, all state changes are reverted. In this case, no gas is returned to the transaction originator because all the remaining gas is consumed.

Layout of a Solidity source code file

In the following subsections we will look at the components of a Solidity source code file.

Version pragma

In order to address compatibility issues that may arise from future versions of the solc version, `pragma` can be used to specify the version of the compatible compiler as, for example, in the following:

```
pragma solidity ^0.5.0
```

This will ensure that the source file does not compile with versions smaller than 0.5.0 and versions starting from 0.6.0.

Import

Import in Solidity allows the importing of symbols from the existing Solidity files into the current global scope. This is similar to `import` statements available in JavaScript, as for example, in the following:

```
Import "module-name";
```

Comments

Comments can be added in the Solidity source code file in a manner similar to C-language. Multiple line comments are enclosed in /* and */, whereas single line comments start with //.

An example Solidity program is as follows, showing the use of pragma, import, and comments:

```
1   pragma solidity ^0.4.0; //specify the compiler version
2 - /*
3   This is a simple value checker contract that checks the value
4   provided and returns boolean value based on the condition
5   expression evaluation.
6   */
7   import "dev.oraclize.it/api.sol";
8 - contract valuechecker {
9       uint price=10;
10      //This is price variable declare and initialized with value 10
11      event valueEvent(bool returnValue);
12      function Matcher (uint8 x) returns (bool)
13 -     {
14          if ( x >= price)
15 -         {
16              valueEvent(true);
17              return true;
18          }
19      }
20  }
```

Sample Solidity program as shown in Remix IDE

This completes a brief introduction to the Solidity language. The language is very rich and under constant improvement. Detailed documentation and coding guidelines are available online at http://solidity.readthedocs.io/en/latest/.

Summary

This chapter started with the introduction of development tools for Ethereum such as Remix IDE. Then we discussed some frameworks such as Truffle along with local blockchain solutions for development and testing such as Ganache, EthereumJS and TestRPC. Other tools such as MetaMask were also explored. Installation of Node was also introduced, as most of the tools are JavaScript and Node based.

In the next chapter we will explore the topic of Web3, a JavaScript API which is used to communicate with Ethereum blockchain using JavaScript.

14
Introducing Web3

In this chapter, we will explore Web3 API. Also, we will see detailed examples on how smart contracts are written, tested, and deployed to the Ethereum blockchain. We will use various tools such as Remix IDE and Ganache to develop and test smart contracts. We will also look at the methods to deploy smart contracts to Ethereum test network and private networks. We will also learn that how HTML and JavaScript frontends can be developed to interact with smart contracts deployed on the blockchain.

We will start with Web3 first and gradually build our knowledge by using various tools and techniques for smart contract development. Finally, we will develop a project using all the techniques that we have learned.

Web3

Web3 is a JavaScript library that can be used to communicate with an Ethereum node via RPC communication. Web3 works by exposing methods that have been enabled over RPC. This allows the development of user interfaces that make use of the Web3 library in order to interact with the contracts deployed over the blockchain.

In order to expose the methods via geth, the following command can be used:

```
$ geth --datadir .ethereum/privatenet/ --networkid 786 --rpc --rpcapi
'web3,net,eth,debug' --rpcport 8001 --rpccorsdomain 'http://localhost:7777'
```

 The --rpcapi flag allows the web3, eth, net, and debug methods.

This is a powerful library and can be explored further by attaching a geth instance. Later in this section, you will be introduced to the concepts and techniques of making use of Web3 via JavaScript/HTML frontends.

The `geth` instance can be attached using the following command:

```
$ geth attach ipc: ~/etherprivate/geth.ipc
```

Once the `geth` JavaScript console is running, Web3 can be queried, for example:

Web3 via geth

Contract deployment

A simple contract can be deployed using geth and interacted with using Web3 via the command-line interface that `geth` provides (console or attach). The following are the steps to achieve that. As an example, the following source code will be used:

```
pragma solidity ^0.4.0;
contract valueChecker
{
    uint price=10;
    event valueEvent(bool returnValue);
    function Matcher (uint8 x) public returns (bool)
    {
        if (x>=price)
        {
            valueEvent(true);
            return true;
        }
    }
}
```

1. Run `geth` client using the following command:

   ```
   $ ./geth --datadir ~/etherprivate/ --networkid 786 --rpc -rpcapi
   'web3,eth,debug,personal'  --rpccorsdomain '*'
   ```

2. You will also want to open another terminal and run the following command. The geth console should already be running by using the following command; if not run it using the following command:

   ```
   $ ./geth attach ipc:/Users/drequinox/etherprivate/geth.ipc
   ```

3. This step will need the Web3 deployment of the contract. This can be obtained from the Remix browser. To learn how to download and use the Remix browser, refer to `Chapter 13`, *Development Tools and Frameworks*. First, paste the following source code in the Remix IDE. We will discuss the Remix IDE in more detail later in this chapter; for now, we are using this IDE only to get the required Web3 deployment object for deployment:

   ```solidity
   pragma solidity ^0.4.0;
   contract valueChecker
   {
       uint price=10;
       event valueEvent(bool returnValue);
       function Matcher (uint8 x) public returns (bool)
       {
           if (x>=price)
           {
               valueEvent(true);
               return true;
           }
       }
   }
   ```

Once the code is pasted in the Remix IDE, it will look like this:

```
1   pragma solidity ^0.4.0;                          ⟳ Start to compile    ☑ Auto compile
2   contract valueChecker
3 ▾ {
4       uint price=10;
5   event valueEvent(bool returnValue);              valueChecker          ⬍     Details    Publish on Swarm
6   function Matcher (uint8 x) public returns (bool)
7 ▾ {
8 ▾     if (x>=price){valueEvent(true);              valueChecker                                          ✕
9       return true;
10
11      }}}
```

Code shown in Remix

4. Now copy the Web3 deployment script by clicking on the **Details** button and copy the function into the clipboard. This can be achieved by clicking on the icon next to **WEB3DEPLOY** caption in the IDE. The Web3 deploy script is shown in the following screenshot:

```
WEB3DEPLOY   ?
                    Copy value to clipboard
var valuecheckerContract = web3.eth.contract([{"constant":false,"inpu
ts":[{"name":"x","type":"uint8"}],"name":"Matcher","outputs":[{"name"
:"","type":"bool"}],"payable":false,"stateMutability":"nonpayable","t
ype":"function"},{"anonymous":false,"inputs":[{"indexed":false,"name"
:"returnValue","type":"bool"}],"name":"valueEvent","type":"event"}]);
var valuechecker = valuecheckerContract.new(
   {
     from: web3.eth.accounts[0],
     data: '0x6060604052600a60005534156100145760008fd5b6101038061002
36000396000f3006060604052600436106603f576000357c0100000000000000000000000
0000000000000000000000000000000000000000000900463ffffffff168063f9d55e2114604
4575b600080fd5b3415604e57600080fd5b6065600480803560ff1690602001909190
5050607f565b604051808215151515815260200191505060405180910390f35b60008
0548260ff1610151560d1577f3eb1a229ff7995457774a4bd31ef7b13b6f4491ad1eb
b8961af120b8b4b6239c6001604051808215151515815260200191505060405180910
390a16001905060d2565b5b9190505600a165627a7a723058205b1d9d0f31b39806b7
782fdb9360af93d5b5f66a36f6f4023ee1aa9ca12782b70029',
     gas: '4700000'
   }, function (e, contract){
    console.log(e, contract);
    if (typeof contract.address !== 'undefined') {
        console.log('Contract mined! address: ' + contract.address +
 ' transactionHash: ' + contract.transactionHash);
     }
  })
```

The Web3 deployment script

The Web3 deployment script is shown in the following code snippet:

```
var valuecheckerContract =
web3.eth.contract([{"constant":false,"inputs":[{"name":"x","type":"
uint8"}],"name":"Matcher","outputs":[{"name":"","type":"bool"}],"pa
yable":false,"stateMutability":"nonpayable","type":"function"},{"an
onymous":false,"inputs":[{"indexed":false,"name":"returnValue","typ
e":"bool"}],"name":"valueEvent","type":"event"}]);
var valuechecker = valuecheckerContract.new(

   {
      from: web3.eth.accounts[0],
      data:
'0x6060604052600a6000553415610014576000080fd5b6101038061002360003960
00f3006060604052600436106003f576000357c010000000000000000000000000000
00000000000000000000000000000000000900463ffffffff168063f9d55e21146044575b
600080fd5b3415604e57600080fd5b6065600480803560ff169060200190190505
0607f565b6040518082151515158152602001915050506040518091039f35b600080
548260ff1610151560d1577f3eb1a229ff7995457774a4bd31ef7b13b6f4491ad1e
bb8961af120b8b4b6239c60016040518082151515158152602001915050506040518
0910390a16001905060d2565b5b9190505600a165627a7a723058205b1d9d0f31b39
806b7782fdb9360af93d5b5f66a36f6f4023ee1aa9ca12782b70029',
      gas: '4700000'
   }, function (e, contract){
   console.log(e, contract);
   if (typeof contract.address !== 'undefined') {
         console.log('Contract mined! address: ' + contract.address
+ ' transactionHash: ' + contract.transactionHash);
      }
  })
```

5. Ensure that the accounts are unlocked and coinbase is set correctly.

First list the accounts, by using the following command, which outputs the account 0, as shown:

```
> personal.listAccounts[0]
"0xcf61d213faa9acadbf0d110e1397caf20445c58f"
```

Now unlock the account using the following command. It will need the passphrase (password) that you used originally when creating this account. Enter the password to unlock the account:

```
> personal.unlockAccount(personal.listAccounts[0])
Unlock account 0xcf61d213faa9acadbf0d110e1397caf20445c58f
Passphrase:
True
```

6. Now open the geth console that has been opened previously, and deploy the contract:

   However, before deploying the contract, make sure that mining is running on the geth node. The command below can be used to start mining under the geth console.

   ```
   > Miner.start(1)
   ```

7. Now paste this Web3 deployment script in the geth console as shown in the following screenshot:

```
> personal.unlockAccount(personal.listAccounts[0])
Unlock account 0xcf61d213faa9acadbf0d110e1397caf20445c58f
Passphrase:
true
> var valuecheckerContract = web3.eth.contract([{"constant":false,"inputs":[{"name":"x","type":"uint8"}],"name":"Matcher","ou
tputs":[{"name":"","type":"bool"}],"payable":false,"stateMutability":"nonpayable","type":"function"},{"anonymous":false,"inpu
ts":[{"indexed":false,"name":"returnValue","type":"bool"}],"name":"valueEvent","type":"event"}]);
undefined
> var valuechecker = valuecheckerContract.new(
...     {
......       from: web3.eth.accounts[0],
......       data: '0x6060604052600a600055341561001457600080fd5b610103806100236000396000f3006060604052600436106100415760003570c01
0000000000000000000000000000000000000000000000900463ffffffff168063f9d55e21146044575b600080fd5b3415604e57600080fd5b6
065600480803560ff1690602001909190505060607f565b60405180821515151581526020019150506060405180910390f35b600080548260ff1610151560d157
7f3eb1a229ff7995457774a4bd31ef7b13b6f4491ad1ebb8961af120b8b4b6239c600160405180821515151581526020019150506060405180910390a160019
05060d2565b5b9190505600a165627a7a723058205b1d9d0f31b39806b7782fdb9360af93d5b5f66a36f6f4023ee1aa9ca12782b70029',
......       gas: '4700000'
......     }, function (e, contract){
......       console.log(e, contract);
......       if (typeof contract.address !== 'undefined') {
.........          console.log('Contract mined! address: ' + contract.address + ' transactionHash: ' + contract.transactionHa
sh);
.........       }
......     })
null [object Object]
undefined
```

The Web3 deployment script deployment using geth

The previous screenshot shows the output as it looks like when the Web3 deployment script is pasted in the geth console for deployment.

You can also see this in the geth logs to verify, you will see messages similar to the one shown as follows:

```
INFO [12-16|13:28:49] Submitted contract creation
fullhash=0x9f7c81a5942b01f2e2446cad6f0acbaa00514326fcf0abf7b7a076d1
72db05d6 contract=0xBD663C5136155cb6d7ED55446888271DCd5092Bc
```

8. After the contract is deployed successfully you can query various attributes related to this contract which we will also use later in this example.

   For example, contract address, ABI definition and so on, as shown in the following screenshot. Remember all these commands are issued via geth console, that we have already opened and used for contract deployment.

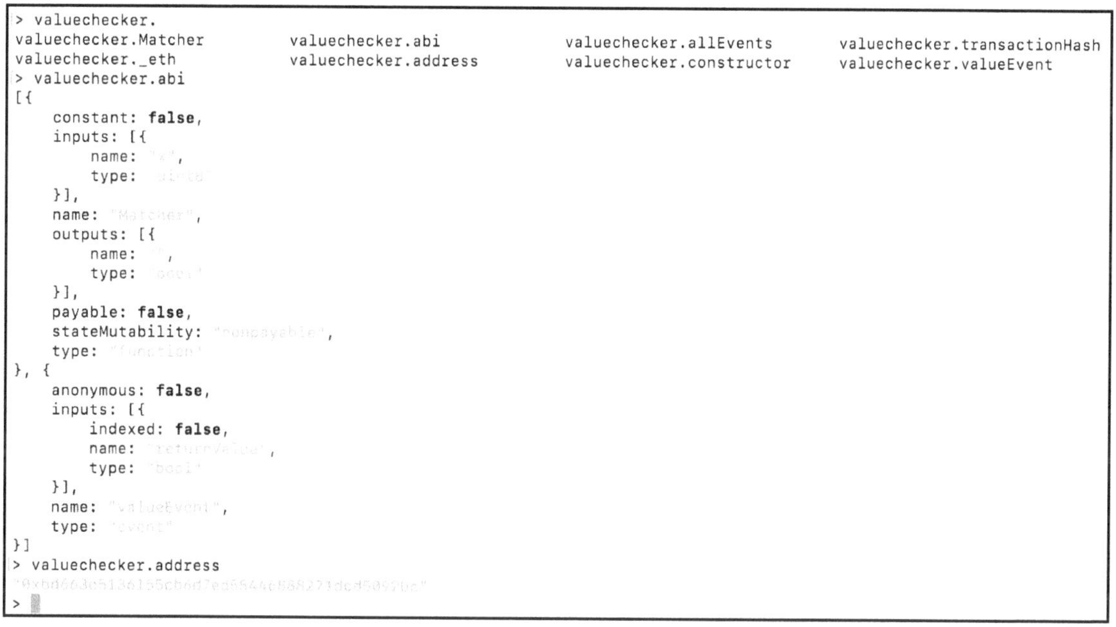

```
> valuechecker.
valuechecker.Matcher        valuechecker.abi        valuechecker.allEvents       valuechecker.transactionHash
valuechecker._eth           valuechecker.address    valuechecker.constructor     valuechecker.valueEvent
> valuechecker.abi
[{
    constant: false,
    inputs: [{
        name: "x",
        type: "uint8"
    }],
    name: "Matcher",
    outputs: [{
        name: ,
        type: "bool"
    }],
    payable: false,
    stateMutability: "nonpayable",
    type: "function"
}, {
    anonymous: false,
    inputs: [{
        indexed: false,
        name: "returnValue",
        type: "bool"
    }],
    name: "valueEvent",
    type: "event"
}]
> valuechecker.address
"0xbd663c5136155cbad7ed6644b588221dc460909c2"
> 
```

Value checker attributes

In order to make interaction with the contract easier, the address of the account can be assigned to a variable, there are a number of methods that are now exposed, and the contract can be further queried now, for example:

```
> eth.getBalance(valuechecker.address)
0
```

We can now call the actual methods in the contract.

There are various methods that have been exposed now, and a list can be seen as follows:

```
> valuechecker.transactionHash
"0x9f7c81a5942b01f2e2446cad6f0acbaa00514326fcf0abf7b7a076d172db05d6
"

> valuechecker.abi
[{
    constant: false,
    inputs: [{
        name: "x",
        type: "uint8"
    }],
    name: "Matcher",
    outputs: [{
        name: "",
        type: "bool"
    }],
    payable: false,
    stateMutability: "nonpayable",
    type: "function"
}, {
    anonymous: false,
    inputs: [{
        indexed: false,
        name: "returnValue",
        type: "bool"
    }],
    name: "valueEvent",
    type: "event"
}]
```

The contract can be further queried as shown here. In the following example, the `Matcher` function is called with the arguments. Arguments, also called parameters, are the values passed to the functions. Remember that in the code, there is a condition that checks that if the value is equal to or greater than 10, then the function returns `true`; otherwise, it returns `false`. This can be seen as follows in the geth console.

Type the following commands in the geth console that is already open.

Pass `12` as an argument, which will return `true` as it is greater than 10.

```
> valuechecker.Matcher.call(12)
True
```

Pass `10` as an argument, which will return `true` as it is equal to 10.

```
> valuechecker.Matcher.call(10)
True
```

Pass `9` as an argument, which will return `false` as it is less than 10.

```
> valuechecker.Matcher.call(9)
false
```

POST requests

It is possible to interact with geth via JSONRPC over HTTP. For this purpose, the curl tool can be used.

 Curl is available at `https://curl.haxx.se/`.

Some examples are shown here to familiarize you with the POST request and show how to make POST requests using curl.

 POST is request method supported by HTTP. You can read more about POST here `https://en.wikipedia.org/wiki/POST_(HTTP)`

Before using the **JSONRPC** interface over **HTTP**, the `geth` client should be started up with appropriate switches, as shown here:

```
--rpcapi web3
```

This switch will enable the web3 interface over HTTP.

The Linux command, `curl`, can be used for the purpose of communicating over HTTP, as shown here in the example.

Retrieve the list of accounts: For example, in order to retrieve the list of accounts using the `personal_listAccounts` method, the following command can be used:

```
$ curl --request POST --data
'{"jsonrpc":"2.0","method":"personal_listAccounts","params": [],"id":4}'
localhost:8545 -H "Content-Type: application/json"
```

This will return the output, a JSON object with the list of accounts:

```
{"jsonrpc":"2.0","id":4,"result":["0xcf61d213faa9acadbf0d110e1397caf20445c5
8f","0x3681e23a71ae8add5b88f01cbda153f1d805dde8"]}
```

In the preceding `curl` command, `--request` is used to specify the request command, `POST` is the request, and `--data` is used specify the parameters and values. Finally, `localhost:8545` is used where the HTTP endpoint from geth is opened.

The HTML and JavaScript frontend

It is desirable to interact with the contracts in a user-friendly manner via a web page. It is possible to interact with the contracts using the web3.js library from HTML/JS/CSS-based web pages. The HTML content can be served using any HTTP web server, whereas web3.js can connect via local RPC to the running Ethereum client (geth) and provide an interface to the contracts on the blockchain. This architecture can be visualized in the following diagram:

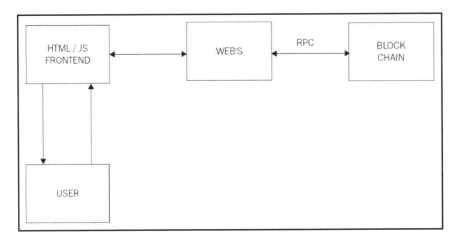

web3.js, frontend, and blockchain interaction architecture

If web3.js is not already installed, use these steps; otherwise, move to the next step.

Installing web3.js

Web3 can be installed via npm by simply issuing the following command:

```
$ npm install web3
```

 It can also be directly downloaded from
https://github.com/ethereum/web3.js.

web3.min.js, downloaded via npm, can be referred in the HTML files. This can be found under node_modules, for example,

/home/drequinox/netstats/node_modules/web3/dist/web3.js. Note that drequinox is specific to the user under which these examples were developed, you will see the user that you are running these commands under.

The file can optionally be copied into the directory where the main application is and can be used from there. Once the file is successfully referred in HTML or JS, Web3 needs to be initialized by providing an HTTP provider. This is usually the link to the localhost HTTP endpoint exposed by the running the geth client. This can be achieved using the following code:

```
web3.setProvider(new web3.providers.HttpProvider('http://localhost:8545'));
```

Once the provider is set, further interaction with the contracts and blockchain can be done using the web3 object and its available methods.

The web3 object can be created using the following code:

```
if (typeof web3 !== 'undefined')
{
    web3 = new Web3(web3.currentProvider);
}
else
{
    web3 = new Web3(new
    Web3.providers.HttpProvider("http://localhost:8545"));
}
```

Example

In the following section, an example will be presented that will make use of web3.js to allow interaction with the contracts via a web page served over a simple HTTP web server. This can be achieved by following these steps:

1. First, create a directory named `/simplecontract/app`, the home directory. This is the directory under your user on Linux. This can be any directory, but in this example home directory is used.

2. Then, create a file named `app.js`, as shown here:

```
var Web3 = require('web3');

if (typeof web3 !== 'undefined') {
  web3 = new Web3(web3.currentProvider);
} else {
  // set the provider you want from Web3.providers
  web3 = new Web3(new
Web3.providers.HttpProvider("http://localhost:8545"));
}
web3.eth.defaultAccount = web3.eth.accounts[0];
//provide ABI
var SimpleContract = web3.eth.contract([
    {
            "constant": false,
            "inputs": [
                    {
                            "name": "x",
                            "type": "uint8"
                    }
            ],
            "name": "Matcher",
            "outputs": [
{
                            "name": "",
                            "type": "bool"
                    }
            ],
            "payable": false,
            "stateMutability": "nonpayable",
            "type": "function"
    },
    {
            "anonymous": false,
            "inputs": [
                    {
                            "indexed": false,
```

```
                              "name": "returnValue",
                              "type": "bool"
                  }
           ],
           "name": "valueEvent",
           "type": "event"
      }
]);

var simplecontract =
SimpleContract.at("0xd9d02a4974cbeb10406639ec9378a782bf7f4dd2");
      console.log(simplecontract);


function callMatchertrue()
{
var txn = simplecontract.Matcher.call(12);
{
};

console.log("return value: " + txn);
}

function callMatcherfalse()
{
var txn = simplecontract.Matcher.call(1);{
};
console.log("return value: " + txn);
}
```

This file contains various elements. The most important is **ABI** (**Application Binary Interface**), which can be queried using geth, generated using solidity compiler or copied directly from remix IDE contract details.

3. Create a file named index.html, as shown here:

```
<html>
<head>
<title>SimpleContract Interactor</title>
<script src="./web3.js"></script>
<script src="./app.js"></script>
</head>
<body>
<button onclick="callMatchertrue()">callTrue</button>
<button onclick="callMatcherfalse()">callFalse</button>
</body>
</html>
```

We are keeping this very simple on purpose, there is no need to use jQuery, React, or Angular here. They are a separate topic and have no connection with Ethereum or blockchain in general.

However, these frontend frameworks are being used commonly for JavaScript frontend development related to blockchain. In order to keep things simple, we are not going to use any frontend JavaScript frameworks here, as the main aim is to focus on blockchain technology and not the HTML, CSS, JavaScript frontend frameworks.

This `app.js` file is the main JavaScript file that contains the code to create a web3 Object. It also provides methods that are used to interact with the contract on the blockchain. An explanation of the code used above is given below.

Creating a web3 object

```
if (typeof web3 !== 'undefined')
{
web3 = new Web3(web3.currentProvider);
}
else
{
web3 = new Web3(new Web3.providers.HttpProvider("http://localhost: 8545"));
}
```

This code checks whether there is already an available provider; if yes, then it will set the provider to the current provider. Otherwise, it sets the `web3` provider to `localhost: 8001`; this is where the local instance of `geth` is running.

Checking availability by calling any web3 method

```
var simplecontract =
SimpleContract.at("0xd9d02a4974cbeb10406639ec9378a782bf7f4dd2");
console.log(simplecontract);
```

This line of code simply uses `console.log` to print the simple contract attributes. Once this call is successful, it means that the `web3` object has been created correctly and `HttpProvider` is available. Any other call can be used to verify the availability, but as a simple example, printing simple contract attributes been used in the preceding example.

Contract functions

Once the web3 object is correctly created and simplecontractinstance is created, calls to the contract functions can be made easily as shown in the following example:

```
function callMatchertrue()
{
var txn = simplecontractinstance.Matcher.call(12);
{
};

console.log("return value: " + txn);
}

function callMatcherfalse()
{
var txn = simplecontractinstance.Matcher.call(1);{
};
console.log("return value: " + txn);
}
```

Calls can be made using simplecontractinstance.Matcher.call and then by passing the value for the argument. Recall the Matcher function in solidity code:

```
function Matcher (uint8 x) returns (bool)
```

It takes one argument x of type uint8 and returns a Boolean value, either true or false. Accordingly, the call is made to the contract, as shown here:

```
var txn = simplecontractinstance.Matcher.call(12);
```

In the preceding example, console.log is used to print the value returned by the function call. Once the result of the call is available in the txn variable, it can be used anywhere throughout the program, for example, as a parameter for another JavaScript function.

Finally, the HTML file named index.html is created with the following code:

```
<html>
<head>
<title>SimpleContract Interactor</title>
<script src="./web3.js"></script>
<script src="./app.js"></script>
</head>
<body>
<button onclick="callMatchertrue()">callTrue</button>
<button onclick="callMatcherfalse()">callFalse</button>
</body>
```

```
</html>
```

It is recommended that a web server be running in order to serve the HTML content (`index.html` as an example). Alternatively, the file can be browsed from the filesystem but that can cause some issues related to serving the content correctly with larger projects; as a good practice, always use a web server.

A quick web server in Python can be started using the following command. This server will serve the HTML content from the same directory that it has been run from. The Python web server is not necessary; it can be an Apache server or any other web container:

```
$ python -m SimpleHTTPServer 7777
Serving HTTP on 0.0.0.0 port 7777 ...
```

Now any browser can be used to view the web page served over TCP port 7777. This is shown in the following example. It should be noted that the output shown here is in the browser's console window. The browser's console must be enabled in order to see the output. For example, in Chrome you can use keyboard shortcuts to open console. On Windows and Linux: *Ctrl + Shift + J*, and on Mac: *Cmd + Option + J* are used:

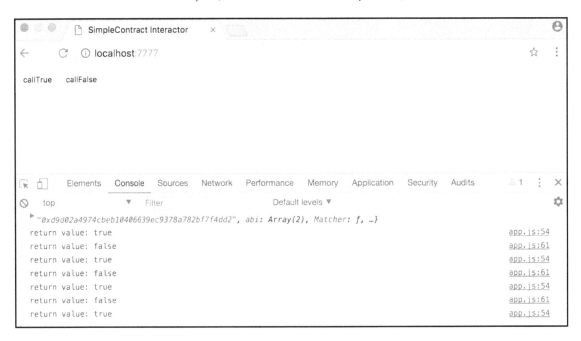

Interaction with the contract

As the values are hardcoded in the code for simplicity, two buttons shown in the screenshot, **callTrue** and **callFalse**, have been created in `index.html`. Both of these buttons call functions with hardcoded values. This is just to demonstrate that parameters are being passed to the contract via Web3 and values are being returned accordingly.

There are two functions being called behind these buttons. The `callMatchertrue()` method has a hardcoded value of `12`, which is sent to the contract using the following code:

```
simplecontractinstance.Matcher.call(12)
```

The return value is printed in the console using the following code, which first invokes the `Matcher` function and then assigns the value to the `txn` variable to be printed later in the console:

```
simplecontractinstance.Matcher.call(1) function callMatchertrue()
{
var txn = simplecontractinstance.Matcher.call(12);{
};
console.log("return value: " + txn);
}
```

Similarly, the `callMatcherfalse()` function works by passing a hardcoded value of `1` to the contract using this:

```
simplecontractinstance.Matcher.call(1)
```

The return value is printed accordingly:

```
console.log("return value: " + txn); function callMatcherfalse()
{
var txn = simplecontractinstance.Matcher.call(1);{
};
console.log("return value: " + txn);
}
```

This example demonstrates how the Web3 library can be used to interact with the contracts on the Ethereum blockchain.

Development frameworks

There are various development frameworks now available for Ethereum. As seen in the examples discussed earlier, it can be quite time-consuming to deploy the contracts via the manual means. This is where Truffle and similar frameworks such as Embark can be used to make the process simpler and quicker. We have chosen truffle because it has a more active developer community and currently is the most widely used framework for Ethereum development. However, note that there is no "best" framework as all frameworks aim to provide methods to make development, testing, and deployment easier. You can read more about embark here: `https://github.com/embark-framework/embark`.

In the next section, you will be introduced to an example project to demonstrate the usage of Truffle framework.

Truffle

We discussed Truffle briefly previously. In this section we will see an example project of Truffle, which will demonstrate how Truffle can be used to develop a full decentralized application. We will see all the steps involved in this process such as initialization, testing, migration, and deployment. First, we will see the initialization process.

Initializing Truffle

Truffle can be initialized by running the following command. First, create a directory for the project, for example:

```
$ mkdir testdapp
```

Then, change directory to `testdapp` and run the following command:

```
$ truffle init
Downloading...
Unpacking...
Setting up...
Unbox successful. Sweet!
Commands:

  Compile:        truffle compile
  Migrate:        truffle migrate
  Test contracts: truffle test
```

Once the command is successful, it will create the directory structure shown here. This can be viewed using the tree command in Linux:

```
$ tree
.
├── contracts
│   └── Migrations.sol
├── migrations
│   └── 1_initial_migration.js
├── test
├── truffle-config.js
└── truffle.js

3 directories, 4 files
```

This command creates three main directories, named contracts, migrations, and test. As seen in the preceding example, a total of 3 directories and 4 files have been created. In the following section, an explanation of all these files and directories is presented.

- contracts: This directory contains solidity contract source code files. This is where Truffle will look for solidity contract files during migration.
- migration: This directory has all the deployment scripts.
- test: As the name suggests, this directory contains relevant test files for applications and contracts.

Finally, Truffle configuration is stored in the truffle.js file, which is created in the root folder of the project from where truffle init was run.

When truffle init is run, it will create a skeleton tree with files and directories. In previous versions of Truffle, this used to produce a project named **MetaCoin**. This project is now available as a *Truffle box*.

As an example, first, you will be introduced to how to use various commands in Truffle in order to test and deploy webpack box, which contains the MetaCoin project. Later, further examples will be shown on how to use Truffle for custom projects.

We will use Ganache as local blockchain to provide the Web3 interface. Make sure that Ganache is running in the background and mining. In the following example it's running on port 7545 with 5 accounts. These options can be changed in the Settings option in Ganache as shown below in the screenshot:

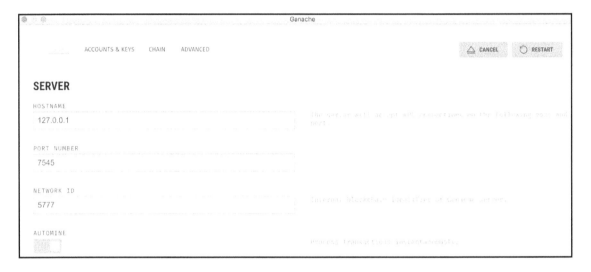

Ganache settings

After successful setup of Ganache, the following steps need to be performed in order to unpack the webpack Truffle box and run the MetaCoin project:

1. First step is to unbox the webpack sample from Truffle:

```
$ truffle unbox webpack
Downloading...
Unpacking...
Setting up...
Unbox successful. Sweet!

Commands:

  Compile:              truffle compile
  Migrate:              truffle migrate
  Test contracts:       truffle test
  Run linter:           npm run lint
  Run dev server:       npm run dev
  Build for production: npm run build
```

2. Edit the `truffle.js` file, if required, and change the port to where Ganache is running. Note the settings provided in the preceding screenshot, *Ganache settings*:

```
$ cat truffle.js
// Allows us to use ES6 in our migrations and tests.
require('babel-register')

module.exports = {
  networks: {
    development: {
      host: 'localhost',
      port: 7545, //This is where ganache is running
      network_id: '*' // Match any network id
    }
  }
}
```

3. Now run the following command to compile all contracts:

```
$ truffle compile
```

This will show the following output:

```
Compiling ./contracts/ConvertLib.sol...
Compiling ./contracts/MetaCoin.sol...
Compiling ./contracts/Migrations.sol...
Writing artifacts to ./build/contracts
```

4. Now, as we are using Ganache as a Web3 provider, we need to edit a file called `app.js` under `app/javascripts/` to edit the connection settings, so that the application can connect to the local Ganache blockchain. Open this file and edit the following code:

```
// fallback - use your fallback strategy (local node / hosted node
+ in-dapp id mgmt / fail)
window.web3 = new Web3(new
Web3.providers.HttpProvider("http://127.0.0.1:9545"));
```

Change this to the following:

```
// fallback - use your fallback strategy (local node / hosted node
+ in-dapp id mgmt / fail)
window.web3 = new Web3(new
Web3.providers.HttpProvider("http://127.0.0.1:7545"));
```

5. Now we can test using the `truffle test` command as shown here:

```
$ truffle test
Using network 'development'.

Compiling ./contracts/ConvertLib.sol...
Compiling ./contracts/MetaCoin.sol...
Compiling ./test/TestMetacoin.sol...
Compiling truffle/Assert.sol...
Compiling truffle/DeployedAddresses.sol...
TestMetacoin
    ✓ testInitialBalanceUsingDeployedContract (164ms)
    ✓ testInitialBalanceWithNewMetaCoin (73ms)

  Contract: MetaCoin
    ✓ should put 10000 MetaCoin in the first account
    ✓ should call a function that depends on a linked library
(248ms)
    ✓ should send coin correctly (185ms)
  5 passing (1s)
```

6. Once testing is completed we can migrate to the blockchain using the following command. Migration will use the settings available in `truffle.js` that we edited in step 2 to point to the port where Ganache is running. This is achieved by issuing the command:

```
$truffle migrate
```

The output is shown below. Notice that when migration runs it will reflect on Ganache; for example, the balance of accounts will go down and you can also view transactions that have been executed. Also notice that the account shown in the screenshot corresponds with what is shown in Ganache:

```
Using network 'development'.

Running migration: 1_initial_migration.js
  Deploying Migrations...
  ... 0x54ac3fff035594cb4f3244ca0115fd206e9bce0a6e19b4964e67fb792e4c4991
  Migrations: 0x2c2b9c9a4a25e24b174f26114e8926a9f2128fe4
Saving successful migration to network...
  ... 0x9b51540f5a7d75a8fc920e3e5e4ec66792ba31fd006bd176901f0e6347af2dba
Saving artifacts...
Running migration: 2_deploy_contracts.js
  Deploying ConvertLib...
  ... 0x4d1f4c386d0b213c154ce5587aa6f625b1c70ff374f4ca0053a82db1074e8765
  ConvertLib: 0xfb88de099e13c3ed21f80a7a1e49f8caecf10df6
  Linking ConvertLib to MetaCoin
  Deploying MetaCoin...
  ... 0xc9f8e7eb12b2cd3d33d73c8ed5858157ebeb7181ea262b19677a081e5e014ce1
  MetaCoin: 0xaa588d3737b611bafd7bd713445b314bd453a5c8
Saving successful migration to network...
  ... 0xd5050afb739a27fba97e027707af14e6e07077227a11a1035d352647a3f644aa
Saving artifacts...
```

Truffle migration

Also, notice that the migration shown in the preceding screenshot is reflected in Ganache with the accounts shown previously.

In Ganache, the list of accounts is displayed as shown in the following screenshot:

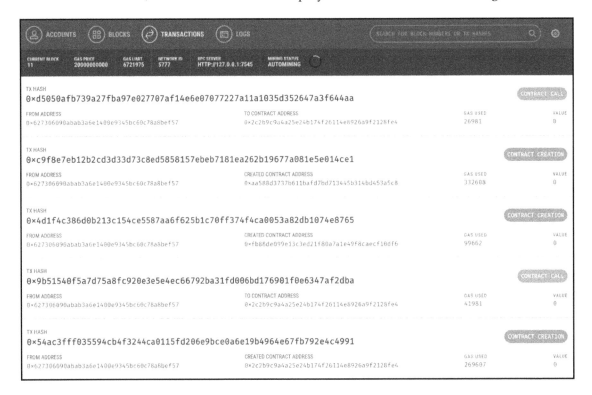

Ganache displaying transactions

Also, notice that Ether has been consumed from the accounts as shown in the following screenshot. You can see **BALANCE** updating in Ganache, as the transactions run:

Ganache displaying accounts

7. Now we can start up the frontend and use the MetaCoin application. First, we will start a dev server using the following command:

```
$ npm run dev
```

This will show the output similar to the following screenshot. If you run this you may see some differences; for example, the username will be different but overall the output will look similar:

```
> truffle-init-webpack@0.0.2 dev /Users/drequinox/dapp1
> webpack-dev-server

Project is running at http://localhost:8080/
webpack output is served from /
Hash: 157d6514272a12586aba
Version: webpack 2.7.0
Time: 6702ms
     Asset        Size  Chunks                    Chunk Names
    app.js     1.65 MB       0  [emitted]  [big]   main
index.html   925 bytes          [emitted]
chunk    {0} app.js (main) 1.63 MB [entry] [rendered]
   [71] ./app/javascripts/app.js 3.64 kB {0} [built]
   [72] (webpack)-dev-server/client?http://localhost:8080 7.95 kB {0} [built]
   [73] ./build/contracts/MetaCoin.json 23.8 kB {0} [built]
  [111] ./~/loglevel/lib/loglevel.js 7.86 kB {0} [built]
  [117] ./~/querystring-es3/index.js 127 bytes {0} [built]
  [119] ./~/strip-ansi/index.js 161 bytes {0} [built]
  [122] ./app/stylesheets/app.css 905 bytes {0} [built]
  [163] ./~/truffle-contract/index.js 2.64 kB {0} [built]
  [197] ./~/url/url.js 23.3 kB {0} [built]
  [199] ./~/web3/index.js 193 bytes {0} [built]
  [233] (webpack)-dev-server/client/overlay.js 3.73 kB {0} [built]
  [234] (webpack)-dev-server/client/socket.js 1.05 kB {0} [built]
  [235] (webpack)/hot nonrecursive ^\.\/log$ 160 bytes {0} [built]
  [236] (webpack)/hot/emitter.js 77 bytes {0} [built]
  [237] multi (webpack)-dev-server/client?http://localhost:8080 ./app/javascripts/app.js 40 bytes {0} [built]
      + 223 hidden modules
webpack: Compiled successfully.
```

Running webpack

8. Now open the web browser and browse to `http://localhost:8080`. This will display the following output:

The MetaCoin example frontend

In the frontend shown, you can now transfer Metacoin to any other account using the MetaCoin frontend application.

These transactions will appear on Ganache as shown here:

Ganache transaction details

You can also interact with the contract using the `truffle console`. We will explore this in the following example.

Interaction with the contract

Truffle also provides a console (a command-line interface) that allows interaction with the contracts. All deployed contracts are already instantiated and ready to use in the console. This is an REPL-based interface that means Read, Evaluate, and Print Loop. Similarly, in the `geth` client (via attach or console), REPL is used via exposing **JSRE** (**JavaScript runtime environment**). The console can be accessed by issuing the following command:

```
$ truffle console
```

This will open a command-line interface, as shown here:

```
drequinox@drequinox-OP7010:~/testdapp$ truffle console
truffle(default)>
```

The truffle console

Once the console is available, various methods can be run in order to query the contract. A list of methods can be displayed by typing the following command and tab-completing:

```
drequinox@drequinox-OP7010:~/testdapp$ truffle console
truffle(default)> MetaCoin.
MetaCoin.__defineGetter__       MetaCoin.__defineSetter__       MetaCoin.__lookupGetter__       MetaCoin.__lookupSetter__
MetaCoin.__proto__              MetaCoin.constructor            MetaCoin.hasOwnProperty         MetaCoin.isPrototypeOf
MetaCoin.propertyIsEnumerable   MetaCoin.toLocaleString         MetaCoin.toString               MetaCoin.valueOf

MetaCoin.apply                  MetaCoin.arguments              MetaCoin.bind                   MetaCoin.call
MetaCoin.caller                 MetaCoin.length                 MetaCoin.name

MetaCoin.abi                    MetaCoin.address                MetaCoin.all_networks           MetaCoin.at
MetaCoin.binary                 MetaCoin.checkNetwork           MetaCoin.class_defaults         MetaCoin.contract_name
MetaCoin.currentProvider        MetaCoin.defaults               MetaCoin.deployed               MetaCoin.events
MetaCoin.extend                 MetaCoin.generated_with         MetaCoin.link                   MetaCoin.links
MetaCoin.network_id             MetaCoin.networks               MetaCoin.new                    MetaCoin.next_gen
MetaCoin.prototype              MetaCoin.setNetwork             MetaCoin.setProvider            MetaCoin.unlinked_binary
MetaCoin.updated_at             MetaCoin.web3
```

Exposed methods

Other methods can also be called in order to interact with the contract; for example, in order to retrieve the address of the contract, the following method can be called using the `truffle console`:

```
truffle(development)> MetaCoin.address
'0xf25186b5081ff5ce73482ad761db0eb0d25abfbf'
truffle(development)>
```

This address is also shown in contract creation transaction in Ganache:

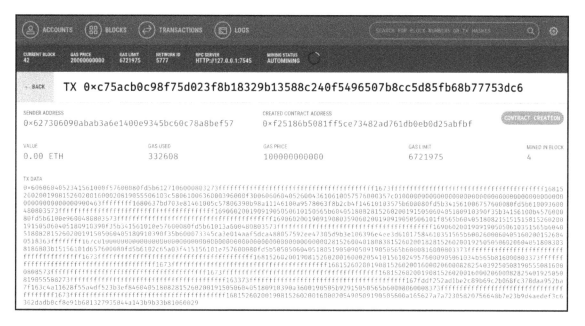

Contract creation transaction shown in Ganache

Few examples of other methods that we can call in the `truffle console` are shown here.

Query the accounts available:

```
truffle(development)> web3.eth.accounts[0]
'0x627306090abab3a6e1400e9345bc60c78a8bef57'
truffle(development)>
```

Query the balance of the contract:

```
truffle(development)> MetaCoin.web3.eth.getBalance(web3.eth.accounts[0])
{ [String: '99922916099998726400'] s: 1, e: 19, c: [ 999229, 16099998726400
] }
truffle(development)>
```

This is the first account shown in Ganache above:

```
0x627306090abaB3A6e1400e9345bC60c78a8BEf57
```

The output returns a string with the value `992299`.

To exit from the `truffle console`, the `.exit` command is used.

This completes our introduction to the sample webpack Truffle box and the MetaCoin application using Truffle. In the next section, we will see how a contract can be developed from scratch and tested and deployed using Truffle, Ganache, and PrivateNet.

Now we will see another example in the next section, which demonstrates that how we can use Truffle for testing and deploying smart contracts.

Another example

An example of a simple contract is shown in the section. This is a simple contract in solidity, which performs only addition. We will see how migrations and tests can be created for this contract.

Follow the steps outline:

1. Create a directory named `simplecontract`:

 `$ mkdir simplecontract`

2. Change directory to `simplecontract`:

 `$ cd simplecontract`

3. Initialize Truffle to create a skeleton structure for smart contract development:

```
$ truffle init
truffle init
Downloading...
Unpacking...
Setting up...
Unbox successful. Sweet!

Commands:

  Compile:        truffle compile
  Migrate:        truffle migrate
  Test contracts: truffle test
```

The tree structure produced by the `init` command is as follows:

```
├──── contracts
│       └──── Migrations.sol
├──── migrations
│       └──── 1_initial_migration.js
├──── test
├──── truffle-config.js
└──── truffle.js
```

4. Place the two files `Addition.sol` and `Migrations.sol` in the `contracts` directory:

`Addition.sol`:

```
pragma solidity ^0.4.2;
contract Addition
{
uint8 x; //declare variable x
// define function addx with two parameters y and z, and modifier
public
    function addx(uint8 y, uint8 z ) public
    {
x = y + z; //performs addition
    }
// define function retrievex to retrieve the value stored, variable x
    function retrievex() constant public returns (uint8)
    {
return x;
    }
}
```

`Migrations.sol`:

```
pragma solidity ^0.4.17;
contract Migrations {
address public owner;
uint public last_completed_migration;
modifier restricted() {
if (msg.sender == owner) _;
}
function Migrations() public {
owner = msg.sender;
}
function setCompleted(uint completed) public restricted {
last_completed_migration = completed;
}
```

```
function upgrade(address new_address) public restricted {
Migrations upgraded = Migrations(new_address);
upgraded.setCompleted(last_completed_migration);
}
}
```

5. Under the `migration` folder, place two files with the `.js` extension as shown here:

`1_initial_migration.js`:

```
var Migrations = artifacts.require("./Migrations.sol");

module.exports = function(deployer) {
deployer.deploy(Migrations);
};
```

`2_deploy_contracts.js`:

```
var SimpleStorage = artifacts.require("Addition");

module.exports = function(deployer) {
deployer.deploy(SimpleStorage);
};
```

6. Under the `test` folder place the following file; this will be used for unit testing:

```
TestAddition.sol
pragma solidity ^0.4.2;

import "truffle/Assert.sol";
import "truffle/DeployedAddresses.sol";
import "../contracts/Addition.sol";

contract TestAddition {

  function testAddition() public {
    Addition adder = Addition(DeployedAddresses.Addition());
    adder.addx(100,100);
    uint returnedResult = adder.retrievex();
    uint expected = 200;

    Assert.equal(returnedResult, expected, "should result 200");
  }
```

In order to interact with the contract, the following methods can be used. As the `Addition` contract is already instantiated and available in the `truffle console`, it becomes quite easy to interact with the contract using various methods.

Run the following command:

```
$ truffle console
```

This will open the `truffle console`, which will allow interaction with the contract.

For example, in order to retrieve the address of the deployed contract, the following method can be called:

```
truffle(development)> Addition.address
'0x345ca3e014aaf5dca488057592ee47305d9b3e10'
```

To call the functions from within the contract, the deployed method is used with contract functions. An example is shown here, in which the `addx` function is called and two parameters are passed:

```
truffle(development)> Addition.at(Addition.address).addx(100,100)
{ tx: '0xd58f346b76c1d878b67e7218bd4f2f4acb53418d4632efafa35bf939f0181cac',
  receipt:
   { transactionHash: '0xd58f346b76c1d878b67e7318bd4f2f4acb53418d4632efafa35bf939f0181cac',
     transactionIndex: 0,
     blockHash: '0x9215cbd4f7e5f2861b08bc8d897c017c65751dbaf4c073c1a6739f97ac4316de',
     blockNumber: 61,
     gasUsed: 27131,
     cumulativeGasUsed: 27131,
     contractAddress: null,
     logs: [],
     status: 1 },
  logs: [] }
truffle(development)> Addition.at(Addition.address).retrievex()
{ [String: '200'] s: 1, e: 2, c: [ 200 ] }
truffle(development)>
```

The truffle console – interaction with the contract

An example project – Proof of Idea

The idea behind this program is to provide a service to notarize a document. This can then be used as proof that at a certain time in the past, the claimant has had access to a certain piece of information. This can be very useful for patent documents.

For example, if someone has come up with an idea, he or she can then create a hash of that document and save it on the blockchain. Due to the immutable nature of blockchain, it can serve as permanent proof that a certain idea (documents) existed at a certain time. There are many ways in which this can be achieved, but the key idea is the same and it works on the principle that hash functions provide a digest of the text or document and are unique.

This can be achieved in several ways by using different hash functions; the key idea is to create a hash of the document or text string and save it on the blockchain. Once the text is hashed and saved, further requests to save that same text can be disallowed by comparing the hash of the document with the already stored hash.

For this example, browser solidity, Truffle, and TestNet (already running Network ID 786, created earlier) will be used.

First, the code for the contract will be written. This can be done using any appropriate text editor or integrated development environment such as the Remix IDE or Visual Studio Code. The Remix IDE can also be used as that too provides a simulated environment for the test. This example will provide you with the opportunity to learn how a contract project can be developed from an idea into a solidity contract source code and finally to deployment.

Let's look at the code line by line:

```
pragma solidity ^0.4.0;
```

This statement ensures that the minimum compiler version is 0.4.0 and the maximum version cannot be greater than 0.4.9. This ensures compatibility between programs:

```
contract PatentIdea {
```

This statement is the start of the contract with the name `PatentIdea`:

```
mapping (bytes32 => bool) private hashes;
```

In the code line above, a mapping is defined, which maps `bytes32` to Boolean, and this is basically a hashmap (dictionary) of `bytes32` mapping to a Boolean value:

```
bool alreadyStored;
```

This is a variable declared with the `alreadyStored` name, which is a Boolean type and can have a `true` or `false` value. This variable is used to hold the return value from the `SaveIdeaHash` function:

```
event ideahashed(bool);
```

An event is declared as well, which will be used to capture the failure or success of the hashing function (SaveIdeaHash). When the event is triggered, it will return a true or false Boolean value.

A function named saveHash is declared, which takes the hash variable of type bytes32 as parameters and saves it in the hash map. This will result in a change of the state of the contract. Note that the function accessibility is changed to private as it is only required internally in the contract and does not need to be exposed publicly:

```
function saveHash(bytes32 hash) private
{
hashes[hash] = true;
}
```

Another function, SaveIdeaHash, is declared, and it takes the variable idea of type string and returns a Boolean (true or false) depending on the outcome of the function:

```
function SaveIdeaHash(string idea) returns (bool)
{
var hashedIdea = HashtheIdea(idea);
if (alreadyHashed(HashtheIdea(idea)))
{
alreadyStored=true; ideahashed(false);
return alreadyStored;
}
saveHash(hashedIdea);
ideahashed(true);
}
```

This function has a variable declared hashedIdea, which is assigned a value after calling the HashtheIdea function described later. Note that this function can also return a value if saved, but it is not shown here for simplicity.

The next function is the alreadyHashed function, which is declared to take the variable named hash of type bytes32 and returns a Boolean (either true or false) after checking the hash in the hash map. This is again declared as a constant and accessibility is set to private:

```
function alreadyHashed(bytes32 hash) constant private returns(bool)
{
return hashes[hash];
}
}
```

The next function is isAlreadyHashed, which checks whether the "idea" is already hashed. This takes the input parameter idea of type string such as "my idea", also declared as a constant, which means that it cannot change the state of the contract and returns either true or false based on the outcome of the execution of the function named alreadyHashed. This function then calls the alreadyHashed function described earlier to check from the hashes map whether the hash is already stored there. This would mean that the same string (idea) has already been hashed and stored (patented):

```
function isAlreadyHashed(string idea) constant returns (bool)
{
var hashedIdea = HashtheIdea(idea);
 return alreadyHashed(hashedIdea);
}
```

Finally, the HashtheIdea function is shown here, which takes the idea variable of type string and is of constant type, which means that it cannot change the state of the contract. It is also declared as private as there is no need to expose this function publicly because it is used only internally in the contract. This function returns the bytes32 type value:

```
function HashtheIdea(string idea) constant private returns (bytes32)
 {
return sha3(idea);
}
```

This function calls solidity's built-in function sha3 and passes a string to it in a variable idea. This function returns the SHA3 hash of the string. The sha3 function is an alias for the keccak256() function available in solidity, which computes the Keccak-256 hash of the string passed to it.

Note that this SHA3 function, used in solidity is not the NIST standard SHA-3; instead, it is Keccak-256, which is the original proposal to NIST for the SHA-3 standard competition. It was later modified slightly and standardized as the SHA-3 standard by NIST. The actual SHA-3 standard hash function will return a different hash compared to Keccak-256 (Ethereum's sha3 function).

The complete contract source code is shown as follows:

```
pragma solidity ^0.4.0;
contract PatentIdea
{
mapping (bytes32 => bool) private hashes;
bool alreadyStored;
event ideahashed(bool);
function saveHash(bytes32 hash) private
{
hashes[hash] = true;
}
function SaveIdeaHash(string idea) returns (bool)
{
var hashedIdea = HashtheIdea(idea);
if (alreadyHashed(HashtheIdea(idea)))
{
alreadyStored=true;
ideahashed(false);
return alreadyStored;
}
saveHash(hashedIdea);
ideahashed(true);
}
function alreadyHashed(bytes32 hash) constant private returns(bool)
{
return hashes[hash];
}
function isAlreadyHashed(string idea) constant returns (bool)
{
var hashedIdea = HashtheIdea(idea);
return alreadyHashed(hashedIdea);
}
function HashtheIdea(string idea) constant private returns (bytes32)
{
return sha3(idea);
}
}
```

This source code can be simulated in browser solidity in order to verify that it is working correctly. Some examples are shown here:

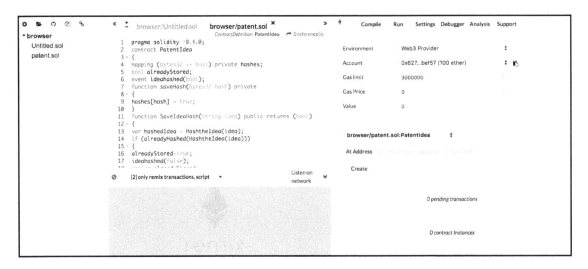

Create contract using browser solidity

Once the contract source code is typed and syntax verification is complete, on the right-hand side panel, a screen similar to the following one shown below will be appear.

This code can be improved in many ways. For example, the date can also be stored in a mapping with the document hash and can be returned when queried. It can be expanded by adding structures and more information related to the patent, but this example was intended to be simple and easy to understand; therefore, too much complexity was avoided. The code provided above is complete and will provide you a full working example of how the "proof of idea" contract can be implemented. You can do further enhancements to this as an exercise.

After clicking on **Create**, two functions from the contract will be exposed, as shown in the following screenshot:

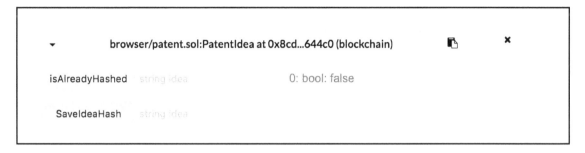

Relevant costs and exposes two methods

Functions **isAlreadyHased** (to check if the idea is already hashed) and **SaveIdeaHash** (to save the new idea string) can now be invoked as shown in the following example:

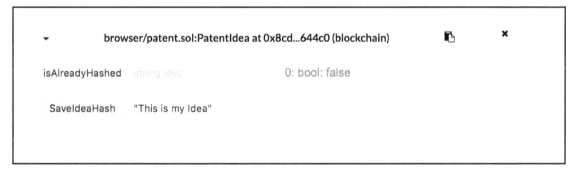

Invoking the SaveIdeaHash function

Now if we look at the logs produced in Remix IDE shown at the bottom of the IDE, we can see helpful details as shown in the following screenshot:

[block:2 txIndex:0] from:0x627...bef57, to:browser/patent.sol:PatentIdea.SaveIdeaHash(string) 0x8cd...644c0, value:0 wei, 1 logs, data:0xe 92...00000, hash:0x783...0a2fc	**Details** Debug

status	1
from	📋 0x627306090abab3a6e1400e9345bc60c78a8bef57
to	📋 browser/patent.sol:PatentIdea.SaveIdeaHash(string) 0x8cdaf0cd259887258bc13a92c0a6da92698644c0
gas	📋 45663 gas
transaction cost	📋 45663 gas
hash	📋 0x7834e933d99861237281906f7f9b92ae8f0ee7c3e9c3005942e4a5efc330a2fc
input	📋 0xe92c848f0000000000000000000000000000000000000000000000000000000000020000000000000000000000000000000000000000000000000000000000000000f54686973206973206d7920496465610000000000000000000000000000000000

decoded input	📋 {
	     "string idea": "This is my Idea"
	 }

decoded output	-

logs	📋📋 [
	     {
	         "topic": "0x50a0231b714fc7ad51309492c3e5b5c3fb79c5aa6646b65abd90b708f30b92e5",
	         "event": "ideahashed",
	         "args": [
	             "true"
	         ]
	     }
	]

value	📋 0 wei

Logs

The log shown valuable information such as:

- `status`: This is `1` in the example, meaning that transaction has been mined and executed successfully.
- `from`: This is the address of the account from, which the contract was initiated.
- `to`: This is the address of the contract on the blockchain.
- `gas`: This shows how much gas is sent.

- `transaction cost`: This shows how much gas is consumed.
- `hash`: This is the hash of the contract.
- `input`: This is input in shown in hex.
- `decoded input`: This shows the decoded input.
- `logs`: This shows transaction logs.
- `value`: This shows the value in Wei in the contract.

Similarly, **isAlreadyHashed** can be called. You can also explore the logs to find more details about the execution:

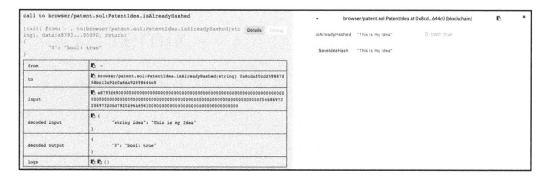

Execute function isAlreadyHashed

If the same string is passed to the function again, it will not be saved, as shown in the following screenshot:

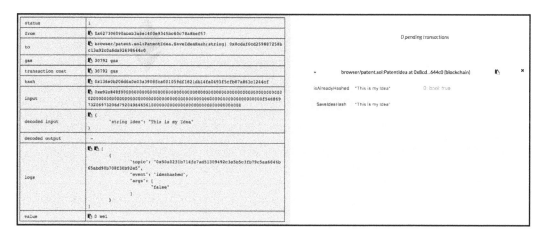

Execute function SaveIdeaHash

Also, note that the event has returned false, indicating that the hash could not be saved and the function returned true, further indicating that the same hash is already saved.

As we have been using Ganache as the local blockchain providing Web3, we can see all the relevant transactions in Ganache Frontend as shown in the following screenshot:

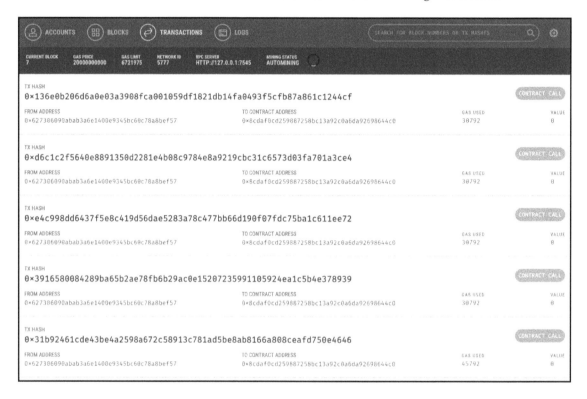

Ganache showing all transactions issued via the Remix IDE

Once the contract is written and simulated in the Remix IDE using Ganache, the next step is to use Truffle to initialize a new project and deploy and test it on the PrivateNet (ID 786), already created in earlier sections:

1. The first step is to create a separate directory for the project:

```
~$ mkdir ideapatent
~$ cd ideapatent/
```

2. The next step is to initialize Truffle and create a new project:

```
~/ideapatent$ truffle init
truffle init
Downloading...
Unpacking...
Setting up...
Unbox successful. Sweet!
Commands:
  Compile:        truffle compile
  Migrate:        truffle migrate
  Test contracts: truffle test
```

It will create a structure as shown here:

```
.
├──── contracts
│     └──── Migrations.sol
├──── migrations
│     └──── 1_initial_migration.js
├──── test
├──── truffle-config.js
└──── truffle.js
```

3. Under the `contracts` folder, create a file named `PatentIdea.sol` and put the source code in the file shown earlier.

4. Edit `truffle.js` to point to the localhost HTTP endpoint. This is our private network 786 created earlier:

```
module.exports = {
  networks: {
    development: {
      host: 'localhost',
      port: 8545,
      network_id: 786
    }
  }
}
```

5. Under the `~/ideapatent/migrations` folder, create the `2_deploy_contracts.js` file so that it looks like the following:

```
2_deploy_contracts.js
var PatentContract = artifacts.require("PatentIdea");

module.exports = function(deployer) {
  deployer.deploy(PatentContract);
};
```

6. Next, run the compilation using Truffle, as shown here:

```
truffle compile
Compiling ./contracts/PatentIdea.sol...
Writing artifacts to ./build/contracts
```

7. Ensure that mining is running in the background and deploy to the network, as shown here:

```
$ truffle migrate
Using network 'development'.

Running migration: 1_initial_migration.js
  Deploying Migrations...
  ...
0x1813f90a123ee23443d10ebec1cf6c58919e10fc36d7de6b063f0cd596c92f97
  Migrations: 0x8cdaf0cd259887258bc13a92c0a6da92698644c0
Saving successful migration to network...
  ...
0xd7bc86d31bee32fa3988f1c1eabce403a1b5d570340a3a9cdba53a472ee8c956
Saving artifacts...
Running migration: 2_deploy_contracts.js
  Deploying PatentIdea...
  ...
0x816dc5e6de1d76152e3680199e71f51b48b79bbe6e0c4e6592633b471ecdea69
  PatentIdea: 0x345ca3e014aaf5dca488057592ee47305d9b3e10
Saving artifacts...
```

8. Once the contract is deployed, it can be interacted with using the `truffle console`. Start the `truffle console` by issuing the following command:

```
$ truffle console
```

9. Once the console is up and running, functions from the deployed contract can be called as shown here.

For example, to register a new idea, type the following commands on the geth console:

```
>PatentIdea.deployed().then(function(instance){app = instance})
truffle(development)>
PatentIdea.deployed().then(function(instance){app = instance})
undefined

>truffle(development)> app.SaveIdeaHash("hello1")
```

This will show the output similar to the following:

```
truffle(development)> PatentIdea.deployed().then(function(instance){app = instance})
undefined
truffle(development)> app.SaveIdeaHash("hello1")
{ tx: '0x597fffed0f869877676b158077c402b09a0ba1cd213c1ba28798e72a1f48af80',
  receipt:
   { blockHash: '0xaf21334ea79cc7f507eca9e6c93f943253fd371d987f0d3593ef3e278e4c77d6',
     blockNumber: 4846,
     contractAddress: null,
     cumulativeGasUsed: 65636,
     from: '0xcf61d213faa9acadbf3d118e1397caf28445c58f',
     gasUsed: 65636,
     logs: [ [Object] ],
     logsBloom: '0x0000000000000000000000000000000000000000000000000000000000000000
0000000000000000000000000000000000000000000000000040000000000000000000000000000000
0000000000000000000000000000000000000000040000020000000000000000000000000000000000',
     root: '0xc9b84ede2a53eef a6e933d697868230565c16570bffcb3ad21fe71c6ce424540',
     to: '0x0694d9db791883c83e10175163d8a58df76a2a84',
     transactionHash: '0x597fffed0f869877676b158077c402b09a0ba1cd213c1ba28798e72a1f48af80',
     transactionIndex: 0 },
  logs:
   [ { address: '0x0694d9db791883c83e10175163d8a58df76a2a84',
       blockNumber: 4846,
       transactionHash: '0x597fffed0f869877676b158077c402b09a0ba1cd213c1ba28798e72a1f48af80',
       transactionIndex: 0,
       blockHash: '0xaf21334ea79cc7f507eca9e6c93f943253fd371d987f0d3593ef3e278e4c77d6',
       logIndex: 0,
       removed: false,
       event: 'ideahashed',
       args: [Object] } ] }
```

Invoking deployed contract methods in the truffle console

If the account is locked, you can unlock it using the following command:

```
> personal.unlockAccount(web3.eth.coinbase, "Password123", 15000)
```

Note that we have used another parameter here, `15000`, which is the duration for which the account will remain unlocked. This is in seconds.

Check whether `"hello1"` is hashed:

```
truffle(development)> app.isAlreadyHashed("hello1");
true
```

Check whether another idea is hashed or not, in this example we've used string `"hello3"`:

```
truffle(development)> app.isAlreadyHashed("hello3");
false
```

This example demonstrated how a contract can be created from scratch, simulated, and deployed on the PrivateNet. In order to deploy this on TestNet or a live blockchain, a similar exercise can be performed. Simply point to the appropriate RPC and use `truffle migrate` to deploy on the blockchain of your choice.

In the next section, some advanced concepts related to Ethereum and blockchain will be discussed.

Oracles

As discussed in `Chapter 9`, *Smart Contracts*, Oracles are real-world data feeds into smart contracts. There are various services available in order to provide Oracles for smart contracts. A rather prominent one is Oraclize, which is available at `http://www.oraclize.it/`. This is especially useful if the smart contract needs, for example, live prices from a third-party source or any other real-life data, such as weather conditions in a particular city.

There are many use cases where Oracles can provide a trusted data feed to smart contracts in order to enable them to make decisions according to real-life events. Oraclize makes it easier for smart contracts to access the Internet in order to get the required data.

In order to utilize Oraclize on Ethereum, a transaction needs to be sent to the Oraclize contract along with the appropriate payment and the query. As a result, Oraclize will retrieve the results based on the query provided in the request transaction and send it back to the contract address. Once the transaction is sent back to the contract, the callback method or fall back function will be called.

At a practical level in solidity, first, the Oraclize library needs to be imported and then all methods that have been inherited from it can be used. Currently, Oraclize is available to be used only on the PrivateNet (Ropsten) and Live Main Net Ethereum blockchain.

Oraclize processing can be visualized as shown in the following diagram:

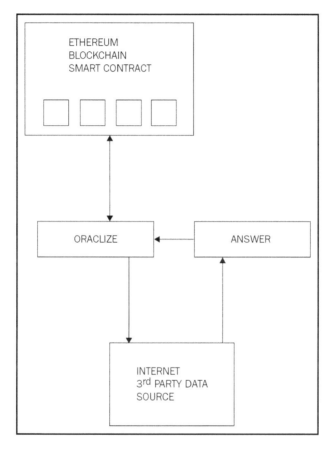

Oraclize data flow

On top we have the Ethereum blockchain and smart contract, to which Oraclize talks via a secure mechanism. Oraclize can request data from external data sources, which can be fed into Oraclize, which can then be sent down to Ethereum blockchain. The answer comes with a TLSNotary proof ensuring the integrity and authenticity of the message. **TLSNotary** proofs are used to provide a cryptographic proof of communication between two parties.

Original research paper of TLSNotary is available
at `https://tlsnotary.org/TLSNotary.pdf`.

The skeleton structure of a solidity contract using Oraclize looks like the one shown here. Note that import works only on the development environment provided on the web by Oraclize; usually, this file needs to be imported manually.

Oraclize API is available at `https://github.com/oraclize/ethereum-api`.

```
import "dev.oraclize.it/api.sol";
contract MyOracleContract is usingOraclize
{
function MyOracleContract(){
}
```

A sample request looks like what is shown in the following example:

```
oraclize_query("URL", "api.somewebsite.net/price?stock=XYZ");
```

Oraclize can also make use of the TLS notary in order to ensure that the feed is secure and provably honest.

Deployment on decentralized storage using IPFS

As discussed in `Chapter 1`, *Blockchain 101*, in order to fully benefit from decentralized platforms, it is desirable that you decentralize the storage and communication layer too in addition to decentralized state/computation (blockchain).

Traditionally, the web content is served via centralized servers, but that part can also be decentralized using distributed filesystems.

The HTML content shown in the earlier examples can be stored on a distributed and decentralized IPFS network in order to achieve enhanced decentralization.

 IPFS is available at `https://ipfs.io/`.

Installing IPFS

IPFS can be installed by following this process:

1. Download the IPFS package using the following command:

   ```
   $ curl https://dist.ipfs.io/go-ipfs/v0.4.4/go- ipfs_v0.4.4_linux-
   amd64.tar.gz -O
   ```

2. Decompress the `.gz` file:

   ```
   $ tar xvfz go-ipfs_v0.4.4_linux-amd64.tar.gz
   ```

3. Move the `ipfs` file to an appropriate folder in order to make it available in the path:

   ```
   $ mv go-ipfs/ipfs /usr/local/bin/ipfs
   ```

4. Initialize the IPFS node:

   ```
   $ ipfs init initializing ipfs node at /home/imran/.ipfs generating
   2048-bit RSA keypair...done
   peer identity: Qmbc726pLS9nUQjUbeJUxcCfXAGaXPD41jAszXniChJz62 to
   get started, enter:
   ipfs cat
   /ipfs/QmYwAPJzv5CZsnA625s3Xf2nemtYgPpHdWEz79ojWnPbdG/readme
   ```

5. Enter the following command to ensure that IPFS has been successfully installed:

IPFS Installation

6. Start the IPFS daemon:

```
$ ipfs daemon

Initializing daemon...
Swarm listening on /ip4/127.0.0.1/tcp/4001 Swarm listening on
/ip4/192.168.0.17/tcp/4001 Swarm listening on
/ip4/86.15.44.209/tcp/4001 Swarm listening on
/ip4/86.15.44.209/tcp/41608 Swarm listening on /ip6/::1/tcp/4001
API server listening on /ip4/127.0.0.1/tcp/5001
Gateway (readonly) server listening on /ip4/127.0.0.1/tcp/8080
Daemon is ready
```

7. Copy files onto IPFS using the following command:

```
~/sampleproject/build$ ipfs add --recursive --progress. added
QmVdYdY1uycf32e8NhMVEWSufMyvcj17w3DkUt6BgeAtx7 build/app.css
added QmSypieNFeiUx6Sq7moAVCsgQhSY3Bh9ziwXJAxqSG5Pcp build/app.js
added QmaJWMjD767GvuwuaLpt5tck9dTVCZPJa9sDcr8vdcJ8pY
build/contracts/ConvertLib.sol.js
added QmQdz9eG2Qd5kwaU86kWebDGPqXBWj1Dmv9MN4BRzt2srf
build/contracts/MetaCoin.sol.js
added QmWpvBjXTP4HutEsYUh3JLDi8VYp73SKNJi4aX1T6jwcmG
build/contracts/Migrations.sol.js
added QmQs7j6NpA1NMueTXKyswLaHKq3XDUCRay3VrC392Q4JDK
build/index.html
added QmPvWzyTEfLQnozDTfqdAAF4W9BUb2cDq5KUUrpHrukseA
build/contracts
added QmUNLLsPACCz1vLxQVkXqqLX5R1X345qqfHbsf67hvA3Nn build/images
added QmSxpucr6J9rX3XQ3MBG8cVzLCrQFFKmMkTmpcNpjbtf3j build
```

8. Now it can be accessed in the browser as follows:

Example Truffle Dapp running on IPFS and served via web host

Note that the URL is pointing to the IPFS filesystem.

9. Finally, in order to make the changes permanent, the following command can be used:

```
$ ipfs pin add QmSxpucr6J9rX3XQ3MBG8cVzLCrQFFKmMkTmpcNpjbtf3j
```

This will show the following output:

```
pinned QmSxpucr6J9rX3XQ3MBG8cVzLCrQFFKmMkTmpcNpjbtf3j recursively
```

The preceding example demonstrated how IPFS can be used to provide decentralized storage for the web part (user interface) of smart contracts.

IPFS can be used with blockchains in another way. As storage is a big issue for blockchains, it is desirable that you are able to save large amounts of data somewhere else and place the links to that data in the blockchain transaction. This way, there will be no need to store large amounts of data on the blockchain and bloat it as a result. IPFS can be used to achieve exactly that by placing the data on IPFS and then storing the IPFS links in blockchain transactions to reference the stored data.

Ethereum's own Swarm protocol is also and works on similar principles. Swarm allows users to run a light client by storing all the blockchain data on it.

This is available with the current version of geth, and a detailed guide is available at
`https://swarm-guide.readthedocs.io/en/latest/introduction.html`.

Swarm is available for use using the provided HTTP API. In order to use Swarm, you need to run a Swarm node. This needs geth and Swarm installed on the node. A Swarm is formed of these Swarm nodes each of these running the geth client and the Swarm client. The protocol used by Swarm is called *bzz*. Each Swarm node is identified by an address called *bzzkey*. This is derived from the Keccak 256-bit hash of the coinbase address of the geth node.

Swarm is composed of various elements called chunks, hashes, and manifests. Chunks are simply pieces of data that are limited to 4K per chunk. This data is identified on the Swarm using a hash, which is generated from the data itself. Finally, manifest is used to describe the access and storage mechanics of the data. It specifies hashes, indexes, and relevant filesystem directories to allow URL-based data retrieval.

For decentralized communication in Ethereum, the **Whisper** protocol provides the decentralized communication layer. This will serve as an identity-based messaging layer for Ethereum. Both Swarm and Whisper are envisaged to be enabling technologies for Web 3.0.

Distributed ledgers

The concept of permissioned distributed ledgers is fundamentally different to a public blockchain. The key idea behind distributed ledgers is that they are permissioned as opposed to an open public blockchain. DLTs do not perform any mining as all the participants are already vetted and known to the network and there is no requirement for mining to secure the network. There is also no concept of digital currency on private permissioned distributed ledgers because the aim of the permissioned blockchain is different from a public blockchain.

In a public blockchain, access is open to everyone and requires some form of incentive and network effect in order to grow; on the contrary, in permissioned DLTs, there are no such requirements. It is possible to build permissioned DLTs using Ethereum in private consortium settings, especially to work within existing financial systems. The key benefit of distributed ledger systems is that they are much faster, governable, and possibly interoperable with the existing financial system.

Summary

This chapter started with the introduction of Web3. We explored various methods to develop smart contracts. Also, we saw how the contract can be tested and verified using local test blockchain before implementation on public blockchain or private production blockchain.

We worked with various tools such as Ganache, the geth client console, and the Remix IDE to develop, test, and deploy smart contracts. Moreover, the Truffle framework was also used to test and migrate contract code. Further, we explored other advanced topics such as Oracles and using IPFS.

In the next chapter, we will see Hyperledger, which is a Linux foundation project to advance the blockchain technologies.

15
Hyperledger

Hyperledger is not a blockchain, but it is a project that was initiated by the Linux Foundation in December 2015 to advance blockchain technology. This project is a collaborative effort by its members to build an open source distributed ledger framework that can be used to develop and implement cross-industry blockchain applications and systems. The principal focus is to develop and run platforms that support global business transactions. The project also focuses on improving the reliability and performance of blockchain systems.

Projects under Hyperledger undergo various stages of development, starting from proposal to incubation and graduating to an active state. Projects can also be deprecated or in end-of-life state where they are no longer actively developed. For a project to be able to move into the incubation stage, it must have a fully working code base along with an active community of developers.

Projects under Hyperledger

There are two categories of projects under Hyperledger. The first is **blockchain projects** and the second category is **relevant tools or modules that support these blockchains**.

Currently, there are five blockchain framework projects under the Hyperledger umbrella: **Fabric**, **Sawtooth Lake**, **Iroha**, **Burrow**, and **Indy**. Under modules, there are the **Hyperledger Cello**, **Hyperledger Composer**, **Hyperledger Explorer**, and **Hyperledger Quilt**. The Hyperledger project currently has more than 200-member organizations and is very active with many contributors, with regular meet-ups and talks organized around the globe.

A brief introduction of all these projects follows, after which we will see more details around the design, architecture, and implementation of Fabric and Sawtooth Lake.

Fabric

The fabric is a blockchain project that was proposed by **IBM** and **DAH** (**Digital Asset Holdings**). This blockchain framework implementation is intended to provide a foundation for the development of blockchain solutions with a modular architecture. It is based on a pluggable architecture where various components, such as consensus engine and membership services, can be plugged into the system as required. It also makes use of container technology which is used to run smart contracts in an isolated contained environment. Currently, its status is *active* and it's the first project to graduate from incubation to active state.

 The source code is available at `https://github.com/hyperledger/fabric`.

Sawtooth Lake

The Sawtooth Lake is a blockchain project proposed by Intel in April 2016 with some key innovations focusing on the decoupling of ledgers from transactions, flexible usage across multiple business areas using transaction families, and pluggable consensus.

Decoupling can be explained more precisely by saying that the transactions are decoupled from the consensus layer by making use of a new concept called **transaction families**. Instead of transactions being individually coupled with the ledger, transaction families are used, which allows for more flexibility, rich semantics, and open design of business logic. Transactions follow the patterns and structures defined in the transaction families.

Some of the innovative elements Intel has introduced include a novel consensus algorithm abbreviated as **PoET**, **Proof of Elapsed Time**, which makes use of **Trusted Execution Environment** (**TEE**) provided by **Intel Software Guard Extensions** (**Intel's SGX**) to provide a safe and random leader election process. It also supports permissioned and permission-less setups.

 This project is available at `https://github.com/hyperledger/sawtooth-core`.

Iroha

Iroha was contributed by Soramitsu, Hitachi, NTT Data, and Colu in September 2016. Iroha is aiming to build a library of reusable components that users can choose to run on their own Hyperledger-based distributed ledgers.

Iroha's primary goal is to complement other Hyperledger projects by providing reusable components written in C++ with an emphasis on mobile development. This project has also proposed a novel consensus algorithm called **Sumeragi**, which is a chain-based Byzantine fault tolerant consensus algorithm.

 Iroha is available at `https://github.com/hyperledger/iroha`.

Various libraries have been proposed and are being worked on by Iroha, including but not limited to a digital signature library (ed25519), a SHA-3 hashing library, a transaction serialization library, a P2P library, an API server library, an iOS library, an Android library, and a JavaScript library.

Burrow

This project is currently in the incubation state. Hyperledger Burrow was contributed by Monax, who develop blockchain development and deployment platforms for business. Hyperledger Burrow introduces a modular blockchain platform and an **Ethereum Virtual Machine** (**EVM**) based smart contract execution environment. Burrow uses proof of stake, Byzantine fault tolerant Tendermint consensus mechanism. As a result, Burrow provides high throughput and transaction finality.

 The source code is available at `https://github.com/hyperledger/burrow`.

Indy

This project is under incubation under Hyperledger. Indy is a distributed ledger developed for building a decentralized identity. It provides tools, utility libraries, and modules which can be used to build blockchain-based digital identities. These identities can be used across multiple blockchains, domains, and applications. Indy has its own distributed ledger and uses **Redundant Byzantine Fault Tolerance** (**RBFT**) for consensus.

 The source code is available at `https://github.com/hyperledger/indy-node`.

Explorer

This project aims to build a blockchain explorer for Hyperledger Fabric that can be used to view and query the transactions, blocks, and associated data from the blockchain. It also provides network information and the ability to interact with chain code.

Currently, there are few other projects that are in incubation under Hyperledger. These projects are aimed to provide tools and utilities to support blockchain networks. These projects are introduced in the following section.

 The source code is available at `https://github.com/hyperledger/blockchain-explorer`.

Cello

The aim behind Cello is to allow easy deployment of blockchains. This will provide an ability to allow "as a service" deployments of blockchain service. Currently, this project is in the incubation stage.

 The source code of Cello is available at `https://github.com/hyperledger/cello`.

Composer

This utility makes the development of blockchain solutions easier by allowing business processes to be described in a business language, while abstracting away the low-level smart contract development details.

 Hyperledger composer is available at `https://hyperledger.github.io/composer/`.

Quilt

This utility implements the Interledger protocol, which facilitates interoperability across different distributed and non-distributed ledger networks.

 Quilt is available at `https://github.com/hyperledger/quilt`.

Currently, all the mentioned projects are in various stages of development.

This list is expected to grow as more and more members are joining Hyperledger project and contributing to the development of blockchain technology. Now in the next section, we will see the reference architecture of Hyperledger, which provides general principles and design philosophy which can be followed to build new Hyperledger projects.

Hyperledger as a protocol

Hyperledger is aiming to build new blockchain platforms that are driven by industry use cases. As there have been many contributions made to the Hyperledger project by the community, Hyperledger blockchain platform is evolving into a protocol for business transactions. Hyperledger is also evolving into a specification that can be used as a reference to build blockchain platforms as compared to earlier blockchain solutions that address only a specific type of industry or requirement.

In the following section, a reference architecture is presented that has been published by the Hyperledger project. As this work is under continuous and rigorous development, some changes are expected in this, but core services are expected to remain unchanged.

The reference architecture

Hyperledger has published a white paper which is available at `https://docs.google.com/document/d/1Z4M_qwILLRehPbVRUsJ3OF8Iir-gqS-ZYe7W-LE9gnE /edit#heading=h.m6iml6hqrnm2`.

This document presents a reference architecture that can serve as a guideline to build permissioned distributed ledgers. The reference architecture consists of various components that form a business blockchain. These high-level components are shown in the reference architecture diagram shown here:

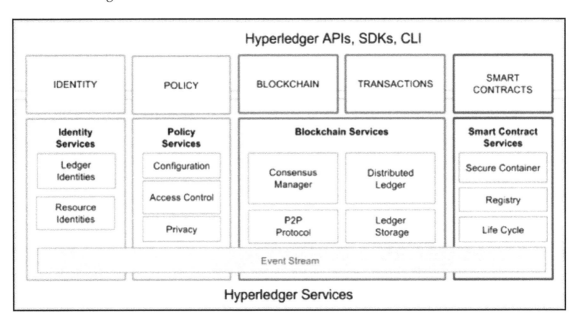

Reference architecture - source: Hyperledger whitepaper

Starting from the left we see that we have five top-level components which provide various services. We will explore all these components in detail.

First is identity, that provides authorization, identification, and authentication services under membership services.

Then is the policy component, which provides policy services.

After this, ledger and transactions come, which consists of the distributed ledger, ordering service, network protocols, and endorsement and validation services. This ledger is updateable only via consensus among the participants of the blockchain network.

Finally, we have the smart contracts layer, which provides chaincode services in Hyperledger and makes use of secure container technology to host smart contracts. We will see all these in more detail in the *Hyperledger Fabric* section shortly.

Generally, from a components point of view Hyperledger contains various elements described here:

- **Consensus layer**: These services are responsible for facilitating the agreement process between the participants on the blockchain network. The consensus is required to make sure that the order and state of transactions is validated and agreed upon in the blockchain network.
- **Smart contract layer**: These services are responsible for implementing business logic as per the requirements of the users. Transaction are processed based on the logic defined in the smart contracts that reside on the blockchain.
- **Communication layer**: This layer is responsible for message transmission and exchange between the nodes on the blockchain network.
- **Security and crypto layer**: These services are responsible for providing a capability to allow various cryptographic algorithms or modules to provide privacy, confidentiality and non-repudiations services.
- **Data stores**: This layer provides an ability to use different data stores for storing state of the ledger. This means that data stores are also pluggable and allows usage of any database backend.
- **Policy services**: This set of services provide the ability to manage different policies required for the blockchain network. This includes endorsement policy and consensus policy.
- **APIs and SDKs**: This layer allows clients and applications to interact with the blockchain. An SDK is used to provide mechanisms to deploy and execute chaincode, query blocks and monitor events on the blockchain.

There are certain requirements of a blockchain service. In the next section, we are going to discuss the design goals of Hyperledger Fabric.

Requirements and design goals of Hyperledger Fabric

There are certain requirements of a blockchain service. The reference architecture is driven by the needs and requirements raised by the participants of the Hyperledger project and after studying the industry use cases. There are several categories of requirements that have been deduced from the study of industrial use cases and are discussed in the following sections.

The modular approach

The main requirement of Hyperledger is a modular structure. It is expected that as a cross-industry fabric (blockchain), it will be used in many business scenarios. As such, functions related to storage, policy, chaincode, access control, consensus, and many other blockchain services should be modular and pluggable. The specification suggests that the modules should be plug and play and users should be able to easily remove and add a different module that meets the requirements of the business.

Privacy and confidentiality

This requirement is one of the most critical factors. As traditional blockchains are permissionless, in the permissioned model like Hyperledger Fabric, it is of utmost importance that transactions on the network are visible to only those who are allowed to view it.

Privacy and confidentiality of transactions and contracts are of absolute importance in a business blockchain. As such, Hyperledger's vision is to provide support for a full range of cryptographic protocols and algorithms. We discussed cryptography in `Chapter 3`, *Symmetric Cryptography* and `Chapter 4`, *Public Key Cryptography*.

It is expected that users will be able to choose appropriate modules according to their business requirements. For example, if a business blockchain needs to be run only between already trusted parties and performs very basic business operations, then perhaps there is no need to have advanced cryptographic support for confidentiality and privacy. Therefore, users should be able to remove that functionality (module) or replace that with a more appropriate module that suits their needs.

Similarly, if users need to run a cross-industry blockchain, then confidentiality and privacy can be of paramount importance. In this case, users should be able to plug an advanced cryptographic and access control mechanism (module) into the blockchain (fabric), which can even allow usage of **hardware of security modules** (**HSMs**).

Also, the blockchain should be able to handle sophisticated cryptographic algorithms without compromising performance. In addition to the previously mentioned scenarios, due to regulatory requirements in business, there should also be a provision to allow implementation of privacy and confidentiality policies in conformance with regulatory and compliance requirements.

Scalability

This is another major requirement which once met will allow reasonable transaction throughput, which will be sufficient for all business requirements and also a large number of users.

Deterministic transactions

This is a core requirement in any blockchain because if transactions do not produce the same result every time they are executed regardless of who and where the transaction is executed, then achieving consensus is impossible. Therefore, deterministic transactions become a key requirement in any blockchain network. We discussed these concepts in `Chapter 9`, *Smart Contracts*.

Identity

In order to provide privacy and confidentiality services, a flexible PKI model that can be used to handle the access control functionality is also required. The strength and type of cryptographic mechanisms is also expected to vary according to the needs and requirements of the users. In certain scenarios, it might be required for a user to hide their identity, and as such, the Hyperledger is expected to provide this functionality.

Auditability

Auditability is another requirement of Hyperledger Fabric. It is expected that an immutable audit trail of all identities, related operations, and any changes is kept.

Interoperability

Currently, there are many blockchain platforms available, but they cannot communicate with each other and this can be a limiting factor in the growth of a blockchain-based global business ecosystem. It is envisaged that many blockchain networks will operate in the business world for specific needs, but it is important that they are able to communicate with each other. There should be a common set of standards that all blockchains can follow in order to allow communication between different ledgers. It is expected that a protocol will be developed that will allow the exchange of information between many fabrics.

Portability

The portability requirement is concerned with the ability to run across multiple platforms and environments without the need to change anything at code level. Hyperledger Fabric is envisaged to be portable, not only at infrastructure level but also at code, libraries, and API levels, so that it can support uniform development across various implementations of Hyperledger.

Rich data queries

The blockchain network should allow rich queries to be run on the network. This can be used to query the current state of the ledger using traditional query languages, which will allow for wider adoption and ease of use.

All aforementioned points describe the requirements, which need to be met to develop blockchain solutions that are in line with the Hyperledger design philosophy. In the next section, we will have a look at Hyperledger Fabric, which is the first project to graduate to active status under Hyperledger.

Fabric

To understand various projects that are under development in the Hyperledger project, it is essential to understand the foundations of Hyperledger first. A few terminologies that are specific to Hyperledger need some clarification before readers are introduced to the more in-depth material.

First, there is the concept of fabric. Fabric can be defined as a collection of components providing a foundation layer that can be used to deliver a blockchain network. There are various types and capabilities of a fabric network, but all fabrics share common attributes such as immutability and are consensus-driven. Some fabrics can provide a modular approach towards building blockchain networks. In this case, the blockchain network can have multiple pluggable modules to perform a various function on the network.

For example, consensus algorithms can be a pluggable module in a blockchain network where, depending on the requirements of the network, an appropriate consensus algorithm can be chosen and plugged into the network. The modules can be based on some particular specification of the fabric and can include APIs, access control, and various other components.

Fabrics can also be designed either to be private or public and can allow the creation of multiple business networks. As an example, Bitcoin is an application that runs on top of its fabric (blockchain network). As discussed earlier in Chapter 1, *Blockchain 101*, blockchain can either be permissioned or permission-less. However, the aim of Hyperledger Fabric is to develop a permissioned distributed ledger.

Fabric is also the name given to the code contribution made by IBM to the Hyperledger foundation and is formally called Hyperledger Fabric. IBM also offers blockchain as a service (IBM Blockchain) via its *IBM Cloud service*.

 It is available at https://www.ibm.com/cloud/.

Now let's have a detailed look at Hyperledger Fabric.

Hyperledger Fabric

The fabric is the contribution made initially by IBM and Digital Assets to the Hyperledger project. This contribution aims to enable a modular, open, and flexible approach towards building blockchain networks.

Various functions in the fabric are pluggable, and it also allows the use of any language to develop smart contracts. This functionality is possible because it is based on container technology (Docker), which can host any language.

Chaincode is sandboxed in a secure container, which includes a secure operating system, chaincode language, runtime environment, and SDKs for Go, Java, and Node.js. Other languages can be supported too in future, if required, but needs some development work. Smart contracts are called chaincode in the fabric. This ability is a compelling feature compared to domain-specific languages in Ethereum, or the limited scripted language in Bitcoin. It is a permissioned network that aims to address issues such as scalability, privacy, and confidentiality. The fundamental idea behind this is modularization, which would allow for flexibility in design and implementation of the business blockchain. This can then result in achieving scalability, privacy, and other desired attributes and fine tune them according to the requirements.

Transactions in the fabric are private, confidential, and anonymous for general users, but they can still be traced and linked to the users by authorized auditors. As a permissioned network, all participants are required to be registered with the membership services to access the blockchain network. This ledger also provided auditability functionality to meet the regulatory and compliance needs required by the user.

Membership services

These services are used to provide access control capability for the users of the fabric network. The following list shows the functions that membership services perform:

- User identity verification
- User registration
- Assign appropriate permissions to the users depending on their roles

Membership services make use of **a certificate authority** in order to support identity management and authorization operations. This CA can be internal (Fabric CA), which is a default interface in Hyperledger Fabric or organization can opt to use an external certificate authority. Fabric CA issues **enrollment certificates** (**E-Certs**), which are produced by **enrollment certificate authority** (**E-CA**). Once peers are issued with an identity, they are allowed to join the blockchain network. There are also temporary certificates issued called T-Certs, which are used for one-time transactions.

All peers and applications are identified using certificate authority. Authentication service is provided by the certificate authority. MSPs can also interface with existing identity services like LDAP.

Blockchain services

Blockchain services are at the core of the Hyperledger Fabric. Components within this category are as follows.

Consensus services

A consensus service is responsible for providing the interface to the consensus mechanism. This serves as a module that is pluggable and receives the transaction from other Hyperledger entities and executes them under criteria according to the type of mechanism chosen.

Consensus in Hyperledger V1 is implemented as a peer called **orderer**, which is responsible for ordering the transactions in sequence into a block. Orderer does not hold smart contracts or ledgers. Consensus is pluggable and currently, there are two types of ordering services available in Hyperledger Fabric:

- **SOLO**: This is a basic ordering service intended to be used for development and testing purposes.
- **Kafka**: This is an implementation of Apache Kafka, which provides ordering service. It should be noted that currently Kafka only provides crash fault tolerance but does not provide byzantine fault tolerance. This is acceptable in a permissioned network where chances of malicious actors are almost none.

In addition to these mechanisms, the **Simple Byzantine Fault Tolerance** (**SBFT**) based mechanism is also under development, which will become available in the later releases of Hyperledger Fabric.

Distributed ledger

Blockchain and world state are two main elements of the distributed ledger. Blockchain is simply a cryptographically linked list of blocks (as introduced in `Chapter 1`, *Blockchain 101*) and world state is a key-value database. This database is used by smart contracts to store relevant states during execution by the transactions. The blockchain consists of blocks that contain transactions. These transactions contain chaincode, which runs transactions that can result in updating the world state. Each node saves the world state on disk in LevelDB or CouchDB depending on the implementation. As Fabric allows pluggable data store, you can choose any data store for storage.

A block consists of three main components called Block header, Transactions (Data) and block metadata.

The following diagram shows a typical block in the Hyperledger Fabric 1.0 with the relevant fields:

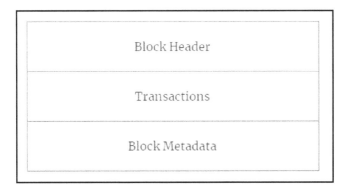

Block structure

Block Header consists of three fields, namely Number, Previous hash, and Data hash.

Transaction is made up of multiple fields such as transaction type, version, timestamp, channel ID, transaction ID, epoch, payload visibility, chaincode path, chaincode name, chaincode version, creator identity, signature, chaincode type, input, timeout, endorser identities and signatures, proposal hash, chaincode events, response status, namespace, read set, write set, start key, end key, list of read, and Merkle tree query summary.

Block Metadata consists of creator identity, relevant signatures, last configuration block number, flag for each transaction included in the block, and last offset persisted (kafka).

The peer to peer protocol

The P2P protocol in the Hyperledger Fabric is built using **google RPC** (**gRPC**). It uses protocol buffers to define the structure of the messages.

Messages are passed between nodes in order to perform various functions. There are four main types of messages in Hyperledger Fabric: **discovery**, **transaction**, **synchronization**, and **consensus**. Discovery messages are exchanged between nodes when starting up in order to discover other peers on the network. Transaction messages are used to deploy, invoke, and query transactions, and consensus messages are exchanged during consensus. Synchronization messages are passed between nodes to synchronize and keep the blockchain updated on all nodes.

Ledger storage

In order to save the state of the ledger, by default, LevelDB is used which is available at each peer. An alternative is to use CouchDB which provides the ability to run rich queries.

Chaincode services

These services allow the creation of secure containers that are used to execute the chaincode. Components in this category are as follows:

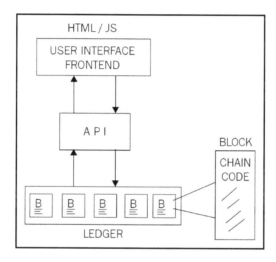

- **Secure container**: Chaincode is deployed in Docker containers that provide a locked down sandboxed environment for smart contract execution. Currently, Golang is supported as the main smart contract language, but any other mainstream languages can be added and enabled if required.
- **Secure registry:** This provides a record of all images containing smart contracts.

Events

Events on the blockchain can be triggered by endorsers and smart contracts. External applications can listen to these events and react to them if required via event adapters. They are similar to the concept of events introduced in solidity in `Chapter 14`, *Introducing Web3*.

APIs and CLIs

An application programming interface provides an interface into the fabric by exposing various REST APIs. Additionally, command-line interfaces that provide a subset of REST APIs and allow for quick testing and limited interaction with the blockchain are also available.

Components of the fabric

There are various components that can be part of the Hyperledger Fabric blockchain. These components include but are not limited to the ledger, chaincode, consensus mechanism, access control, events, system monitoring and management, wallets, and system integration components.

Peers

Peers participate in maintaining the state of the distributed ledger. They also hold a local copy of the distributed ledger. Peers communicate via gossip protocol. There are three types of peers in the Hyperledger Fabric network:

- **Endorsing peers** or endorsers which simulate the transaction execution and generate a read-write set. Read is a simulation of transaction's reading of data from the ledger and write is the set of updates that would be made to the ledger if and when the transaction is executed and committed to the ledger. Endorses execute and endorse transactions. It should be noted that an endorser is also a committer too. Endorsement policies are implemented with chaincode and specify the rules for transaction endorsement.
- **Committing peers** or committers which receives transaction endorsed by endorsers, verify them and then update the ledger with the read-write set. A committer verifies the read-write set generated by the endorsers along with transaction validation.
- **Submitters** is the third type of peers which has not been implemented yet. It is on the development roadmap and will be implemented

Orderer nodes

Ordering nodes receive transactions from endorsers along with read-write sets, arrange them in a sequence, and send those to committing peers. Committing peers then perform validation and committing to the ledger.

All peers make use of certificates issued by membership services.

Clients

Clients are software that makes use of APIs to interact with the Hyperledger Fabric and propose transactions.

Channels

Channels allow the flow of confidential transactions between different parties on the network. They allow using the same blockchain network but with separate blockchains. Channels allow only members of the channel to view the transaction related to them, all other members of the network will not be able to view the transactions.

World state database

World state reflects all committed transaction on the blockchain. This is basically a key-value store which is updated as a result of transactions and chaincode execution. For this purpose, either LevelDB or CouchDB is used. LevelDB is a key-value store whereas CouchDB stores data as JSON objects which allows rich queries to run against the database.

Transactions

Transaction messages can be divided into two types: **deployment transactions** and **invocation transactions**. The former is used to deploy new chaincode to the ledger, and the latter is used to call functions from the smart contract. Transactions can be either public or confidential. Public transactions are open and available to all participants whilst confidential transactions are visible only in a channel open to its participants.

Membership Service Provider (MSP)

MSP is a modular component that is used to manage identities on the blockchain network. This provider is used to authenticate clients who want to join the blockchain network. We have discussed certificate authority is some detail earlier in this chapter. CA is used in MSP to provide identity verification and binding service.

Smart contracts

We discussed smart contracts in good detail in `Chapter 9`, *Smart Contracts*. In Hyperledger Fabric same concept of smart contracts is implemented but they are called chain code instead of smart contracts. They contain conditions and parameters to execute transactions and update the ledger. Chaincode is usually written in Golang and Java.

Crypto service provider

As the name suggests this is a service that provides cryptographic algorithms and standards for usage in the blockchain network. This service provides key management, signature and verification operations, and encryption-decryption mechanisms. This service is used with the membership service to provide support for cryptographic operations for elements of blockchain such as endorsers, clients, and other nodes and peers.

After this introduction to this component of Hyperledger Fabric, in the next section, we will see what an application looks like when on a Hyperledger network.

Applications on blockchain

A typical application on Fabric is simply composed of a user interface, usually written in JavaScript/HTML, that interacts with the backend chaincode (smart contract) stored on the ledger via an API layer:

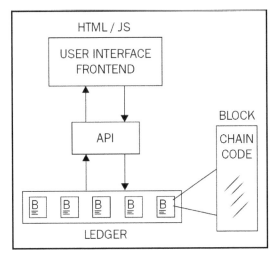

A typical Fabric application

Hyperledger provides various APIs and command-line interfaces to enable interaction with the ledger. These APIs include interfaces for identity, transactions, chaincode, ledger, network, storage, and events.

Chaincode implementation

Chaincode is usually written in Golang or Java. Chaincode can be public (visible to all on the network), confidential, or access controlled. These code files serve as a smart contract that users can interact with via APIs. Users can call functions in the chaincode that result in a state change, and consequently updates the ledger.

There are also functions that are only used to query the ledger and do not result in any state change. Chaincode implementation is performed by first creating the chaincode shim interface in the code. Shim provides APIs for accessing state variables and transaction context of chain code. It can either be in Java or Golang code.

The following four functions are required in order to implement the chaincode:

- `Init()`: This function is invoked when chaincode is deployed onto the ledger. This initializes the chaincode and results in making a state change, which accordingly updates the ledger.
- `Invoke()`: This function is used when contracts are executed. It takes a function name as parameters along with an array of arguments. This function results in a state change and writes to the ledger.
- `Query()`: This function is used to query the current state of a deployed chaincode. This function does not make any changes to the ledger.
- `4()`: This function is executed when a peer deploys its own copy of the chaincode. The chaincode is registered with the peer using this function.

The following diagram illustrates the general overview of Hyperledger Fabric, note that peers cluster at the top includes all types of nodes such as endorsers, committers, Orderers, and so on.

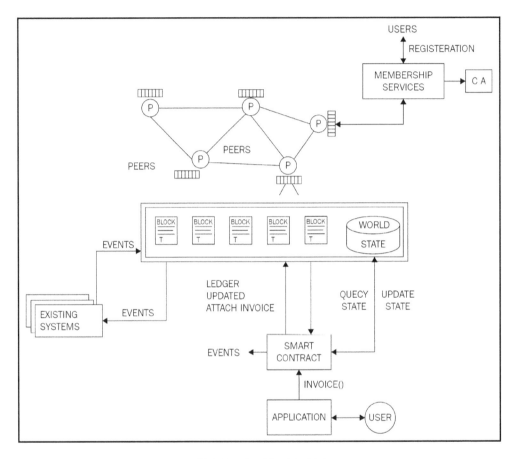

A high-level overview of Hyperledger Fabric

The preceding diagram shows that peers shown at the top middle communicate with each and each node has a copy of blockchain. On the top-right corner, the membership services are shown which validate and authenticate peers on the network by using a **certificate authority** (**CA**). At the bottom of the image, a magnified view of blockchain is shown where by existing systems can produce events for the blockchain and also can listen for the blockchain events, which then can optionally trigger an action. At the bottom right-hand side, a user's interaction is shown with the application which talks to the smart contract via the `invoice()` method, and smart contracts can query or update the state of the blockchain.

The application model

Any blockchain application for Hyperledger Fabric follows the MVC-B architecture. This is based on the popular MVC design pattern. Components in this model are Model, View, Control, and Blockchain:

- **View logic**: This is concerned with the user interface. It can be a desktop, web application, or mobile frontend.
- **Control logic**: This is the orchestrator between the user interface, data model, and APIs.
- **Data model**: This model is used to manage the off-chain data.
- **Blockchain logic**: This is used to manage the blockchain via the controller and the data model via transactions.

The IBM cloud service offers sample applications for blockchain under its blockchain as a service offering. It is available at
`https://www.ibm.com/blockchain/platform/`. This service allows users to create their own blockchain networks in an easy-to-use environment.

Consensus in Hyperledger Fabric

The consensus mechanism in Hyperledger Fabric consists of three steps:

1. **Transaction endorsement**: This process endorses the transactions by simulating the transaction execution process.
2. **Ordering**: This is a service provided by the cluster of orderers which takes endorsed transactions and decide on a sequence in which the transactions will be written to the ledger.
3. **Validation and commitment**: This process is executed by committing peers which first validates the transactions received from the orderers and then commit that transaction to the ledger.

These steps are shown in the following flowchart:

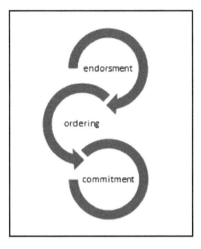

The consensus flow

The transaction life cycle in Hyperledger Fabric

There are several steps that are involved in a transaction flow in Hyperledger Fabric. These steps are shown in the following diagram below

A quick summary of the process can be visualized in the following diagram:

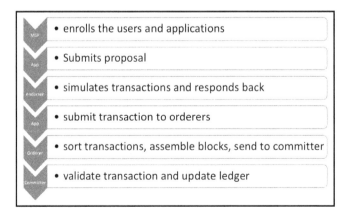

The transaction life cycle

The steps are described below in detail:

1. Transaction proposal by clients. This is the first step where a transaction is proposed by the clients and sent to endorsing peers on the distributed ledger network. All clients need to be enrolled via membership services before they can propose transactions.
2. The transaction is simulated by endorsers which generates a read-write (RW) set. This is achieved by executing the chaincode but instead of updating the ledger, only a read-write set depicting any reads or updates to the ledger is created.
3. The endorsed transaction is sent back to the application.
4. Submission of endorsed transactions and read-write (RW) sets to the ordering service by the application.
5. The ordering service assembles all endorsed transactions and read-write sets in order into a block, and sorts them by channel ID.
6. Ordering service broadcasts the assembled block to all committing peers.
7. Committing peers validate the transactions.
8. Committing peers update the ledger.
9. Finally, notification of success or failure of the transaction by committing peers is sent back to the clients/applications.

The following diagram represents the above-mentioned steps and Fabric architecture from transaction flow point of view:

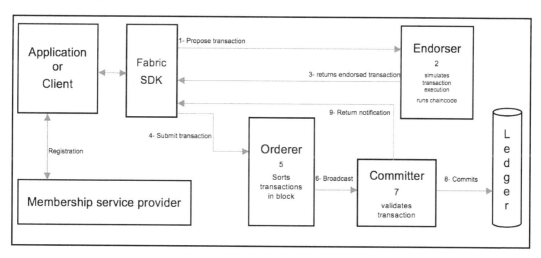

The transaction flow architecture

As seen in the preceding diagram, the first step is to propose transactions which a client does via an SDK. Before this, it is assumed that all clients and peers are registered with the Membership service provider.

With this topic, our introduction to Hyperledger Fabric is complete. In the next section, we will see another Hyperledger project named Sawtooth Lake.

Sawtooth Lake

Sawtooth Lake can run in both permissioned and non-permissioned modes. It is a distributed ledger that proposes two novel concepts: the first is the introduction of a new consensus algorithm called **Proof of Elapsed Time** (**PoET**); and the second is the idea of **transaction families**.

A description of these novel proposals is given in the following sections.

PoET

PoET is a novel consensus algorithm that allows a node to be selected randomly based on the time that the node has waited before proposing a block. This concept is in contrast to other leader election and lottery-based proof of work algorithms, such as the PoW used in Bitcoin where an enormous amount of electricity and computer resources are used in order be elected as a block proposer; for example in the case of Bitcoin. PoET is a type of Proof of Work algorithm but, instead of spending computer resources, it uses a trusted computing model to provide a mechanism to fulfill the Proof of Work requirements. PoET makes use of Intel's SGX architecture (Software Guard Extensions) to provide a trusted execution environment (TEE) to ensure randomness and cryptographic security of the process.

It should be noted that the current implementation of Sawtooth Lake does not require real hardware SGX-based TEE, as it is simulated for experimental purposes only and as such should not be used in production environments. The fundamental idea in PoET is to provide a mechanism of leader election by waiting randomly to be elected as a leader for proposing new transactions.

PoET, however, has a limitation which has been highlighted by Ittay Eyal. This limitation is called the *stale chips* problem.

 The research paper is available at https://eprint.iacr.org/2017/179.pdf.

This limitation results in hardware wastage, which can result in the waste of resources. There is also a possibility of hacking the chip's hardware, which could result in system compromise and undue incentivizing to miners.

Transaction families

A traditional smart contract paradigm provides a solution that is based on a general-purpose instruction set for all domains. For example, in the case of Ethereum, a set of opcodes has been developed for the EVM that can be used to build smart contracts to address any type of requirements for any industry.

While this model has its merits, it is becoming clear that this approach is not very secure as it provides a single interface into the ledger with a powerful and expressive language, which potentially offers a larger attack surface for malicious code. This complexity and generic virtual machine paradigm have resulted in several vulnerabilities that were found and exploited recently by hackers. A recent example is the **DAO hack** and further **Denial of Services** (**DoS**) attacks that exploited limitations in some EVM opcodes. The DAO hack was discussed in `Chapter 9`, *Smart Contracts*.

A model shown in the following figure describes the traditional smart contract model, where a generic virtual machine has been used to provide the interface into the blockchain for all domains:

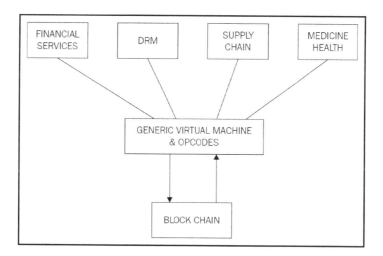

The traditional smart contract paradigm

In order to address this issue, Sawtooth Lake has proposed the idea of transaction families. A transaction family is created by decomposing the logic layer into a set of rules and a composition layer for a specific domain. The key idea is that business logic is composed within transaction families, which provides a more secure and powerful way to build smart contracts. Transaction families contain the domain-specific rules and another layer that allows for creating transactions for that domain. Another way of looking at it is that transaction families are a combination of a data model and a transaction language that implements a logic layer for a specific domain. The data model represents the current state of the blockchain (ledger) whereas the transaction language modifies the state of the ledger. It is expected that users will build their own transaction families according to their business requirements.

The following diagram represents this model, where each specific domain, like financial services, **digital rights management** (**DRM**), supply chain, and the health industry, has its own logic layer comprised of operations and services specific to that domain. This makes the logic layer both restrictive and powerful at the same time. Transaction families ensure that operations related to only the required domain are present in the control logic, thus removing the possibility of executing needless, arbitrary and potentially harmful operations:

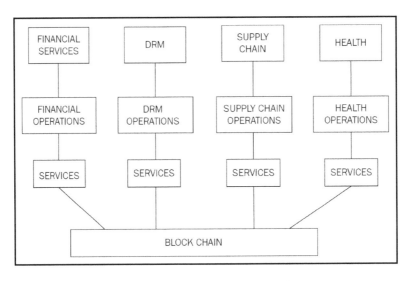

The Sawtooth (transaction families) smart contract paradigm

Intel has provided three transaction families with Sawtooth: Endpoint registry, Integerkey, and MarketPlace.

- **Endpoint registry** is used for registering ledger services
- **Integerkey** is used for testing deployed ledgers
- **MarketPlace** is used for selling, buying, and trading operations and services

Sawtooth_bond has been developed as a proof of concept to demonstrate a bond trading platform.

 It is available at `https://github.com/hyperledger/sawtooth-core/tree/master/extensions/bond`.

Consensus in Sawtooth

Sawtooth has two types of consensus mechanisms based on the choice of network. PoET, as discussed previously, is a trusted executed environment-based lottery function that elects a leader randomly based on the time a node has waited for block proposal.

There is another consensus type called **quorum voting**, which is an adaptation of consensus protocols built by Ripple and Stellar. This consensus algorithm allows instant transaction finality, which is usually desirable in permissioned networks.

The development environment – Sawtooth Lake

In this section, a quick introduction is given on how to set up a development environment for Sawtooth Lake. There are a few prerequisites that are required in order to set up the development environment.

Examples in this section assume a running Ubuntu system and the following:

- Vagrant, at least version 1.9.0, available at
  `https://www.vagrantup.com/downloads.html`.
- VirtualBox, at least 5.0.10 r104061, available at
  `https://www.virtualbox.org/wiki/Downloads`.

Once both of the prerequisites are downloaded and installed successfully, the next step is to clone the repository.

```
$ git clone https://github.com/IntelLedger/sawtooth-core.git
```

This will produce an output similar to the one shown in the following screenshot:

```
drequinox@drequinox-OP7010:~/project$ git clone https://github.com/IntelLedger/sawtooth-core.git
Cloning into 'sawtooth-core'...
remote: Counting objects: 12527, done.
remote: Compressing objects: 100% (964/964), done.
remote: Total 12527 (delta 452), reused 0 (delta 0), pack-reused 11515
Receiving objects: 100% (12527/12527), 9.26 MiB | 1.76 MiB/s, done.
Resolving deltas: 100% (8131/8131), done.
Checking connectivity... done.
```

The GitHub Sawtooth clone

Once Sawtooth is cloned correctly, the next step is to start up the environment. First, run the following command to change the directory to the correct location and then start the vagrant box:

```
$ cd sawtooth-core/tools
$ vagrant up
```

This will produce an output similar to the following screenshot:

```
drequinox@drequinox-OP7010:~/project/sawtooth-core/tools$ vagrant up
Could not determine vagrant user.
VAGRANT_BOX = ubuntu/xenial64
VAGRANT_FORWARD_PORTS = true
VAGRANT_MEMORY = 2048
VAGRANT_CPUS = 2
Proxyconf plugin not found
Install: vagrant plugin install vagrant-proxyconf
Bringing machine 'default' up with 'virtualbox' provider...
==> default: Box 'ubuntu/xenial64' could not be found. Attempting to find and install...
    default: Box Provider: virtualbox
    default: Box Version: >= 0
==> default: Loading metadata for box 'ubuntu/xenial64'
    default: URL: https://atlas.hashicorp.com/ubuntu/xenial64
==> default: Adding box 'ubuntu/xenial64' (v20161221.0.0) for provider: virtualbox
    default: Downloading: https://atlas.hashicorp.com/ubuntu/boxes/xenial64/versions/20161221.0.0/providers/virtualbox.bo
x
    default: Progress: 1% (Rate: 1709k/s, Estimated time remaining: 0:04:04)
```

The vagrant up command

If at any point vagrant needs to be stopped, the following command can be used:

```
$ vagrant halt
```

Or:

```
$ vagrant destroy
```

halt will stop the vagrant machine, whereas destroy will stop and delete vagrant machines.

Finally, the transaction validator can be started by using the following commands. First ssh into the vagrant Sawtooth box:

```
$ vagrant ssh
```

When the vagrant prompt is available, run the following commands. First build the Sawtooth Lake core using following command:

```
$ /project/sawtooth-core/bin/build_all
```

When the build has completed successfully, in order to run the transaction validator, issue the following commands:

```
$ /project/sawtooth-core/docs/source/tutorial/genesis.sh
```

This will create the genesis block and clear any existing data files and keys. This command should show an output similar to the following screenshot:

```
ubuntu@ubuntu-xenial:/project/sawtooth-core$ /project/sawtooth-core/docs/source/tutorial/genesis.sh
writing file: /home/ubuntu/sawtooth/keys/base000.wif
writing file: /home/ubuntu/sawtooth/keys/base000.addr
```

Genesis block and keys generation

The next step is to run the transaction validator, and change the directory as shown follows:

```
$ cd /project/saw-toothcore
```

Run the transaction validator:

```
$ ./bin/txnvalidator -v -F ledger.transaction.integer_key --config
/home/ubuntu/sawtooth/v0.json
```

```
ubuntu@ubuntu-xenial:/project/sawtooth-core$ ./bin/txnvalidator -v -F ledger.transaction.integer_key --config /home/ubuntu/sawtu
oth/v0.json
[22:08:22 INFO    validator_cli] validator started with arguments: ['./bin/txnvalidator', '-v', '-F', 'ledger.transaction.intege
r_key', '--config', '/home/ubuntu/sawtooth/v0.json']
[22:08:22 INFO    validator_cli] read signing key from /home/ubuntu/sawtooth/keys/base000.wif
[22:08:24 WARNING validator_cli] validator pid is 10937
[22:08:24 INFO    gossip_core] listening on IPv4Address(UDP, '0.0.0.0', 33713)
[22:08:24 INFO    global_store_manager] create blockstore from file /home/ubuntu/sawtooth/data/base000_state.dbm with flag c
[22:08:24 INFO    validator] set administration node to None
[22:08:24 INFO    validator] starting ledger base000 with id 1K5RNedZ at network address ('127.0.0.1', 33713)
[22:08:24 INFO    web_api] listen for HTTP requests on (ip='localhost', port=8800)
[22:08:24 INFO    validator_cli] adding transaction family: ledger.transaction.integer_key
[22:08:24 INFO    journal_core] restore ledger state from persistence
[22:08:24 INFO    global_store_manager] add block 60af3ec894fa1cb0 to the queue for loading
[22:08:24 INFO    global_store_manager] load block 60af3ec894fa1cb0 from storage
[22:08:24 INFO    journal_core] commit head: 60af3ec894fa1cb0
[22:08:26 INFO    validator] ledger connections using RandomWalk topology
[22:08:26 INFO    random_walk] initiate random walk topology update
[22:08:26 INFO    validator] ledger initialization complete
[22:08:29 INFO    journal_core] process initial transactions and blocks
[22:08:29 INFO    validator] register endpoint 1K5RNedZ with name base000
[22:08:29 INFO    journal_core] build transaction block to extend 60af3ec8 with 1 transactions
[22:08:29 INFO    wait_timer] wait timer created; TIMER, 5.00, 33.69, HE2DQNJWGI2DCNJQ
```

Running transaction validator

The validator node can be stopped by pressing *Ctrl + C*. Once the validator is up and running, various clients can be started up in another terminal window to communicate with the transaction validator and submit transactions.

For example, in the following screenshot, the market client is started up to communicate with the transaction validator. Note that keys under `/keys/mkt.wif` are created by using the following command:

```
./bin/sawtooth keygen --key-dir validator/keys mkt
```

```
ubuntu@ubuntu-xenial:/project/sawtooth-core$ ./bin/mktclient --name market --keyfile validator/keys/mkt.wif
//UNKNOWN> help

Documented commands (type help <topic>):
========================================
EOF         dump          exit        liability     selloffer   tokenstore
account     echo          help        map           session     waitforcommit
asset       exchange      holding     offers        sleep
assettype   exchangeoffer holdings    participant   state

Miscellaneous help topics:
==========================
symbols   names

//UNKNOWN> participant reg --name market --description "the market"
transaction ff652e63dadeaf32 submitted
//market> ▮
```

mktclient for marketplace transaction family

This completes our basic introduction to Sawtooth. The example shown above is also quite basic but demonstrates that how Sawtooth Lake works.

Sawtooth Lake is also under continuous development and therefore, it is recommended that readers keep an eye on documentation available at `http://intelledger.github.io/` to keep up with the latest developments.

 There is an excellent online page where official Sawtooth lake examples are provided. The page is available at `https://sawtooth.hyperledger.org/examples/`. Readers are encouraged to visit this page and explore these sample projects.

Now in the next section we will see an introduction to Corda. It should be noted that Corda is not yet an official project under Hyperledger; however, it may become a member very soon. Therefore, for now, this is being discussed under Hyperledger, but in the future, it may not become part of Hyperledger.

Corda

Corda is not a blockchain by definition because it does not contain blocks of bundled transactions, but it falls under the category of distributed ledgers. It provides all benefits that a blockchain can. Traditional blockchain solutions, as discussed before, have the concept of transactions that are bundled together in a block and each block is linked back cryptographically to its parent block, which provides an immutable record of transactions. This is not the case with Corda.

Corda has been designed entirely from scratch with a new model for providing all blockchain benefits, but without a traditional blockchain. It has been developed purely for the financial industry to solve issues arising from the fact that each organization manages their own ledgers and thus have their own view of *truth*, which leads to contradictions and operational risk. Moreover, data is also duplicated at each organization, which results in an increased cost of managing individual infrastructures and complexity. These are the types of problems within the financial industry that Corda aims to resolve by building a decentralized database platform.

 The Corda source code is available at `https://github.com/corda/corda`. It is written in a language called Kotlin, which is a statically typed language targeting the **Java Virtual Machine (JVM)**.

Architecture

The main components of the Corda platform include state objects, contract code, legal prose, transactions, consensus, and flows. We will now explore them in more detail.

State objects

State objects represent the smallest unit of data that represent a financial agreement. They are created or deleted as a result of a transaction execution. They refer to **contract code** and **legal prose.** Legal prose is optional and provides legal binding to the contract. However, contract code is mandatory in order to manage the state of the object. It is required in order to provide a state transition mechanism for the node according to the business logic defined in the contract code. State objects contain a data structure that represents the current state of the object. A state object can be either current (live) or historic (no longer valid).

For example, in the following diagram, a state object represents the current state of the object. In this case, it is a simple mock agreement between **Party A** and **Party B** where **Party ABC** has paid **Party XYZ 1,000 GBP**. This represents the current state of the object; however, the referred contract code can change the state via transactions. State objects can be thought of as a state machine, which are consumed by transactions in order to create updated state objects.

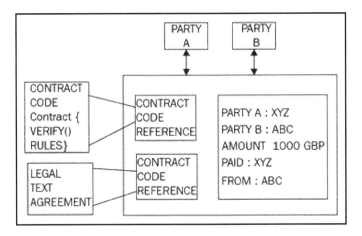

An example state object

Transactions

Transactions are used to perform transitions between different states. For example, the state object shown in the preceding diagram is created as a result of a transaction. Corda uses a Bitcoin-style UTXO-based model for its transaction processing. The concept of state transition by transactions is same as in Bitcoin. Similar to Bitcoin, transactions can have none, single, or multiple inputs, and single or multiple outputs. All transactions are digitally signed.

Moreover, Corda has no concept of mining because it does not use blocks to arrange transactions in a blockchain. Instead, notary services are used in order to provide temporal ordering of transactions. In Corda, new transaction types can be developed using JVM bytecode, which makes it very flexible and powerful.

Consensus

The consensus model in Corda is quite simple and is based on notary services that are discussed in a later section of this chapter. The general idea is that the transactions are evaluated for their uniqueness by the notary service and, if they are unique (that is, unique transaction inputs), they are signed by consensus services as valid. There can be single or multiple clustered notary services running on a Corda network. Various consensus algorithms like PBFT or Raft can be used by notaries to reach consensus.

There are two main concepts regarding consensus in Corda: **consensus over state validity** and **consensus over state uniqueness**. The first concept is concerned with the validation of the transaction, ensuring that all required signatures are available and states are appropriate. The second concept is a means to detect double-spend attacks and ensures that a transaction has not already been spent and is unique.

Flows

Flows in Corda are a novel idea that allows the development of decentralized workflows. All communication on the Corda network is handled by these flows. These are transaction-building protocols that can be used to define any financial flow of any complexity using code. Flows run as an asynchronous state machine and they interact with other nodes and users. During the execution, they can be suspended or resumed as required.

Components

The Corda network has multiple components. All these components are described in the upcoming sections.

Nodes

Nodes in a Corda network operated under a trust-less model and run by different organizations. Nodes run as part of an authenticated peer-to-peer network. Nodes communicate directly with each other using the **Advanced Message Queuing Protocol** (**AMQP**), which is an approved international standard (ISO/IEC 19464) and ensures that messages across different nodes are transferred safely and securely. AMQP works over **Transport Layer Security** (**TLS**) in Corda, thus ensuring privacy and integrity of data communicated between nodes.

Nodes also make use of a local relational database for storage. Messages on the network are encoded in a compact binary format. They are delivered and managed by using the **Apache Artemis message broker** (**Active MQ**). A node can serve as a network map service, notary, Oracle, or a regular node. The following diagram shows a high-level view of two nodes communicating with each other:

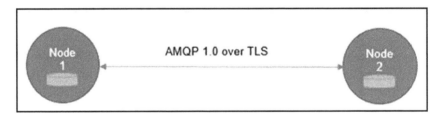

Two nodes communicating in a Corda network

In the preceding diagram, **Node 1** is communicating with **Node 2** over a TLS communication channel using the AMQP protocol, and the nodes have a local relational database for storage.

The permissioning service

A permissioning service is used to provision TLS certificates for security. In order to participate in the network, participants are required to have a signed identity issued by a root certificate authority. Identities are required to be unique on the network and the permissioning service is used to sign these identities. The naming convention used to recognize participants is based on the X.500 standard. This ensures the uniqueness of the name.

Network map service

This service is used to provide a network map in the form of a document of all nodes on the network. This service publishes IP addresses, identity certificates, and a list of services offered by nodes. All nodes announce their presence by registering to this service when they first startup, and when a connection request is received by a node, the presence of the requesting node is checked on the network map first. Put another way, this service resolves the identities of the participants to physical nodes.

Notary service

In a traditional blockchain, mining is used to ascertain the order of blocks that contain transactions. In Corda, notary services are used to provide transaction ordering and timestamping services. There can be multiple notaries in a network and they are identified by composite public keys. Notaries can use different consensus algorithms like BFT or Raft depending on the requirements of the applications. Notary services sign the transactions to indicate validity and finality of the transaction which is then persisted to the database.

Notaries can be run in a load-balanced configuration in order to spread the load across the nodes for performance reasons; and, in order to reduce latency, the nodes are recommended to be run physically closer to the transaction participants.

Oracle service

Oracle services either sign a transaction containing a fact, if it is true, or can themselves provide factual data. They allow real-world feed into the distributed ledgers. Oracles were discussed in `Chapter 9`, *Smart Contracts*.

Transactions

Transactions in a Corda network are never transmitted globally but in a semi-private network. They are shared only between a subset of participants who are related to the transaction. This is in contrast to traditional blockchain solutions like Ethereum and Bitcoin, where all transactions are broadcasted to the entire network globally. Transactions are digitally signed and either consume state(s) or create new state(s).

Transactions on a Corda network are composed of the following elements:

- **Input references**: This is a reference to the states the transaction is going to consume and use as an input.
- **Output states**: These are new states created by the transaction.
- **Attachments**: This is a list of hashes of attached ZIP files. ZIP files can contain code and other relevant documentation related to the transaction. Files themselves are not made part of the transaction, instead, they are transferred and stored separately.
- **Commands**: A command represents the information about the intended operation of the transaction as a parameter to the contract. Each command has a list of public keys, which represents all parties that are required to sign a transaction.
- **Signatures**: This represents the signature required by the transaction. The total number of signatures required is directly proportional to the number of public keys for commands.
- **Type**: There are two types of transactions namely, normal or notary changing. Notary changing transactions are used for reassigning a notary for a state.
- **Timestamp**: This field represents a bracket of time during which the transaction has taken place. These are verified and enforced by notary services. Also, it is expected that if strict timings are required, which is desirable in many financial services scenarios, notaries should be synced with an atomic clock.
- **Summaries:** This is a text description that describes the operations of the transaction.

Vaults

Vaults run on a node and are akin to the concept of wallets in bitcoin. As the transactions are not globally broadcasted, each node will have only that part of data in their vaults that is considered relevant to them. Vaults store their data in a standard relational database and as such can be queried by using standard SQL. Vaults can contain both on ledger and off ledger data, meaning that it can also have some part of data that is not on ledger.

CorDapp

The core model of Corda consists of state objects, transactions, and transaction protocols, which when combined with contract code, APIs, wallet plugins, and user interface components results in constructing a **Corda distributed application** (**CorDapp**).

Smart contracts in Corda are written using Kotlin or Java. The code is targeted for JVM.

JVM has been modified slightly in order to achieve deterministic results of execution of JVM bytecode. There are three main components in a Corda smart contract as follows:

- Executable code that defines the validation logic to validate changes to the state objects.
- State objects represent the current state of a contract and either can be consumed by a transaction or produced (created) by a transaction.
- Commands are used to describe the operational and verification data that defines how a transaction can be verified.

The development environment – Corda

The development environment for Corda can be set up easily using the following steps. Required software includes the following:

- JDK 8 (8u131), which is available at
  `http://www.oracle.com/technetwork/java/javase/downloads/index.html`.
- IntelliJ IDEA Community edition, which is free and available at
  `https://www.jetbrains.com/idea/download`.
- H2 database platform independent ZIP, and is available at
  `http://www.h2database.com/html/download.html`.
- Git, which is available at `https://git-scm.com/downloads`.
- Kotlin language, which is available for IntelliJ, and more information can be found at `https://kotlinlang.org/`.

Gradle is another component that is used to build Corda. It is available at `https://gradle.org`.

Once all these tools are installed, smart contract development can be started. CorDapps can be developed by utilizing an example template available at `https://github.com/corda/cordapp-template`.

 Detailed documentation on how to develop contract code is available at `https://docs.corda.net/`.

Corda can be cloned locally from GitHub using the following command:

```
$ git clone https://github.com/corda/corda.git
```

When the cloning is successful, you should see output similar to the following:

```
Cloning into 'corda'...
remote: Counting objects: 74695, done.
remote: Compressing objects: 100% (67/67), done.
remote: Total 74695 (delta 17), reused 0 (delta 0), pack-reused 74591
Receiving objects: 100% (74695/74695), 51.27 MiB | 1.72 MiB/s, done.
Resolving deltas: 100% (42863/42863), done.
Checking connectivity... done.
```

Once the repository is cloned, it can be opened in IntelliJ for further development. There are multiple samples available in the repository, such as a bank of Corda, interest rate swaps, demo, and traders demo. Readers can find them under the `/samples` directory under `corda` and they can be explored using IntelliJ IDEA IDE.

Summary

In this chapter, we have gone through an introduction to the Hyperledger project. Firstly, the core ideas behind the Hyperledger project were discussed, and a brief introduction to all projects under Hyperledger was provided. Three main Hyperledger projects were discussed in detail, namely Hyperledger Fabric, Sawtooth lake, and Corda. All these projects are continuously improving and changes are expected in the next releases. However, the core concepts of all the projects mentioned above are expected to remain unchanged or change only slightly. Readers are encouraged to visit the relevant links provided within the chapter to see the latest updates.

It is evident that a lot is going on in this space and projects like Hyperledger from the Linux Foundation are playing a pivotal role in the advancement of blockchain technology. Each of the projects discussed in this chapter has novel approaches towards solving the issues faced in various industries, and any current limitations within the blockchain technology are also being addressed, such as scalability and privacy. It is expected that more projects will soon be proposed to the Hyperledger project, and it is envisaged that with this collaborative and open effort blockchain technology will advance tremendously and will benefit the community as a whole.

In the next chapter, alternative blockchain solutions and platforms will be introduced. As blockchain technology is growing very fast and has attracted lot of research interest there are many new projects that have emerged recently. We will discuss those projects in the next chapter.

16
Alternative Blockchains

This chapter is intended to provide an introduction to alternative blockchain solutions. With the success of Bitcoin and subsequent realization of the potential of blockchain technology, a Cambrian explosion started that resulted in the development of various blockchain protocols, applications, and platforms. Some projects did not gain much traction, for example as an estimate 46% of ICOs have failed this year, but many have succeeded in creating a solid place in this space.

In this chapter, readers will be introduced to alternative blockchains and platforms such as Kadena, Ripple, and Stellar. We will explore the projects that either are new blockchains on their own or provide support to other existing blockchains by providing SDKs, frameworks, and tools to make development and deployment of blockchain solutions easier. The success of Ethereum and Bitcoin has resulted in various projects that spawned into existence by leveraging the underlying technologies and concepts introduced by them. These new projects add value by addressing the limitations in the current blockchains such as scalability and or enhancing the existing solutions by providing an additional layer of user-friendly tools on top of them.

Blockchains

In this section, an introduction to new blockchain solutions will be given, and later sections will cover various platforms and development kits that complement existing blockchains. For example, Kadena is a new private blockchain with novel ideas such as Scalable BFT. Various concepts such as sidechains, drivechains, and pegging have also been introduced with this growth of blockchain technologies. This chapter will cover all these technologies and related concepts in detail. Of course, it's not possible to cover all **alternative chains** (**altchains**) and platforms, but all those platforms have been included in this chapter that is related to blockchains, covered in the previous chapters, or are expected to gain traction soon.

We will explore Kadena, Ripple, Stellar, Quorum and various other blockchains in the section.

Kadena

Kadena is a private blockchain that has successfully addressed scalability and privacy issues in blockchain systems. A new Turing incomplete language, called Pact, has also been introduced with Kadena that allows the development of smart contracts. A key innovation in Kadena is its Scalable BFT consensus algorithm, which has the potential to scale to thousands of nodes without performance degradation.

Scalable BFT is based on the original Raft algorithm and is a successor of Tangaroa and Juno. Tangaroa, which is a name given to an implementation of Raft with fault tolerance (a BFT Raft), was developed to address the availability and safety issues that arose from the behavior of Byzantine nodes in the Raft algorithm, and Juno was a fork of Tangaroa that was developed by JPMorgan. Consensus algorithms are discussed in `Chapter 1`, *Blockchain 101* in more detail.

Both of these proposals have a fundamental limitation—they cannot scale while maintaining a high level of high performance. As such, Juno could not gain much traction. Private blockchains have the more desirable property of maintaining high performance as the number of nodes increase, but the aforementioned proposals lack this feature. Kadena solves this issue with its proprietary Scalable BFT algorithm, which is expected to scale up to thousands of nodes without any performance degradation.

Moreover, confidentiality is another significant aspect of Kadena that enables privacy of transactions on the blockchain. This security service is achieved by using a combination of key rotation, symmetric on-chain encryption, incremental hashing, and Double Ratchet protocol.

Key rotation is used as a standard mechanism to ensure the security of the private blockchain. It is used as a best practice to thwart any attacks if the keys have been compromised, by periodically changing the encryption keys. There is native support for key rotation in Pact smart contract language.

Symmetric on-chain encryption allows encryption of transaction data on the blockchain. These transactions can be automatically decrypted by the participants of a particular private transaction. Double Ratchet protocol is used to provide key management and encryption functions.

Scalable BFT consensus protocol ensures that adequate replication and consensus has been achieved before smart contract execution. The consensus is achieved by following the process described here.

This is how a transaction originates and flows in the network:

1. First, a new transaction is signed by the user and broadcasted over the blockchain network, which is picked up by a leader node that adds it to its immutable log. At this point, an incremental hash is also calculated for the log. Incremental hash is a type of hash function that allows computation of hash messages in the scenario where, if a previous original message which is already hashed is slightly changed, then the new hash message is computed from the already existing hash. This scheme is quicker and less resource intensive compared to a conventional hash function where an altogether new hash message is required to be generated even if the original message has only changed very slightly.

2. Once the transaction is written to the log by the leader node, it signs the replication and incremental hash and broadcasts it to other nodes.

3. Other nodes after receiving the transaction, verify the signature of the leader node, add the transaction into their own logs, and broadcast their own calculated incremental hashes (quorum proofs) to other nodes. Finally, the transaction is committed to the ledger permanently after an adequate number of proofs are received from other nodes.

A simplified version of this process is shown in the following diagram, where the leader node is recording the new transactions and then replicating them to the follower nodes:

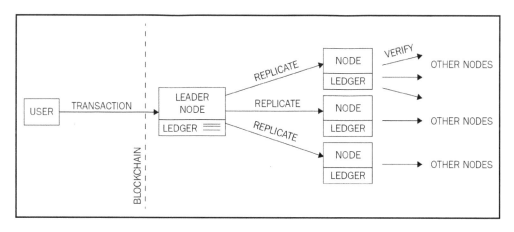

Consensus mechanism in Kadena

Once the consensus is achieved, a smart contract execution can start and takes a number of steps, as follows:

1. First, the signature of the message is verified.
2. Pact smart contract layer takes over.
3. Pact code is compiled.
4. The transaction is initiated and executes any business logic embedded within the smart contract. In case of any failures, an immediate rollback is initiated that reverts that state back to what it was before the execution started.
5. Finally, the transaction completes and relevant logs are updated.

 Pact has been open sourced by Kadena and is available for download at `http://kadena.io/pact/downloads.html`.

This can be downloaded as a standalone binary that provides a REPL for Pact language. An example is shown here where Pact is run by issuing the `./pact` command in Linux console:

```
drequinox@drequinox-OP7010:~/Downloads$ ./pact
pact> 1234
1234
pact> (+ 1 2)
3
pact> (if (= (+ 1 2) 3 "OK" "ERROR")
(interactive):1:31: error: unexpected
    EOF, expected: ")", ";", "{",
    Boolean false, Boolean true,
    Decimal literal, Integer literal,
    String literal, Symbol literal,
    list literal, pact, sexp, space
(if (= (+ 1 2) 3 "OK" "ERROR")<EOF>
                              ^
pact> (if (= (+ 1 2) 3) "OK" "ERROR")
"OK"
pact>
```

Pact REPL, showing sample commands and error output

A smart contract in Pact language is usually composed of three sections: keysets, modules, and tables. These sections are described here:

- **Keysets**: This section defines relevant authorization schemes for tables and modules.
- **Modules**: This section defines the smart contract code encompassing the business logic in the form of functions and pacts. Pacts within modules are composed of multiple steps and are executed sequentially.
- **Tables:** This section is an access-controlled construct defined within modules. Only administrators defined in the admin keyset have direct access to this table. Code within the module is granted full access, by default to the tables.

Pact also allows several execution modes. These modes include contract definition, transaction execution, and querying. These execution modes are described here:

- **Contract definition:** This mode allows a contract to be created on the blockchain via a single transaction message.
- **Transaction execution:** This mode entails the execution of modules of smart contract code that represent business logic.
- **Querying**: This mode is concerned with simply probing the contract for data and is executed locally on the nodes for performance reason. Pact uses LISP-like syntax and represents in the code exactly what will be executed on the blockchain, as it is stored on the blockchain in human-readable format. This is in contrast to Ethereum's EVM, which compiles into bytecode for execution, which makes it difficult to verify what code is in execution on the blockchain. Moreover, it is Turing incomplete, supports immutable variables, and does not allow null values, which improves the overall safety of the transaction code execution.

It is not possible to cover the complete syntax and functions of Pact in this limited length chapter; however, a small example is shown here, that shows the general structure of a smart contract written in Pact. This example shows a simple addition module that defines a function named `addition` that takes three parameters. When the code is executed it adds all three values and displays the result.

The following example has been developed using the online Pact compiler available at http://kadena.io/try-pact/.

```
 1   ;Begin transaction with optinal NAME.
 2 - (begin-tx) 'testTransaction
 3   ;Set transaction data in JSON format or pact types
 4   (env-data { "keyset": {"keys": ["admin"], "pred": "keys-any"}})
 5   ;Define keyset as NAME with KEYSET
 6   (define-keyset 'admin-keyset (read-keyset "keyset"))
 7   ;Set transaction signature KEYS
 8   (env-keys ["admin"])
 9   ;define module using syntax (module NAME KEYSET [DOCSTING] DEFS . . .)
10   (module additionModule 'admin-keyset
11   ;define function that takes three arguments x y z
12   (defun addition (x y z) (+ x (+ y z))))
13   ;Commit transaction.
14   (commit-tx)
15   ;use the function addition
16   (use 'additionModule)
17   ;run the function addition and format result
18   (format "Result : {} " [(addition 100 200 300)])
```

Sample Pact code

When the code is run, it produces the output shown as follows:

```
Begin Tx Just 1
testTransaction
Setting transaction data
Keyset defined
Setting transaction keys
Loaded module "additionModule"
  , hash "eaf647f843b2e88b5009253fe4eeca6f8890a646da76b4(
Commit Tx Just 1
Using "additionModule"
Result : 600
```

The output of the code

As shown in the preceding example, the execution output matches exactly with the code layout and structure, which allows for greater transparency and limits the possibility of malicious code execution.

Kadena is a new class of blockchains introducing the novel concept of **pervasive determinism** where, in addition to standard public/private key-based data origin security, an additional layer of fully deterministic consensus is also provided. It provides cryptographic security at all layers of the blockchain including transactions and consensus layer.

 Relevant documentation and source code for Pact can be found here `https://github.com/kadena-io/pact`.

Kadena has also introduced a public blockchain in January, 2018 which is another leap forward in building blockchains with massive throughput. The novel idea in this proposal is to build a PoW parallel chain architecture. This scheme works by combining individually mined chains on peers into a single network. The result is massive throughput capable of processing more than 10,000 transactions per second.

 The original research paper is available at `http://kadena.io/docs/chainweb-v15.pdf`.

Ripple

Introduced in 2012, Ripple is a currency exchange and real-time gross settlement system. In Ripple, the payments are settled without any waiting as opposed to traditional settlement networks, where it can take days for settlement.

It has a native currency called **Ripples** (**XRP**). It also supports non-XRP payments. This system is considered similar to an old traditional money transfer mechanism known as *Hawala*. This system works by making use of agents who take the money and a password from the sender, then contact the payee's agent and instruct them to release funds to the person who can provide the password. The payee then contacts the local agent, tells them the password and collects the funds. An analogy to the agent is gateway in Ripple. This is just a very simple analogy; the actual protocol is rather complex but principally it is the same.

The Ripple network is composed of various nodes that can perform different functions based on their type:

- **User nodes**: These nodes use in payment transactions and can pay or receive payments.
- **Validator nodes**: These nodes participate in the consensus mechanism. Each server maintains a set of unique nodes, which it needs to query while achieving consensus. Nodes in the **Unique Node List** (**UNL**) are trusted by the server involved in the consensus mechanism and will accept votes only from this list of unique nodes.

Ripple is sometimes not considered a truly decentralized network as there are network operators and regulators involved. However, it can be considered decentralized due to the fact that anyone can become part of the network by running a validator node. Moreover, the consensus process is also decentralized because any changes proposed to make on the ledger have to be decided by following a scheme of super majority voting. However, this is a hot topic among researchers and enthusiasts and there are arguments against and in favor of each school of thought. There are some discussions online that readers can refer to for further exploration of these ideas.

You can find these online discussions at the following links:

- https://www.quora.com/Why-is-Ripple-centralized
- https://thenextweb.com/hardfork/2018/02/06/ripple-report-bitmex-centralized/
- https://www.reddit.com/r/Ripple/comments/6c8j7b/is_ripple_centralized_and_other_related_questions/?st=jewkor7bamp;sh=e39bc635

Ripple maintains a globally distributed ledger of all transactions that are governed by a novel low-latency consensus algorithm called **Ripple Protocol Consensus Algorithm** (**RPCA**). The consensus process works by achieving an agreement on the state of an open ledger containing transactions by seeking verification and acceptance from validating servers in an iterative manner until an adequate number of votes are achieved. Once enough votes are received (a super majority, initially 50% and gradually increasing with each iteration up to at least 80%) the changes are validated and the ledger is closed. At this point, an alert is sent to the whole network indicating that the ledger is closed.

Original research paper for RPCA is available at `https://ripple.com/files/ripple_consensus_whitepaper.pdf`.

In summary, the consensus protocol is a three-phase process:

- **Collection phase**: In this phase validating nodes gather all transactions broadcasted on the network by account owners and validate them. Transactions, once accepted, are called candidate transactions and can be accepted or rejected based on the validation criteria.
- **Consensus phase**: After the collection phase the consensus process starts, and after achieving it the ledger is **closed**.
- **Ledger closing phase**: This process runs asynchronously every few seconds in rounds and, as result, the ledger is opened and closed (updated) accordingly:

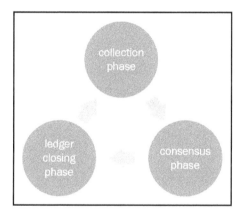

Ripple consensus protocol phases

In a Ripple network, there are a number of components that work together in order to achieve consensus and form a payment network. These components are discussed individually here:

- **Server**: This component serves as a participant in the consensus protocol. Ripple server software is required in order to be able to participate in consensus protocol.
- **Ledger**: This is the main record of balances of all accounts on the network. A ledger contains various elements such as ledger number, account settings, transactions, timestamp, and a flag that indicates the validity of the ledger.

- **Last closed ledger**: A ledger is closed once consensus is achieved by validating nodes.
- **Open ledger**: This is a ledger that has not been validated yet and no consensus has been reached about its state. Each node has its own open ledger, which contains proposed transactions.
- **Unique Node List:** This is a list of unique trusted nodes that a validating server uses in order to seek votes and subsequent consensus.
- **Proposer**: As the name suggests, this component proposes new transactions to be included in the consensus process. It is usually a subset of nodes (UNL defined in the previous point) that can propose transactions to the validating server.

Transactions

Transactions are created by the network users in order to update the ledger. A transaction is expected to be digitally signed and valid in order for it to be considered as a candidate in the consensus process. Each transaction costs a small amount of XRP, which serves as a protection mechanism against denial of service attacks caused by spamming.

There are different types of transaction in the Ripple network. A single field within the Ripple transaction data structure called `TransactionType` is used to represent the type of the transaction. Transactions are executed by using a four-step process:

1. First, transactions are prepared whereby an unsigned transaction is created by following the standards
2. The second step is signing, where the transaction is digitally signed to authorize it
3. After this, the actual submission to the network occurs via the connected server
4. Finally, the verification is performed to ensure that the transaction is validated successfully

Roughly, the transactions can be categorized into three types, namely payments related, order related, and account and security related. All these types are described in the following section.

Payments related

There are several fields in this category that result in certain actions. All these fields are described as follows:

- `Payment`: This transaction is most commonly used and allows one user to send funds to another.
- `PaymentChannelClaim`: This is used to claim Ripples (XRP) from a payment channel. A payment channel is a mechanism that allows recurring and unidirectional payments between parties. This can also be used to set the expiration time of the payment channel.
- `PaymentChannelCreate`: This transaction creates a new payment channel and adds XRP to it in *drops*. A single drop is equivalent to 0.000001 of an XRP.
- `PaymentChannelFund`: This transaction is used to add more funds to an existing channel. Similar to the `PaymentChannelClaim` transaction, this can also be used to modify the expiration time of the payment channel.

Order related

This type of transaction includes following two fields:

- `OfferCreate`: This transaction represents a limit order, which represents an intent for the exchange of currency. It results in creating an offer node in the consensus ledger if it cannot be completely fulfilled.
- `OfferCancel`: This is used to remove a previously created offer node from the consensus ledger, indicating withdrawal of the order.

Account and security-related

This type of transaction includes the fields listed as follows. Each field is responsible for performing a certain function:

- `AccountSet`: This transaction is used to modify the attributes of an account in the Ripple consensus ledger.
- `SetRegularKey`: This is used to change or set the transaction signing key for an account. An account is identified using a base-58 Ripple address derived from the account's master public key.
- `SignerListSet`: This can be used to create a set of signers for use in multisignature transactions.
- `TrustSet`: This is used to create or modify a trust line between accounts.

A transaction in Ripple is composed of various fields that are common to all transaction types. These fields are listed as follows with a description:

- Account: This is the address of the initiator of the transaction.
- AccountTxnID: This is an optional field which contains the hash of another transaction. It is used to chain the transaction together.
- Fee: This is the amount of XRP.
- Flags: This is an optional field specifying the flags for the transaction.
- LastLedgerSequence: This is the highest sequence number of the ledger in which the transaction can appear.
- Memos: This represents optional arbitrary information.
- SigningPubKey: This represents the public key.
- Signers: This represent signers in a multisig transaction.
- SourceTag: This represents either sender or reason of the transaction.
- SourceTag: This represents either sender or reason of the transaction.
- TxnSignature: This is the verification digital signature for the transaction.

Interledger

Interledger is a simple protocol that is composed of four layers: Application, Transport, Interledger, and Ledger. Each layer is responsible for performing various functions under certain protocols. These functions and protocols are described in the following section.

 The specifications of this protocol are available at: https://interledger.org/rfcs/0003-interledger-protocol/draft-9.html

Application layer

Protocols running on this layer govern the key attributes of a payment transaction. Examples of application layer protocols include **Simple Payment Setup Protocol** (**SPSP**) and **Open Web Payment Scheme** (**OWPS**). SPSP is an Interledger protocol that allows secure payment across different ledgers by creating connectors between them. OWPS is another scheme that allows consumer payments across different networks.

Once the protocols on this layer have run successfully, protocols from the transport layer will be invoked in order to start the payment process.

Transport layer

This layer is responsible for managing payment transactions. Protocols such as **Optimistic Transport Protocol** (**OTP**), **Universal Transport Protocol** (**UTP**) and **Atomic Transport Protocol** (**ATP**) are available currently for this layer. OTP is the simplest protocol, which manages payment transfers without any escrow protection, whereas UTP provides escrow protection. ATP is the most advanced protocol, which not only provides an escrowed transfer mechanism but in addition, makes use of trusted notaries to further secure the payment transactions.

Interledger layer

This layer provides interoperability and routing services. This layer contains protocols such as **Interledger Protocol** (**ILP**), **Interledger Quoting Protocol** (**ILQP**), and **Interledger Control Protocol** (**ILCP**). ILP packet provides the final target (destination) of the transaction in a transfer. ILQP is used in making quote requests by the senders before the actual transfer. ILCP is used to exchange data related to routing information and payment errors between connectors on the payment network.

Ledger layer

This layer contains protocols that enable communication and execution of payment transactions between connectors. **Connectors** are basically objects that implement the protocol for forwarding payments between different ledgers. It can support various protocols such as simple ledger protocol, various blockchain protocols, legacy protocols, and different proprietary protocols.

Ripple connect consists of various Plug and Play modules that allow connectivity between ledgers by using the ILP. It enables the exchange of required data between parties before the transaction, visibility, fee management, delivery confirmation, and secure communication using transport layer security. A third-party application can connect to the Ripple network via various connectors that forward payments between different ledgers.

All layers described in the preceding sections make up the architecture of Interledger Protocol. Overall, Ripple is a solution that is targeted for the financial industry and makes real-time payments possible without any settlement risk. As this is a very feature-rich platform, covering all aspects of it are not possible in this chapter.

 Ripple documentation for the platform are available at `https://ripple.com/`.

Stellar

Stellar is a payment network based on blockchain technology and a novel consensus model called **Federated Byzantine Agreement** (**FBA**). FBA works by creating quorums of trusted parties. **Stellar Consensus Protocol** (**SCP**) is an implementation of FBA.

Key issues identified in the Stellar whitepaper are the cost and complexity of current financial infrastructure. This limitation warrants the need for a global financial network that addresses these issues without compromising the integrity and security of the financial transaction. This requirement has resulted in the invention of SCP which is a provably safe consensus mechanism.

 Original research paper for SCP is available at `https://www.stellar.org/papers/stellar-consensus-protocol.pdf`.

It has four main properties, which are described here:

- **Decentralized control**: This allows participation by anyone without any central party
- **Low latency**: This addresses the much-desired requirement of fast transaction processing
- **Flexible trust**: This allows users to choose which parties they trust for a specific purpose
- **Asymptotic security**: This makes use of digital signatures and hash functions for providing the required level of security on the network

The Stellar network allows transfer and representation of the value of an asset by its native digital currency, called **Lumens,** abbreviated as **XLM**. Lumens are consumed when a transaction is broadcasted on the network, which also serves as a deterrent against denial of service attacks.

At its core, the Stellar network maintains a distributed ledger that records every transaction and is replicated on each Stellar server (node). The consensus is achieved by verifying transactions between servers and updating the ledger with updates. The Stellar ledger can also act as a distributed exchange order book by allowing users to store their offers to buy or sell currencies.

There are various tools, SDKs, and software that make up the Stellar network.

The core software is available at `https://github.com/stellar/stellar-core`.

Rootstock

Before discussing **Rootstock (RSK)** in detail, it's important to define and introduce some concepts that are fundamental to the design of Rootstock. These concepts include sidechains, drivechains, and two-way pegging. The concept of the sidechain was originally developed by Blockstream.

 Blockstream's online presence is at `https://blockstream.com`.

Two-way pegging is a mechanism by which value (coins) can transfer between one blockchain to another and vice versa. There is no real transfer of coin between chains. The idea revolves around the concept of locking the same amount and value of coins in a bitcoin blockchain (main chain) and unlocking the equivalent number of tokens in the secondary chain.

Bearing this definition in mind, sidechains can be defined as described in the following section.

Sidechain

This is a blockchain that runs in parallel with a main blockchain and allows transfer of value between them. This means that tokens from one blockchain can be used in the sidechain and vice versa. This is also called a pegged sidechain because it supports two-way pegged assets.

Drivechain

This is a relatively new concept, where control on unlocking the locked bitcoins (in main chain) is given to the miners who can vote when to unlock them. This is in contrast to sidechains, where consensus is validated though simple payment verification mechanism in order to transfer the coins back to the main chain.

Rootstock is a smart contract platform which has a two-way peg into bitcoin blockchain. The core idea is to increase the scalability and performance of the bitcoin system and enable it to work with smart contracts. Rootstock runs a Turing complete deterministic virtual machine called **Rootstock Virtual Machine** (**RVM**). It is also compatible with the EVM and allows solidity-compiled contracts to run on Rootstock. Smart contracts can also run under the time-tested security of bitcoin blockchain. The Rootstock blockchain works by merge mining with bitcoins. This allows Rootstock blockchain to achieve the same security level as Bitcoin. This is especially true for preventing double spends and achieving settlement finality. It allows scalability, up to 400 transactions per second due to faster block times and other design considerations.

The research paper is available at, should you want to explore it further
`https://uploads.strikinglycdn.com/files/ec5278f8-218c-407a-af3c-ab71a910246d/RSK%20White%20Paper%20-%20Overview.pdf`.

RSK has released the main network called Bamboo, RSK MainNet which is a beta currently.

It is available at `http://www.rsk.co/`.

Quorum

This is a blockchain solution built by enhancing the existing Ethereum blockchain. There are several enhancements such as transaction privacy and a new consensus mechanism that has been introduced in Quorum. Quorum has introduced a new consensus model known as QuorumChain, which is based on a majority voting and time-based mechanism. Another feature called Constellation is also introduced which is a general-purpose mechanism for submitting information and allows encrypted communication between peers. Furthermore, permissions at node level is governed by smart contracts. It also provides a higher level of performance compared to public Ethereum blockchains.

Several components make up the Quorum blockchain ecosystem. These are listed in the following subsections.

Transaction manager

This component enables access to encrypted transaction data. It also manages local storage on nodes and communication with other transaction managers on the network.

Crypto Enclave

As the name suggests, this component is responsible for providing cryptographic services to ensure transaction privacy. It is also responsible for performing key management functions.

QuorumChain

This is the key innovation in Quorum. It is a BFT consensus mechanism which allows verification and circulation of votes via transactions on the blockchain network. In this scheme, a smart contract is used to manage the consensus process and nodes can be given voting rights to vote on which new block should be accepted. Once an appropriate number of votes is received by the voters, the block is considered valid. Nodes can have two roles, namely Voter or Maker. The **Voter** node is allowed to vote, whereas the **Maker** node is the one that creates a new block. By design, a node can have either right, none, or only one.

Network manager

This component provides an access control layer for the permissioned network.

A node in the quorum network can take several roles, for example, a Maker node that is allowed to create new blocks. Transaction privacy is provided using cryptography and the concept that certain transactions are meant to be viewable only by their relevant participants. This idea is similar to Corda's idea of private transactions that was discussed in `Chapter 15`, *Hyperledger*. As it allows both public and private transactions on the blockchain, the state database has been divided into two databases representing private and public transactions. As such, there are two separate Patricia-Merkle trees that represent the private and public state of the network. A private contract state hash is used to provide consensus evidence in private transactions between transacting parties.

Transaction in a Quorum network consists of various elements such as the recipient, the digital signature of the sender, which is used to identify the transaction originator, optional Ether amount, the optional list of participants that are allowed to see the transaction, and a field that contains a hash in case of private transactions.

A transaction goes through several steps before it can reach its destination. These steps are described as follows in detail:

1. User applications (DApps) send the transaction to the Quorum node via an API exposed by the blockchain network. This also contains the recipient address and transaction data.

2. The API then encrypts the payload and applies any other necessary cryptographic algorithm in order to ensure the privacy of the transaction and is sent to the transaction manager. The hash of the encrypted payload is also calculated at this step.

3. After receiving the transaction, the transaction manager validates the signature of the transaction sender and stores the message.

4. The hash of the previously encrypted payload is sent to the Quorum node.

5. Once the Quorum node starts to validate a block that contains the private transaction, it requests more relevant data from the transaction manager.

6. Once this request is received by the transaction manager, it sends the encrypted payload and relevant symmetric keys to the requestor Quorum node.

7. Once the Quorum node has all the data, it decrypts the payload and sends it to the EVM for execution. This is how Quorum achieves privacy with symmetric encryption on the blockchain, while it is able to use native Ethereum protocol and EVM for message transfer and execution respectively.

A similar concept, but quite different in a few aspects, has been proposed before in the form of **HydraChain**, which is based on Ethereum blockchain and allows the creation of permissioned distributed ledgers.

 Quorum is available for download at `https://github.com/jpmorganchase/quorum`.

Tezos

Tezos is a generic self-amending cryptographic ledger, which means that it not only allows decentralized consensus on the state of the blockchain but also allows consensus on how the protocol and nodes are evolved over time. Tezos has been developed to address limitations in the Bitcoin protocol such as issues arising from hard forks, cost, and mining power centralization due to PoW, limited scripting ability, and security issues. It has been developed in a purely functional language called OCaml.

The original research paper is available at https://www.tezos.com/ static/papers/white_paper.pdf.

The architecture of Tezos distributed ledger is divided into three layers: the network layer, consensus layer, and transaction layer. This decomposition allows the protocol to be evolved in a decentralized fashion. For this purpose, a generic network shell is implemented in Tezos that is responsible for maintaining the blockchain, which is represented by a combination of consensus and transaction layer. This shell provides an interface layer between the network and the protocol.

A concept of seed protocol has also been introduced, which is used as a mechanism to allow stakeholders on the network to approve any changes to the protocol.

Tezos blockchain starts from a seed protocol compared to a traditional blockchain that starts from a genesis block.

This seed protocol is responsible for defining procedures for amendments in the blockchain and even the amendment protocol itself. The reward mechanism in Tezos is based on a PoS algorithm, therefore there is no mining requirement.

Contract script language has been developed in Tezos for writing smart contracts, which is a stack-based Turing complete language. Smart contracts in Tezos are formally verifiable, which allows the code to be mathematically proven for its correctness.

Tezos has recently completed crowdfunding via ICO of 232 million USD. Their public network is due to be released in Q1 2018.

Tezos code is available at https://github.com/tezos/tezos.

Storj

Existing models for cloud-based storage are all centralized solutions, which may or may not be as secure as users expect them to be. There is a need to have a cloud storage system that is secure, highly available, and above all decentralized. Storj aims to provide blockchain based, decentralized, and distributed storage. It is a cloud shared by the community instead of a central organization. It allows execution of storage contracts between nodes that act as autonomous agents. These agents (nodes) execute various functions such as data transfer, validation, and perform data integrity checks.

The core concept is based on **Distributed Hash Tables** (**DHTs**) called **Kademlia**, however this protocol has been enhanced by adding new message types and functionalities in Storj. It also implements a peer to peer **publish/subscribe** (**pub/sub**) mechanism known as **Quasar**, which ensures that messages successfully reach the nodes that are interested in storage contracts. This is achieved via a bloom filter-based storage contract parameters selection mechanism called **topics**.

Storj stores files in an encrypted format spread across the network. Before the file is stored on the network, it is encrypted using AES-256-CTR symmetric encryption and is then stored piece by piece in a distributed manner on the network. This process of dissecting the file into pieces is called **sharding** and results in increased availability, security, performance, and privacy of the network. Also, if a node fails the shard is still available because by default a single shard is stored at three different locations on the network.

It maintains a blockchain, which serves as a shared ledger and implements standard security features such as public/private key cryptography and hash functions similar to any other blockchain. As the system is based on hard drive sharing between peers, anyone can contribute by sharing their extra space on the drive and get paid with Storj's own cryptocurrency called **Storjcoin X** (**SJCX**). SJCX was developed as a *Counterparty* asset and makes use of Counterparty (Bitcoin blockchain based) for transactions. This has been migrated to Ethereum now.

 A detailed discussion is available at `https://blog.storj.io/post/158740607128/migration-from-counterparty-to-ethereum`. Storj code is available at `https://github.com/Storj/`.

MaidSafe

This is another distributed storage system similar to Storj. Users are paid in Safecoin for their storage space contribution to the network. This mechanism of payment is governed by *proof of resource*, which ensures that the disk space committed by a user to the network is available, if not then the payment of Safecoin will drop accordingly. The files are encrypted and divided into small portions before being transmitted on to the network for storage.

Another concept of **opportunistic caching** has been introduced with MaidSafe, which is a mechanism to create copies of frequently accessed data physically closer to where the access requests are coming from, which results in high performance of the network. Another novel feature of the SAFE network is that it automatically removes any duplicate data on the network, thus resulting in reduced storage requirements.

Moreover, the concept of **churning** has also been introduced, which basically means that data is constantly moved across the network so that the data cannot be targeted by malicious adversaries. It also keeps multiple copies of data across the network to provide redundancy in case a node goes offline or fails.

BigchainDB

This is a scalable blockchain database. It is not strictly a blockchain itself but complements blockchain technology by providing a decentralized database. At its core it's a distributed database but with the added attributes of a blockchain such as decentralization, immutability, and handling of digital assets. It also allows usage of NoSQL for querying the database.

It is intended to provide a database in a decentralized ecosystem where not only processing is decentralized (blockchain) or the filesystem is decentralized (for example, IPFS) but the database is also decentralized. This makes the whole application ecosystem decentralized.

 This is available at `https://www.bigchaindb.com/`.

MultiChain

MultiChain has been developed as a platform for the development and deployment of private blockchains. It is based on bitcoin code and addresses security, scalability, and privacy issues. It is a highly configurable blockchain platform that allows users to set different blockchain parameters. It supports control and privacy via a granular permissioning layer. Installation of MultiChain is very quick.

 Link to installation files are available at http://www.multichain.com/download-install/.

Tendermint

Tendermint is a software that provides a BFT consensus mechanism and state machine replication functionality to an application. Its main motivation is to develop a general purpose, secure, and high-performance replicated state machine.

There are two components in Tendermint, which are described in the following section.

Tendermint Core

This is a consensus engine that enables secure replication of transactions on each node in the network.

Tendermint Socket Protocol (TMSP)

This is an application interface protocol that allows interfacing with any programming language to process transactions.

Tendermint allows decoupling of the application process and consensus process, which allows any application to benefit from the consensus mechanism.

The Tendermint consensus algorithm is a round-based mechanism where validator nodes propose new blocks in each round. A locking mechanism is used to ensure protection against a scenario where two different blocks are selected for committing at the same height of the blockchain. Each validator node maintains a full local replicated ledger of blocks that contain transactions. Each block contains a header, which consists of the previous block hash, timestamp of the proposal of block, the current block height, and the Merkle root hash of all transactions present in the block.

Tendermint has recently been used in **Cosmos** (`https://cosmos.network`) which is a network of blockchains that allows interoperability between different chains running on BFT consensus algorithm. Blockchains on this network are called zones. The first zone in Cosmos is called Cosmos hub, which is, in fact, a public blockchain and is responsible for providing connectivity service to other blockchains. For this purpose, the hub makes use of **Inter Blockchain Communication** (**IBC**) protocol. IBC protocol supports two types of transactions called `IBCBlockCimmitTx` and `IBCPacketTx`. The first type is used to provide proof of the most recent block hash in a blockchain to any party, whereas the latter type is used to provide data origin authentication. A packet from one blockchain to another is published by first posting a proof to the target chain. The receiving (target) chain checks this proof in order to verify that the sending chain has indeed published the packet. In addition, it has its own native currency called Atom. This scheme addresses scalability and interoperability issues by allowing multiple blockchains to connect to the hub.

 Tendermint is available at `https://tendermint.com/`.

Platforms and frameworks

This section covers various platforms that have been developed to enhance the experience of existing blockchain solutions.

Eris

Eris is not a single blockchain, it is an open modular platform developed by Monax for development of blockchain-based ecosystem applications. It offers various frameworks, SDKs, and tools that allow accelerated development and deployment of blockchain applications.

The core idea behind the Eris application platform is to enable development and management of ecosystem applications with a blockchain backend. It allows integration with multiple blockchains and enables various third-party systems to interact with various other systems.

This platform makes use of smart contracts written in Solidity language. It can interact with blockchains such as Ethereum or Bitcoin. The interaction can include connectivity commands, start, stop, disconnection, and creation of new blockchains. Complexity related to setup and interaction with blockchains have been abstracted away in Eris. All commands are standardized for different blockchains, and the same commands can be used across the platform regardless of the blockchain type being targeted.

An ecosystem application can consist the Eris platform, enabling the API gateway to allow legacy applications to connect to key management systems, consensus engines, and application engines. The Eris platform provides various toolkits that are used to provide various services to the developers. These modules are described as follows:

- **Chains**: This allows the creation of and interaction with blockchains.
- **Packages**: This allows the development of smart contracts.
- **Keys**: This is used for key management and signing operations.
- **Files**: This allows working with distributed data management systems. It can be used to interact with filesystems such as IPFS and data lakes.
- **Services**: This exposes a set of services that allows the management and integration of ecosystem applications.

Several SDKs has also been developed by Eris that allow the development and management of ecosystem applications. These SDKs contain smart contracts that have been fully tested and address specific needs and requirements of business. For example, a finance SDK, insurance SDK, and logistics SDK. There is also a base SDK that serves as a basic development kit to manage the life cycle of an ecosystem application.

Monax has developed its own permissioned blockchain client called `eris:db`. It is a PoS-based blockchain system that allows integration with a number of different blockchain networks. The `eris:db` client consists of four components:

- **Consensus**: This is based on the Tendermint consensus mechanism, discussed before
- **Virtual machine**: Eris uses EVM, as such it supports Solidity compiled contracts
- **Permissions layer**: Being a permissioned ledger, Eris provides an access control mechanism that can be used to assign specific roles to different entities on the network

- **Interface**: This provides various command-line tools and RPC interfaces to enable interaction with the backend blockchain network

The key difference between Ethereum blockchain and `eris:db` is that `eris:db` makes use of a **Practical Byzantine Fault-Tolerance** (**PBFT**) algorithm, which is implemented as a deposit-based Proof of Stake (DPOS system) whereas Ethereum uses PoW. Moreover, `eris:db` uses the ECDSA `ed22519` curve scheme whereas Ethereum uses the `secp256k1` algorithm. Finally, it is permissioned with an access control layer on top whereas Ethereum is a public blockchain.

Eris is a feature-rich application platform that offers a large selection of toolkits and services to develop blockchain-based applications.

 It is available at `https://monax.io/`.

Summary

This chapter started with the introduction of alternative blockchains and is divided into two main sections discussing blockchains and platforms. Blockchain technology is a very thriving area, as such changes are quite rapid in existing solutions and new relevant technologies or tools are being introduced almost every day. In this chapter, a careful selection of platforms and blockchains was introduced. Several solutions were considered that complement material covered in previous chapters, for example, Eris, which supports blockchain development. New blockchains such as Kadena, various new protocols such as Ripple, and concepts such as sidechains and drivechains were also discussed.

The material covered in this chapter is intended to provide a strong foundation for more in-depth research into areas that readers are interested in. As said before, blockchain is a very fast-moving field, and there are many other blockchain proposals projects such as Tau-Chain, HydraChain, Elements, CREDITS, and many more that have not been discussed in this chapter. Readers are encouraged to keep an eye on the developments in this field to keep themselves up to date with advancement in this rapidly growing area.

In the next chapter, we will explore that how blockchain can be used out of its original usage, that is, cryptocurrencies. We will cover various use cases and especially usage of blockchain in IoT.

17
Blockchain – Outside of Currencies

Digital currencies were the first-ever application of blockchain technology, arguably without realizing its real potential. With the invention of Bitcoin, the concept of blockchain was introduced for the very first time, but it was not until 2013 that the true potential of blockchain technology was realized with its possible application in many different industries, other than cryptocurrencies. Since then many use cases of blockchain technology in various industries have been proposed, including but not limited to finance, the Internet of Things, digital rights management, government, and law.

In this chapter, four main industries namely the Internet of Things, government, health, and finance, have been selected, with the aid of use cases, for discussion.

 In 2010, discussion started regarding BitDNS, a decentralized naming system for domains on the internet. Then Namecoin (`https://wiki.namecoin.org/index.php?title=History`) started in April 2011 with a different vision as compared to Bitcoin whose sole purpose is to provision electronic cash. This can be considered first example of blockchain usage other than purely cryptocurrencies.
After this by 2013, many ideas emerged. Since 2013 this trend is growing exponentially.

Internet of Things

The **Internet of Things** (**IoT**) for short has recently gained much traction due to its potential for transforming business applications and everyday life. IoT can be defined as a network of computationally intelligent physical objects (any object such as cars, fridges, industrial sensors, and so on) that are capable of connecting to the internet, sensing real-world events or environments, reacting to those events, collecting relevant data, and communicating it over the internet.

This simple definition has enormous implications and has led to exciting concepts, such as wearables, smart homes, smart grids, smart connected cars, and smart cities, that are all based on this basic concept of an IoT device. After dissecting the definition of IoT, four functions come to light as being performed by an IoT device. These include **sensing**, **reacting**, **collecting**, and **communicating**. All these functions are performed by using various components on the IoT device.

Sensing is performed by sensors. Reacting or controlling is performed by actuators, the collection is a function of various sensors, and communication is performed by chips that provide network connectivity. One thing to note is that all these components are accessible and controllable via the internet in the IoT. An IoT device on its own is perhaps useful to some extent, but if it is part of a broader IoT ecosystem, it is more valuable.

A typical IoT can consist of many physical objects connecting with each other and to a centralized cloud server. This is shown in the following diagram:

A typical IoT network

Source: IBM

Elements of IoT are spread across multiple layers, and various reference architectures exist that can be used to develop IoT systems. A five-layer model can be used to describe IoT, which contains a physical object layer, device layer, network layer, services layer, and application layer. Each layer or level is responsible for various functions and includes multiple components. These are shown in the following diagram:

| Application Layer |
| Transportation, financial, insurance and many others |
| Management Layer |
| Data processing, analytics, security management |
| Network Layer |
| LAN, WAN, PAN, Routers |
| Device Layer |
| Sensors , Actuators, smart devices |
| Physical Objects |
| People, cars, homes etc. etc. |

IoT five-layer model

Now we will examine each layer in detail.

Physical object layer

These include any real-world physical objects. It includes people, animals, cars, trees, fridges, trains, factories, homes, and in fact anything that is required to be monitored and controlled can be connected to the IoT.

Device layer

This layer contains things that make up the IoT such as sensors, transducers, actuators, smartphones, smart devices, and **Radio-Frequency Identification** (**RFID**) tags. There can be many categories of sensors such as body sensors, home sensors, and environmental sensors based on the type of work they perform. This layer is the core of an IoT ecosystem where various sensors are used to sense real-world environments. This layer includes sensors that can monitor temperature, humidity, liquid flow, chemicals, air, pressure, and much more. Usually, an **Analog to Digital Converter** (**ADC**) is required on a device to turn the real-world analog signal into a digital signal that a microprocessor can understand.

Actuators in this layer provide the means to enable control of external environments, for example, starting a motor or opening a door. These components also require digital to analog converters to convert a digital signal into analog. This method is especially relevant when control of a mechanical component is required by the IoT device.

Network layer

This layer is composed of various network devices that are used to provide Internet connectivity between devices and to the cloud or servers that are part of the IoT ecosystem. These devices can include gateways, routers, hubs, and switches. This layer can include two types of communication.

First there is the horizontal means of communication, which includes radio, Bluetooth, Wi-Fi, Ethernet, LAN, Zigbee, and PAN and can be used to provide communication between IoT devices. Second, we have communication to the next layer, which is usually through the internet and provides communication between machines and people or other upper layers. The first layer can optionally be included in the device layer as it physically is residing on the device layer where devices can communicate with each other at the same layer.

Management layer

This layer provides the management layer for the IoT ecosystem. This includes platforms that enable processing of data gathered from the IoT devices and turn that into meaningful insights. Also, device management, security management, and data flow management are included in this layer. It also manages communication between the device and application layers.

Application layer

This layer includes applications running on top of the IoT network. This layer can consist of many applications depending on the requirements such as transportation, healthcare, financial, insurance, or supply chain management. This list, of course, is not an exhaustive list by any stretch of the imagination; there is a myriad of IoT applications that can fall into this layer.

With the availability of cheap sensors, hardware, and bandwidth, IoT has gained popularity in recent years and currently has applications in many different areas including healthcare, insurance, supply chain management, home automation, industrial automation, and infrastructure management. Moreover, advancements in technology such as the availability of IPv6, smaller and powerful processors, and better internet access have also played a vital role in the popularity of IoT.

The benefits of IoT range from cost saving to enabling businesses to make vital decisions and thus improve performance based on the data provided by the IoT devices. Even in domestic usage IoT equipped home appliances can provide valuable data for cost saving. For example, smart meters for energy monitoring can provide valuable information on how the energy is being used and can convey that back to the service provider. Raw data from millions of things (IoT devices) is analyzed and provides meaningful insights that help in making timely and efficient business decisions.

The usual IoT model is based on a centralized paradigm where IoT devices usually connect to a cloud infrastructure or central servers to report and process the relevant data back. This centralization poses certain possibilities of exploitation including hacking and data theft. Moreover, not having control of personal data on a single, centralized service provider also increases the possibility of security and privacy issues. While there are methods and techniques to build a highly secure IoT ecosystem based on the normal IoT model, there are specific much more desirable benefits that blockchain can bring to IoT. A blockchain-based IoT model differs from the traditional IoT network paradigm.

According to IBM, blockchain for IoT can help to build trust, reduce costs, and accelerate transactions. Additionally, decentralization, which is at the very core of blockchain technology, can eliminate single points of failure in an IoT network. For example, a central server perhaps is not able to cope with the amount of data that billions of IoT devices (things) are producing at high frequency. Also, the peer-to-peer communication model provided by blockchain can help to reduce costs because there is no need to build high-cost centralized data centers or implementation of complex public key infrastructure for security. Devices can communicate with each other directly or via routers.

As an estimate of various researchers and companies, by 2020 there will be roughly 22 billion devices connected to the internet. With this explosion of billions of devices connecting to the internet, it is hard to imagine that centralized infrastructures will be able to cope with the high demands of bandwidth, services, and availability without incurring excessive expenditure. Blockchain-based IoT will be able to solve scalability, privacy, and reliability issues in the current IoT model.

Blockchain enables *things* to communicate and transact with each other directly and with the availability of smart contracts, negotiation, and financial transactions can also occur directly between the devices instead of requiring an intermediary, authority, or human intervention. For example, if a room in a hotel is vacant, it can rent itself out, negotiate the rent, and can open the door lock for a human who has paid the right amount of funds. Another example could be that if a washing machine runs out of detergent, it could order it online after finding the best price and value based on the logic programmed in its smart contract.

The aforementioned five-layer IoT model can be adapted to a blockchain-based model by adding a blockchain layer on top of the network layer. This layer will run smart contracts, and provide security, privacy, integrity, autonomy, scalability, and decentralization services to the IoT ecosystem. The management layer, in this case, can consist of only software related to analytics and processing, and security and control can be moved to the blockchain layer. This model can be visualized in the following diagram:

Application Layer Transportation, financial, insurance and many others
Management Layer Data processing, analytics
Blockchain Layer Security, P2P (M2M) autonomous transactions, decentralization, smart contracts
Network Layer LAN, WAN, PAN, Routers
Device Layer Sensors , Actuators, smart devices
Physical Objects People, cars, homes etc. etc.

Blockchain-based IoT model

In this model, other layers would perhaps remain the same, but an additional blockchain layer will be introduced as a middleware between all participants of the IoT network.

It can also be visualized as a peer-to-peer IoT network after abstracting away all the layers mentioned earlier. This model is shown in the following diagram where all devices are communicating and negotiating with each other without a central command and control entity:

Blockchain-based direct communication model, source: IBM

It can also result in cost saving which is due to easier device management by using a blockchain based decentralized approach. The IoT network can be optimized for performance by using blockchain. In this case, there will be no need to store IoT data centrally for millions of devices because storage and processing requirements can be distributed to all IoT devices on the blockchain. This can result in completely removing the need for large data centers for processing and storing the IoT data.

Blockchain-based IoT can also thwart denial of service attacks where hackers can target a centralized server or data center more efficiently, but with blockchain's distributed and decentralized nature, such attacks are no longer possible. Additionally, if as estimated there will be billions of devices connected to the internet soon, it will become almost impossible to manage security and updates of all those devices from traditional centrally-owned servers. Blockchain can provide a solution to this problem by allowing devices to communicate with each other directly in a secure manner and even request firmware and security updates from each other. On a blockchain network, these communications can be recorded immutably and securely which will provide auditability, integrity, and transparency to the system. This mechanism is not possible with traditional peer-to-peer systems.

In summary, there are clear benefits that can be reaped with the convergence of IoT and blockchain and a lot of research and work in academia and industry are already in progress. There are various projects already proposed providing blockchain-based IoT solutions. For example, IBM Blue Horizon and IBM Bluemix are IoT platforms supporting blockchain IoT platforms. Various start-ups such as Filament have already proposed novel ideas on how to build a decentralized network that enables devices on IoT to transact with each other directly and autonomously driven by smart contracts.

In the following section, a practical example is provided on how to build a simple IoT device and connect it to the Ethereum blockchain. This IoT device is connected to the Ethereum blockchain and is used to open a door (in this case the door lock is represented by an LED) when the appropriate amount of funds is sent by a user on the blockchain. This is a simple example and requires a more rigorously-tested version to implement it in production, but it demonstrates how an IoT device can be connected, controlled, and responded to in response to certain events on an Ethereum blockchain.

IoT blockchain experiment

This example makes use of a Raspberry Pi device which is a **Single Board Computer** (**SBC**). The Raspberry Pi is a SBC developed as a low-cost computer to promote computer education but has also gained much more popularity as a tool of choice for building IoT platforms. A Raspberry Pi 3 Model B is shown in the following picture. You may be able to use earlier models too, but those have not been tested:

Raspberry Pi Model B

In the following section, an example will be discussed where a Raspberry Pi will be used as an IoT device connected to the Ethereum blockchain and will act in response to a smart contract invocation.

First, the Raspberry Pi needs to be set up. This can be done by using NOOBS which provides an easy method of installing Raspbian or any other operating system.

 This can be downloaded and installed from the link `https://www.raspberrypi.org/downloads/noobs/`.
Alternatively, only Raspbian can be installed from the link `https://www.raspberrypi.org/downloads/raspbian/`.
Another alternative available at `https://github.com/debian-pi/raspbian-ua-netinst` can also be used to install a minimal non-GUI version of Raspbian OS.

For this example, NOOBS has been used to install Raspbian, as such the rest of the exercise assumes Raspbian is installed on the SD memory card of the Raspberry Pi. The command output in the following screenshot shows that which architecture the operating system is running on. In this case, it is `armv71`; therefore ARM-compatible binary for Geth will be downloaded.

The platform can be confirmed by running the command `uname -a` in a terminal window in Raspberry Pi Raspbian operating system.

Raspberry Pi architecture

Once the Raspbian operating system is installed, the next step is to download the appropriate Geth binary for the Raspberry Pi ARM platform.

The download and installation steps are described in detail:

1. Geth download. Note that in the following example a specific version is downloaded however other versions are available which can be downloaded from `https://geth.ethereum.org/downloads/`.

   We can use `wget`, to download the `geth` client images:

   ```
   $ wget https://gethstore.blob.core.windows.net/builds/geth-linux-arm7-1.5.6-2a609af5.tar.gz
   ```

    Other versions are also available, but it's recommended that you download this version, as this is the one that has been used in examples in this chapter.

2. Unzip and extract into a directory. The directory named `geth-linux-arm7-1.5.6-2a609af5` will be created automatically with the `tar` command shown next:

```
$ tar -zxvf geth-linux-arm7-1.5.6-2a609af5.tar
```

This command will create a directory named `geth-linux-arm7-1.5.6-2a609af5` and will extract the Geth binary and related files into that directory. The Geth binary can be copied into `/usr/bin` or the appropriate path on Raspbian to make it available from anywhere in the operating system. When the download is finished, the next step is to create the genesis block.

3. The same genesis block needs to be used that was created previously in `Chapter 12`, *Ethereum Development Environment*. The genesis file can be copied from the other node on the network. This is shown in the following screenshot. Alternatively, an entirely new genesis block can be generated.

```
{
        "nonce": "0x0000000000000042",
        "timestamp": "0x00",
        "parentHash":
"0x0000000000000000000000000000000000000000000000000000000000000000",
        "extraData": "0x00",
        "gasLimit": "0x8000000",
        "difficulty": "0x0400",
        "mixhash":
"0x0000000000000000000000000000000000000000000000000000000000000000",
        "coinbase": "0x3333333333333333333333333333333333333333",
        "alloc": {
        },
        "config": {
            "chainId": 786,
            "homesteadBlock": 0,
            "eip155Block": 0,
            "eip158Block": 0
        }
}
```

4. Once the `genesis.json` file is copied onto the Raspberry Pi; the following command can be run to generate the genesis block. It is important that the same genesis block is used that was generated previously otherwise the nodes will effectively be running on separate networks:

```
$ ./geth init genesis.json
```

This will show the output similar to the one shown in the following screenshot:

```
pi@raspberrypi:~/geth-linux-arm7-1.5.6-2a609af5 $ ./geth init genesis.json
I0110 23:37:15.714795 cmd/utils/flags.go:612] WARNING: No etherbase set and no accounts found as default
I0110 23:37:15.715283 ethdb/database.go:83] Allotted 128MB cache and 1024 file handles to /home/pi/.ethereum/geth/chaindata
I0110 23:37:15.794383 ethdb/database.go:176] closed db:/home/pi/.ethereum/geth/chaindata
I0110 23:37:15.794723 ethdb/database.go:83] Allotted 128MB cache and 1024 file handles to /home/pi/.ethereum/geth/chaindata
I0110 23:37:15.923300 core/genesis.go:93] Genesis block already in chain. Writing canonical number
I0110 23:37:15.923895 cmd/geth/chaincmd.go:131] successfully wrote genesis block and/or chain rule set: f2b2ffed01907a845a01d1dea21e5a
ec021e8e68b5ec9ffccb82df
```

Initialize genesis file

5. After genesis block creation, there is a need to add peers to the network. This can be achieved by creating a file named `static-nodes.json`, which contains the enode ID of the peer that `geth` on the Raspberry Pi will connect for syncing:

```
pi@raspberrypi:~/.ethereum $ cat static-nodes.json
[
"enode://44352ede5b9e792e437c1c0431c1578ce3676a87e1f588434aff1299d30325c233c8d426fc
57a25380481c8a36fb3be2787375e932fb4885885f6452f6efa77f@192.168.0.19:30301"
]
```

Static nodes configuration

This information can be obtained from the Geth JavaScript console by running the following command, and this command should be run on the peer to which Raspberry Pi is going to connect:

```
> admin.nodeInfo
```

This will show the output similar to the one shown in the following screenshot:

```
> admin.nodeInfo
{
  enode: "enode://44352ede5b9e792e437c1c0431c1578ce3676a87e1f588434aff1299d30325c233c8d426fc57a25380481c8a36fb3
87375e932fb4885885f6452f6efa77f@[::]:30301",
  id: "44352ede5b9e792e437c1c0431c1578ce3676a87e1f588434aff1299d30325c233c8d426fc57a25380481c8a36fb3be2787375e9
4885885f6452f6efa77f",
```

geth nodeInfo

After this step, further instructions presented in the following sections can be followed to connect Raspberry Pi to the other node on the private network. In the example, the Raspberry Pi will be connected to the network ID `786` created in `Chapter 12`, *Ethereum Development Environment.* The key is to use the same genesis file created previously and different port numbers. Same genesis file will ensure that clients connect to the same network in which the genesis file originated from.

Different ports are not a strict requirement, however, if the two nodes are running under a private network and access from an environment external to the network is required then a combination of DMZ, router and port forwarding will be used. Therefore, it is recommended to use different TCP ports to allow port forwarding to work correctly. The `--identity` switch shown in the following command for first node set up, which hasn't been introduced previously, allows for an identifying name to be specified for the node.

First node setup

First, the `geth` client needs to be started on the first node using the following command:

```
$ geth --datadir .ethereum/privatenet/ --networkid 786 --maxpeers 5 --rpc --rpcapi web3,eth,debug,personal,net --rpcport 9001 --rpccorsdomain "*" --port 30301 --identity "drequinox"
```

This will give the output similar to the following:

```
imran@drequinox-OP7010:~$ geth --datadir .ethereum/privatenet/ --networkid 786 --maxpeers 5 --rpc --rpcapi web3,eth,debug,personal,net --rpcport 9001 --rpccorsdomain "*" --port 30301 --identity "drequinox"
I0110 23:26:46.032878 ethdb/database.go:83] Allotted 128MB cache and 1024 file handles to /home/imran/.ethereum/privatenet/geth/chaindata
I0110 23:26:46.072986 ethdb/database.go:176] closed db:/home/imran/.ethereum/privatenet/geth/chaindata
I0110 23:26:46.073243 node/node.go:175] instance: Geth/drequinox/v1.5.2-stable-c8695209/linux/go1.7.3
I0110 23:26:46.073258 ethdb/database.go:83] Allotted 128MB cache and 1024 file handles to /home/imran/.ethereum/privatenet/geth/chaindata
I0110 23:26:46.082654 eth/backend.go:193] Protocol Versions: [63 62], Network Id: 786
I0110 23:26:46.083188 core/blockchain.go:214] Last header: #7991 [999c534f…] TD=11652654509
I0110 23:26:46.083203 core/blockchain.go:215] Last block: #7991 [999c534f…] TD=11652654509
I0110 23:26:46.083210 core/blockchain.go:216] Fast block: #7991 [999c534f…] TD=11652654509
I0110 23:26:46.083929 p2p/server.go:336] Starting Server
I0110 23:26:48.239776 p2p/discover/udp.go:217] Listening, enode://44352ede5b9e792e437c1c0431c1578ce3676a87e1f588434aff1299d30325c233c8d426fc57a25380481c8a36fb3be2787375e932fb4885885f6452f6efa77f@[::]:30301
I0110 23:26:48.239893 p2p/server.go:604] Listening on [::]:30301
I0110 23:26:48.240913 node/node.go:340] IPC endpoint opened: /home/imran/.ethereum/privatenet/geth.ipc
I0110 23:26:48.241212 node/node.go:410] HTTP endpoint opened: http://localhost:9001
I0110 23:42:58.206205 eth/backend.go:479] Automatic pregeneration of ethash DAG ON (ethash dir: /home/imran/.ethash)
I0110 23:42:58.206217 miner/miner.go:136] Starting mining operation (CPU=8 TOT=9)
```

geth on first node

Once this is started up, it should be kept running, and another `geth` instance should be started from the Raspberry Pi node.

Raspberry Pi node setup

On Raspberry Pi, the following command is required to be run to start `geth` and to sync it with other nodes (in this case only one node). The following is the command:

```
$ ./geth --networkid 786 --maxpeers 5 --rpc --rpcapi
web3,eth,debug,personal,net --rpccorsdomain "*" --port 30302 --identity
"raspberry"
```

This should produce the output similar to the one shown in the following screenshot. When the output contains the row displaying `Block synchronisation started` it means that the node has connected successfully to its peer.

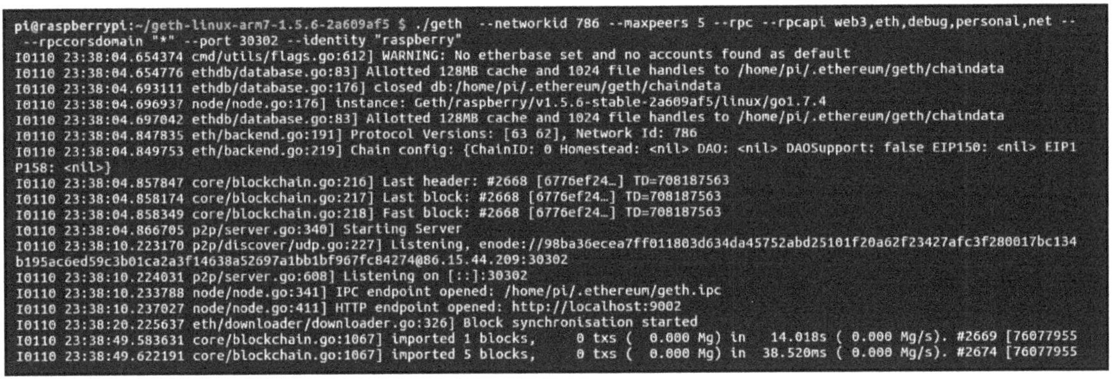

geth on the Raspberry Pi.

This can be further verified by running commands in the `geth` console on both nodes as shown in the following screenshot. The `geth` client can be attached by simply running the following command on the Raspberry Pi:

```
$ geth attach
```

This will open the JavaScript `geth` console for interacting with the `geth` node. We can use `admin.peers` command to see the connected peers:

```
> admin.peers
[{
    caps: ["eth/62", "eth/63"],
    id: "44352ede5b9e792e437c1c0431c1578ce3676a87e1f588434aff1299d30325c233c8d426fc57a25380481c8a36fb3be2787375e932f
b4885885f6452f6efa77f",
    name: "Geth/drequinox/v1.5.2-stable-c8695209/linux/go1.7.3",
    network: {
      localAddress: "192.168.0.21:56550",
      remoteAddress: "192.168.0.19:30301"
    },
    protocols: {
      eth: {
        difficulty: 11719415397,
        head: "0x2d32c90b4c9dacea9a109b0ae52c1ebf511915bb618a2d3c55a80a63852e89f6",
        version: 63
      }
    }
}]_
```

geth console admin peers command running on Raspberry Pi

Similarly, we can attach to the `geth` instance by running the following command on the first node:

```
$ geth attach ipc:.ethereum/privatenet/geth.ipc
```

Once the console is available `admin.peers` can be run to reveal the details about other connected nodes as shown in the following screenshot:

```
> admin.peers
[{
    caps: ["eth/62", "eth/63"],
    id: "98ba36ecea7ff011803d634da45752abd25101f20a62f23427afc3f280017bc134833dd5ba400bb195ac6ed59c3b01
ca2a3f14638a52697a1bb1bf967fc84274",
    name: "Geth/raspberry/v1.5.6-stable-2a609af5/linux/go1.7.4",
    network: {
      localAddress: "192.168.0.19:30301",
      remoteAddress: "192.168.0.21:56512"
    },
    protocols: {
      eth: {
        difficulty: 11700366117,
        head: "0x1188f58b4900a1d771d333141ea9400d78400bb8e561494ab436519ae64e1e34",
        version: 63
      }
    }
}]
```

geth console admin peers command running on the other peer

Once both nodes are up-and-running further prerequisites can be installed to set up the experiment. Installation of Node.js and the relevant JavaScript libraries is required.

Installing Node.js

The required libraries and dependencies are listed here. First Node.js and npm need to be updated on the Raspberry Pi Raspbian operating system. For this the following steps can be followed:

1. Install latest Node.js on the Raspberry Pi using the following command:

   ```
   $ curl -sL https://deb.nodesource.com/setup_7.x | sudo -E bash -
   ```

   This should display output similar to the following. The output is quite large therefore only the top part of the output is shown in the following screenshot:

Node.js installation

2. Run the update via `apt-get`:

   ```
   $ sudo apt-get install nodejs
   ```

   Verification can be performed by running the following command to ensure that the correct versions of Node.js and npm are installed, as shown in the following screenshot:

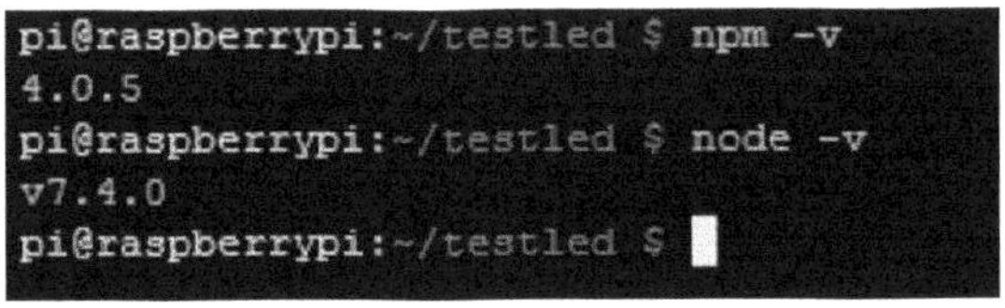

npm and node installation verification

It should be noted that these versions are not a necessity; any of the latest version of npm and Node.js should work. However, the examples in this chapter make use of npm 4.0.5 and node v7.4.0, so it is recommended that readers use the same version in order to avoid any compatibility issues.

3. Install Ethereum `web3` npm, which is required to enable JavaScript code to access the Ethereum blockchain:

 Make sure that specific version of `web3` shown in the screenshot is installed or a version similar to this for example 0.20.2. This is important because by default version 1.0.0-beta.26 (at the time of writing) will be installed which is beta and is under development. Therefore `web3` 0.20.2 or 0.18.0 stable version should be used for this example. Readers can install this version by using `$ npm install web3@0.20.2`.

```
pi@raspberrypi:~/testled $ npm install web3
testled@1.0.0 /home/pi/testled
└─┬ web3@0.18.0
  └── bignumber.js@2.0.7  (git+https://github.com/debris/bignumber.js.git#94d7146671b9719e00a09c29b01a691bc85048c2)

npm WARN testled@1.0.0 No repository field.
pi@raspberrypi:~/testled $ 
```

npm install web3

4. Similarly, npm `onoff` can be installed, which is required to communicate with the Raspberry Pi and control GPIO:

```
$ npm install onoff
```

```
pi@raspberrypi:~/testled $ npm install onoff --save
testled@1.0.0 /home/pi/testled
└── onoff@1.1.1

npm WARN testled@1.0.0 No repository field.
pi@raspberrypi:~/testled $ 
```

Onoff installation

When all the prerequisites are installed, hardware setup can be performed. For this purpose, a simple circuit is built using a breadboard and a few electronic components.

The hardware components are listed as follows:

- **LED**: The abbreviation of **Light Emitting Diode**, this can be used as a visual indication for an event.
- **Resistor**: A 330 ohm component is required which provides resistance to passing current based on its rating. It is not necessary to understand the theory behind it for this experiment; any standard electronics engineering text covers all these topics in detail.

- **Breadboard**: This provides a means of building an electronic circuit without requiring soldering.
- **T-Shaped cobbler**: This is inserted on the breadboard as shown in the following photo and provides a labeled view of all **General Purpose I/O** (**GPIO**) pins for the Raspberry Pi.
- **Ribbon cable connector**: This is simply used to provide connectivity between the Raspberry Pi and the breadboard via GPIO. All these components are shown in the following picture:

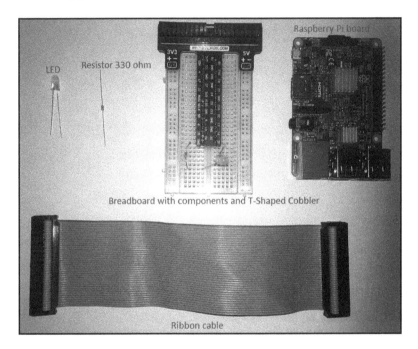

Required components

Circuit

As shown in the following picture, the positive leg (long leg) of the LED is connected to pin number **21** of the GPIO, and the negative (short leg) is connected to the resistor, which is then connected to the **ground** (**GND**) pin of the GPIO. Once the connections are set up the ribbon cable can be used to connect to the GPIO connector on the Raspberry Pi simply.

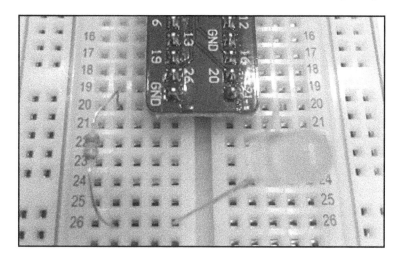

Connections for components on the breadboard

Once the connections are set up correctly, and the Raspberry Pi has been updated with the appropriate libraries and Geth, the next step is to develop a simple, smart contract that expects a value. If the value provided to it is not what it expects it does not trigger an event; otherwise if the value passed matches the correct value, the event triggers which can be read by the client JavaScript program running via Node.js. Of course, the Solidity contract can be very complicated and can also deal with the Ether sent to it, and if the amount of Ether is equal to the required amount, then the event can trigger. However, in this example, the aim is to demonstrate the usage of smart contracts to trigger events that can then be read by JavaScript program running on Node.js, which then, in turn, can trigger actions on IoT devices using various libraries.

The smart contract source code is shown as follows:

```
1   pragma solidity ^0.4.0;
2 - contract simpleIOT {
3       uint roomrent = 10;
4       event roomRented(bool returnValue);
5 -     function getRent (uint8 x) public returns (bool) {
6 -         if (x==roomrent) {
7               roomRented(true);
8               return true;
9           }
10      }
11  }
```

Solidity code for simple IOT

The online Solidity compiler (Remix IDE) can be used to run and test this contract. The **Application Binary Interface** (**ABI**) required for interacting with the contract is also available in the **Details** section as shown in the following screenshot:

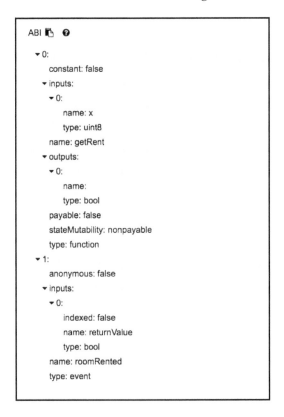

ABI from Remix IDE

The following is the ABI of the contract:

```
[
    {
        "constant": false,
        "inputs": [
            {
                "name": "x",
                "type": "uint8"
            }
        ],
        "name": "getRent",
        "outputs": [
            {
                "name": "",
                "type": "bool"
            }
        ],
        "payable": false,
        "stateMutability": "nonpayable",
        "type": "function"
    },
    {
        "anonymous": false,
        "inputs": [
            {
                "indexed": false,
                "name": "returnValue",
                "type": "bool"
            }
        ],
        "name": "roomRented",
        "type": "event"
    }
]
```

There are two methods by which the Raspberry Pi node can connect to the private blockchain via the web3 interface. The first is where the Raspberry Pi device is running its own geth client locally and maintains its ledger, but with resource-constrained devices, it is not possible to run a full geth node or even a light node in a few circumstances. In that case, the second method, which uses web3 provider can be used to connect to the appropriate RPC channel. This will be shown later in the client JavaScript Node.js program.

A comparison of both of these approaches is shown in the following diagram:

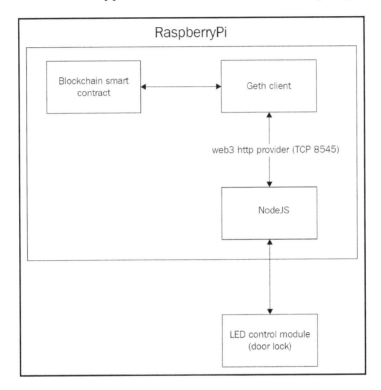

Application architecture of room rent IoT application (IoT device with local ledger)

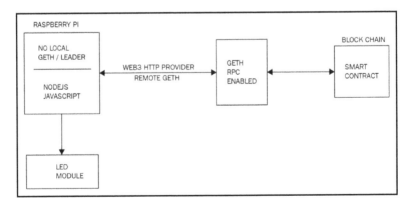

Application architecture of room rent IoT application (IoT device without local ledger)

There are obvious security concerns which arise from exposing RPC interfaces publicly; therefore, it is recommended that this option is used only on private networks and if required to be used on public networks appropriate security measures are put in place, such as allowing only the known IP addresses to connect to the `geth` RPC interface. This can be achieved by a combination of disabling peer discovery mechanisms and HTTP-RPC server listening interfaces.

More information about this can be found using `geth help`. The traditional network security measures such as firewalls, **Transport Layer Security** (**TLS**) and certificates can also be used but have not been discussed in this example. Now Truffle can be used to deploy the contract on the private network ID `786` to which at this point the Raspberry Pi is connected. Truffle deploy can be performed simply by using the following shown command; it is assumed that `truffle init` and other preliminaries discussed in `Chapter 12`, *Ethereum Development Environment* has already been performed:

```
$ truffle migrate
```

It should produce the output similar to the following screenshot:

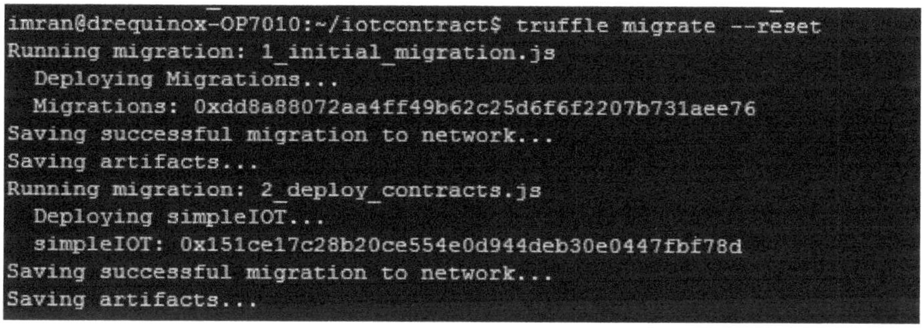

Truffle deploy

Once the contract is deployed correctly, JavaScript code can be developed that will connect to the blockchain via `web3`, listen for the events from the smart contract in the blockchain, and turn the LED on via the Raspberry Pi. The JavaScript code of the `index.js` file is shown as follows:

```
var Web3 = require('web3');
if (typeof web3 !== 'undefined')
{
    web3 = new Web3(web3.currentProvider);
}else
{
    web3 = new Web3(new
```

```
Web3.providers.HttpProvider("http://localhost:9002"));
    //http-rpc-port
}
var Gpio = require('onoff').Gpio;
var led = new Gpio(21,'out');
var coinbase = web3.eth.coinbase;
var ABIString =
'[{"constant":false,"inputs":[{"name":"x","type":"uint8"}],"name":"getRent"
,"outputs":[{"name":"","type":"bool"}],"payable":false,"stateMutability":"n
onpayable","type":"function"},{"anonymous":false,"inputs":[{"indexed":false
,"name":"returnValue","type":"bool"}],"name":"roomRented","type":"event"}]'
;
var ABI = JSON.parse(ABIString);
var ContractAddress = '0x975881c44fbef4573fef33cccec1777a8f76669c';
web3.eth.defaultAccount = web3.eth.accounts[0];
var simpleiot = web3.eth.contract(ABI).at(ContractAddress);
var event = simpleiot.roomRented( {}, function(error, result) { if (!error)
{
    console.log("LED On");
    led.writeSync(1);
}
});
```

Note that in the preceding example the contract address
`'0x975881c44fbef4573fef33cccec1777a8f76669c'` for variable `var`
`ContractAddress` is specific to the deployment and it will be different when readers run this example. Simply change the address in the file to what you see after deploying the contract.

Also, note that the HTTP-RPC server listening port on which Geth has been started on Raspberry Pi. By default, it is TCP port `8545`. Remember to change this according to your Raspberry Pi setup and Geth configuration. It is set to `9002` in the preceding example code because Geth running on Raspberry Pi is listening on `9002` in the example. If it's listening to a different port on your Raspberry Pi, then change it to that port:

```
web3 = new Web3(new Web3.providers.HttpProvider("http://localhost:9002"));
```

When Geth starts up it shown which port it has HTTP endpoint listening on. This is also configurable with `--rpcport` in `geth` by specifying the port number value as a parameter to the flag.

This JavaScript code can be placed in a file on the Raspberry Pi, for example, `index.js`. It can be run by using the following command:

```
$ node index.js
```

This will start the program, which will run on Node.js and listen for events from the smart contract. Once the program is running correctly, the smart contract can be invoked by using the Truffle console as shown in the following screenshot.

In this case, the `getRent` function is called with parameter `10`, which is the expected value:

```
truffle(development)> simpleiot.getRent(10)
```

Interaction with the contract

After the contract is mined, `roomRented` will be triggered, which will turn on the LED.

In this example, it is a simple LED, but it can be any physical device such as a room lock that can be controlled via an actuator. If all works well, the LED will be turned on as a result of the smart contract function invocation as shown in the following picture:

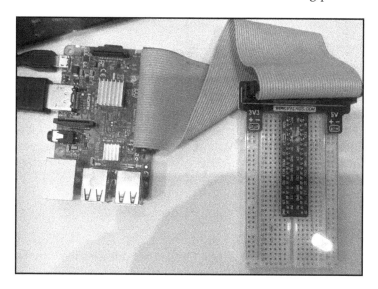

Raspberry Pi with LED control

Also, on node side it will display output similar to the one shown here:

```
$ node index.js
LED On
```

As demonstrated in the preceding example, a private network of IoT devices can be built that runs a `geth` client on each of the nodes and can listen for events from smart contracts and trigger an action accordingly. The example shown is simple on purpose but demonstrates the underlying principles of an Ethereum network that can be built using IoT devices along with smart contract-driven control of the physical devices.

In the next section, other applications of the blockchain technology in government, finance, and health will be discussed.

Government

There are various applications of blockchain being researched currently that can support government functions and take the current model of e-government to the next level. First, in this section, some background for e-government will be provided, and then a few use cases such as e-voting, homeland security (border control), and electronic IDs (citizen ID cards) will be discussed.

Government or electronic government is a paradigm where information and communication technology are used to deliver public services to citizens. The concept is not new and has been implemented in various countries around the world, but with blockchain, a new avenue of exploration has opened up. Many governments are researching the possibility of using blockchain technology for managing and delivering public services including but not limited to identity cards, driving licenses, secure data sharing among various government departments and contract management. Transparency, auditability, and integrity are attributes of blockchain that can go a long way in effectively managing various government functions.

Border control

Automated border control systems have been in use for decades now to thwart illegal entry into countries and prevent terrorism and human trafficking.

Machine-readable travel documents and specifically biometric passports have paved the way for automated border control; however current systems are limited to a certain extent and blockchain technology can provide solutions. A **Machine Readable Travel Document** (**MRTD**) standard is defined in document ICAO 9303 (`https://www.icao.int/publications/pages/publication.aspx?docnum=9303`) by the **International Civil Aviation Organization** (**ICAO**) and has been implemented by many countries around the world.

Each passport contains various security and identity attributes that can be used to identify the owner of the passport and also circumvent attempts at tampering with the passports. These include biometric features such as retina scan, fingerprints, facial recognition, and standard ICAO specified features including **Machine Readable Zone** (**MRZ**) and other text attributes that are visible on the first page of the passport.

One key issue with current border control systems is data sharing whereby the systems are controlled by a single entity and data is not readily shared among law enforcement agencies. This lack of the ability to share data makes it challenging to track suspected travel documents or individuals. Another issue is related to the immediate implementation of blacklisting of a travel document, for example, when there is an immediate need to track and control suspected travel documents. Currently, there is no mechanism available to blacklist or revoke a suspected passport immediately and broadcast it to the border control ports worldwide.

Blockchain can provide a solution to this problem by maintaining a blacklist in a smart contract which can be updated as required and any changes will be immediately visible to all agencies and border control points thus enabling immediate control over the movement of a suspected travel document. It could be argued that traditional mechanisms like PKIs and peer-to-peer networks can also be used for this purpose, but they do not provide the benefits that a blockchain can provide. With blockchain, the whole system can be simplified without the requirement of complex networks and PKI setups which will also result in cost reduction. Moreover, blockchain based systems will provide cryptographically guaranteed immutability which helps with auditing and discourages any fraudulent activity.

The full database of all travel documents perhaps cannot be stored on the blockchain currently due to scalability issues, but a backend distributed database such as BigchainDB, IPFS, or Swarm can be used for that purpose. In this case, a hash of the travel document with the biometric ID of an individual can be stored in a simple smart contract, and a hash of the document can then be used to refer to the detailed data available on the distributed filesystem such as IPFS. This way, when a travel document is blacklisted anywhere on the network, that information will be available immediately with the cryptographic guarantee of its authenticity and integrity throughout the distributed ledger. This functionality can also provide adequate support in anti-terrorism activities, thus playing a vital role in the homeland security function of a government.

A simple contract in Solidity can have an array defined for storing identities and associated biometric records. This array can be used to store the identifying information about a passport. The identity can be a hash of MRZ of the passport or travel document concatenated with the biometric record from the RFID chip. A simple Boolean field can be used to identify blacklisted passports. Once this initial check passes, further detailed biometric verification can be performed by traditional systems and eventually when a decision is made regarding the entry of the passport holder that decision can be propagated back to the blockchain, thus enabling all participants on the network to immediately share the outcome of the decision.

A high-level approach to building a blockchain-based border control system can be visualized as shown in the following diagram. In this scenario, the passport is presented for scanning to an RFID and page scanner which reads the data page and extracts machine-readable information along with a hash of the biometric data stored in the RFID chip. At this stage, a live photo and retina scan of the passport holder is also taken. This information is then passed on to the blockchain where a smart contract is responsible for verifying the legitimacy of the travel document by first checking its list of blacklisted passports and then requesting more data from the backend IPFS database for comparison. Note that the biometric data such as photo or retina scan is not stored on the blockchain, instead only a reference to this data in the backend (IPFS or BigchainDB) is stored in the blockchain.

If the data from the presented passport matches with what is held in the IPFS as files or in BigchainDB and also pass the smart contract logical check, then the border gate can be opened.

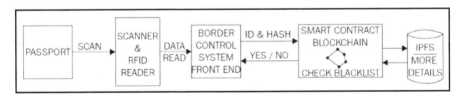

Automated border control using blockchain

After verification, this information is propagated throughout the blockchain and is instantly available to all participants on the border control blockchain. These participants can be a worldwide consortium of homeland security departments of various nations.

Voting

Voting in any government is a key function and allows citizens to participate in the democratic election process. While voting has evolved into a much more mature and secure process, it still has limitations that need to be addressed to achieve a desired level of maturity. Usually, the limitations in current voting systems revolve around fraud, weaknesses in operational processes, and especially transparency. Over the years, secure voting mechanisms (machines) have been built which make use of specialized voting machines that promised security and privacy, but they still had vulnerabilities that could be exploited to subvert the security mechanisms of those machines. These vulnerabilities can lead to serious implications for the whole voting process and can result in mistrust in the government by the public.

Blockchain-based voting systems can resolve these issues by introducing end-to-end security and transparency in the process. Security is provided in the form of integrity and authenticity of votes by using public key cryptography which comes as standard in a blockchain. Moreover, immutability guaranteed by blockchain ensures that votes cast once cannot be cast again. This can be achieved through a combination of biometric features and a smart contract maintaining a list of votes already cast. For example, a smart contract can maintain a list of already casted votes with the biometric ID (for example a fingerprint) and can use that to detect and prevent double casting. Secondly, **Zero-Knowledge Proofs** (**ZKPs**) can also be used on the blockchain to protect voters' privacy on the blockchain.

 Some companies are already providing such services, one example is `https://polys.me/blockchain/online-voting-system`. Recently, presidential elections were held in Sierra Leone using blockchain technology, making it the first country to use blockchain technology for elections (`https://www.coindesk.com/sierra-leone-secretly-holds-first-blockchain-powered-presidential-vote/`).

Citizen identification (ID cards)

Electronic IDs or national ID cards are issued by various countries around the world at present. These cards are secure and possess many security features that thwart duplication or tampering attempts. However, with the advent of blockchain technology, several improvements can be made to this process.

Digital identity is not only limited to just government-issued ID cards; it is a concept that applies to online social networks and forums too. There can be multiple identities used for different purposes. A blockchain-based online digital identity allows control over personal information sharing. Users can see who used their data and for what purpose and can control access to it. This is not possible with the current infrastructures which are centrally controlled. The key benefit is that a single identity issued by the government can be used easily and in a transparent manner for multiple services via a single government blockchain. In this case, the blockchain serves as a platform where a government is providing various services such as pensions, taxation, or benefits and a single ID is being used for accessing all these services. Blockchain, in this case, provides a permanent record of every change and transaction made by a digital ID, thus ensuring integrity and transparency of the system. Also, citizens can notarize birth certificates, marriages, deeds, and many other documents on the blockchain tied with their digital ID as a proof of existence.

Currently, there are successful implementations of identity schemes in various countries that work well, and there is an argument that perhaps blockchain is not required in identity management systems. Although there are several benefits such as privacy and control over the usage of identity information due to the current immaturity of blockchain technology, perhaps it is not ready for use in real-world identity systems. However, research is being carried out by various governments to explore the usage of blockchain for identity management.

Moreover, laws such as the right to be forgotten can be quite difficult to incorporate into blockchain due to its immutable nature.

Miscellaneous

Other government functions where blockchain technology can be implemented to improve cost and efficiency include the collection of taxes, benefits management and disbursement, land ownership record management, life event registration (marriages, births), motor vehicle registration, and licenses. This is not an exhaustive list, and over time many functions and processes of a government can be adapted to a blockchain-based model. The key benefits of blockchain such as immutability, transparency, and decentralization can help to bring improvements to most of the traditional government systems.

Health

The health industry has also been identified as another major industry that can benefit by adapting blockchain technology. Blockchain provides an immutable, auditable, and transparent system that traditional peer-to-peer networks cannot. Also, blockchain provides a cost-effective, simpler infrastructure as compared to traditional complex PKI networks. In healthcare, major issues such as privacy compromises, data breaches, high costs, and fraud can arise from lack of interoperability, overly complex processes, transparency, auditability, and control. Another burning issue is counterfeit medicines; especially in developing countries, this is a major cause of concern.

With the adaptability of blockchain in the health sector, several benefits can be realized, ranging from cost saving, increased trust, faster processing of claims, high availability, no operational errors due to complexity in the operational procedures, and preventing the distribution of counterfeit medicines.

From another angle, blockchains that are providing a digital currency as an incentive for mining can be used to provide processing power to solve scientific problems that can help to find cures for certain diseases. Examples include FoldingCoin, which rewards its miners with FLDC tokens for sharing their computer's processing power for solving scientific problems that require unusually large calculations.

 FoldingCoin is available at `http://foldingcoin.net/`.

Another similar project is called CureCoin which is available at `https://www.curecoin.net/`. It is yet to be seen that how successful these projects will be in achieving their goals but the idea is very promising.

Finance

Blockchain has many applications in the finance industry. Blockchain in finance is the hottest topic in the industry currently, and major banks and financial organizations are researching to find ways to adapt blockchain technology primarily due to its highly-desired potential to cost-save.

Insurance

In the insurance industry, blockchain technology can help to stop fraudulent claims, increase the speed of claim processing, and enable transparency. Imagine a shared ledger between all insurers that can provide a quick and efficient mechanism for handling intercompany claims. Also, with the convergence of IoT and blockchain, an ecosystem of smart devices can be imagined where all these things can negotiate and manage their insurance policies controlled by smart contracts on the blockchain.

Blockchain can reduce the overall cost and effort required to process claims. Claims can be automatically verified and paid via smart contracts and the associated identity of the insurance policyholder. For example, a smart contract with the help of Oracle and possibly IoT can make sure that when the accident occurred, it can record related telemetry data and based on this information can release payment. It can also withhold payment if the smart contract after evaluating conditions of payment concludes that payment should not be released. For example, in a scenario where an authorized workshop did not repair the vehicle or was used outside a designated area and so on and so forth. There can be many conditions that a smart contract can evaluate to process claims and choice of these rules depend on the insurer, but the general idea is that smart contracts in combination with IoT and Oracle can automate the entire vehicle insurance industry.

Several start-ups such as Dynamis have proposed smart contract-based peer-to-peer insurance platforms that run on Ethereum blockchain. This is initially proposed to be used for unemployment insurance and does not require underwriters in the model.

 It is available at `http://dynamisapp.com/`.

Post-trade settlement

This is the most sought-after application of blockchain technology. Currently, many financial institutions are exploring the possibility of using blockchain technology to simplify, automate, and speed up the costly and time-consuming post-trade settlement process.

To understand the problem better, the trade life cycle is described briefly. A trade life cycle contains three steps: execution, clearing, and settlement. Execution is concerned with the commitment of trading between two parties and can be entered into the system via front office order management terminals or exchanges. Clearing is the next step whereby the trade is matched between the seller and buyer based on certain attributes such as price and quantity. At this stage, accounts that are involved in payment are also identified. Finally, the settlement is where eventually the security is exchanged for payment between the buyer and seller.

In the traditional trade life cycle model, a central clearinghouse is required to facilitate trading between parties which bears the credit risk of both parties. The current scheme is somewhat complicated, whereby a seller and buyer have to take a complicated route to trade with each other. This comprises of various firms, brokers, clearing houses, and custodians but with blockchain, a single distributed ledger with appropriate smart contracts can simplify this whole process and can enable buyers and sellers to talk directly to each other.

Notably, the post-trade settlement process usually takes two to three days and has a dependency on central clearing houses and reconciliation systems. With the shared ledger approach, all participants on the blockchain can immediately see a single version of truth regarding the state of the trade. Moreover, the peer-to-peer settlement is possible, which results in the reduction of complexity, cost, risk, and the time it takes to settle the trade. Finally, intermediaries can be eliminated by making use of appropriate smart contracts on the blockchain. Also, regulators can also see view the blockchain for auditing and regulatory requirements.

This can be very useful in implementing MIFID-II regulation requirements (`https://www.fca.org.uk/markets/mifid-ii`).

Financial crime prevention

Know Your Customer (**KYC**), and **Anti Money Laundering** (**AML**) are the key enablers for the prevention of financial crime. In the case of KYC, currently, each institution maintains their own copy of customer data and performs verification via centralized data providers. This can be a time-consuming process and can result in delays in onboarding a new client.

Blockchain can provide a solution to this problem by securely sharing a distributed ledger between all financial institutions that contain verified and true identities of customers. This distributed ledger can only be updated by consensus between the participants thus providing transparency and auditability. This can not only reduce costs but also enable meeting regulatory and compliance requirements in a better and consistent manner.

In the case of AML, due to the immutable, shared, and transparent nature of blockchain, regulators, can easily be granted access to a private blockchain where they can fetch data for relevant regulatory reporting. This will also result in reducing complexity and costs related to the current regulatory reporting paradigm where data is fetched from various legacy and disparate systems and aggregated and formatted together for reporting purposes. Blockchain can provide a single shared view of all financial transactions in the system that are cryptographically secure, authentic, and auditable, thus reducing the costs and complexity associated with the currently employed regulatory reporting methods.

Media

Critical issues in the media industry revolve around content distribution, rights management, and royalty payments to artists. For example, digital music can be copied many times without any restriction and any attempts to apply copy protection have been hacked in some way or other. There is no control over the distribution of the content that a musician or songwriter produces; it can be copied as many times as needed without any restriction and consequently has an impact on the royalty payments. Also, payments are not always guaranteed and are based on traditional airtime figures. All these issues revolving around copy protection and royalty payments can be resolved by connecting consumers, artists, and all players in the industry, allowing transparency and control over the process. Blockchain can provide a network where digital music is cryptographically guaranteed to be owned only by the consumers who pay for it. This payment mechanism is controlled by a smart contract instead of a centralized media agency or authority. The payments will be automatically made based on the logic embedded within the smart contract and number of downloads.

 A recent example of such an initiative is Musicoin (`https://musicoin. org`).

Moreover, illegal copying of digital music files can be stopped altogether because everything is recorded and owned immutably in a transparent manner on the blockchain. A music file, for example, can be stored with owner information and timestamp which can be traced throughout the blockchain network. Furthermore, the consumers who own a legal copy of some content are cryptographically tied to the content they have, and it cannot be moved to another owner unless permissioned by the owner. Copyrights and transfers can be managed easily via blockchain once all digital content is immutably recorded on the blockchain. Smart contracts can then control the distribution and payment to all concerned parties.

Summary

There are many applications of blockchain technology, and as discussed in the chapter they can be implemented in various industries to bring about multiple benefits to existing solutions. In this chapter, five main industries that can benefit from blockchain have been discussed. First IoT was discussed, which is another revolutionary technology on its own; and by combining it with the blockchain, several fundamental limitations can be addressed, which brings about tremendous benefits to the IoT industry. More focus has been given to IoT as it is the most prominent and most ready candidate for adapting blockchain technology.

Already, practical use cases and platforms have emerged in the form of **Platform as a Service** (**PaaS**) for blockchain-based IoT such as the IBM Watson IoT blockchain. IBM Blue Horizon is also now available for experimentation, which is a decentralized blockchain-based IoT network. Second, applications in the government sector were discussed whereby various government processes such as homeland security, identification cards, and benefit disbursements can be made transparent, secure, and more robust.

Furthermore, issues in the finance sector were discussed with possible solutions that blockchain technology could provide. Although the finance sector is exploring the possibilities of using blockchain with high energy and enthusiasm, it is still far away from production-ready blockchain-based systems. Finally, some aspects of the health sector and music industry were also discussed. All these use cases and much more in the industry stand on pillars provided by core attributes of blockchain technology such as decentralization, transparency, reliability, and security. However, certain challenges need to be addressed before blockchain technology can be adapted fully; these will be discussed in the next chapter.

18
Scalability and Other Challenges

This chapter aims to provide an introduction to various challenges that need to be addressed before blockchains can become a mainstream technology. Even though various use cases and proof of concept systems have been developed and the technology works well for many of the scenarios, there still is a need to address some fundamental limitations that are present in blockchains in order to make this technology more adaptable.

At the top of the list of these issues comes scalability and then privacy. Both of these are important limitations to address, especially as blockchains are envisioned to be used in privacy-demanding industries too. There are specific requirements around confidentiality of transactions in finance, law, and health, whereas scalability is generally a concern where blockchains do not meet the adequate performance levels expected by the users. These two issues are becoming inhibiting factors toward blockchain technology's wider acceptance.

A review of currently proposed and ongoing research in these two specific areas will be presented throughout this chapter. In addition to privacy and security, other challenges include regulation, integration, adaptability, and security in general. Although, in Bitcoin blockchain security is bulletproof and has stood the test of time, there still are some caveats that may allow security to be compromised to an extent in some subtle scenarios. Also, there are some reasonable security concerns in other blockchains, such as Ethereum, regarding smart contracts, denial of service attacks, and large attack surface. All of these will be discussed in detail in the following sections.

Scalability

This problem has been a focus of intense debate, rigorous research, and media attention for the last few years.

This is the single most important problem that could mean the difference between wider adaptability of blockchains or limited private use only by consortiums. As a result of substantial research in this area, many solutions have been proposed, which are discussed in the following section.

From a theoretical perspective, the general approach toward tackling the scalability issue generally revolves around protocol-level enhancements. For example, a commonly mentioned solution to Bitcoin scalability is to increase its block size. Other proposals include off-chain solutions that offload certain processing to off-chain networks, for example, off-chain state networks. Based on the aforementioned solutions, generally, the proposals can be divided into two categories: **on-chain solutions** that are based on the idea of changing fundamental protocols on which the blockchain operates, and **off-chain solutions** that make use of network and processing resources off-chain in order to enhance the blockchain.

Another approach to addressing limitations in blockchains has been recently proposed by Miller and others in their position paper *On Scaling Decentralized Blockchains* available at https://doi.org/10.1007/978-3-662-53357-4_8. In this paper, it is shown that a blockchain can be divided into various abstract layers called **planes**. Each plane is responsible for performing specific functions. These include the network plane, consensus plane, storage plane, view plane, and side plane. This abstraction allows bottlenecks and limitations to be addressed at each plane individually and in a structured manner. A brief overview of each layer is given in the following subsections with some references to the Bitcoin system.

Network plane

First, the network plane is discussed. A key function of the network plane is transaction propagation. It has been identified in the aforementioned paper that in Bitcoin, this plane underutilizes the network bandwidth due to the way transaction validation is performed by a node before propagation and duplication of transaction propagation, first in the transaction broadcast phase, and then after mining in a block.

It should be noted that this issue was addressed by BIP 152 (*Compact Block Relay*, https://github.com/bitcoin/bips/blob/master/bip-0152.mediawiki).

Consensus plane

The second layer is called the consensus plane. This layer is responsible for mining and achieving consensus. Bottlenecks in this layer revolve around limitations in PoW algorithms whereby increasing consensus speed and bandwidth results in compromising the security of the network due to an increase in the number of forks.

Storage plane

The storage plane is the third layer, which stores the ledger. Issues in this layer revolve around the need for each node to keep a copy of the entire ledger, which leads to certain inefficiencies, such as increased bandwidth and storage requirements. Bitcoin has a method available called **pruning**, which allows a node to operate without the need to keep the full blockchain in its storage. Pruning means that when a Bitcoin node has downloaded the blockchain and validated it, it deletes the old data that it has already validated. This saves storage space. This functionality has resulted in major improvements from a storage point of view.

View plane

Next on the list is the view plane, which proposes an optimization which is based on the proposal that bitcoin miners do not need the full blockchain to operate, and a view can be constructed out of the complete ledger as a representation of the entire state of the system, which is sufficient for miners to function. Implementation of views will eliminate the need for mining nodes to store the full blockchain.

Finally, the side plane has been proposed by the authors of the aforementioned research paper. This plane represents the idea of off-chain transactions whereby the concept of payment or transaction channels is used to offload the processing of transactions between participants but is still backed by the main Bitcoin blockchain.

The aforementioned model can be used to describe limitations and improvements in current blockchain designs in a structured manner. Also, there are several general strategies that have been proposed over the last few years which can address the limitations in current blockchain designs such as Ethereum and Bitcoin. These approaches are also characterized and discussed individually in the following section.

Block size increase

This is the most debated proposal for increasing blockchain performance (transaction processing throughput). Currently, Bitcoin can process only about three to seven transactions per second, which is a major inhibiting factor in adapting the Bitcoin blockchain for processing microtransactions. Block size in Bitcoin is hardcoded to be 1 MB, but if the block size is increased, it can hold more transactions and can result in faster confirmation time. There are several **Bitcoin Improvement Proposals** (**BIPs**) made in favor of block size increase. These include BIP 100, BIP 101, BIP 102, BIP 103, and BIP 109.

An excellent account of historic references and discussion is available at `https://en.bitcoin.it/wiki/Block_size_limit_controversy`.

In Ethereum, the block size is not limited by hardcoding; instead, it is controlled by a gas limit. In theory, there is no limit on the size of a block in Ethereum because it's dependent on the amount of gas, which can increase over time. This is possible because miners are allowed to increase the gas limit for subsequent blocks if the limit has been reached in the previous block. Bitcoin SegWit has addressed this issue by separating witness data from transaction data which resulted in more space for transactions. Other proposals for Bitcoin include Bitcoin Unlimited, Bitcoin XT and Bitcoin Cash. Readers can refer back to `Chapter 5`, *Introducing Bitcoin*, for more details.

For more information refer to the following links:

- `https://www.bitcoinunlimited.info`
- `https://bitcoinxt.software`
- `https://www.bitcoincash.org`

Block interval reduction

Another proposal is to reduce the time between each block generation. The time between blocks can be decreased to achieve faster finalization of blocks but may result in less security due to the increased number of forks. Ethereum has achieved a block time of approximately 14 seconds.

This is a significant improvement from the Bitcoin blockchain, which takes 10 minutes to generate a new block. In Ethereum, the issue of high orphaned blocks resulting from smaller times between blocks is mitigated by using the **Greedy Heaviest Observed Subtree** (**GHOST**) protocol whereby orphaned blocks (uncles) are also included in determining the valid chain. Once Ethereum moves to **Proof of Stake** (**PoS**), this will become irrelevant as no mining will be required and almost immediate finality of transactions can be achieved.

Invertible Bloom Lookup Tables

This is another approach that has been proposed to reduce the amount of data required to be transferred between the Bitcoin nodes. **Invertible Bloom Lookup Tables** (**IBLTs**) were originally proposed by Gavin Andresen, and the key attraction in this approach is that it does not result in a hard fork of Bitcoin if implemented. The key idea is based on the fact that there is no need to transfer all transactions between nodes; instead, only those that are not already available in the transaction pool of the syncing node are transferred. This allows quicker transaction pool synchronization between nodes, thus increasing the overall scalability and speed of the Bitcoin network.

Sharding

Sharding is not a new technique and has been used in distributed databases for scalability such as MongoDB and MySQL. The key idea behind sharding is to split up the tasks into multiple chunks that are then processed by multiple nodes. This results in improved throughput and reduced storage requirements. In blockchains, a similar scheme is employed whereby the state of the network is partitioned into multiple shards. The state usually includes balances, code, nonce, and storage. Shards are loosely coupled partitions of a blockchain that run on the same network. There are a few challenges related to inter-shard communication and consensus on the history of each shard. This is an open area for research.

State channels

This is another approach proposed for speeding up the transaction on a blockchain network. The basic idea is to use side channels for state updating and processing transactions off the main chain; once the state is finalized, it is written back to the main chain, thus offloading the time-consuming operations from the main blockchain.

State channels work by performing the following three steps:

1. First, a part of the blockchain state is locked under a smart contract, ensuring the agreement and business logic between participants.
2. Now off-chain transaction processing and interaction is started between the participants that update the state only between themselves for now. In this step, almost any number of transactions can be performed without requiring the blockchain and this is what makes the process fast and a best candidate for solving blockchain scalability issues. However, it could be argued that this is not a real on-blockchain solution such as, for example, sharding, but the end result is a faster, lighter, and robust network which can prove very useful in micropayment networks, IoT networks, and many other applications.
3. Once the final state is achieved, the state channel is closed and the final state is written back to the main blockchain. At this stage, the locked part of the blockchain is also unlocked.

This process is shown in the following diagram:

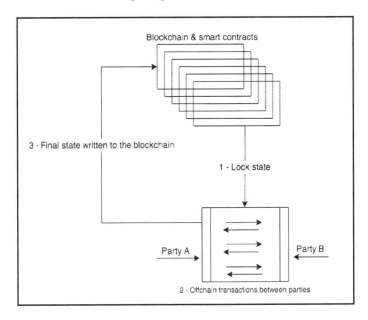

State channels

This technique has been used in the Bitcoin lightning network and Ethereum's Raiden.

Private blockchain

Private blockchains are inherently fast because no real decentralization is required and participants on the network do not need to mine; instead, they can only validate transactions. This can be considered as a workaround to the scalability issue in public blockchains; however, this is not the solution to the scalability problem. Also, it should be noted that private blockchains are only suitable in specific areas and setups such as enterprise environments where all participants are known.

Proof of Stake

Instead of using **Proof of Work** (**PoW**), PoS algorithm based blockchains are fundamentally faster. PoS was explained in greater detail in `Chapter 8`, *Alternative Coins*.

Sidechains

Sidechains can improve scalability indirectly by allowing many sidechains to run along with the main blockchain while allowing usage of perhaps comparatively less secure and faster sidechains to perform transactions but still pegged with the main blockchain. The core idea of sidechains is called a two-way peg, which allows transfer of coins from a parent chain to a sidechain and vice versa.

Subchains

This is a relatively new technique recently proposed by Peter R. Rizun which is based on the idea of weak blocks that are created in layers until a strong block is found. Weak blocks can be defined as those blocks that have not been able to be mined by meeting the standard network difficulty criteria but have done enough work to meet another weaker difficulty target. Miners can build subchains by layering weak blocks on top of each other unless a block is found that meets the standard difficulty target.

At this point, the subchain is closed and becomes the strong block. Advantages of this approach include reduced waiting time for the first verification of a transaction. This technique also results in a reduced chance of orphaning blocks and speeds up transaction processing. This is also an indirect way of addressing the scalability issue. Subchains do not require any soft fork or hard fork to implement but need acceptance by the community.

The subchains research paper is available at
`https://www.ledgerjournal.org/ojs/index.php/ledger/article/view/40`.

Tree chains (trees)

There are also other proposals to increase Bitcoin scalability, such as tree chains that change the blockchain layout from a linearly sequential model to a tree. This tree is basically a binary tree which descends from the main Bitcoin chain. This approach is similar to sidechain implementation, eliminating the need for major protocol change or block size increase. It allows improved transaction throughput. In this scheme, the blockchains themselves are fragmented and distributed across the network in order to achieve scalability.

Moreover, mining is not required to validate the blocks on the tree chains; instead, users can independently verify the block header. However, this idea is not ready for production yet and further research is required in order to make it practical.

The original idea was proposed in the research paper
`https://eprint.iacr.org/2016/545.pdf`.

In addition to the aforementioned general techniques, some Bitcoin-specific improvements have also been proposed by Christian Decker
(`https://scholar.google.ch/citations?user=ZaeGlZIAAAAJ&hl=en`) in his book *On the Scalability and Security of Bitcoin*. This proposal is based on the idea of speeding up propagation time as the current information propagation mechanism results in blockchain forks. These techniques include minimization of verification, pipelining of block propagation, and connectivity increase. These changes do not require fundamental protocol-level changes; instead, these changes can be implemented independently in the Bitcoin node software.

With regards to verification minimization, it has been noted that the block verification process is contributing toward propagation delay. The reason behind this is that a node takes a long time to verify the uniqueness of the block and transactions within the block. It has been suggested that a node can send the inventory message as soon as the initial PoW and block validation checks are completed. This way, propagation can be improved by just performing the first *difficulty check* and not waiting for transaction validation to finish.

Block propagation

In addition to the preceding proposal, pipelining of block propagation has also been suggested, which is based on the idea of anticipating the availability of a block. In this scheme, the availability of a block is already announced without waiting for actual block availability, thus reducing the round-trip time between nodes. Finally, the problem of long distances between transaction originator and nodes also contributes toward the slowdown of block propagation. It has been shown in the research conducted by Christian Decker that connectivity increase can reduce propagation delay of blocks and transactions. This is possible because, if at any one time the Bitcoin node is connected to many other nodes, it will result in reducing the distance between nodes and can speed up information propagation on the network.

An elegant solution to scalability issues will most likely be a combination of some or all of the aforementioned general approaches. A number of initiatives taken in order to address scalability and security issues in blockchains are now almost ready for implementation or already implemented. For example, Bitcoin **Segregated Witness** (**SegWit**) is a proposal that can help massively with scalability and only needs a soft fork in order for it to be implemented. The key idea behind so-called *SegWit* is to separate signature data from the transactions, which resolves the transaction malleability issue and allows block size increase, thus resulting in increased throughput.

Bitcoin-NG

Another proposal, Bitcoin-NG, which is based on the idea of microblocks and leader election, has gained some attention recently. The core idea is to split blocks into two types, namely leader blocks (also called key blocks) and microblocks:

- **Leader blocks**: These are responsible for PoW whereas microblocks contain actual transactions.
- **Micro blocks**: These do not require any PoW and are generated by the elected leader every block-generation cycle. This block-generation cycle is initiated by a leader block. The only requirement is to sign the microblocks with the elected leader's private key. The microblocks can be generated at a very high speed by the elected leader (miner), thus resulting in increased performance and transaction speed.

On the other hand, an Ethereum mauve paper written by Vitalik Buterin has been presented at Ethereum Devcon2 in Shanghai; it describes the vision of a scalable Ethereum. The mauve proposal is based on a combination of sharding and implementation of PoS algorithm. Certain goals such as efficiency gain via PoS, maximally fast block time, economic finality, scalability, cross-shard communication, and censorship resistance have been identified in the paper.

Mauve paper is available at `https://docs.google.com/document/d/1maFT3cpHvwn29gLvtY4WcQiI6kRbN_nbCf3JlgR3m_8/edit#`.

Plasma

Another recent scalability proposal is **Plasma**, which has been proposed by Joseph Poon and Vitalik Buterin. This proposal describes the idea of running smart contracts on root blockchain (Ethereum MainNet) and have child blockchains that perform high number of transactions to feedback small amounts of commitments to the parent chain. In this scheme, blockchains are arranged in a tree hierarchy with mining performed only on the root (main) blockchain which feeds the proofs of security down to child chains. This is also called a Layer-2 system, like state channels also operate on Layer 2, and not on the main chain.

 The research paper is available at `http://plasma.io`.

Privacy

Privacy of transactions is a much-desired property of blockchains. However, due to its very nature, especially in public blockchains, everything is transparent, thus inhibiting its usage in various industries where privacy is of paramount importance, such as finance, health, and many others. There are different proposals made to address the privacy issue and some progress has already been made. Several techniques, such as **Indistinguishability Obfuscation** (**IO**), usage of homomorphic encryption, ZKPs, and ring signatures.

All these techniques have their merits and demerits and are discussed in the following sections.

Indistinguishability Obfuscation

This cryptographic technique may serve as a silver bullet to all privacy and confidentiality issues in blockchains but the technology is not yet ready for production deployments. IO allows for code obfuscation, which is a very ripe research topic in cryptography and, if applied to blockchains, can serve as an unbreakable obfuscation mechanism that will turn smart contracts into a black box.

The key idea behind IO is what's called by researchers a *multilinear jigsaw puzzle*, which basically obfuscates program code by mixing it with random elements, and if the program is run as intended, it will produce expected output but any other way of executing would render the program look random and garbage. This idea was first proposed by Shai and others in their research paper *Candidate Indistinguishability Obfuscation and Functional Encryption for all circuits*.

 This research paper is available at `https://doi.org/10.1109/FOCS.2013.13`.

Homomorphic encryption

This type of encryption allows operations to be performed on encrypted data. Imagine a scenario where the data is sent to a cloud server for processing. The server processes it and returns the output without knowing anything about the data that it has processed. This is also an area ripe for research and fully homomorphic encryption that allows all operations on encrypted data is still not fully deployable in production; however, major progress in this field has already been made. Once implemented on blockchains, it can allow processing on ciphertext which will allow privacy and confidentiality of transactions inherently. For example, the data stored on the blockchain can be encrypted using homomorphic encryption and computations can be performed on that data without the need for decryption, thus providing privacy service on blockchains. This concept has also been implemented in a project named *Enigma* which is available online at (`https://www.media.mit.edu/projects/enigma/overview/`) by MIT's Media Lab. Enigma is a peer-to-peer network which allows multiple parties to perform computations on encrypted data without revealing anything about the data.

 Original research is available at `https://crypto.stanford.edu/craig/`.

Zero-Knowledge Proofs

ZKPs have recently been implemented in Zcash successfully, as seen in Chapter 8, *Alternative Coins*. More specifically, **SNARK** (short for **Succinct Non-Interactive Argument of Knowledge**) have been implemented in order to ensure privacy on the blockchain.

The same idea can be implemented in Ethereum and other blockchains also. Integrating Zcash on Ethereum is already a very active research project being run by the Ethereum R&D team and the Zcash Company.

 The original research paper is available at https://eprint.iacr.org/2013/879.pdf.
Another excellent paper is here
http://chriseth.github.io/notes/articles/zksnarks/zksnarks.pdf.

There is a recent addition to the family of ZKPs called **Zero-Knowledge Succinct Transparent Argument of Knowledge** (**ZK-STARKs**) which is an improvement on ZK-SNARKs in the sense that ZK-STARKs consume a lot less bandwidth and storage as compared to ZK-SNARKs. Also, they do not require the initial, somewhat controversial, trusted setup that is required for ZK-SNARKs. Moreover, ZK-STARKs are much quicker than ZK-SNARKs as they do not make use of elliptic curves and rely on hashes.

 The original research paper for ZK-STARKs is available here https://eprint.iacr.org/2018/046.pdf.

State channels

Privacy using state channels is also possible, simply due to the fact that all transactions are run off-chain and the main blockchain does not see the transaction at all except for the final state output, thus ensuring privacy and confidentiality.

Secure multiparty computation

The concept of secure multiparty computation is not new and is based on the notion that data is split into multiple partitions between participating parties under a secret sharing mechanism which then does the actual processing on the data without the need of the reconstructing data on a single machine. The output produced after processing is also shared between the parties.

Usage of hardware to provide confidentiality

Trusted computing platforms can be used to provide a mechanism by which confidentiality of transaction can be achieved on a blockchain, for example, by using Intel **Software Guard Extension** (**SGX**), which allows code to be run in a hardware-protected environment called an **enclave**. Once the code runs successfully in the isolated enclave, it can produce a proof called a **quote** that is attestable by Intel's cloud servers. However, it is a concern that trusting Intel will result in some level of centralization and is not in line with the true spirit of blockchain technology. Nevertheless, this solution has its merits and, in reality, many platforms already use Intel chips anyway, therefore trusting Intel may be acceptable by some in some cases.

If this technology is applied on smart contracts then, once a node has executed the smart contract, it can produce the quote as a proof of correct and successful execution and other nodes will only have to verify it. This idea can be further extended by using any **Trusted Execution Environment** (**TEE**) which can provide the same functionality as an enclave and is available even on mobile devices with **Near Field Communication** (**NFC**) and a secure element.

CoinJoin

CoinJoin is a technique which is used to anonymize the bitcoin transactions by mixing them interactively. The idea is based on forming a single transaction from multiple entities without causing any change in inputs and outputs. It removes the direct link between senders and receivers, which means that a single address can no longer be associated with transactions, which could lead to the identification of the users. CoinJoin needs cooperation between multiple parties that are willing to create a single transaction by mixing payments. Therefore, it should be noted that, if any single participant in the CoinJoin scheme does not keep up with the commitment made to cooperate for creating a single transaction by not signing the transactions as required, then it can result in a denial of service attack.

In this protocol, there is no need for a single trusted third party. This concept is different from mixing a service which acts as a trusted third party or intermediary between the bitcoin users and allows shuffling of transactions. This shuffling of transactions results in the prevention of tracing and the linking of payments to a particular user.

Confidential transactions

Confidential transactions make use of Pedersen commitments in order to provide confidentiality. Commitment schemes allow a user to commit to some value while keeping it secret with the capability of revealing it later. Two properties that need to be satisfied in order to design a commitment scheme are binding and hiding.

Binding makes sure that the committer is unable to change the chosen value once committed, whereas the **hiding** property ensures that any adversary is unable to find the original value to which the committer made a commitment. Pedersen commitments also allow addition operations and preserve commutative property on the commitments, which makes it specifically useful for providing confidentiality in bitcoin transactions. In other words, it supports homomorphic encryption of values. Using commitment schemes allows the hiding of payment values in a bitcoin transaction. This concept is already implemented in the Elements Project (`https://elementsproject.org/`).

MimbleWimble

The MimbleWimble scheme was proposed somewhat mysteriously on the Bitcoin IRC channel and since then has gained a lot of popularity. MimbleWimble extends the idea of confidential transactions and CoinJoin, which allows aggregation of transactions without requiring any interactivity. However, it does not support the use of Bitcoin scripting language along with various other features of standard Bitcoin protocol. This makes it incompatible with existing Bitcoin protocol. Therefore, it can either be implemented as a sidechain to Bitcoin or on its own as an alternative cryptocurrency.

This scheme can address privacy and scalability issues both at once. The blocks created using the MimbleWimble technique do not contain transactions as in traditional Bitcoin blockchains; instead, these blocks are composed of three lists: an input list, output list, and something called **excesses** which are lists of signatures and differences between outputs and inputs. The input list basically references to the old outputs, and the output list contains confidential transactions outputs. These blocks are verifiable by nodes by using signatures, inputs, and outputs to ensure the legitimacy of the block. In contrast to Bitcoin, MimbleWimble transaction outputs only contain pubkeys, and the difference between old and new outputs is signed by all participants involved in the transactions.

Security

Even though blockchains are generally secure and make use of asymmetric and symmetric cryptography as required throughout the blockchain network, there still are few caveats that can result in compromising the security of the blockchain.

There are a few examples of transaction malleability, eclipse attacks, and the possibility of double spending in bitcoin that, in certain scenarios, have been shown to work by various researchers. Transaction malleability opens up the possibility of double withdrawal or deposit by allowing a hacker to change a transaction's unique ID before the Bitcoin network can confirm it, resulting in a scenario where it would seem that transactions did not occur. BIP 62 is one of the proposals along with SegWit that have suggested solutions to solve this issue. It should be noted that this is a problem only in the case of unconfirmed transactions, that is, scenarios where operational processes rely on unconfirmed transactions. In the case of normal applications that only rely on confirmed transactions, this is not an issue.

Information eclipse attacks in Bitcoin can result in double spending. The idea behind eclipse attacks is that the Bitcoin node is tricked into connecting only with the attacker node IPs. This opens up the possibility of a 51 % attack by the attacker. This has been addressed to some extent in Bitcoin client v0.10.1.

Smart contract security

Recently, a lot of work has been started in smart contract security and, especially, formal verification of smart contracts is being discussed and researched. This was all triggered especially due to the infamous DAO hack.

Formal verification is a process of verifying a computer program to ensure that it satisfies certain formal statements. This is now a new concept and there are a number of tools available for other languages that achieve this; for example, Frama-C (`https://frama-c.com`) is available for analyzing C programs. The key idea behind formal verification is to convert the source program into a set of statements that is understandable by the automated provers.

For this purpose, Why3 (`http://why3.lri.fr`) is commonly used, and a formal verifier for Solidity also makes use of that. An experimental but operational verifier is available in browser Solidity already.

Smart contract security is of paramount importance now, and many other initiatives have also been taken in order to devise methods that can analyze Solidity programs and find bugs. A recent and seminal example is Oyente, which is a tool built by researchers and has been introduced in their paper *Making Smart Contracts Smarter*.

Oyente is available at `https://github.com/melonproject/oyente`.

Several security bugs in smart contracts have been discovered and analyzed in this paper. These include transaction ordering dependence, timestamp dependence, mishandled exceptions such as call stack depth limit exploitation, and reentrance vulnerability. The transaction ordering dependency bug basically exploits the scenarios where the perceived state of a contract might not be what the state of the contract changes to after execution.

This weakness is a type of race condition. It is also called frontloading and is possible due to the fact that the order of transactions within a block can be manipulated. As all transactions first appear in the memory pool, the transactions there can be monitored before they are included in the block. This allows a transaction to be submitted before another transaction, thus leading to controlling the behavior of a smart contract.

Timestamp dependency bugs are possible in scenarios where the timestamp of the block is used as a source of some decision-making within the contract, but timestamps can be manipulated by the miners. Call stack depth limit is another bug that can be exploited due to the fact that the maximum call stack depth of EVM is 1,024 frames. If the stack depth is reached while the contract is executing then, in certain scenarios, the send or call instruction can fail, resulting in non-payment of funds. The call stack depth bug was addressed in the EIP 50 hard fork `https://github.com/ethereum/EIPs/blob/master/EIPS/eip-150.md`.

The reentrancy bug was exploited in the DAO attack to siphon out millions of dollars into a child DAO. The reentrancy bug basically means that a function can be called repeatedly before the previous (first) invocation of the functions has completed. This is particularly unsafe in Ether withdrawal functions in Solidity smart contracts.

In addition to the aforementioned bugs, there are several other problems that should be kept in mind while writing contracts. These bugs include that fact that if sending funds to another contract, handle it carefully because send can fail and even if throw is used as a *catch-all* mechanism, it will not work.

Other standard software bugs such as integer overflow and underflow are also quite significant and any use of integer variables should be carefully implemented in Solidity. For example, a simple program where uint8 is used to parse through elements of an array with more than 255 elements can result in an endless loop. This occurs because uint8 is limited to 256 numbers.

In the following sections, two examples of contract verification will be shown using Remix IDE, Why3 and Oyente respectively.

Formal verification and analysis

Security analysis of Solidity code is now available as a feature in the solidity online IDE called Remix. The code is analyzed for vulnerabilities and reported in the **Analysis** tab of the remix IDE:

```
Security

  ☑ Transaction origin: Warn if tx.origin is used

  ☑ Check effects: Avoid potential reentrancy bugs

  ☑ Inline assembly: Use of Inline Assembly

  ☑ Block timestamp: Semantics maybe unclear

  ☑ Low level calls: Semantics maybe unclear

  ☑ Block.blockhash usage: Semantics maybe unclear

  ☑ Selfdestruct: Be aware of caller contracts.


Gas & Economy

  ☑ Gas costs: Warn if the gas requirements of functions are too high.

  ☑ This on local calls: Invocation of local functions via this


Miscellaneous

  ☑ Constant functions: Check for potentially constant functions

  ☑ Similar variable names: Check if variable names are too similar

  ☑ no return: Function with return type is not returning

  ☑ Guard Conditions: Use require and appropriately


    Run        Auto run


Potential Violation of Checks-Effects-Interaction pattern in <i>Fund.withdraw()</i>: Could    ✖
potentially lead to re-entrancy vulnerability.
more
```

Remix IDE analysis options

A sample output of the same contract with reentrancy bug is shown in the bottom of the preceding screenshot.

This tool analyzes several categories of vulnerabilities including, security, gas, and economy. As shown in the preceding screenshot the analysis tool has successfully detected the reentrancy bug, details of which are shown at the bottom of the screen.

Why3 can also be used for formally analyzing Solidity code.

 Why3 is available at `http://why3.lri.fr/try/`.

In the following example, a simple Solidity code that defines the z variable as the maximum limit of `uint` is shown. When this code runs, it will result in returning 0, because `uint z` will overrun and start again from 0. This can also be verified using Why3, which is shown here:

```
1  pragma solidity ^0.4.8;
2 ▾ contract Overflow {
3      uint z;
4 ▾    function x() returns (uint y) {
5          z = 2**256-1;
6          return z+1;
7      }
8  }
```

This tab provides support for formal verification of Solidity contracts.
This feature is still in development and thus also not yet well documented, but you can find some information here. The compiler generates input
Please paste the text below into http://why3.lri.fr/try/ to actually perform the verification. We plan to support direct integration in the future.

Solidity online compiler with formal verification

Conversion from Solidity to Why3 compliant code used to be available in Solidity online compiler but it is no longer available. Therefore, the following example is only for completeness purposes and to shed light on an important class of bugs which can go undetected with traditional tools. In this example, integer overflow is shown as an example.

The following example shows that Why3 successfully checks and reports integer overflow errors. This tool is under heavy development but is still quite useful. Also, this tool or any other similar tool is not a silver bullet. Even formal verification generally should not be considered a panacea because specifications in the first place should be defined appropriately:

```
27    use import mach.int.Unsigned
28    use import UInt256
29    exception Revert
30    exception Return
31    type state = {
32        mutable _z: uint256
33    }
34    type account = {
35        mutable balance: uint256;
36        storage: state
37    }
38    val external_call (this: account): bool
39        ensures { result = false -> this = (old this) }
40        writes { this }
41    let rec _x (this: account):
42            (uint256)
43        writes { this }
44        =
45        let prestate = {balance = this.balance; storage = {_z
46        let _y: ref uint256 = ref (of_int 0) in
47        try
48        begin
49            this.storage._z <- (of_int 1157920892373161954235
50            begin _y := (this.storage._z + (of_int 1)); raise
51        end;
```

Task list

- UInt256
- Address
- Contract_Overflow
- VC for _x
  - integer overflow
  - integer overflow
  - integer overflow
  - integer overflow (unknown)

Split and prove
- Prove (default)
- Prove (100 steps)
- Prove (1000 steps)
- Clean

Why3

Oyente tool

Currently, Oyente is available as a Docker image for easy testing and installation. It is available at `https://github.com/melonproject/oyente` and can be downloaded and tested.

In the following example, a simple contract taken from Solidity documentation that contains a reentrancy bug has been tested and it is shown that Oyente successfully analyzes the code and finds the bug:

```
1    pragma solidity ^0.4.0;
2 -  contract Fund {
3        mapping(address => uint) shares;
4 -      function withdraw() public {
5            if (msg.sender.call.value(shares[msg.sender])())
6                shares[msg.sender] = 0;
7        }
8    }
```

Contract with reentrancy bug, source: solidity documentation

This sample code contains a reentrancy bug which basically means that if a contract is interacting with another contract or transferring Ether, it is effectively handing over the control to that other contract. This allows the called contract to call back into the function of the contract from which it has been called without waiting for completion. For example, this bug can allow calling back into the withdraw function shown in the preceding example again and again, resulting in getting Ethers multiple times. This is possible because the share value is not set to 0 until the end of the function, which means that any later invocations will be successful, resulting in withdrawing again and again.

An example is shown of Oyente running to analyze the contract shown here and as can be seen in the following output, the analysis has successfully found the reentrancy bug. The bug is proposed to be handled by a combination of the Checks-Effects-Interactions pattern described in the solidity documentation:

```
                    root@fa9ef6ac8455: /home/oyente/oyente
(venv)root@fa9ef6ac8455:/home/oyente/oyente# python oyente.py a1.sol
Contract Fund:
Running, please wait...
            ============ Results ============
            CallStack Attack:       False
THIS IS A CALLLLLLLLLL
{'path_condition': [Iv >= 0, init_Is >= Iv, init_Ia >= 0, If(Id_0/
    2695994666715063979466701508701963067363714442254057248110361024921 ==
    1020253707,
    1,
    0) !=
0, Not(Iv != 0)], 'Is': Is, 'Iv': Iv, 'some_var_1': some_var_1, 'Id_0': Id
_0, 'Ia_store_some_var_1': Ia_store_some_var_1, 'Ia': Ia}

 This is the global state
{'Ia': {'some_var_1': 0}, 'miu_i': 3L, 'balance': {'Ia': init_Ia + Iv, 'Is
': init_Is - Iv}}
{64: 96, 0: Is & 14615016373309029182036848327162830196559325429 75, 32: 0}

CALL params

Is & 14615016373309029182036848327162830196559325429 75

Ia_store_some_var_1


=>>>>>> New PC: []

Reentrancy_bug? True

Added True
            Concurrency Bug:        False
            Time Dependency:        False
            Reentrancy bug exists:  True
            ====== Analysis Completed ======
(venv)root@fa9ef6ac8455:/home/oyente/oyente# █
```

Oyente tool detecting solidity bugs

Oyente is also available in analysis tools for smart contacts at `https://oyente.melon.fund`. A sample output is shown here.

With this example, we conclude our introduction to security and analysis tools for solidity. This is a very rich area of research and more and more tools are expected to be available with time.

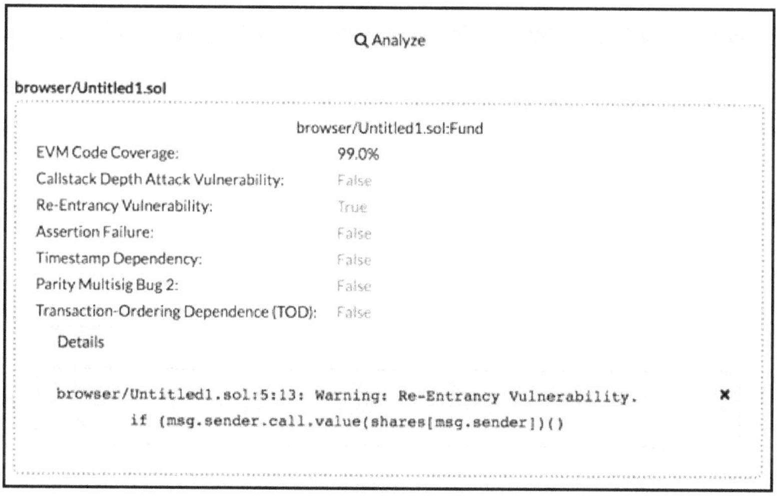

Oyente analysis

Summary

In this chapter, readers have been introduced to the security, confidentiality, and privacy aspects of blockchain technology. Privacy was discussed, which is another major inhibiting factor in adapting public blockchains for various industries. Next, smart contract security, which is a very hot topic currently, was discussed. It is a deep and extensive subject but a brief introduction on various aspects has been given, which should serve as a solid ground for further research in this area.

For example, formal verification on its own is a vast area for research. Furthermore, examples of formal verification have also been provided to give readers an idea of what tools are available. It should be noted that the tools mentioned earlier are under heavy development and lack various desirable features. Also, documentation is quite scarce; therefore, readers are encouraged to keep an eye on developments, especially around formal verification and developments related to the Ethereum mauve paper, as it is going to develop rapidly very soon. The field of blockchain security and especially smart contract security is so ripe now that a whole book can be written on the subject.

There are many experts and researchers in academia and the commercial sector exploring this area and soon there will be many automated tools available for the verification of smart contracts. There is an online tool available already at `https://securify.ch` which analyses smart contract code to find security vulnerabilities.

19
Current Landscape and What's Next

Blockchain technology is changing and will continue to change the way we conduct our day-to-day business. It has challenged existing business models and has the promise of great benefits regarding cost saving, and greater efficiency and transparency. This chapter will explore the latest developments, emerging trends, issues, and future predictions about this technology.

We finish this book by presenting some topics related to open research problems and improvements related to blockchain technology.

Emerging trends

Blockchain technology is under rapid change and intense development due to the deep interest in it by academics and the commercial sector. As the technology is becoming mature, a few trends have started to emerge recently. For example, private blockchains have recently gained quite a lot of attention due to their specific use cases in finance. Also, enterprise blockchains are another new trend that is aiming to develop blockchain solutions that meet enterprise-level efficiency, security, and integration requirements. Some of the trends are listed here and discussed.

Application-specific blockchains (ASBCs)

Currently, an inclination toward ASBCs is noticed, whereby a blockchain or distributed ledger is specially developed for only one application in mind and is focused on a specific industry, for example, Everledger, (`https://www.everledger.io`) which is a blockchain that has been developed to be used for providing an immutable tracing history and audit trail for diamonds and other high-value items. This approach thwarts any fraud attempts because everything related to ownership, authenticity, and value of the items is verified and recorded on the blockchain. This result is precious for insurance and law enforcement agencies.

Enterprise-grade blockchains

As blockchains in their original form are not ready for use at enterprise level due to privacy and scalability issues, a recent trend in developing enterprise-grade blockchains has emerged, whereby various companies have started to provide enterprise-grade blockchain solutions that are ready to be deployed and integrated at an enterprise level. Requirements such as testing, documentation, integration, and security are all addressed already in this type of solution and can be implemented with minimal or no change at the enterprise level.

This concept is in contrast to public blockchains, which are unregulated and do not meet specific enterprise-level security requirements. This also implies that enterprise-grade blockchains are usually supposed to be implemented in private configurations; however, public enterprise-grade blockchain implementation is also a possibility. In recent years, many technology start-ups have started to offer enterprise-grade blockchain solutions such as Bloq, Tymlez, Chain, Colu, ChainThat, ChromaWay and many others. This trend continues to grow, and years to come will see more technology initiatives like this.

Private blockchains

With the need for privacy and confidentiality, a major focus is on developing private distributed ledgers that can be used within a group of trusted participants. As public blockchains, due to their open and comparatively less secure nature, are not suitable for industries such as finance, medicine, and law, private blockchains hold the promise to address this limitation and bring end users one step closer to reaping the benefits of blockchains while meeting all security and privacy requirements.

Public blockchains are less secure because generally, they do not provide privacy and confidentiality services. Private blockchains allow the participants or a subset of participants to be in full control of the system, thus making it desirable for use in finance and other industries where privacy and control are required.

Ethereum can be used in both private and public modes, whereas there are a few projects that have been developed solely as private blockchains, such as Hyperledger and Corda. We discussed both of these in `Chapter 15`, *Hyperledger*.

Start-ups

In recent years, many technology start-ups have emerged that are working on blockchain projects and are offering solutions specific to this technology. There is a significant increase in the number of start-ups that are offering blockchain consultancy and solutions.

 You can visit the link `https://angel.co/blockchains`, which currently shows a list of 1927 blockchain start-ups.

Strong research interest

Blockchain technology has stimulated intense research interest both in academia and the commercial sector. In recent years, the interest has dramatically increased, and now major institutions and researchers around the world are exploring this technology. This growth in interest is primarily because blockchain technology can help to make businesses efficient, reduce costs, and make things transparent. Academic interest is around addressing hard problems in cryptography, consensus mechanisms, performance, and addressing other limitations in blockchains.

As blockchain technology comes under the broader umbrella of distributed systems, many researchers from distributed computing research have focused their research on blockchain technology. For example, UCL has a dedicated department, the UCL Research Centre for Blockchain Technologies, which focuses on blockchain technology research.

Another example is the ETH Zurich distributed computing group (`https://disco.ethz.ch`) that has published seminal research regarding blockchain technology. A recent journal called the *Ledger Journal* has recently published its first issue of research papers.

It is available at http://www.ledgerjournal.org/ojs/index.php/ledger.

There are now teams and departments dedicated to blockchain research and development in various academic and commercial institutes.

Although the initiatives mentioned here are not an exhaustive list by any stretch of the imagination, it is still a solid indication that this is a subject of extreme interest for researchers, and more research and development is expected to be seen in 2018 and beyond. Another organization called **The Initiative for Cryptocurrencies & Contracts** (**IC3**), is also researching smart contract and blockchain technologies. IC3 aims to address performance, confidentiality, and safety issues in blockchains and smart contracts and runs multiple projects to address these issues.

More information about projects running in IC3 is available online at http://www.initc3.org/.

Standardization

Blockchain technology is not yet mature enough to be able to integrate with existing systems readily. Even, as the current technology stands, two blockchain networks cannot easily talk to each other. Standardization will help to improve **interoperability**, **adaptability**, and **integration** aspects of blockchain technology. Some attempts have been made recently to address this, and the most notable out of these attempts is the establishment of ISO/TC 307, which is a technical committee with the scope of standardizing blockchain and distributed ledger technology.

The aim of the committee revolves around increasing interoperability and data interchange between users, applications, and systems. On the other hand, the recent creation of consortia and open source collaborative efforts such as R3 and Hyperledger has helped with standardization of this technology by sharing ideas, tools, and code with other participants. R3 works with a consortium of more than 80 banks that all have similar goals, which in a way results in standardization. Hyperledger, on the other hand, has a reference architecture that can be used to build blockchain systems and is supported by the Linux Foundation and many other participants from the industry.

Another example is the open chain standard, which is a protocol developed for financial networks. The chain OS1 standard is already available, which was built in collaboration with major financial institutions around the world. This standard allows faster settlement of transactions and direct peer-to-peer transaction routing. It aims to address regulatory, security, and privacy requirements in blockchain technologies. OS1 also provides a framework for smart contract development and allows the participant to meet AML and KYC requirements easily.

Smart contract standardization efforts have also started with a seminal paper authored by Lee and others, which formally defines the smart contract templates and presents a vision for future research and necessities in smart contract related research and development.

 This paper is available at `https://arxiv.org/abs/1608.00771v2`.

Moreover, some discussion on this topic has been carried out in `Chapter 18`, *Scalability and Other Challenges* and `Chapter 9`, *Smart Contracts*.

All of the efforts mentioned here are a clear indication that very soon, standards will emerge in the industry that will further make adoption of blockchain technology easier and quicker. Standards will also result in exponential growth of the blockchain industry because the availability of standards will eliminate hurdles such as interoperability.

Enhancements

Various enhancements and suggestions to further develop existing blockchains have been made over the last few years. Most of these suggestions have been made in response to security vulnerabilities and to address inherent limitations in blockchain technology. There are certain limitations in blockchain technology, such as scalability, privacy, and interoperability, that are required to be addressed before it can become mainstream like any other technology.

Recently, there have been tremendous efforts made toward addressing scalability issues in blockchain technology, which have been discussed in `Chapter 18`, *Scalability and Other Challenges*. Also, blockchain-specific improvement proposals such as **BIPs** (short for **Bitcoin Improvement Proposals**) and **EIPs** (short for **Ethereum Improvement Proposals**) are regularly made by developers to address various concerns in these systems.

Some recent and notable improvement proposals for both of these chains will be discussed later in the chapter. Moreover, recent advancements such as state channels are examples that blockchain technology is improving rapidly and very soon will evolve as a mature and more practical technology.

Real-world implementations

Many proofs of concept have been developed in recent years, especially in 2017, using blockchain technology. A few application-specific implementations emerged, such as Everledger for diamond tracking and filament for the IoT but are still lacking in various areas.

This seems not too far now as many proofs of concept have already been developed and proved to work; the next stage is to implement these in real-life scenarios. For example, recently, a group of seven banks agreed to build a **Digital Trade Chain** (**DTC**) that will simplify the trade finance process.

DTC related information is available at `http://www.bankingtech.com/2017/10/ibm-and-eight-banks-unleash-we-trade-platform-for-blockchain-powered-commerce/`.

Concrete, real-life, end-to-end implementations are also now becoming available, even in finance industry such as **Australian Securities Exchange** (**ASX**) replacing it legacy post trade system with blockchain.

The information regarding this project from ASX is available at `https://www.asx.com.au/services/chess-replacement.htm`.

Consortia

In recent years there has been various consortia and shared open source efforts started. This trend is expected to grow in the coming years, and more and more consortia, committees, and open source efforts will emerge soon. A prime example is R3, which has developed Corda with a consortium of the world's largest financial organizations.

Answers to technical challenges

Already, due to intense research effort and interest from the community in blockchain technology, answers to various challenges have started to emerge. For example, the concept of state channels has been developed as a response to scalability and privacy issues on the blockchain. Using state channels, the Bitcoin lightning network and Ethereum's Raiden are already almost ready for implementation.

 This is work in progress, however and updates are available here `https://github.com/raiden-network/raiden/milestones`.

Moreover, various blockchain solutions emerged, such as Kadena, that directly addressed the confidentiality issues in blockchains. Other concepts such as Zcash, CoinJoin, and confidential transactions have also been developed and were discussed in `Chapter 8`, *Alternative Coins*. This trend will also continue to grow in years to come, and even if almost all fundamental challenges are addressed in blockchain technology, further enhancement and optimization will never stop.

Convergence

Convergence of other technologies with blockchains brings about major benefits. At their core, blockchains provide resilience, security, and transparency, which, when combined with other technologies, results in a very powerful technology that complements each other. For example, the IoT can gain major benefits when implemented via blockchains, such as integrity, decentralization, and scalability. **Artificial Intelligence** (**AI**) is expected to gain benefits from blockchain technology, and in fact, within blockchain technology, AI can be implemented in the form of **Autonomous Agents** (**AAs**). More examples and the aforementioned converging technologies would be discussed in detail in later sections in the chapter.

Education of blockchain technology

While blockchain technology has spurred a great interest among technologists, developers, and scientists throughout almost every industry around the world, there is a lack of formal learning resources and educational material. As this is a new technology, various courses are now being offered by various reputed institutions such as Princeton University that introduce the technology to anyone who wants to learn about this technology.

For example, Princeton University has started a cryptocurrency and digital currencies course that is delivered online (`https://online.princeton.edu/course/bitcoin-and-cryptocurrency-technologies`). Many private organizations are also offering similar online and classroom training courses. More efforts like this will be seen soon due to the popularity and acceptance of blockchain technology.

Employment

There is a recent trend emerging in the job market whereby recruiters are now looking for blockchain experts and developers who can program for blockchains. This is especially relevant to the financial industry, and recently many start-ups and large organizations have started to hire blockchain specialists. This trend is of course expected to grow as the technology gains more acceptance and maturity. There is also concern about the lack of blockchain developers, which undoubtedly will be addressed as the technology progresses and more and more developers either gain experience on a self-learning basis or gain formal training from some training providers.

Cryptoeconomics

New fields of research are emerging with blockchains, most notably, cryptoeconomics, which is the study of protocols governing the decentralized digital economy. With the advent of blockchains and cryptocurrencies, research in this area has also grown. Cryptoeconomics has been defined as a combination of mathematics, cryptography, economics, and game theory by Vitalik Buterin.

 There is an excellent presentation available at `https://vitalik.ca/files/intro_cryptoeconomics.pdf`.

Research in cryptography

Even though cryptography was an area of keen interest and research for many decades before Bitcoin invention, blockchain technology has resulted in renewed interest in this field. With the advent of blockchains and related technologies, there is a significant increase in the interest in cryptography also. Especially in the area of financial cryptography, new research is being carried out and published regularly.

Technologies such as ZKPs, fully homomorphic encryption, and functional encryption are being researched for their use in blockchains. In the form of Zcash, already ZKPs have been implemented for the first time at a practical level. It can be seen that blockchains and cryptocurrencies have helped with the advancement of cryptography and especially financial cryptography.

New programming languages

There is also an increased interest in the development of programming languages for developing smart contracts. The efforts are more focused on domain-specific languages, for example, Solidity for Ethereum and Pact for Kadena. This is just a start, and many new languages are likely to be developed as the technology advances.

Hardware research and development

When it was realized in 2010 that current methods are not efficient for mining bitcoins, miners started shifting toward optimizing mining hardware. These initial efforts included usage of GPUs, and then **Field-Programmable Gate Arrays** (**FPGAs**) were used after GPUs reached their limit. Very quickly after that, **Application-Specific Integrated Circuits** (**ASICs**) emerged, which increased the mining power significantly. This trend is expected to grow further as now there is more research into further optimizing ASICs by parallelizing and decreasing the die size.

Moreover, GPU programming initiatives are also expected to grow because new cryptocurrencies are emerging quite regularly now and many of them make use of PoW algorithms that can benefit from GPU processing capabilities. For example, recently Zcash has spurred interest in GPU mining rigs and related programming using NVIDIA CUDA and OpenCL. The aim is to use multiple GPUs in parallel for optimizing mining operations. Also, some research has been in the field of using trusted computing hardware such as Intel's **Software Guard Extensions** (**SGX**) to address security issues on blockchains. Also, Intel's SGX has been used in a novel consensus algorithm called **Proof of Elapsed Time** (**PoET**) which has been discussed in `Chapter 15`, *Hyperledger*. Another project, the 21 Bitcoin Computer, was developed, which serves as a platform for developers to learn Bitcoin technology and easily develop applications for the Bitcoin platform.

The hardware research and development trend are expected to continue, and soon many more hardware scenarios will be explored.

Research in formal methods and security

With the realization of security issues and vulnerabilities in smart contract programming languages, there is now a keen interest in the formal verification and testing of smart contracts before production deployments. For this, various efforts are already underway, including Why3 for Ethereum's Solidity. Hawk is another example that has been developed to allow smart contract confidentiality.

Alternatives to blockchains

As the blockchain technology advanced in recent years, researchers started to think about the possibility of creating platforms that can provide guarantees and services which a blockchain provides but without the need for a blockchain. This has resulted in development of R3's Corda, which in fact is not really a blockchain because it is not based on the concept of blocks containing transactions; instead, it is based on the concept of a state object that transverses throughout the Corda network according to the requirements and rules of the network participants representing the latest state of the network. Other examples include IOTA, which is an IoT blockchain which makes use of a **Directed Acyclic Graph** (**DAG**) as a distributed ledger named Tangle, instead of conventional blockchain with blocks. This ledger is claimed to have addressed scalability issues along with high-level security which even protects against quantum computing based attacks. It should be noted that Bitcoin is also somewhat protected against quantum attacks because the quantum attacks can only work on exposed public keys which are only revealed on the blockchain if both send and receive transactions are made. If the public key is not revealed, which is the case in unused addresses or the addresses that may have only used to receive bitcoins, then quantum safety can be guaranteed. In other words, using a different address for each transaction protects against quantum attacks. Also, in Bitcoin, it is quite easy to change to another quantum signature protocol if required.

Interoperability efforts

Recent realization of limitations around interoperability of blockchains has resulted in the development of systems that can work across multiple blockchains. A recent example is Qtum, which is a blockchain that is compatible with both Ethereum and Bitcoin blockchains. It makes use of Bitcoin's UTXO mechanism for transfer of value and an EVM for smart contracts. This means that Ethereum projects can be ported onto Qtum without requiring any change.

Blockchain as a Service

With the current level of maturity of cloud platforms, many companies have started to provide **Blockchain as a Service** (**BaaS**). The most prominent examples are Microsoft's Azure, where Ethereum blockchain is provided as a service, and IBM's Bluemix platform, that provides IBM BaaS. This trend is only expected to grow in the next few years, and more companies will emerge that provide BaaS. **Electronic Government as a Service** (**eGaaS**) is another example which is, in fact, BaaS but provides application-specific blockchains for governance functions (http://egaas.org). This project aims to organize and control any activity without document circulation and bureaucratic overhead.

Efforts to reduce electricity consumption

It is evident from Bitcoin's blockchain that the PoW mechanism is very inefficient. Of course, this computation secures the Bitcoin network but there is no other benefit of this computation, and it wastes much electrical energy. To reduce this waste, now there is more focus on greener options such as PoS algorithms which do not need enormous resources like Bitcoin's PoW algorithm. This trend is expected to grow, especially with PoS planned for Ethereum.

Other challenges

Apart from security and privacy, discussed in Chapter 18, *Scalability and Other Challenges*, several other hurdles should be addressed before the mainstream adoption of blockchains can be realized. These include regulation, government control, immature technology, integration with existing systems, and implementation costs.

Regulation

Regulation is considered one of the most significant challenges that need to be addressed. The core issue is that blockchains and especially cryptocurrencies are not recognized as a legal currency by any government. Even though in some cases, it has been classified as money in the US and Germany, it is still far from being accepted as a regular currency. Moreover, blockchains in their current state are not recognized as a platform that can be used by financial institutions. No financial regulatory body has yet accepted it as a platform that can be authorized to be used.

There are, however, various initiatives taken by regulatory authorities around the world to research and propose regulations. Bitcoin in its current state is fully unregulated, even though some attempts have been made by governments to tax the bitcoin. In the UK, under the EU VAT directive, bitcoin transactions are exempt from **Value Added Tax** (**VAT**), but this may change after Brexit. However, **Capital Gains Tax** (**CGT**) may still be applicable in some scenarios.

Some regulation attempt is expected very soon from financial regulatory authorities generally regarding blockchain technology, especially after the recent announcement by the **Financial Conduct Authority** (**FCA**) in the UK that it may approve some companies that are using blockchain.

It is a general concern that the blockchain technology is not ready for production deployments. Even though the Bitcoin blockchain has evolved into a solid blockchain platform and is used in production, it is not suitable for every scenario. This is especially true in the case of sensitive environments such as finance and health. However, this situation is changing very quickly and we've already seen in this chapter various examples of new blockchain projects, that have been implemented in real life such as ASX blockchain post trade solution. This trend is expected to grow as ample efforts discussed previously in this chapter are being made to improve the technology and address any technical limitations such as scalability and privacy.

Security is also another general concern which has been highlighted by many researchers and is especially applicable to the finance and health sectors. A report by the **European Union Agency for Network and Information Security** (**ENISA**) has highlighted distributed ledger specific concerns that should be addressed.

 The report is available at `https://www.enisa.europa.eu/news/enisa-news/enisa-report-on-blockchain-technology-and-security`.

Some concerns highlighted in the report include smart contract management, key management, **Anti Money Laundering** (**AML**), and anti-fraud tools. Also, the need for **regulation**, **audit**, **control**, and **governance** has been highlighted in the report.

Integration with existing legacy systems is also a prime concern. It is not clear how blockchains can be integrated with the existing financial systems.

Hurdles toward adoption are more or less related to regulatory, security, and interoperability. Integration with existing systems can be carried out in several ways.

Dark side

With the key attributes of censorship resistance and decentralization, blockchain technology can help to improve transparency and efficiency in many walks of life, but this somewhat unregulated nature of this technology means that it can be used by criminals for illegal activities too. For example, compare a scenario where if some illegal content is published over the internet it can be immediately shut down by approaching the concerned authorities and website service providers, but this is not possible in blockchains.

Once something is there on the blockchain, it is almost impossible to revert it. This means that any unacceptable content, once published on the blockchain, cannot be removed. If the blockchain is used for distributing immoral content, then there is no way for anyone to shut it down. This poses a serious challenge and it seems that some regulation and control is beneficial in this scenario, but how can a blockchain be regulated? That is another critical question. It may not be prudent to create the regulatory laws first and then see if blockchain technology adapts to that because it might disrupt innovation and progress in this technology. It would be more sensible to let the blockchain technology grow first, just like the internet and when it reaches a critical mass then governing bodies can call for applying some regulation around the implementation and usage of blockchain technology.

There are various examples where the Dark Web is used in conjunction with bitcoin to perform illegal activities. For example, Silk Road, which was used to sell illegal drugs over the internet, used bitcoins for payments and the Dark Web using onion URLs which are only visible with Tor. Although Silk Road was shut down after months of effort by law enforcement agencies, new similar sites started to emerge. Now, other alternatives are available that similar offer services; as such, generally, this type of problem remains a big concern.

Imagine that an illegal website is on IPFS and a blockchain; there is no easy way of shutting it down. It is clear that absence of control and regulation can encourage criminal activity and similar issue like Silk Road will keep arising. Further development of totally anonymous transaction capabilities such as Zcash could provide another layer of protection for criminals but at the same time may be quite useful in various legitimate scenarios. It depends on that who is using the technology; anonymity can be good in many scenarios, for example in the health industry where patient records should be kept private and anonymous but may not be appropriate if it can also be used by criminals to hide their activities.

One solution might be to introduce intelligent bots or AAs or even contracts that are programmed with regulatory logic embedded within them. They are most likely to be programmed by regulators and law enforcement agencies and live on the blockchain as a means to provide governance and control. For example, a blockchain could be designed in such a way that every smart contract has to go through a controller contract that scrutinizes the code logic and provides a regulatory mechanism to control the behavior of the smart contract.

It may also be possible to get each smart contract's code to be inspected by regulatory authorities, and once a smart contract code has a certain level of authenticity attached to it in the form of certificates issued by a regulator, it can be deployed on the blockchain network. This concept of binary signing is akin to the concept of the already established concept of code signing whereby executables are digitally signed as a means to confirm that the code is bona fide and is not malicious. This idea is more applicable in the context of semiprivate or regulated blockchains, where a certain degree of control is required by a regulatory authority, for example, in finance. It means that there is some degree of trust required to be placed in a trusted third party (regulator) which may not be desirable due to deviation from the concept of full decentralization. However, to address this, the blockchain itself can be used to provide a decentralized, transparent, and secure certificate issuance and digital signing mechanism.

Blockchain research

While major innovations have been made in blockchain technology in recent years, the area is still very ripe for further research. Some selected research topics are listed as follows with some information about existing challenges and state of the art. Some ideas are also presented in the following subsections on how to address these issues.

Smart contracts

Significant progress has been made in this area to define the key requirements of smart contracts and development of templates. However, further research is required in the area of making smart contracts more secure and safe.

Centralization issues

This is true for especially Bitcoin mining centralization, there is a growing concern about how Bitcoin can be decentralized again.

Limitations in cryptographic functions

Cryptography used in the Bitcoin blockchain is exceptionally secure and has stood the test of time. In other blockchains, similar security techniques are used and are also very secure. However, specific security issues such as the possibility of generation and usage of duplicate signature nonces in elliptic curve digital signature schemes (leading to private key recovery attack), collisions in hash functions, and a possibility of quantum attacks that may break the underlying cryptographic algorithms remain an exciting area of research.

Consensus algorithms

Research in PoS algorithms or alternatives to PoW is also an important area of research. This is especially relevant due to the fact the current Bitcoin network's power consumption is expected to reach almost 125 TWh by the end of 2018. Currently it is almost equivalent to the country of Israel in terms of electricity consumption. It has also been suggested that instead of performing an inefficient or single-purpose type of work as is the case with Bitcoin's PoW, the network power can be used to solve some mathematical or scientific problems. Also, alternatives such as PoS algorithms have already gained much traction and are due to be implemented in major blockchains, for example, Ethereum's Casper. However, so far, PoW remains the best option for securing a public blockchain.

Scalability

A detailed discussion has already been carried out on scalability in `Chapter 18`, *Scalability and Other Challenges*; briefly, it is sufficient to say in this section that while some progress has already been made, still there is a need for more research to enable on-chain scalability and further improve off-chain solutions such as state channels. Some initiatives like block size increase and transaction-only blockchains (without blocks) have been proposed to address scalability issues that increase the capacity of the blockchain itself instead of using side channels. Examples of without blocks implementation include IOTA (Tangle). It is a DAG which is used to store transactions as compared to traditional blockchain solutions where a block is used to store transactions. This makes it inherently faster as compared to block-based blockchains such as Bitcoin where waiting time between block generations is at least approximately 10 minutes.

Code obfuscation

Code obfuscation by using indistinguishability obfuscation can be used as a means to provide confidentiality and privacy in the blockchain. However, this is still not practical, and major research effort is required to achieve this.

Notable projects

Following is a list of notable projects in the blockchain space that is currently in progress. In addition to these projects, there is also a myriad of start-ups and companies working in the blockchain space and offering blockchain-related products.

Zcash on Ethereum

A recent project by the Ethereum R&D team is the implementation of Zcash on Ethereum. This is an exciting project whereby developers are trying to create a privacy layer for Ethereum using ZK-SNARKs already used in Zcash project. With Zcash implementation on Ethereum, the aim is to create a platform that allows applications such as voting where privacy is of paramount importance.

It will also allow the creation of anonymous tokens on Ethereum that can be used in a number of applications.

CollCo

This is a project developed by Deutsche Borse which is based on the Hyperledger code base and is used for managing commercial bank cash transfers. **Collateralized Coin** (**CollCo**) provides a blockchain-based platform that allows real-time transfer of commercial bank money while still relying on traditional capabilities provided by Eurex Clearing CCP. This is a major project that can be used to address inefficiencies in the post-trade settlement processes.

Cello

As of February 2017, this is the most recent addition to Hyperledger project. This project aims to provide on-demand BaaS which will make deployments and management of multiple blockchains convenient and easy for users. It is envisioned that Cello will support all future and current Hyperledger blockchains, such as Fabric and Sawtooth Lake.

Qtum

This project is based on the idea of combining capabilities of Bitcoin and Ethereum blockchains. Qtum makes use of the Bitcoin code base but uses Ethereum's EVM for smart contract execution. Ethereum smart contracts can run using Bitcoin's UTXO (unspent transactions) model.

 It is available at `https://qtum.org/`.

Bitcoin-NG

This is another proposal for addressing scalability, throughput, and speed issues in the Bitcoin blockchain. **Next Generation** (**NG**) protocol is based on a mechanism of leader election which verifies transactions as soon as they occur, as compared to Bitcoin's protocols, where the time between blocks and block size are the key limitations concerning scalability.

Solidus

This is a new cryptocurrency which provides a solution for selfish mining while addressing scaling and performance issues. It also addresses confidentiality issues. It is based on permissionless Byzantine consensus. The protocol in its current state is comparatively complex and is an open area for research.

 Original research paper is available at `https://eprint.iacr.org/2017/317.pdf`.

Hawk

This is a project that is aiming to address privacy issues of smart contracts in blockchains. It is a smart contract system that allows encryption of transactions on the blockchain. Hawk can generate a secure protocol for interaction with blockchains automatically without the need for manually programming the cryptographic protocol.

Town-Crier

This is a project that is aiming to provide real-world, authentic feed into smart contracts. This system is based on Intel's SGX trusted hardware technology. This is a step further in Oracle design whereby smart contracts can request data from online sources while preserving confidentiality.

SETLCoin

This is a system built by Goldman Sachs and is filed for the patent under the *Cryptographic currency for securities settlement* application. As the name suggests, this cryptocurrency coin can be used for fast and efficient settlement. The technology makes use of virtual wallets to exchange assets over the network between peers and allows immediate settlement via ownership of SETLCoin.

TEEChan

This is novel idea of using **Trusted Execution Environments** (**TEEs**) to provide a scalable and efficient solution for scaling the Bitcoin blockchain. This is similar to the concept of payment channels whereby off-chain channels are used for faster transfer of transactions. The principal attraction in this idea is that it is implementable on Bitcoin blockchain without the need for any changes in the Bitcoin network because it is an off-the-chain solution.

There is, however, a small caveat that this solution does require trusting Intel for remote attestation (verification) as Intel's SGX CPUs are used to provide TEEs. This is not a desirable property in decentralized blockchains; however, it should be noted that the confidentiality of transactions is still preserved even if remote attestation is used as remote attester (Intel) cannot see the contents of the communication between users. This limitation makes it debatable that whether it is an entirely decentralized and trustless solution or not.

Falcon

Falcon is a project that helps Bitcoin to scale by providing a fast relay network for broadcasting Bitcoin blocks over the network. The core idea revolves around a technique to reduce orphan blocks, thus helping with the overall scalability of the Bitcoin network. The technique used for this purpose has been called application-level cut-through routing.

Bletchley

This project has been introduced by Microsoft, indicating the commitment by Microsoft to blockchain technology. Bletchley allows the use of Azure cloud services to build blockchains in a user-friendly manner. A major concept introduced by Bletchley is called cryptlets, which can be thought of like an advanced version of Oracles that reside outside the blockchain and can be called by smart contracts using secure channels. These can be written in any language and execute within a secure container.

There are two types of cryptlets: **utility cryptlets** and **contract cryptlets**. The first type is used to provide basic services such as encryption and basic data fetching from external sources, whereas the latter is a more intelligent version that is created automatically when a smart contract is created on the chain and resides off the chain but still linked to the on-chain contract. Due to this off-chain existence, there is no need to execute the contract cryptlets on all nodes of the blockchain network. Therefore, this approach results in increased performance of the blockchain.

The whitepaper is available at `https://github.com/Azure/azure-blockchain-projects/blob/master/bletchley/bletchley-whitepaper.md`.

Casper

This is the Proof of Stake algorithm for Ethereum in development. Significant research has already been conducted in this area and is expected to be implemented in 2017. The nodes become bonded validators in a Casper-based Ethereum network and are required to pay a security deposit for them to be able to propose new blocks.

Casper research paper is available at `https://github.com/ethereum/research/blob/master/papers/casper-basics/casper_basics.pdf`.

Miscellaneous tools

Some tools that have not been discussed previously are listed in the following subsections and introduced briefly to make readers aware of the myriad of development options available for blockchains. This list includes platforms, utilities, and tools that can be used for blockchain development.

Solidity extension for Microsoft Visual Studio

This extension provides IntelliSense, autocompletion, and templates for DApps, and works within the familiar Visual Studio IDE, making it easier for developers to familiarize themselves with Ethereum development.

 You can download this extension from: `https://marketplace.visualstudio.com/items?itemName=ConsenSys.Solidity`.

MetaMask

This is a DApp browser that is similar to Mist from a DApp browsing point of view but allows users to run Ethereum DApps within the browser without the requirement of running a full Ethereum node.

 This is available from `https://metamask.io/` and can be installed as a Chrome plugin.

Stratis

This is a blockchain development platform that allows the creation of custom private blockchains and works in conjunction with the main Stratis blockchain (Stratis chain) for security reasons. It allows provisioning of major blockchains such as Bitcoin, Ethereum, and Lisk easy. Also, it allows development using C# .NET technologies. It is also available via Microsoft Azure as BaaS.

This is available at `https://stratisplatform.com/`.

Embark

This is a development framework for Ethereum which allows similar functionality to Truffle, which is discussed in `Chapter 14`, *Introducing Web3*. It allows automatic deployment of smart contracts, easier integration with JavaScript, and, especially, easier integration with IPFS. This is a very feature-rich framework, and many more functionalities are available. It can be installed via npm.

This framework is available at GitHub: `https://github.com/iurimatias/embark-framework`.

DAPPLE

This is another framework for Ethereum that allows easier development and deployment of smart contracts by taking care of more complex tasks. It can be used for package management, contract building, and deployment scripting.

This is also available via npm. It is also available via GitHub at `https://github.com/nexusdev/dapple`.

Meteor

This is a full-stack development framework for single-page applications. It can be used for Ethereum DApp development. There is a development environment available in meteor, and it allows easier and easy development of complex DApps.

It is available at `https://www.meteor.com/` and Ethereum-specific DApp building information is available at `https://github.com/ethereum/wiki/wiki/Dapp-using-Meteor`.

uPort

This platform is built on Ethereum and provides a decentralized identity management system. This allows users to have full control over their identity and personal information. This is based on the idea of reputation systems enables users to attest each other and build trust.

 This is available at `https://www.uport.me/`.

INFURA

This project aims to provide enterprise-level Ethereum and IPFS nodes. INFURA consists of Ethereum nodes, IPFS nodes, and a service layer named Ferryman which provides routing and load balancing services.

Convergence with other industries

Convergence of blockchain with IoT has been discussed at length in `Chapter 18`, *Scalability and Other Challenges*. Briefly, it can be said that due to the authenticity, integrity, privacy, and shared nature of blockchains, IoT networks will benefit greatly from blockchain technology. This can be realized in the form of an IoT network that runs on a blockchain and makes use of a decentralized mesh network for communication to facilitate **Machine-to-Machine** (**M2M**) communication in real time. All this data which is generated as a result of M2M communication can be used in the machine learning process to augment the functionality of Artificially Intelligent DAOs or simple AAs. AAs can act as agents in a **Distributed Artificial Intelligence** (**DAI**) environment provided by a blockchain and can learn over time using machine learning processes.

AI is a field of computer science that endeavors to build intelligent agents that can make rational decisions based on the scenarios and environment that they observe around them. Machine learning plays a vital role in AI by making use of raw data as a learning resource. A key requirement in AI-based systems is the availability of authentic data that can be used for machine learning and model building. The explosion of data coming out IoT devices, smartphone's, and other data acquisition means that AI and machine learning is becoming more and more powerful.

There is, however, a requirement of authenticity of data. Once consumers, producers, and other entities are on a blockchain, the data that is generated as a result of interaction between these entities can be readily used as an input to machine learning engines with a guarantee of authenticity. This is where AI converges with blockchains. It could be argued that if an IoT device is hacked, it can send malformed data to the blockchain. This issue is mitigated because an IoT device is part of the blockchain (as a node) and has all security properties applied to it as a standard node in the blockchain network. These properties include incentivization of good behavior, rejection of malformed transactions, and strict verification of transactions and various other checks that are part of blockchain protocol. Therefore, even if an IoT device is somehow hacked, it would be treated as a Byzantine node by the blockchain network and would not cause any adverse impact on the network.

Moreover, the possibility of combining intelligent Oracles, intelligent, smart contracts, and AAs will give rise to **Artificially Intelligent Decentralized Autonomous Organizations (AIDAOs)** that can act on behalf of humans to run entire organizations on their own. This is another side of AI that can become norm in the future. However, more research is required to realize this vision.

Also, convergence of blockchain technology with other fields such as 3D printing, virtual reality, augmented reality, and the gaming industry is also envisaged. For example, in a multiplayer online game, blockchain's decentralized approach allows for more transparency and can ensure that no central authority is gaining unfair advantage by manipulating the game rules. All these topics are active areas of research currently and more interest and development are expected in these areas soon.

Future

The year 2017 was predicted to be the year when blockchain technology is implemented in real-world production environments and move from the **Proof of Concept** (**PoC**) and theoretical stage of previous years. It is true to some extent that companies have implemented some pilot projects but large-scale production implementations are yet to be seen. It is expected that within year 2018 we will see some organization implementing full scale blockchain based projects. In 2019, it is expected that almost 20% of central banks will be using blockchain.

 Original research is available here https://papers.ssrn.com/sol3/papers.cfm?abstract_id=3040224.

In years to come, this trend is only expected to grow. There are few careful predictions being made in the section that is based on the current advancement and speed of progress in the concerned field.

All of these predictions are likely to come true between the years 2020 and 2050:

- The IoT will run on multiple blockchains and will give rise to an M2M economy. This can include energy devices, autonomous cars, and house hold accessories.
- Medical records will be shared securely while preserving the privacy of patients between various private blockchains run by consortia of health providers. It may well be a single private blockchain shared among all service providers including pharmacies, hospitals, and clinics.
- Elections will be held via decentralized web applications with a backend of blockchains transparently and securely.
- Financial institutions will be running many private blockchains to share data between participants and for internal processes.
- Financial institutions will be making use of semiprivate blockchains that will provide identity information for AML and KYC functions and will be shared between many or all of the financial institutions around the world.
- Immigration and border control related activities will be recorded on the blockchain and passport control will be conducted via a blockchain shared between all ports of entries and border agencies around the world.
- Governments will run interdepartmental blockchain to provide government services such as pension disbursement, benefit disbursement, land ownership records, birth registrations and other citizen services. This way auditability, trust and sense of security will develop among citizens.
- Research in cryptography and distributed systems will reach new heights and universities, and educational establishment will offer dedicated courses on cryptoeconomics, cryptocurrencies, and blockchains.
- Artificially Intelligent DAOs will prevail on blockchains that will make rational decisions on behalf of humans.
- A publicly available regulated blockchain run by the government will be used on day-to-day basis by citizens to perform their day-to-day activities, for example tax payments, TV license registration and marriage registrations.
- BaaS will be provided as standard to anyone who wishes to run their business or day-to-day transactions on a blockchain. In fact, it could be envisaged that just like the Internet, blockchains will seamlessly integrate into our daily lives and people will be using them without knowing much about the underlying technology and infrastructure.

- Blockchains will normally be used to provide **Digital Rights Management** (**DRM**) services for arts and media and can be used to deliver content to the consumers, enabling direct communication between consumer and the producer. This will eliminate the need for any central party to govern the licensing and rights managing of valuable goods.
- Existing cryptocurrencies such as Bitcoin will continue to grow in value, and with the availability of state channels and scalability efforts, this trend is only expected to grow.
- Cryptocurrency investment will greatly increase, and a new cryptoeconomic society will emerge.
- Bitcoin value will reach tens of thousands of dollars per coin.
- Digital identities will be routinely managed on the blockchain, and different government functions such as voting, taxation, and funds disbursement will be conducted via blockchain-enabled platforms.
- Financial institutions and clearing houses will start to introduce blockchain-based solutions for their customers in 2018.

Summary

Blockchains are going to change the world. The revolution has already started, and it is only expected to grow at an exponential scale. This chapter has explored various projects and the current state of blockchain technology.

First, a few trends were discussed that are expected to continue as the technology progresses further. There is deep research interest in blockchain technology by many researchers and organizations around the world, and some research topics have also been introduced in this chapter. Furthermore, convergence with other fields such as the IoT and AI has also been discussed.

Finally, some predictions regarding the growth of blockchain technology have been made. Most of these predictions are likely to come true within the next decade or so, while some may take a longer time. Blockchain technology has the potential to change the world, and a few positive signs have already been seen in the form of successful PoC implementations and a growing number of enthusiasts and developers taking an interest in this technology. Very soon, blockchains will be intertwined with our lives just as the Internet is now. This chapter is just a modest overview of the vast and tremendous potential of blockchains, and in the near future, exponential growth and further adoption of this technology is expected.

Another Book You May Enjoy

If you enjoyed this book, you may be interested in another book by Packt:

Building Blockchain Projects

Narayan Prusty

ISBN: 978-1-78712-214-7

- Walk through the basics of the Blockchain technology
- Implement Blockchain's technology and its features, and see what can be achieved using them
- Build DApps using Solidity and Web3.js
- Understand the geth command and cryptography
- Create Ethereum wallets
- Explore consortium blockchain

Leave a review – let other readers know what you think

Please share your thoughts on this book with others by leaving a review on the site that you bought it from. If you purchased the book from Amazon, please leave us an honest review on this book's Amazon page. This is vital so that other potential readers can see and use your unbiased opinion to make purchasing decisions, we can understand what our customers think about our products, and our authors can see your feedback on the title that they have worked with Packt to create. It will only take a few minutes of your time, but is valuable to other potential customers, our authors, and Packt. Thank you!

Index

D

Lightning Source UK Ltd.
Milton Keynes UK
UKHW030831161119
353665UK00006B/243/P